Of Arms and Men

OF ARMS AND MEN

A History of War, Weapons, and Aggression

ROBERT L. O'CONNELL

New York   Oxford
OXFORD UNIVERSITY PRESS
1989

Oxford University Press

Oxford   New York   Toronto
Delhi   Bombay   Calcutta   Madras   Karachi
Petaling Jaya   Singapore   Hong Kong   Tokyo
Nairobi   Dar es Salaam   Cape Town
Melbourne   Auckland

and associated companies in
Berlin   Ibadan

Library of Congress Cataloging-in-Publication Data

O'Connell, Robert L.
Of arms and men : a history of war, weapons, and aggression /
Robert L. O'Connell.
p.   cm.   Bibliography: p.   Includes index.
ISBN 0-19-505359-1
1. Military art and science—History.   2. War.   I. Title.
U27.026 1989   355'.009—dc19   88-19526   CIP

Printed in the United States of America
on acid-free paper

To Benjie, Jessica, and Lucy
whose love gave this life

PREFACE

Every book has a moment of conception. This one's came during an extended luncheon with Mike MccGwire of the Brookings Institution, as I complained for what must have been hours over my dissatisfaction at the way weapons have traditionally been studied. "How can we ever deal with these things effectively, until we look at them more openly and with fewer preconceptions?" Perhaps as much in self-defense as anything else, he replied: "Well then, why don't you do it?" Mike MccGwire is a thoughtful and enthusiastic man; but he is also an ex-Royal Navy officer, and his voice had the ring of authority. It occurred to me for the first time maybe I really could do such a thing. So began an eight-year intellectual odyssey.

As part of the Ph.D. glut of the mid-1970s, I was a historian by training, but found myself working in military intelligence. My job was interesting, and my background provided me with some useful perspectives on the present course of arms. Nevertheless, the two never really came together in a way which took full advantage of the insights I believed lay fallow in the field of military history. Yet now, armed with Mike's suggestion, I thought I saw a means to this end. It was clear that weapons were very old and that the military profession was a highly traditional one. It also stood to reason that the accumulated rituals of military life would have been deeply conditioned by the succession of arms, and that contemporary weapons choice should logically be an extension of this condition. Technology might appear dominant. Yet culture was subtle and pervasive. Therefore it made sense to go to the very origins of these phenomena, and begin reconstructing the matrix of thought and action from which weapons have sprung. Much of what I found surprised me. And the conclusions I have reached are far from what I might have anticipated. Yet at my journey's end, I do have the sense that I have been on the right track, and that my work will serve as a useful guidepost to those who venture onward.

Meanwhile along the way I have accumulated numerous debts of gratitude. Although I can never repay most of those who helped me, I can at least thank them. First I want to acknowledge a few scholars whose work had a particular influence on this book. Among them are Edward O. Wilson, John U. Nef, William H. McNeill, Elting Morison, John Keegan, John Dower, I. F. Clarke, and Eric J. Leed. I also want to thank several of my colleagues at the U.S. Arms Control and Disarmament Agency for their advice and guidance. Archelaus Turrentine, Robert Guth, John Tierney, Col. Charles Hertel, Steven Lawrence, and particularly Col. Garnett C. Brown were kind enough to read the manuscript and make numerous valuable comments. At the U.S. Army Foreign Science and Technology Center, Herbert Ely has been a constant source of encouragement, Gerald Halbert was extremely generous with his private library, and Stephen Eitelman provided computer support for my index. The research for the book was done primarily at the Alderman Library of the University of Virginia, the Library of the U.S. Department of State, and the Pentagon Library. The staffs of all three could not have been more helpful or cooperative. Nancy Lane, senior editor at Oxford University Press, and Peter Kracht, assistant editor, rescued my manuscript from obscurity and have been primarily responsible for bringing it to print. No amount of thanks can express my gratitude to them both. At the University of Virginia I want to thank Joseph Kett and John Casey for their continued interest in my work, and in particular Norman A. Graebner, who introduced a generation of students to the world of power, and demonstrated by his personal example that decency and an effective approach to this world were not incompatible ends.

Finally, I want to thank my friends Gordon Bowen and Charles Shaffer, my wife Benjie, and my mother Dorothea O'Connell for listening to my endless talk on the subject, staying awake during my impromptu readings, and putting up with me during what must have seemed an endless project.

Charlottesville, Virginia   R.L.O.
Fall 1988

CONTENTS

Of Arms and Men

 Chapter 1

MECHANISMS

I

War has fallen upon hard times. The true sport of kings appears no longer worthy of Clausewitz's famous dictum "A mere continuation of policy by other means."[1] From our own perspective the phrase has the ring of black humor, a grotesque mockery of reality. Two centuries of increasingly pointless, financially disastrous, and above all, lethal conflicts, culminating in the discovery and proliferation of nuclear weapons, have rendered this venerable institution virtually incapable of performing any of the roles classically assigned to it.

At the level of superpower interaction, it is only a slight exaggeration to say that war could only occur through accident or madness. Scenarios for limited engagement are constantly being mulled over by strategists on both sides. Yet the political gains are so nebulous, and the firebreaks to escalation so weak, that neither presumes the other reckless enough to make a move. Even if a purely conventional war could be fought by the superpowers, it is quite possible that large-scale, long-term radiation would still result from the destruction of nuclear power plants. Moreover, there are signs that modern Soviet and American precision-guided munitions have become so accurate as to render this form of combat almost equally suicidal—at least for those doing the fighting. Meanwhile, reality will grant no such guarantee that the nuclear threshold will not be breached. This is the essence of deterrence. And it must be conceded that it has meant peace, albeit of a very uneasy sort, to the industrialized world for over four decades.

Yet there is still accident and madness. Unfortunately, deterrence is neither foolproof nor capable of preventing conventional war among the third-tier powers who do not possess such armaments.

The threat of nuclear sanctions against a non-nuclear belligerent is essentially a hollow one. The inevitable political price and danger of third-party nuclear retaliation are simply too great for such an initiative to be taken seriously. So beneath the baleful but helpless gaze of the nuclear few, the small fish are left to fight among themselves with relative impunity. In the words of Zbigniew Brzezinski: "War today is a luxury that only the weak and the poor can afford."[2]

This is not meant to imply that wars at this level are cheap. Quite the contrary, luxuries are never cheap. The astronomical cost and destructiveness of high-intensity combat are so out of phase with the fragility of Third World economies that the proposition remains unattractive to all but the most desperate. Even when serious fighting does break out, as in the case of the Gulf War, the realities of Third World logistics are such that full-scale combat cannot be sustained on anything more than a spasmodic basis, each spasm being generally too short for either party to gain a significant advantage.

Of course Vietnam has demonstrated that effective guerrilla campaigns can be waged practically endlessly. Yet her present position as one of the world's ten poorest nations testifies to the costs. If it cannot exactly be said that war on this level does not pay, we can confidently assert that the wages are not good.

II

This brings us to one of the central paradoxes of the age. If war is such an unsavory proposition, how can it be that weapons—at once the tools of its prosecution and the prime cause of its present relative futility—retain such a remarkable allure to even the most unlikely nations?

It is a question that invites strong opinions. Those repelled by the illogic of the situation have operated mostly on the level of accusation, ascribing motivation ranging from paranoia to megalomania to simple greed. On the other hand, apologists tend to ignore the basic contradictions posed by modern weapons and concentrate instead on the intricacies of deterrence and national strategy. In neither case has there been much incentive to look seriously at the roots of the problem.

Undeniably, a great deal of time and effort have been spent studying weapons. Yet almost without exception, researchers have stopped short of asking the most basic questions about them. Beyond the most literal definition, what in fact are they? What do they mean to us? Does this meaning shift with time and culture? Not only are these topics not being addressed by the military and intelligence communities, but with a few notable exceptions, they have been ignored by academe.[3]

This is not hard to fathom. Questions of values and preference, when applied to armaments, are unlikely to yield comfortable answers. The accepted rules of weapons advocacy leave little room for considerations beyond the threat and, grudgingly, economics. Anything else tends to diffuse the threat and the absolute necessity of building weapons to meet it. Nevertheless, it is possible to point to a number of instances, both recent and historical, when the beliefs and institutions of those involved made it difficult, if not impossible, to accept a particular weapon in spite of a clearly demonstrated combat superiority. Nor is this so hard to understand. Weapons are among man's oldest and most significant artifacts; it makes sense that their development would be affected by their users' attitudes toward them.

However, these attitudes, or at least our perception of them, remain at a crude level of definition. In part this is a matter of scale. Weapons give every impression of having grown beyond the traditional categories used to think about them. There is an aura of unreality about megatonnage that must confound rational attempts to come to grips with instruments capable of such statistics. To say this, however, merely skirts the issue. The fear engendered by these weapons—a backdrop of unimaginable horror lying just beneath the surface—has led to a sort of paralysis of inquiry. Almost by mutual consent we avoid looking too closely or asking too many of the wrong kinds of questions.

Hence, stereotypes perpetuate themselves and will continue to do so as long as analysis remains narrowly focused on tactical-technical factors, the threat, and economics. By virtue of an odd sort of consensus of opposites, weapons are generally perceived as matter-of-fact objects mechanisms with little more symbolic and cultural significance than a pair of pliers or a stillson wrench. This would be acceptable so long as the contracted field of vision was capable of resolving some of the major contradictions surrounding armaments. Yet this has not proved to be the case.

It is a fundamental premise of this study that the relationship between man and his weapons is a great deal more intimate and complex than heretofore has been admitted. The length of time we have been using them, the profound effect they have had on political and military systems, and the psychological impact of their death-dealing capacity all argue strongly that weapons are very special devices, artifacts of the greatest significance.

It is remarkable that this is not more obvious. Yet the destructiveness of weapons technology is so great, the special skills required for its generation so inaccessible, and its internal logic so compelling that the illusion of human nonparticipation has become exceedingly seductive—especially when there is every reason to disavow the product. This a dangerous fantasy. It is true that once a developmental sequence has begun, the technological imperative becomes nearly absolute. But at the beginning and end of every such sequence is a point when human choice can and does exert itself. These preferences are as much a part of the arms competition as thermal imaging sights and look down–shoot down radar.

What is needed is an expanded context which considers arms not as something alien to ourselves but as tangible manifestations of some of our basic fantasies and experiences. Man is simply not a matter-of-fact creature. What is important to him is so on a number of different levels and for a variety of reasons. To understand the paradox of weapons development it is necessary to look deeply within ourselves and face up to the contradictory impulses that are at the root of the dilemma.

III

Before this can be done, however, weapons must be addressed on their own terms. They are, after all, mechanisms designed to achieve purpose. Neither tactical and strategic ends nor the nature of military organizations has proved greatly change-able—only technology, and this is a relatively recent phenomenon. Modern weapons development is not necessarily without precedent. Rather, there is a tendency for situations and responses to repeat themselves in recognizable patterns. Thus, many of the weapons in use today have long histories and have arrived at their present form through a process that can best be termed evolutionary.

Like so many things having to do with weapons, these statements might appear self-evident were it not for the long shadow cast by nuclear weapons, obscuring continuity and making the past seem quaint and irrelevant. To some degree this may be true. Yet it is also true that we have little else to guide us.

To call weapons evolutionary requires further explanation. Clearly, the mechanisms involved are only analogous, not identical. Life follows the paths of possibility spontaneously through mutation. Weapons follow possibility as a result of a two-way (or more) interaction; the path is contrived. Yet it follows the maze just as relentlessly, driven by the same life-and-death issues. Moreover, as it branches out along the line of least resistance, weapons technology betrays many of the same, or at least analogous, tendencies in its creations.

For example, peculiar features such as accuracy, range, mobility, or impenetrability are characteristically seized upon as critical and successively improved in a manner which causes the weapon as a whole to become increasingly specialized. In doing so there is also a decided tendency, paralleled in nature, toward growth. While certain types of weapons, warships for instance, are more prone to growth than others, it can be said as a rule of thumb that each iteration of a modern weapon will exceed its predecessor in one or several of the parameters of size, weight, and complexity. This persistent phenomenon is a major complicating factor in military planning since growth ordinarily implies increasing cost, a factor directly at odds with the very strong military urge to possess large numbers. Nonetheless, size usually prevails. Overtly, the technological advantage embodied in growth is normally sufficient to insure that this occurs. Yet on another level it is also true that military men habitually equate size with power, and that, historically, large weapons have been preferred. Only in rare instances has a smaller, cheaper weapon played on the overspecialization of the traditional armament in order to defeat it.

Now it should be emphasized that this last occurrence, the wholesale obsolescence of a significant class of weapon, remains, even today, exceptional. In fact, weapon types have always been remarkably stable. Thus, many of the weapons in today's arsenals have not only functional equivalents in the distant past but also traceable lineages. Operating principles, of course, have changed. Yet the tasks of war, and the images these conjure up, have not. Hence, the bolt shot from a catapult was intended for the same purpose as the surface-to-surface missile, just as was the phalanx in relation to the armored division, or the trireme and the heavy cruiser. Certainly, some areas have been added very recently. Neither submarine and antisubmarine nor air and antiair weapons had recognizable predecessors much more than a hundred years ago. Weapons operating at the edge of space have been with us barely forty years. Nevertheless, much that remains in contemporary stockpiles is very old in origin.

This fact is of major significance to military attitudes toward armaments. The evolutionary development of weapons within stable functional categories is a critical factor to the "culture" that surrounds armaments since it provides the physical bridge by which traditional values are transmitted forward in time. Thus, weapons development becomes something of a self-fulfilling prophecy, with even revolutionary technology classically being handled by military organizations in a manner calculated to integrate it into familiar compartments. Hence, the Americans' bringing back battleships to carry cruise missiles, or the Russians' resurrecting the battle cruiser class after a forty-year hiatus, should not be seen as aberrations. Rather, they represent very characteristic behavior. On the other hand, in cases such as the submarine, where no usable ancestry is available, the tendency is toward suppression.

Yet some change is beyond circumvention. Just twice in recorded history have there arrived weapons technologies of such fundamental importance that they changed everything, not simply military relationships but politics itself. But if the gun and nuclear weapons cast men immediately into a new era, the process of accommodation remained slow. Warriors persisted in behavior so inappropriate to the new context that it frequently spelled suicide. And when this finally ceased, they continued dragging along everything salvable from their old way of life.

This goes far beyond pertinacity. There is within the military mind a deep and abiding need for order arising out of the very chaos of warfare. The continuing need to make predictions about matters so volatile by its nature requires a steady frame of reference. Weapons, then, tend to be viewed in a manner which makes their effects most calculable.

This is true even in the extreme case represented by an arms race, a phenomenon generally characterized by the rapid numerical expansion of one or a few weapons—a sort of military-industrial equivalent of a population explosion.

However, the mechanisms which drive weapons proliferation, unlike most forms of natural reproduction, offer alternatives. Generally known as threat-response patterns, they can be reduced to two basic types. First, an adversary weapon can be met with a *counter-response,* an item of military hardware designed specifically to oppose the threat—a surface-to-air missile versus a bomber, for example. On the other hand, there is the possibility of acquiring a weapon basically equivalent to the one held by the adversary. This can be termed a *symmetrical response.* While there are some variations within these categories, it can be said that most weapons historically come about as a result of these two mechanisms. This is not to say that all threats will necessarily be responded to, or that there is in reality such a tight causal chain in weapons programs as was supposed by the action-reaction theories of the 1960s. It only presumes that in those cases where there is weapons competition, the results will normally be either symmetrical responses or counters. Further, it is possible to say with some confidence that the symmetrical responses greatly outnumber the counters.

And with good reason. Counters, although representing a persistent thread in military technologies, are generally unpopular precisely because they are exceedingly difficult to estimate in terms of military effectiveness. Basically, they are the weapons of the weak or the desperate. Unable to match an opponent in a particular class of armaments, the inferior party seeks the radical alternative of neutralizing that class. However, being based on a single presumed weakness in an adversary weapon, counters are inherently unstable and subject to adversary palliatives or counter-counter measures. For this reason counter-based weapons deployment cycles tend to be very rapid and volatile.

The safer, more stable course is to build weapons basically like, though perhaps a bit better than, the other fellow's. So long as he cooperates by fielding weapons in fixed categories, as is generally the case, it pays to outnumber him in these categories. Prospective success or failure then becomes largely a matter of counting. Inscriptions indicate that the Pharaohs and the warrior kings of Mycenae kept track of their chariots no less anxiously than NATO commanders fret over the tank ratio in Europe. Significantly, the ratio of antitank guided missiles to tanks is much less discussed.

Granted, in time of war these factors are mitigated somewhat by the greater opportunities to collect data on weapons performance and by the heavy rewards paid to those equipped with superior weapons, no matter what their characteristics. Nevertheless, peace is the normal condition of military organizations, and it is from within this context that most planning for war must take place.

Thus, symmetry and numbers have long been the essence of the military balance. So much so that not only military men but arms controllers have fallen under their spell. Indeed, it was they who sanctified these concepts in their most extreme form, mutually assured destruction.

All of this is no accident. These notions play on the insecurities of both soldier and diplomat, bending their ears with the promise of order. For military men this prospect is particularly seductive. The concept of like fighting like imposes at least some measure of decorum and predictability upon the chaos of battle. In addition, symmetry, by implication, is intrinsically hierarchical and therefore compatible with the world view of the rank-conscious military. Ideally, battles tend to be planned and perceived in terms of a series of discrete actions between increasingly more heavily armed opponents. In the realm of naval architecture, an area particularly suited to differentiation by size, these tendencies became formalized and exaggerated in the venerable hierarchy of ships, a concept dependent on the assumption that like will normally fight like.

Ideally, that is. The major shortcoming of symmetry is also the major weakness of negotiated arms control. Reality is forever mocking theory with incompatible detail and rampant ambiguity. It has been argued that recent weapons deployment patterns are more a product of bureaucratic machinations within the states building them than they are a reaction to stimuli from without. Certainly, organizational dynamics are responsible for a considerable amount of "slop" and discontinuity in actual responses. Yet common sense as well as observed behavior argue strongly that no country can afford to ignore what type and number of weapons a potential enemy is currently fielding. A natural preference for symmetrical force structures is highly logical, for the reasons outlined above.

Most assuredly, this does not deny the existence of tendencies in other directions. And in fact these tendencies are a persistent source of frustration to both force planners and arms controllers. For symmetry to become truly reliable in a predictive sense, force structures would have to become qualitatively identical. Yet secrecy, technology, and the perennial urge to build a better weapon all militate against this happening in reality. Hence, both force planners and diplomats are obliged to balance incompatibility against incompatibility in an endless effort to approximate the ideal. Inevitably, the action retreats to ever-greater levels of detail, with the participants frequently losing track of larger issues and new developments.

Nevertheless, from a macro perspective symmetry almost automatically continues to assert itself. In effect, what generally happens in the world's armories parallels the biological concept of an evolutionary stable strategy. Just as the gene pool oscillates as it searches for equilibrium, so arms preferences vary somewhat over time. Yet the major tendency will be toward stability and symmetrical developments. Counters, like recessive genes, will continue to exist because they play on the weaknesses of the primary type. Yet they cannot achieve dominance because such dominance would prove chaotic. Weapons are expensive. They often take a long time to build. To exist in a situation in which the rate of obsolescence normally exceeds the rate of deployment—an environment where, at any one point in time, no one has a good idea what will work and what won't—is to exist under conditions that are organizationally intolerable. This is one reason why tactically superior weapons are at times relegated to institutional limbo.

Besides numerical competition (for which there is presumably an upward limit defined by manpower and resources) the major functional variable affecting the equilibrium of a symmetrical armament pattern is technology. Because of it, weapons are constantly changing or threatening to change. Yet the rate and manner in which this goes on is much misunderstood.

Standing near the end of the twentieth century, it is easy to see weapons technology as a process out of control, carrying mankind toward an abyss. It is beyond dispute that the rate of weapons development has accelerated remarkably since approximately 1830. Yet our present perception of the process and its dynamism has been distorted, like so much else, by the fires of nuclear weaponry.

Doubtless, the collective impact of the many advances surrounding modern armaments—rocket and gas turbine technology, material advances, computers, electronic sensing and guidance—would have been extremely significant, perhaps even revolutionary, had fission and fusion never been discovered. But nuclear weapons are largely responsible for the allegorical overtones which hang about the process—that sense of foreboding which accompanies practically every new weapon development.

Yet the arrival of atomic energy, however significant, is not all-encompassing. In this respect it can be compared to the arrival of man in nature. Certainly, man has come to dominate nature. Nevertheless, much that constitutes life on earth continues to operate in its own way, though ultimately subject to this larger force. So it is with weapons technology. Nuclear arms hold sway over all strategy. Yet below them other arms continue to evolve according to their own logic. The process has speeded up, certainly, but it is still explainable in terms of what has already transpired.

Throughout most of human history the rate of weapons innovation has been very slow. So slow, in fact, that we sometimes have trouble comprehending it. To a mind immersed in the twentieth century it is puzzling that so simple a device as the stirrup—the one link needed to turn an armored horseman into an effective lancer—could have completely eluded antiquity and not become widespread until the early Middle Ages. Naturally, we wonder, "Didn't people realize that superior weapons were a life-and-death matter? That with them victory could be snatched from defeat?"

Of course they did. The Persians had just this in mind when they lined up scythed chariots before Alexander's cavalry at Gaugamela, so did the landlubber Romans when they introduced the boarding bridge to help them get at the swift Carthaginian galleys. Yet armaments research and development of the scale and continuity calculated to explore every avenue of possibility are exclusively products of the industrial era. History is replete with examples of timely weapons innovations. But their frequency is sporadic—brief flurries of activity followed by long periods in which virtually nothing happened.

Much the same thing can be said of learning itself. And in fact there is some coincidence between historical clusters of weapons developments and periods noted for generalized creativity. The Hellenistic period following the conquest of Alexander the Great constituted such a time frame. The Italian Renaissance marked another. These were times of energy and optimism, brief spans when tradition loosened its grip on men's minds and freed them to explore possibility.

This serves to illustrate the degree to which arms development is a captive not only of time and place but also of knowledge itself. To show how this works, we have only to consider the technologies which have dominated weapons development over the last half century. With the exception of gas turbines and rockets which work on chemical energy, all of them—fission, fusion, laser applications, and solid-state electronics—are founded on an understanding of relativistic physics and quantum mechanics. Without these it not only becomes impossible to implement such technologies, it becomes impossible to even conceive of them.

Weapons technology, then, must forever wait upon the revelation of basic principles capable of exploitation. When this has stopped, or is occurring very slowly, the process of improving arms must soon run out of possibilities.

This proposition can be inverted to illustrate another important aspect of the topic—its inevitability. The principles upon which weapons work are a function of the laws that govern the physical universe. They are timeless and eternal, awaiting only the investigative powers necessary to uncover them. Although there has never been a case of two isolated individuals painting the same picture or composing the same symphony, scientific principles repeatedly have been formulated simultaneously. This is because art springs from the soul, a unique and spontaneous creation of the individual. Science, on the other hand, is anchored in what has been and always will be. Nuclear weapons were simply out there waiting for us. When we reached a certain point, an encounter was virtually inevitable.

This is worth mentioning because it serves to dispel some of the guilt engendered by modern weaponry. The compulsion for self-castigation which pervades so much of the writing on the subject may give vent to very real emotions, but it is neither particularly enlightening nor very realistic.

The state which contemporary arms have reached is as irrevocable as original sin. Even if we were able to rid ourselves of the most dangerous devices through effective disarmament, the memory of these weapons and how they were built, the knowledge that they could be built, would linger indefinitely. Given man's nature and capabilities, along with the record of the past, it seems rather more likely that weapons technology will continue to move forward, though quite possibly at a considerably slower rate. Although transformations as basic as the one wrought by nuclear weapons are rare indeed, other principles yielding still other weapons await us in the future.

While the end of this process can only be guessed at, its immediate goals are endlessly apparent. Weapons are improved to gain a military advantage, pure and simple. Yet the dreams of an absolute superiority of arms—Maxim gun–firing Europeans versus spear-bearing West Africans—is a fleeting one, both rare in occurrence and short in duration. This aspect of weapons technology is analogous to bicycle racing in that a great deal more effort is required to lead than to follow. Moreover, it is inherently difficult for the leader to increase his advantage beyond a certain point.

Keeping secret weapons secret implies much more than simply the physical denial of vital pieces of equipment. It means effective control over concepts and theory. Indeed, the most basic bit of information about a new weapon, the fact that someone, somewhere made it work, is likely to be the most critical to a researcher struggling independently with the same concept. This is why the Russians subscribe to *Aviation Week*.

So it is that the social dynamics of technology reinforce the other pressures tending toward symmetry in armaments. There is, of course, a leitmotif of futility hanging about the process. The image of mankind transfixed by a receding dream of security, pulling itself along, sluglike, to ever-greater levels of potential destructiveness, is so ridiculous as to cause wonder at its continued existence. Yet it is our own fears and ambitions, sublimated through the international political system, which cause the chimera of absolute technical advantage to remain an attractive one. It must not be overlooked that men really do die in battle. Individually, they lose everything. Ultimately, it is the strength of the desire to avoid such a fate, and perhaps to inflict it on others, however self-defeating this may be from a larger perspective, which propels men toward better weapons.

All of this serves to emphasize the degree to which arms development remains a human, as well as a technological, concern. The relationship, though, is one of coexistence, not syncretism. Together they interact eccentrically, like a cam gyrating in first one direction, then the other. Hence, beneath the facade of printouts and statistics, the most fundamental decisions about weapons (the fleet needs surface ships; an air force isn't an air force without manned warplanes) are primarily reflections of human motives and considerations. Once these initial conditions are set, however, the logic of technology becomes nearly irresistible, at times sweeping us toward destinations never contemplated or desired. Because so much of this is a function of the physical universe and the laws that govern it, the process is, in a very real sense, beyond our control. It has proved possible to modulate the rate of occurrence, but the course and consequences are largely immutable.

The human input is not, however. Neither a suit of armor nor a battleship is technologically predestined. They are products of tradition and, above all, the men who made them.

IV

What follows will explore the relationship between man and armaments in a roughly chronological fashion, concentrating on events in the West, since it is this weapons tradition which produced arms as we now know them. While the emphasis will be historical, it is hoped that the spirit will remain eclectic, drawing from the worlds of biology, psychology, anthropology, sociology, art, literature, and popular culture when they appear to shed light on the subject. A special effort, however, will be made to view man's aggressive and weapons-related conduct in the context of animal behavior. Not only has this proved a particularly fertile field of inquiry over the last two decades, but it provides a very broad and morally neutral context in which to examine a subject which frequently has been viewed from an emotionally charged and categorical perspective.

Good intellectual history is always speculative. It is meant to stimulate thought as well as chronicle it. This study proceeds in that spirit. Too much has been taken for granted about weapons for too long. The reader is not asked to agree with all that will be presented here, only to think seriously about these matters, to wonder about the nature of armaments and man's attachment to them.

It is impossible to separate weapons from war and politics. They are interwoven threads in a single tapestry. However, because this book is focused on armaments, the history of the West will be viewed from an unusual standpoint. It will be divided into three periods based on the source of energy by which the principle weapons of the day derived their power. Thus, there will be an era of mechanical weapons, an era of chemical energy–based weapons, and an era of nuclear weapons. This is obviously a convention.[4] But it is also true that the transition from era to era had a profound effect, not only on warlike behavior but on political systems and, thus, history itself. Further, it can be demonstrated that much of the evolution of armaments has transpired during these transitional periods and that this has been a major source of the turbulence characteristic of these times. This is of more than academic interest since we live in such a period.

Finally, it is inevitable that the selective interpretation of people and events deep in the past will raise questions of relevance and the inadvertent projection of contemporary values onto that which is long gone. Yet it is also true that man's basic nature has not changed, nor has the life-and-death aspect of battle. Only technology has changed.

 Chapter 2

DIALOGUE WITH THE SPHINX

I

When we are faced with something we don't understand, there is a tendency to reduce it to its simplest terms. Two ways of doing this are definition and retrospection, the idea in both cases being to arrive at a core or embryonic form which is somehow more comprehensible. While this doesn't always work, it is often helpful in cases such as weapons where there is no clear path of investigation.

The act of approaching the concept of a weapon through definition is instructive. Taking "an instrument or device for use in attack or defense in combat, fighting, or war"[1] as a starting point, complications immediately set in. Consider, for example, the concept of being "for use in attack or defense." Many objects, some of them clearly dedicated to other functions—an ice pick, for instance—might reasonably be deemed "for use" in a pinch. Yet their inclusion tends to diffuse the concept and add ambiguity as to what actually constitutes a weapon. Nevertheless, turning a blind eye to them seems worse since it establishes the kind of rigid category which has so constricted thought on armaments in the past. But unless all the sharp objects in the world are to be considered, some qualifications had better be added. Therefore, it seems best to turn from the passive to the active voice—from "for use" to "used"—and add "primarily" to narrow things still further. While this does not preclude an occasional pitchfork or sledgehammer, it at least draws the focus in on what we mostly want to talk about.

Having established that, another problem immediately takes its place. Who exactly is being attacked or defended against? It is readily apparent that "the enemy" and "the other fellow" are not the only candidates; nor are "combat, fighting, or war" the only conditions in which weapons might be used. Weapons can be and frequently are employed against other species. Indeed, hunting supported man for much the greater portion of his existence.

Once this is clarified, it becomes possible to broaden the context still further. Don't other animals possess "instruments used primarily for attack and defense"? Unquestionably, they do. In fact, to answer otherwise is to divorce the study of weapons from its biological heritage. Certainly, those studying human aggression have not been willing to make such a concession in terms of animal aggression. Yet this is precisely what has happened in the case of weapons, which heretofore have been studied as an exclusively human phenomenon. Again, this can be traced partly to a problem of definition.

Clearly, there are some fairly fundamental differences between weapons in nature and those of mankind. The former, manifesting themselves in tusks, antlers, and the like, are quite literally a part of the user—attached physically and a product of the species' genetic evolution. Human weapons,[2] on the other hand, are distinguished as being noncontiguous (the exceptions being our teeth and fingernails, both poorly adapted for aggression) and consciously selected. While these differences are substantial, they don't appear to be crucial in light of the original definition.

The essence of a weapon is its ability to do damage to, or prevent damage from, another organism.[3] Ultimately, it is this functional capability, not detachability or origin, which causes a weapon to be a weapon.

Granted, this presupposes a very broad conceptual framework. Moreover, it can be argued that such a definition, by adopting as its central criterion, a more or less universalized statement of function, tends to obscure the vast differences among weapons—between a sharp stick and an intercontinental ballistic missile, for example. To a degree, it does. But it also may be that only a very broad understanding of what constitutes a weapon can provide the necessary perspective to come to grips with this destructiveness. The mouth of a shark, the branch grasped by a frightened chimp, the bow of the hunter, and an F-16 in the hands of a young fighter pilot may have little in common morphologically. Yet functionally they are linked together, benchmarks in a single strand of evolution.

If this bridge is established, it is possible to see that weapons are truly ancient, far older than man—perhaps nearly as old as life itself. It is among the stingers of colonial invertebrates and the body armor of Paleozoic crustaceans that the genesis of weaponry is to be found. Man is but the inheritor of this long tradition. This is important because, among other things, it tends to dispel at least some of the stigma surrounding the topic. Too frequently, weapons development is viewed as fundamentally unnatural, a particular curse of mankind that sets him at cross-purposes with the mechanisms of his environment.

This is far from true. The world of nature is essentially a violent one. This reality has been somewhat obscured by the tendency of researchers to concentrate on intraspecific aggression (strife among members of the same species), an area where effective restraints on combatants have frequently evolved. Yet predation, certainly a major, if not the major, source of violent encounters, can be subject to no such mitigating influences. Animals hunt to kill and eat other animals. With few exceptions, if given a choice, they will choose as their victims the youngest and most helpless.[4] Restraint only comes with fear or satiation, and even in the latter case, both the Serengeti lion and the hyena have been observed to kill wantonly when it is convenient to do so.[5]

While the Hobbesian nature of nature can be overdrawn, it remains true that only a miniscule portion of any nondomesticated species dies of old age.[6] Disease and, especially, starvation are major factors. Yet many are killed.[7] And in every mortal encounter a fang or a talon, a tusk or a claw plays a critical role. This is equally true in intraspecific aggression, where some of the most original and bizarre specializations have taken place. Seen in this light the world of nature becomes an armed camp, the scene of weapons competitions that have gone on for millions, and in a few instances billions, of years.[8] In some cases the entire physique of a species comes to be dominated by a particular weapon adaptation. Others are less affected. Yet almost all animals come to possess some form of tangible self-defense equipment. Conceptually, at least, man has simply been following this long-established precedent.

To say that nature creates weapons in profusion is also to recognize that there are a variety of possible uses to which they can be put. Quite obviously, aggression and weapons are intimately related. Yet the relationship is a complex one. For instance, although weapons adaptations are normally employed in the service of aggression, it is possible to point to several, such as shells and specialized retreat mechanisms, which have evolved primarily to thwart attacks. Edward Wilson, Dolf Zillman, and other sociobiologists have shown that aggression in nature is an extremely complex phenomenon,[9] with a variety of purposes such as territoriality, dominance, sexuality, and survival coming in to play. Because weapons are so much a part of the phenomenon, they are bound to share this complexity and diversity of intent. While it is true that animals often apply the same weapons toward several different ends, this is not necessarily the case. Deer, for example, use their antlers only in social combat, while relying on their front hooves to ward off predators.[10] On the other hand, piranha fish, much feared for their teeth, never bite other piranhas, but instead strike at them with their tail fins.[11]

Such diversity of function implies that lethality is only one of several motivating factors in the development of nature's arsenal. Yet the patterns have not been thoroughly explored. As is typical of the area in general, no study primarily dedicated to natural weapon adaptations appears to exist. Therefore, any generalization made on the subject must be very tentative and conditional. Nonetheless, several persistent characteristics of arms development in nature seem quite apparent.

Despite considerable multifunctionality, it does seem possible to draw some gross distinctions between weapons evolved for predation and those primarily oriented around conflict within a species. In the former instance the ruthless, matter-of-fact nature of the killing seems in some ways to be paralleled by the conservative, almost prosaic nature of the instruments. This statement appears to be backed up by the stability of the forms involved, especially in the vertebrates. The enduring nature of submarine predator design is obvious. Hence, large sharks, evolutionarily stabilized for hundreds of millions of years, remain, in terms of killing mechanisms, very similar to the much more recent and physiologically more sophisticated killer whale. Both are big, fast swimmers and possessors of effective but fairly generalized teeth. From this gross perspective, mammalian land carnivores also appear to be built along parallel lines—quadrupeds making use of tearing teeth and specialized claws. As with predatory fish, the major variation within the groupings appear to be size. Therefore, with minor changes in detail, a domestic cat could serve as a scale model for its larger feline cousins.

It also seems possible to say that sex is not a major factor in upsetting the stability of predatory arms. Since it is not unusual for both genders to engage in the hunt, it is both logical and apparent that the distribution of predatory weapons is reasonably uniform. Again, size seems to be the predominant variable.

To a considerable degree these tendencies are reflected in defensive adaptations against predation. While there have been innumerable experiments with protective coloration and/or noxious taste and smell in the course of evolution, a basic reliance on fairly stable shell forms, body armor, and specialized retreat mechanisms, has remained a favorite survival strategy. Consequently, the chitin of the beetle, the shell of the tortoise, and the horny armor of the armadillo are, in defensive terms at least, very analogous to one another.

There are certainly exceptions to these trends of conservatism and uniformity. Birds of prey are spectacular adaptations to the possibilities of attack from above. In the reptilian order, the legless serpent form and the largest extinct macropods, (bipedal, using the tail for balance) are obviously alternatives to the quadruped mold. The huge number of species in the class Insecta has produced a galaxy of variation. Yet even here certain general design patterns appear to exist.

Neither has the form of weapons of prey changed a great deal. Nor have the advantages of efficiency in the kill mechanism driven evolution into audacious functional experimentation. Beyond poison and penetration, little else has been tried. This may be due to the very simplicity and stability of the original proposition. To eat and avoid being eaten, the rules have never changed.

Whatever the driving forces, natural weapons of prey are notable for their unobstrusive and generalized nature. While there are numerous examples of predators with spectacular physiques, the actual killing instuments are seldom out of proportion to the body. If the elongated fangs of the saber-toothed tiger strike us as impressive, it is perhaps notable that he is no longer with us.

The basically straightforward nature of predatory weapons stands in marked contrast to the complexity and diversity found in animal armaments specialized for intraspecific combat. Here there is no simple proposition restraining developmental ingenuity. Instead, combat is undertaken for a variety of motives, including sex, territory, and dominance.[12] Moreover, there is no particular genetic advantage in actually killing the adversary, although this does occur.[13]

Rather, intraspecific violence is characteristically ritualized, with the instruments of combat often being specialized to serve the ends of these ceremonial confrontations.[14] The antlers of the deer and the moose are therefore designed for locking and pushing rather than penetration, while the horns of the bighorn sheep are elaborately specialized for their spectacular butting matches. In cases such as those of predators possessing lethal instruments, their use is often avoided or mitigated in some way during intraspecific combat. Rattlesnakes, for instance, do not bite each other but determine dominance through elaborate wrestling matches.[15] On the other hand, wild boars and northern elephant seals do attack conspecifics with their tusks, but each tries to take the blows on the shoulders and chest, areas protected with heavy layers of skin.[16]

These are not isolated occurrences. It is the norm for animals in combat to follow a set body of rules, of which weapon use forms an important part. Characteristically, arms are matched symmetrically. Unlike predatorial interaction, where practically any means of offense or defense is employed without hesitation, intraspecific aggression is focused on attaining dominance through a fairly narrow range of aggressive activities. Occasionally, in the heat of battle, alternate means might be resorted to, but in general the contest centers around a single weapon type.[17] In all of these confrontations, potential lethality is further circumscribed by the fact that combat is overwhelmingly individualized. Whereas predators, particularly mammals, frequently hunt in groups, ganging up is rare in aggression among conspecifics. These are ceremonial duels between single combatants; their essential function is to settle individual disputes.[18]

Not surprisingly, sexual differences are deeply involved in these matters. While conspecific violence among females does exist, this sort of fighting is largely the province of the male.[19] For this reason conspecific weapon distribution is also heavily skewed in the direction of males. Moreover, it is also true that this sort of fighting does not emerge, in earnest at least, until puberty, with the weapons it requires often being classed as secondary sex characteristics. In certain species such as red deer, the very size of the weapon and not the actual contest between conspecifics at times determines dominance.[20]

Other animals such as elephants seem extraordinarily well endowed with tangible armaments, given the relatively tame nature of internecine conflict and the relative absence of predators large enough to pose a real threat. Since behavior is highly labile, much more so than physiological adaptation, it is possible to conceive of a situation in which a species might evolve a formidable weapon, only later to have the intraspecific combat upon which it was based extinguished. This, however, would seem to be an unusual occurrence. A rather more likely driving force in the development of weapons among nonpredators is threat. As opposed to predatory weapons, the natural armaments of vegetarians such as ungulates often give the impression of being oversized and unwieldy. They are, on the other hand, very formidable to look at.

It is of course possible to confuse our own preconceptions of what a weapon should be with its actual nature. Yet from the standpoint of functional efficiency, to contemplate the spectacle of a mammal so festooned with antlers that it can barely stand, or the horn of a Hercules beetle, so long as to actually exceed the length of the creature's body,[21] is to engage in an exercise bordering on the fantastic. Discounting an evolutionary propensity for black humor, such cases would seem to indicate that the ability to intimidate is in fact a driving force in arms adaptation. Certainly, other forms of threat posturing are common enough in nature. Numerous species react to danger with physiological functions aimed at making them appear bigger. It is not hard to imagine that this principle might be extended to natural armaments. Both Konrad Lorenz and Edward Wilson appear to agree that the natural progression of intraspecific aggression is in the direction of increasing ritualization.[22] Seen in this light, the transition from instruments of death to instruments of bluff makes sense.

This statement and the ones which precede it are highly speculative. It could be argued, for example, that the consideration of animal arms, virtually irrespective of the beasts to which they are attached, is meaningless. Certainly, sociobiological evidence has been used in the past to promote dubious conclusions.

Yet the fundamental dichotomy between predatory and nonpredatory instruments does appear to be more than just a matter of assembling anecdotes. The homogeneity of predatory arms as opposed to the diversity of those specialized for fighting coequals, the singular role of sex and maleness in intraspecific weapons development, and, finally, the contrast between the unpretentiousness of weapons of prey and the apparent role of threat in the evolution of intraspecific types— these all appear to be basic trends which cut across a wide number of species, especially vertebrates.

It must be conceded that the degree to which valid analogies to human weapons trends can be drawn remains open to question. The study of armaments is a field basically lacking a theoretical or conceptual structure. Until the mechanisms of causation are better understood, it is difficult to assess how similar or dissimilar they are to those operating in the world of nature. Nevertheless, it is also true that the parallels between animal behavior and much more sophisticated human activities have shed considerable light on our own motivations. Meanwhile, the construction of a framework capable of explaining contemporary arms development has to start somewhere. It seems logical to begin with the world which existed when man arrived on the scene.

II

Yet the influence of this world on weapons development is not necessarily limited to sociobiological mechanisms. Man is a thinking being. He does more than react to his environment; he can profit from its example. Therefore, it is not unreasonable that observations of animals hunting and fighting with each other would have had some effect on the tools man chose to conduct the same activities. Yet it is doubtful that he approached the subject analytically, noting, for instance, the basic differences in predatory and nonpredatory adaptations. Man, especially prescientific man, is essentially a symbolizer, a mythmaker.[23] He naturally grasps things as a whole, seeking their essence. Animals, then, were ready sources of archetypes as man sought to define in his own imagination what a weapon might be. Moreover, these paradigms were symbolic, not literal. They were capable of embodiment at a number of different technical levels, thereby assuming an element of timelessness. Images might lay dormant for several millennia, only to be dredged up to help provide the cultural matrix for weapons made possible by our growing ingenuity. It is probable, therefore, that the Romans placed the iron image of a ram's head at the end of their battering engines for much the same reason the

U.S. Air Force named a Mach 2 fighter aircraft the Eagle. In neither case was functional identity sought, only the symbolic obduracy of the male sheep or the swooping suddenness of the bird of prey. However, man's tendency to attribute animal characteristics to his weaponry has always been a limited phenomenon, hedged in on one side by his access to nature (microscopic organisms, for instance, were clearly beyond his purview until recently) and on the other by the fundamental lack of similarity between certain of his arms and any known or admired beast.

Nonetheless, animals, especially predators, have always provided at least some of the cultural context and creative impulse for weaponry. Whether through names or tactics or aesthetic valuation, these archetypes subtly condition our preconceptions and decisions. Moreover, like so much of the culture that hangs about weaponry, these images are ancient, traceable to the dawn of our awareness. The world of nature is a part of our armories in a way that transcends the immediacy of technology. It is our heritage. It should not be overlooked.

But ultimately weapons are about man, not animals. Though they may not be alien to the world of nature, they are primarily our own creation and our own dilemma. We must look to ourselves for answers.

To do this, however, requires that we go to the source of the problem, that we approach as nearly as possible the point at which man first picked up a rock or stick with malicious intent. It is here, if anywhere, that the basic proposition should be most clearly outlined.

Yet what appears to be the first hominid weapons bearer is known to be a man only in the technical sense that he is in the general line of our descent.[24] He was, in fact, a transitional creature, still far from modern man in physical size and cranial capacity. Therefore, an examination of the origins of weaponry by necessity leads to an examination of the origins of humanity. While there are alternative explanations, it remains highly plausible that the two are inextricably linked. Man became man, in part, because he held a weapon in his hand.[25]

Other than genetic analysis, which is in its infancy, anthropologists presently studying the origins of mankind are thrown back on two basic perspectives: archaeology and behavioral analogies with either primates or recent primitive human societies. Yet neither of the lenses is really capable of adequate resolution, the one being far too narrow in the glimpse it gives us and the other lacking clarity.

Undeniably, anthropologists have learned much from primate groups and human hunting-and-gathering societies. Yet the fact remains that all are far removed from the first weapons users, not only in time and space but also in speciation. Therefore, the richness of available ethnological detail is constantly being confounded by uncertainty as to how far comparisons can be carried—the so-called fallacy of the contemporary ancestor.[26] Broad patterns of behavior are perhaps transferable, but one-to-one analogies must remain suspect.

Archaeological evidence, on the other hand, though subject to varying interpretation, is on much firmer ground theoretically. But it is sparse to the extreme. To ponder the data—a few fossilized skulls, some pelvic and leg bones, and an eerie set of 3.75-million-year-old footprints—is to carry on a dialogue with the

Sphinx. Because the clues are so few, understanding requires imagination. But unlike the original riddle posed to Oedipus,[27] the key is that man always walked on two legs.

All the physical data—the placement of the spinal cord at the base of the skull, the breadth of the pelvis, and those footprints set for an eternity in the fresh volcanic ash of Tanzania—establish that protoman walked upright, probably as easily and as naturally as we do. Moreover, there is general agreement that this feature—which, among other things, freed up the hands—was the critical breaking point between man and the apes, the key feature that set him on his evolutionary way.[28]

It is also apparent from the evidence that these hominids, *Australopithecus*, to be more precise, were small—slight of build and probably no more than 1.5 meters tall—and virtually without natural armaments, not even a decent set of canines such as those of the baboon. Moreover, remains of pigs, antelopes, and other mammals specialized for life on the grasslands, found in association with hominids, indicate strongly that he lived not in the tropical forests that are the traditional home of the great apes but on the savannas with the teeming herds of herbivores and the big cats and other carnivores which preyed upon them.[29]

For whatever reason, this creature that was to become man left his ancient home and wandered out on new and inhospitable terrain. It appears that he began as a vegetarian, perhaps eking out a living, as Clifford Jolly suggests, by gathering seeds, an occupation that would seem to place a premium on digital manipulation. Yet food was probably scarce and danger a relatively constant fact of life. Despite some evidence indicating that primate flesh is unpalatable to large carnivores,[30] he, like his grassland-dwelling cousin the baboon, must have been subject to some predation.

Hunger and fear drove him toward change. It may have begun as modestly as digging for grubs and progressed gradually to scavenging. But man developed a taste for meat.

Moreover, at some point in this progression, he learned to use weapons. While the exact sequence of events may never be established, it could well have happened during the scavenging stage, possibly in the defense of carcasses brought down by one of the larger predators or simply to help him pry and eat the flesh. It need not have been a purposeful act, just a fortuitous accident later reinforced by operant conditioning. Yet gradually he came to realize that these previously useless objects, taken up in a hand preshaped for grasping and thrown or wielded with a body made nimble through bipedalism, could be transformed into deadly instruments—that he could take the offense. It was here that the hominid became a hunter.[31]

It was an amazing transition. Whether its time was relatively compressed or several hundred thousand years elapsed, hunting brought about an abrupt change in man's destiny. Undoubtedly, his success in these areas was based on a nexus of skills. Stealth, deception, relentlessness, and the ability to anticipate results all played a role. Yet it was weapons that made the killing possible.

Although the weapon may not have been the first tool, it did mark mankind's first great success with tools. The realization that he could supplement his own

Figure 1. A band of early men (*Homo habilis*) drives rival predators from a newly fallen dinothere, c. two million B.C. Reprinted by permission of the artist, Sara Landry, from Edward O. Wilson, *Sociobiology: The New Synthesis* copyright © 1975, 1980 by the President and Fellows of Harvard College.

physiognomy, artificially adapting himself for specific situations, was the beginning of culture.[32] With weapons early man was taking evolution into his own hands. He was no longer limited to a specific environment. If he lacked fur, he might clothe himself against the cold with the fur of other species. Artificial shelter, even boats, became possibilities. The options were literally unlimited.

Yet the users of early weapons, late *Australopithecus* and *Homo habilis,* were unlikely to have dwelled on the future. In their eyes the virtues of these devices were undoubtedly grounded in the here and now. For the first time hunger and fear were no longer absolutes.

It is apparent that early man, once he began hunting, moved relatively quickly to big game, prey much larger than himself. Numerous skulls fractured by blunt objects indicate that he attacked and killed the now-extinct giant baboon. In addition to antelope, giant sivatheres (horned giraffes) and dinotheres (elephantlike beasts with tusks curving downward) appear to have numbered among his victims.[33]

Concentrating on the killing of big animals made good sense. This sort of ''bonanza strategy,'' while difficult, has been shown to be economically sound by analysis of protein consumption among contemporary human hunters.[34] Large carcasses simply have a great deal more meat than small ones. Therefore, while periods of hunger and reliance on small prey and gathering lingered to remind him of the past, early man for the first time could look forward to regular intervals of protein glut and satiation.[35]

More was involved than just food. The psychological impact of weapons must have been profound. One has only to compare the demeanor of antelope, ever vigilant, to the posture of a pride of protein-besotted lions strewn heedlessly about the veldt, to understand the enormous difference in outlook between predator and prey. With weapons, even primitive ones, early man was transformed into a creature to be reckoned with, destined to become the most wanton and deadly of hunters. Because a variety of arms gave him the flexibility to stalk practically every type of terrestrial beast, most animals came to fear and avoid him—even when he was alone. Thus, weapons also served to isolate man, to build a barrier between himself and the natural world from which he sprang. It is a persistent cultural fantasy to look back to a time of human innocence and harmlessness, a time when man did not kill for a living. Yet the possession of weapons made it unlikely that the curtain of fear separating man from animal—at least wild animal—would ever be raised.

At first weapons must have been very primitive, nothing more than conveniently shaped rocks and sharp sticks. Gradually, however, steady reinforcement and a ready access to a variety of animal spare parts led man to increasingly efficient use of borrowed natural weapons—the long limb bones of antelope as clubs, for example, and their horns as daggers. At some point in this sequence— a point which defies precise location since all the evidence has either been destroyed or is archaeologically indistinguishable from other common forms—early man began to fashion his armaments, to sharpen sticks and bones, even chipping rocks to give them an edge.

Louis Leakey[36] and others believe that by the time of *Homo habilis,* roughly 1.5 million years ago, man had advanced to the point of inventing the bola. If true, this is significant since it constitutes the first example of a truly artificial weapon. There are simply no models in nature for launching stones through centrifugal force. Moreover, the bola provided a real standoff capability, always an attractive means of avoiding injury. Yet it, like the sling and the bow, placed definite limits on the size of the prey it could bring down with anything other than a fantastically lucky shot.

To kill a really large, thick-skinned animal required close confrontation and eventually either penetration or a heavy blow, or blows, to the head. It follows that, even at this early date, arms had begun a conceptual divergence. On one hand there were the standoff weapons, safe to use but limited in effect. On the other were penetration implements and the club, short-ranged to the extreme, backed by natural precedent, and, in this context at least, inherently decisive. But to use them required not only skill but raw courage—the willingness to close in on something larger, stronger, and often lethally aroused.

Even armed with his improvised panoply, an early representation of the genus *Homo* was no match for many of the victims he stalked. Therefore, group hunting, presumably modeled on the behavior of other predators, became a necessity with big game. Moreover, it was probably a significant factor in later social evolution. Specifically, this sort of close cooperation in killing would logically appear to have preadapted man for military organization and true warfare.[37] Yet this would come much later.

III

For most of human existence, man's killing proclivities probably remained fastened on other species. Yet this must be labeled as a matter of opinion. In fact, the nature and extent of intraspecific violence and its relationship to the discovery of weapons by early man is a highly controversial matter. Partly because it involves issues of deep significance to the survival of contemporary man, the topic has become overgrown with polemic and simplistic explanations. Certainly, the evidence is scarce and ambiguous enough to accommodate a wide range of viewpoints. Genetic analysis may prove more definitive, but for now, as with most problems dealing with Pliocene ethnology, the Sphinx tells us what she will and no more.

If there is such a thing as a popular vision of the subject, it is probably the one set forth in the memorable prologue to the film *2001: A Space Odyssey,* in which one of the members of a beleaguered band of monkey-men, presumably under the influence of an extraterrestrial artifact, picks up a conveniently shaped animal bone and promptly bashes in the skull of the nearest attacking conspecific. Disregarding the theme of outside intervention, it is possible to maintain that weapons were first enlisted to the cause of manslaughter, not hunting. Yet it is also quite possible to believe that man, prior to the weapon, was a pacific creature with no prior history of intraspecific aggression. Or that, if he did have such a history, it had a negligible effect on weapons use, which became essentially a reflection of acquired predatory behavior.[38]

Quite possibly the truth is more complex than any of these explanations allows. Yet it must be derived more as a matter of logic than evidence. Given the general tendency to satisfy basic needs first, early man would have had a good deal more interest in filling his stomach than in fighting his fellows. And it appears most likely that his ingenuity would have focused in this direction first. Although the possibility of cannibalism and the relationship of dominance to food access are complicating factors, it is most reasonable to assume that weapon use did not begin with conflict between conspecifics.

Yet to dismiss the influence of preestablished patterns of intraspecific competition on the eventual development and use of weapons also seems unwise. With the possible exception of the eastern mountain gorilla, hostility and some form of aggression, however ritualized, have been found throughout the primate order.[39] This being the case, it is likely that man exhibited at least some aggressive behavior prior to the point at which he discovered weapons. It seems only natural that when he did take up arms against himself, the preestablished framework of conflict would assert itself.

Supporting this hypothesis are several characteristic features of human weapons use. It is, for example, highly differentiated by sex. While mythical and historical exceptions can be cited (Artemis the huntress, the Amazons, Joan of Arc), combat and weapons innovation have always been the province of the male. Moreover, men build weapons not only to kill with but also to threaten. Whether it be in the form of a larger club, a terrible monster engraved on a breastplate, or the excruciating logic of deterrence, the urge to intimidate appears over and over. The phenomenon of the champion, the single superbly equipped warrior, also asserts itself throughout military history. Despite a general willingness to employ weapons in groups, man has demonstrated a consistent penchant for individual combat right up to the present. Finally, the urge to bring weapons under a specific body of rules and regulations would seem to have more than just a pragmatic basis. The ritualization of combat, as opposed to the more laissez-faire approach exemplified in predatory behavior, has always provided a major theme in weapons development, and one that cannot be attributed wholly to humanistic motives. Rather, it follows that the inclination to fight by the rules, to use similar weapons in a prescribed fashion, is a vestige of intraspecific combat. It is undeniable that violence reflecting hunting behavior—the urge to band together in groups, to kill excessively and in any way possible, to include both sexes and the young as victims—at times seems to make a mockery of these conventions. Yet it is difficult to dismiss the more ethical strain.

Rather, it appears that these two poles of aggression exist in a state of dynamic tension and together define the parameters of human violence. Given certain conditions, one will tend to dominate for a while, but inevitably the other will make its presence known. Because of their usefulness in describing and encapsulating major thematic concerns, the terms *predatory* and *intraspecific* will be referred to frequently in this study. However, in the historical context they are not meant to be understood as connoting scientific precision but rather as metaphors which describe behavior that is consistent and apparently deeply rooted.

If rules for fighting did exist prior to weaponry, they probably never precluded killing an opponent. Konrad Lorenz has theorized that, since our progenitors were once not dependent upon killing for a living, the need for specific inhibitory mechanisms against conspecific bloodshed present in a number of predators was not anticipated in the ancestral gene pool.[40] Moreover, Jane Goodall's observations of the repeated lethal attacks by the "northern" group on the "southern" group among the chimpanzees of Gombe seem to bear this out by analogy.[41] Thus, it follows that the introduction of armaments, with their death-dealing capacity, must have posed a great challenge to the primitive hominid social structure. It has even been suggested that some of the early hominid strains met extinction, not at the hands of *Homo erectus*, but because they proved incapable of controlling weapons use among their own kind.[42] From this perspective, man's survival, at least up to the dangerous present, is prima facie evidence that he learned to keep the violence within acceptable limits.

Yet what this actually meant in terms of day-to-day life is subject to wide disagreement. One school founded by Raymond Dart has labeled early man a "confirmed killer" and points to an array of physical evidence indicating an extremely high level of interpersonal violence.[43] M. K. Roper, for example, subjected the remains of 169 pre–*Homo sapiens* to intensive analysis and concluded that in 33 percent of the sample cases apparent injuries (e.g., skull fractures likely to have been inflicted with a blunt instrument) could be attributed to armed aggression.[44]

Yet it should be noted that these and other studies are based on very small samples of very old and incomplete evidence. It is possible to read a great deal more into these data than can be logically supported by the hunting-and-gathering way of life to which early man was universally wed. Ethnologists make note of the high degree of internal cooperation necessary to make such an arrangement work, especially in an arduous environment. Subject to some variation, it can be said that anthropological studies of contemporary hunting-and-gathering cultures generally reveal a relatively low-key existence in which teamwork is emphasized and hostility and aggression are more or less permanently muted.[45] (However, this too could be the result of natural selection in which the shy, peaceful people who did not engage in combat survived in forest relict zones.)

Nonetheless, observed behavior still indicates that the focus of violence, when it does come into play, is almost always external to the band and takes the form of extended blood quarrels. Yet here too, economic reality sets at least some theoretical limits on the duration and intensity of the bloodshed. This type of life simply does not afford the long-term food surpluses necessary for extended military campaigns. Moreover, the general absence of nonportable material goods, necessitated by nomadic shifts in hunting grounds, removes at least one major motive behind armed aggression.

Man during the formative era was not a numerous creature. Living in bands of twenty to forty and earning a living on the grasslands demanded that he wander over relatively large areas, territories too broad to defend. Contact with other bands was probably limited and, in case of hostilities, possible to break off through simple withdrawal. For early man, unlike today's hunter-gatherers locked in perpetual feuds with neighbors, there was almost always someplace else to go.

Most probably fighting was, as it is now among contemporary hunting-and-gathering people, a sporadic, highly personalized affair, homicidal in intent and, occasionally, in effect, but lacking a sustained economic and political motivation beyond that of revenge and, sometimes, women. Under such conditions, ambush and raiding are the preferred modes of operation, and the target often is a single "enemy." Pitched battles, when they occur, represent tactical failure. The object of the foray is rout, not prolonged combat. In such an environment the attacking party will close only if surprise is reasonably certain; otherwise the aim is to stay at long range and exchange missiles.[46]

From the perspective of the participants this makes perfect sense. What are frequently referred to as "wars" in this context are really only extensions of personal disputes. Armies are collections of individuals, fighting, in most cases, more out of loyalty to some injured party than to the group and its aspirations. Lacking a stronger, more unifying purpose, the combat potential of such a force is limited by the participants' willingness to assume risk, which is usually low. This type of combat is therefore inherently indecisive and produces few casualties. Given the motivating factors, it could hardly be otherwise.[47]

Thus, the portrait of early man drenched in his own blood seems considerably overdrawn. If his life was dangerous, it was probably more due to hunting than fighting. Here the willingness to work as part of a team, to move in and kill at close quarters was founded on the solid base of economic reality. Probably, as weapons slowly improved through the Pleistocene, the deadliness of interpersonal combat did in fact increase. Yet it was hunting and not fighting which drove these improvements.

Gradually, as his proficiency and intelligence grew, early man began to methodically work stone, particularly flint, to fashion more and more useful hand axes. The discovery of fire would have allowed him to char-harden the tips of wooden staves to produce effective spear forms. These two trends converged at some point at which some pioneering craftsman began lashing hand axes and stone points to wooden extensions to produce truly effective axes and spears. As this technique of hafting improved, stone artifacts would eventually begin to be shaped specifically to be joined to other materials.[48]

Skill and workmanship progressed slowly through the Lower and Middle Pleistocene until approximately forty thousand years ago, when a sort of takeoff point was reached. It is tempting to associate this stage, known as the Upper Paleolithic, with the finalization of our physical evolution and, as P. Lieberman and others have suggested, the development of true speech,[49] certainly a potent force in not only innovation but diffusion. While this last assertion is basically unprovable, it does seem apparent that some important threshold was passed and that from this point innovations occurred at an entirely more rapid rate than before.

Although this applied to the gamut of human activities, weapons certainly constituted an important part of the technical revolution, with the throwing stick, the spear thrower, the harpoon, the sling, and the bow appearing around this time.[50]

Of particular significance was the bow. A truly ingenious device, it took advantage of a number of mechanical principles to maximize lethality while retaining a high degree of light weight and portability. Allowing first the storage and then the sudden and precise release of human energy, the simple bow generated significant range (up to fifty meters) and velocity (up to seventy meters a second) and capitalized on the shape of the projectile (long and thin) to effectively convert this energy into penetrating power. Deadly against game up to the size of antelope,[51] the bow was eminently well suited to the type of combat typical among hunter-gatherers.

At once safe and deadly, it was the ideal weapon of harassment. A combatant might spend an afternoon shooting away at long range with little fear of injury. Yet if the opportunity arose, he could move in closer and swiftly, silently dispatch an enemy with a single shot. It is not surprising, therefore, that the earliest actual image of combat, a Mesolithic cave painting at Morela la Vella in Spain, depicts men fighting with bows.[52] Conceptually at least, the picture is a familiar one. The action is confused. The participants appear to be on the run, perhaps hoping to rip off a few quick shots before retreating. Moreover, all the combatants are armed symmetrically; only the bow is used.

The scene captures in a single visual metaphor the essence of primitive combat. No doubt it was vicious, at times as atrocious as man's growing imagination could make it. Yet there are no signs of organization or a strong economic motivation. Only with the coming of agriculture, and later politics, would true warfare become part of the human experience. Then there would be something to steal and governments to organize the theft.

Yet the tools of war were ready. Hunting had taught men to kill in groups. It had also nurtured the mechanisms of death. With the exception of the sword and body armor, both of which require metal, and the crossbow, all the major imple-

Figure 2. Mesolithic cave painting at Morela la Vella, Spain, which is the earliest depiction of men fighting, c. 20,000 B.C. From Irenaus Eibl-Eibesfeldt, *Krieg und Frieden aus der Sicht der Verhaltensforschung* © R. Piper GmbH & Co. KG, Munchen 1975, 1984.

ments of personal combat used prior to the invention of firearms were introduced during the hunting-and-gathering stage. Indeed, they made this way of life possible.

The criticalness of arms to such an economy—an economy which, after all, provided the environment in which man reached his final form—raises a number of issues of primary importance. Is there in fact a direct causal link between the development and use of weapons and our own physical and mental evolution? While it would not be hard to recruit a chorus of scholars willing to denounce this proposition, there are a number of reasons to suspect that it could be true nonetheless.

Certainly, defense mechanisms, both behavioral and physical, are commonly transmitted through the genes of species other than man. There is also little doubt that the making and using of weapons was of great significance experientially—both as a means of developing dexterity and hand-eye coordination and as a stimulus to accurate observation and generalization from nature. To be sure, there were other useful crafts which must have preoccupied early man in much the same way. Yet none was so intimately related to his long-term survival. Logically at least, weapons are the kind of vital adaptation which is normally favored heavily by natural selection.

Further supporting this supposition is the virtual universality of arms in human societies. Doubtless, cultures have been uncovered that do not possess implements of war. Yet in the history of ethnological research only one small group, the Phi Tong Luang, has been found not to have even weapons to hunt with.[53] (A second candidate, the Tasaday, a group of twenty-five individuals living what appeared to be an arboreal existence in the Philippines archipelago, has recently been alleged to have been a hoax set up by the Marcos regime to boost tourism.) While it is not a certainty, this sort of unanimity is often taken to indicate genetic, rather than cultural, transmission.

If this is true, if the urge to build and use weapons is literally a part of our gene pool, what does it mean?

Basically, no one knows and no one will know until the biochemical basis for human behavior is better defined. Even so, the idea of men gathering compulsively around engineering tables and churning out tank designs like bees building a nest is so ridiculous as to be rejected by even the most deterministic. Believers in genetic transmission of behavior patterns talk in terms of inherent predispositions toward different skills and activities. They concede that both man and his behavior are extremely complex and that if there is a genetic component to our actions, it is conditioned by the environment—the "interactionist paradigm."

Even so, the genetic transmission of at least some weapons-related behavior might help explain a number of phenomena, from the fascination of little boys with war toys to the pursuit of excessive and at times tactically and strategically irrelevant arms races in the face of all reason.

It also seems that a genetic dimension would have definite implications for the perceived relationship between war and weapons. According to conventional wisdom, weapons are a direct result of war, or at least the threat of war. If it could be shown that the two exist more or less independently, that the urge to build weapons stems from factors other than the immediate possibility of combat, then our attitudes toward both might change. Contemporary efforts to ameliorate the effects of mass violence seem to approach the problem with the assumptions that war is basically inevitable and that it is weapons development which can most effectively be controlled or even reversed.

Nevertheless, few would question that true warfare is purely a cultural adaptation, and a rather late one at that.[54] Weapons, on the other hand, may be much more deeply rooted. If the skein could be unraveled and the genetic strands separated scientifically from the cultural, we would be on much firmer ground in predicting what might and might not work in the way of arms control and peace research. Conceivably, new strategies might be developed which would take our hereditary proclivities into account and even turn them to our advantage.

This is, of course, speculation. Yet one element cannot so easily be dismissed. Weapons are far older and more intimately related to our species than warfare. If we came into this world armed, it was not necessarily as soldiers.

Chapter 3

GENESIS

I

Organized warfare was part of nature long before man arrived on the scene. The coordinated rapacity and obvious political intent with which certain of the social insects conduct aggression demonstrate that, behaviorally, there is nothing uniquely human about joining an army or fighting as part of it. Whether it be meeting-engagements between legions of specialized warriors or elaborate defenses of nests to avoid enslavement, most functional aspects of human warfare are accurately reflected in the miniature depredations of a creature such as *Eciton burchelli*.

Yet the key difference has to do with motivation. Driver ants wage war because their genes demand that they wage war. Man, on the other hand, invented his version of the phenomenon. It is a cultural instrument, a product of his imagination. This is why, as Quincy Wright recognized forty years ago, the study of animal aggression and primitive human conflict can be taken only so far in the explanation of conscious, organized warfare.[1] They are essentially static, while war is dynamic—invented for a specific purpose and changing with that purpose. To understand its true nature we must follow this path and trace its development.

The best estimate is that war, true war, began somewhere between seven and nine thousand years ago[2]—although it could have been much earlier—not as an aberration of the human psyche, but as the culmination of a revolutionary change in man's economic and social life. Prior to this transitional period, man had been a nomad, going where the game went. However, as early as 20,000 years ago and for reasons still unclear, scattered groups began settling down and foraging more intensively for a broader array of smaller foods. Shelter and possessions no longer had to be portable, but could become more substantial and elaborate. Food was stored. There is evidence of social and political differentiation.

Somewhat later, other groups began making the transition from hunters to herdsmen. For them, mobility probably remained central, but it was men who decided when and in what direction. Control, moreover, implied ownership. Thus, flocks became property, objects of value to be protected.

In both cases, the implications for human relations, and ultimately politics, were enormous. For this was the way of the future. Yet the process apparently took place in fits and starts. There is evidence of several complex foraging communities which evolved, collapsed, and disappeared. For the food they stored was essentially meat, easily spoiled. In the end, it seems these cultures simply crashed through this unstable resource base. But it is possible, though there is no specific evidence, that violence was involved. For the keys to societal conflict, property and politics, were in place, albeit in a rudimentary form.

True war probably required a more robust economic engine. The roots of agriculture appear to go back thirteen or fourteen thousand years to a few Mideastern cultures (the Natufians were archetypes) that harvested abundant and storable wild grains. Gradually, over three or four thousand years, planting and cultivating took hold. As techniques improved, fertile, well-watered land, especially, began to produce regular and substantial surpluses. By degrees a nexus of property grew up around the agricultural community. Wealth accumulated, and upon it grew not only civilization but covetousness and the will to power.

Jacob Bronowski has created a logical scenario for war's genesis. He argues persuasively that organized theft lies at the root of true warfare. Thus it may have begun when nomads—pastoralists or possibly advanced hunter-gatherers—having learned to steal from each other, descended on the fertile valleys and oases of the agriculturalist to rob his surpluses.[3] Women and revenge, the traditional motivators, presumably still played a role in these depredations, but it was this new factor, property, which provided the impetus that had been missing previously.

Although this dynamic—the nomadic outlander periodically sweeping down upon the sedentary agrarian—would remain a major theme in the history of aggression until at least the time of Genghis Khan, it was the agriculturalist response that would provide the major substance for our warlike past.[4] Having suffered at the hands of the interloper, agrarian communities gradually learned to defend themselves. In doing so they discovered that their more efficient economic systems imparted certain advantages in terms of time and available resources to be expended on martial activities. Similarly, it must soon have become apparent that a capable defense against nomadic marauders might be turned against their fellow plant growers in order to obtain better land, women, possessions, or even political dominion. Archaelogically in the Mideast, these changes are registered in two ways: the appearance of weapons, such as the mace and later the battle-ax, which were clearly optimized for combat, not hunting, and the introduction of massive encircling walls and fortifications around centers of population.

In the latter case, the mid-1950s discovery and subsequent excavation of the massive stoneworks at Jericho demonstrated that such measures were undertaken considerably earlier (ca. 7000 B.C.) and were technically a good deal more advanced than anyone had hitherto suspected.[5] Moreover, their size (up to seven meters tall) and sophistication (a large moat nine meters wide and three meters deep had been scooped out of the rock at the foot of the wall) implied equally potent means of attack. This precocity is symptomatic of the entire epoch of war up until the invention of gunpowder. While it is not exactly accurate to say that military systems emerged full-blown at the dawn of history, a remarkable amount was finalized very early, with the details being worked out, forgotten, and periodically rediscovered over a span of five thousand years.

The era began, however, with one great innovation, and that was metal. For reaping grain, slicing up carcasses, or trimming skins, stone tools served very well. Yet in combat the wielder of metallic weapons had a tremendous advantage over adversaries whose stone-based arms were all too prone to shatter at a critical moment. Moreover, the toughness and ductility of metal made it possible to extend the length of the dagger to produce, by the middle of the third millennium B.C., a true sword,[6] an instrument whose reach, maneuverability, and capacity to inflict both slash and puncture wounds rendered it practically ideal for the kind of close-in combat which would become the specialty of the warrior class.

To be efficient, however, swords required a metal harder and stronger than the copper that was smelted initially. Here, again, the progress of metallurgy serves to illustrate the point about precocity. Very rapidly, probably by 3500 B.C.,[7] certain groups in the Middle East had learned how to alloy copper with tin to produce bronze, a substance which not only could be cast into complex forms, but, after cold-working, produced weapons of sufficient tensile strength and hardness to rival those of iron for certain uses until Roman times, when tempering came to be understood. Yet it is worth noting that iron, too, was used very early, Anatolian armorers having experimented with ferrous blades at least as far back as 2500 B.C.[8]

Clearly, the major limitation on early metallurgy was less a matter of technology than availability. Deposits of tin, in particular, were not only scarce and capriciously scattered in this part of the world but relatively difficult to extract. Under the circumstances, it was practically inevitable that the bulk of what metal there was would be channeled into weaponry, and that governmental structures would expand, in part, to control its acquisition and distribution.[9]

For at this level the relationship between metallurgy, weaponry, and politics is intimate and self-reinforcing. Hence, the superior cutting and penetrating qualities of metal called forth a defensive reciprocal in metal and metal-reinforced helmets, torso protection and shields, objects destined to become virtual prerequisites of honorific combat for thousands of years. Yet the influence of metal was hardly limited to the stimulation of new weapons. Metal points and socketed heads greatly increased the lethality of holdovers from an earlier era—the spear, the ax, and the bow. In the latter case, especially, metal-tipped arrows, propelled by bows rendered much more powerful through composite construction, combined to produce a weapon that not only was vastly improved in range and penetration but necessitated further metallic protection. This was characteristic: The need for metal fed upon itself.

Yet the advantages of metal-armed troops, in terms of their ability to coerce, were too clear to ignore. Moreover, the organization necessary to obtain such armaments also served to reinforce their effectiveness. As Stanislav Andreski notes, it is well known that coercion, like any mass-oriented activity, benefits from economies of scale. Hence, it is a great deal easier for a force of one thousand to control a population of one hundred thousand than it is for one man to control one hundred.[10] As armies grew, therefore, so did the potential for enforcing social discipline and, eventually, the capacity to dominate much larger populations. Similarly, the evolution of internal control—the maintenance of order and discipline within a military force—not only improved fighting efficiency but exerted a significant influence on the emerging body politic. Hierarchies, particularly those based on multiples of ten, so suited for military command structures, naturally extended themselves to the ordering of life in general—so much so that the Pyramids seem at times less monuments than giant organization charts.[11]

Yet for all this emphasis on the emerging power of groups and organizations, it is important to remember that war is still based on the life and death of the individual. Moreover, just as pyramids reach a pinnacle, so political structures were generally capped by one man with more to win or lose than any other. Hence, individual combat would remain a persistent and important theme in warfare throughout the period under study.

II

The idea of warfare as the prime motivating force and major preoccupation of emerging urban societies must strike some as entirely overdrawn. Generally, the appearance of civilization is perceived as having broadened and enriched life, not simply militarized it. Also, it can be said that such an approach is unidimensional in that it ignores significant variations in societal evolution, along with a host of other causal factors such as religion and kinship. If the matter is looked at from our own historical perspective, a vantage point largely devoid, at least in the industrialized world, of daily hunger and internecine violence, all of this must be conceded. The picture is a distorted one.

Yet when seen through the eyes of the participants, this seems much less true. The image which emerges from monuments, inscriptions, and the writings of contemporaries is that of a dangerous world where attack could come from any quarter and only the militarily strong survived. In such an environment the successful society was, by definition, the society successful at waging war.

For example, although the Greek city-state of the fifth century B.C. is remembered today chiefly for the magnificence of its cultural achievements, it is more likely that it was respected by contemporaries primarily for the deadly efficiency of its heavy infantry and naval squadrons. Moreover, there is reason to believe the Greeks saw themselves in much the same light. Lest this seem exaggerated, it is instructive to consider that the three greatest Greek historians, the three greatest of antiquity, for that matter—Herodotus, Thucydides, and Polybius—all chose major wars as the centerpieces of their works. Nor were they alone. Practically every history preserved from this period, and later the Middle Ages, concerns itself with war and conquest. Quite simply, these were seen as the chief events of the day and the ones thought most worthy of recording.

Other aspects of culture were similarly, though perhaps less uniformly, infused with the martial spirit. In many cases the very gods were warlike, fighting among themselves in titanic struggles which defined the state of the art in bellicosity.

These and other less-exalted examples of heroism often functioned as a sort of cultural reservoir, providing a pool of available stories and events suitable for graphic representation and linguistic embellishment.

In particular, the orally composed epic poems which form the basis for so many national literatures are repositories for such tales, startling the modern reader with their gory heroics and unabashed celebration of homicide and the warrior ethic. This is significant since it can be argued that monuments, inscriptions, and even histories were generally commissioned by the very parties doing the fighting and were therefore indicative of only a small segment of society. Yet epics such as the *Iliad* or the *Chanson de Roland* were not mandated. They arose as a form of mass entertainment and were necessarily reflections of the popular consciousness.

Judging by the content, it was far from pacific. It may be that men were intrinsically no more violent than they are today. Yet their acceptance, even celebration, of force as the final arbiter of human affairs is striking. Until law took hold of men's minds, might literally meant right. In intersocietal terms this spelled endless warfare.

Of course, there were numerous variations. Some states were obviously more aggressive than others. The frequency of wars for all seems to have been affected by long-term climatic and demographic trends.[12] Bribery and diplomacy often acted as surrogates for actual combat. But in the last analysis, it remains true that until at least the commercial revolution of the seventeenth century A.D. dominant states and empires achieved that status ultimately through an ability to wage war.

An awareness of the importance of warfare during the period under consideration is critical to the study of armaments. Lacking this, it is impossible to appreciate the significance of the fact that weapons were not relentlessly improved over time by societies ambitious for power and conquest.

Such forbearance was not without exception. There is certainly evidence to show at least a sporadic awareness that better weapons could provide a decisive margin of superiority in battle, and, occasionally—particularly in time of crisis—this did lead to fundamental improvements. Also, it does seem that politically ambitious states were, in fact, somewhat more innovative than their more passive counterparts. Yet even in these cases, which are rare, the momentum was never sustained, and in fact novel arms frequently fell into disuse.

Thus, weapons development until at least the mid–nineteenth century A.D. is best described as cyclical rather than linear. To a remarkable degree the same basic variables continued to reassert themselves, though not necessarily in the same combinations. This is not because men didn't care about weapons. Quite the contrary, they revered them. Nor was it necessarily due to a dearth of technology, though the means available were often very primitive. Rather, the key to stability seems to lie more in the fact that arms were so bound up with ritual and culture— not just biology and tradition but economic and political reality—that fundamental changes often implied a restructuring of society itself.

To see how and why this was true requires that we take up the historical record and examine in a roughly chronological order the manner in which it revealed itself. Yet such a trek through time poses a number of immediate difficulties. A subject of this magnitude, pursued for so long by so many, implies a journey far beyond the resources of the present study. In our case, only through ruthlessly selecting our stopping points will it be possible to descend to the level of detail necessary to show why it was that certain cultures came to fight and bear arms as they did. The key, then, becomes picking the military entities which were truly significant to the development of war and weaponry. This must be an arbitrary process. The reasoning behind the choices made here is complex and will gradually become apparent in the narrative. Yet one guiding criterion should be stipulated at the outset. Modern weaponry is a derivative of Western culture and civilization. Thus, while our tour through history will not exclude nonoccidental cultures entirely, it will be highly skewed in the direction of the West. No doubt much important military history will be missed, but so was it missed by those who brought our armaments to their present level of destructiveness.

III

The earliest organized military forces for which hard evidence is available are those of Mesopotamia, specifically the cluster of city-states (Ur, Kish, Lagash, Erech, Suruppack, Larsa, and Umma) known collectively as Sumer.[13] This is a purely generic term, though. The Sumerian communities never willingly formed anything that resembled a single political unit, but fell instead into a pattern of constant intramural warfare, in many ways similar to that which would prevail in ancient Greece and on the Italian peninsula during the Renaissance.

As best can be reconstructed, they began as outlanders, coming down out of Persia and settling in lower Mesopotamia sometime during the fourth millennium.[14] Here they built their cities out of brick made from the abundant mud of the Tigris and the Euphrates and kept cuneiform records inscribed in the same substance. Of these, the most famous relate to a fragmentary epic cycle surrounding the life of Gilgamesh of Erech, an actual person but also quite literally the first hero in written literature and a model for those who would follow.[15]

From a military perspective the Gilgamesh epic is particularly interesting in the manner in which it relates to Sumerian fighting forces and in its remarkable foreshadowing of the *Iliad*'s effect on the development of Greek heavy infantry. For at the core of the matter is a singular contradiction: Gilgamesh was an individual combatant and his countrymen were not. Armed with a battle-ax (surnamed "Might of Heroism," the first of a long line of titled weapons) and a coat of mail probably scaled with bronze, but not a bow, he was obviously oriented toward close combat.[16] So were his retainers, though they seem to have relied on the spear.[17]

Yet perhaps more suggestive than armament was Gilgamesh's relationship to his men. Clearly, this was not one of blind obedience. Quite the contrary, when Gilgamesh plans to fight the rulers of Kish over water rights, he must put the question before an assembly of warriors, which immediately rejects the idea and only later reconsiders.[18] If Gilgamesh ruled Erech, he did so with the consent of the governed.

Figure 3. "Stele of Vultures" a Sumerian stele from Telloh, Early Dynatic III, depicting a fully developed phalanx, third millennium B.C. Courtesy of the Musées Nationaux Louvre, Paris.

This takes on particular significance in light of a remarkable artifact, a limestone victory monument dated 2500 B.C., the Stele of Vultures. Here the basic dichotomy between the individual warrior and group combatants is illustrated in the most startling way. The Stele of Vultures depicts Eannat of Lagash leading his troops into battle, the hero at the head of his army, yet the infantry behind him is extraordinary indeed. Packed shoulder to shoulder, advancing behind a barrier of locked rectangular shields reinforced with bronze disks, and presenting a hedgehog of spearheads protruding from several rows back, this mass constitutes a full-fledged phalanx. This is an important distinction since there is a decided tendency to overlook or discount the significance of this Sumerian development.[19]

This is not surprising. It is incredibly out of context, coming almost two thousand years before the "advanced" Greeks took up the formation. Moreover, rather than being the product of a sustained technical evolution, it appears to have burst virtually full-blown upon the scene. Why this is so is suggested by the behavior of Gilgamesh's men. They are clearly people with a stake in society, the very types necessary for a style of warfare which demands that the participants both fight at close range and face danger in a cooperative fashion. Such qualities are impossible to bring out in any but highly motivated troops. Therefore, although the phalanx was clearly an innovation in the technical sense, it is perhaps better thought of as a sort of limited military option, available for those with the right kind of government but otherwise unusable. This type of absolute constraint, whether politically, economically, or sociologically based, would appear to have been a significant factor in the diffusion and development of weapons technologies up to modern times.

The apparent tension in Sumer between the individualized warrior and the phalanx also had political implications. It is interesting that the Stele of Vultures depicts phalangites and the individual warrior as similarly dressed and protected. While this obviously has something to do with both being specialized for close combat, it is also true that possessing and wearing appropriate regalia was a prime determinant of social status in numerous traditional societies.[20] Thus, the phalangite's adoption of aristocratic arms, a phenomenon which would be repeated in ancient Greece, not only reflects the community's growing ability to accumulate metal but implies an act of social mobility.

Despite the importance of political factors, these preferences also appear to draw on deeper roots. Thus, the confrontational style of Sumerian warfare seems to find its analogue in the Pleistocene hunt. In both cases the greatest rewards and dangers were to be found at close range, where the virtues of courage and cooperation were most severely tested. It was natural, therefore, that the weapons appropriate for fighting at such distances—the spear, the sword, the ax, and the dagger—tended to take on the prestige associated with physical bravery. But it was more than just a matter of status and weapons. The manifest lethality of the Sumerian phalanx and its successors indicated that the outlook of the hunt, with its casual ruthlessness and willingness to kill without mercy, had now become imprinted on warfare, allowing men to commit acts of mass violence unprecedented except in the broken bodies of a herd of mastodons run off a cliff. It was here that men learned to kill wantonly, and it was this terrible capacity which they turned on themselves when they transferred it to warfare.

Yet it also seems that the influence of the hunt was balanced and somewhat mitigated by the tradition of intraspecific aggression, especially in the perpetuation of single combat. There were, of course, pragmatic and political reasons. But the prominence of individualized fighting in so many divergent cultures indicates a deeper motivation. Apparently, something remained to remind antagonists that males of the same species most naturally settled disputes in pairs. On the other hand, it is obvious but still worth reiterating, that women were excluded from Sumerian and, until very recently, virtually all subsequent forms of organized combat (sieges and wars with genocidal overtones being special exceptions). In this regard it would appear that, rather than serving as the equivalent of the hunt (an activity in which female predators frequently participate), warfare preserved the intraspecific role of the female as prize and object of combat. If nothing else, this helps to account for the aura of sexuality which has hung about war and weapons throughout history, serving as both a thematic equipoise to its ruthlessness and an indication of the complexity of the subject and the motives behind it.

But if these undercurrents are important clues to help us understand why war developed as it did, the phenomenon remains basically about economics and politics. And on these grounds the Sumerians were shortly to be superseded by a new type of state with a different style of warfare. The phalanx and the endless quarrels between small entities would be replaced by empire, absolute rule, and the bow.

IV

His name was Sargon, and he began life around 2300 B.C., the illegitimate son, legend has it, of a Semite girl who abandoned him, Moses-like, in a cradle of reeds. He was, however, fished out of the Euphrates and grew up among the Sumerians, rising quickly—apparently on raw talent—to the important position of royal cupbearer to Ur-Zababa of Kish. But when the ambitious Lugalzaggesi of Umma dethroned and perhaps killed Sargon's patron, he took matters into his own hands, staging a successful surprise attack against Lugalzaggesi's capital, Erech, and later defeating the remains of his troops in two pitched battles.[21]

The ancient home of Gilgamesh had fallen. Lugalzaggesi was led away in chains, and Sargon was launched on a military career that would lead to victory in, according to his own count, thirty-four major battles and the establishment of a domain that would stretch eventually from the Mediterranean to the Persian Gulf.[22] Not only did he subdue all of Sumer, but under his leadership armies from the Mesopotamian plains for the first time sought to take and hold the surrounding highlands, thus reversing a centuries-old pattern of conquest.[23]

This campaign is of particular interest militarily since it has been cited by Richard Humble and others[24] as accounting for the disappearance of the Sumerian phalanx. While it is certainly true that close infantry formations are nearly impossible to maintain in hilly, broken terrain, it is also a fact that Sargon and his empire had removed the political foundation of the phalanx. Though the Sumerian kings had never been above lording their power over their weaker rivals, Sargon had created something else, a new type of dominion which took much fuller advantage of the power latent in military organizations. He was the architect of the world's first predatory transnational tyranny, a political form remarkable for its persistence and steadfast in its reliance on absolute rule, rigid hierarchies, and, above all, force as the major mechanism of expansion and cohesion.

Such a societal structure necessarily influenced the evolution of its military instrumentalities. At the core, Sargon's Akkadian Empire consisted of a small Semitic warrior class living off the labor of a few artisans and an ethnically heterogeneous mass of peasants. Because the latter group had no more than a marginal loyalty to the state, it is logical to assume that they lacked the aggressiveness and steadiness to fight at close range. Indeed, as Stanislav Andreski notes, the proverbial passivity of the peasantry is largely responsible for the despotic penchant for foreign mercenaries.[25] Yet in the ancient world such troops were notoriously fickle and expensive, while economies of scale continued to prompt tyrannies of this nature to field very large peasant-based armies.

Under the circumstances a heavy reliance on the bow was practically inevitable since it provided meaningful lethality without necessitating hand-to-hand combat. While the physical evidence is slim, the existence of at least two Akkadian fragments depicting the use of the composite bow (the first such representation) has led Yigael Yadin and others to hypothesize that this new weapon—its power magnified by the careful lamination of bone, keratin, and sinew to a wooden core—provided the margin of superiority over the Sumerians.[26]

Yet in actual tactical terms it is probable that the peasant archers were merely expected to keep up a fairly steady stream of arrows. In this sort of army the decisive maneuver element was composed of those with the most at stake, the ruler and his retainers, who were generally armed for close combat, though the bow was often carried too.

Also, it would be surprising if the Akkadian nobility did not ride into battle on chariots similar to the four-wheeled, onager-drawn vehicles of the Sumerians. This was a weapon peculiarly suited to, even archetypical of, this kind of warfare. Most sources agree it was essentially worthless as an engine of destruction.[27] Yet as an instrument of intimidation its impact was sufficient to win it a stable place in the Eurasian hero-oriented army until at least the time of Alexander. For the speed and power implied in this multiequine vehicle served as a reliable means of terrorizing the weakly motivated, fulfilling the traditional role of bluff in intraspecific combat. Meanwhile, it further reinforced the heroic warrior's image of himself as far more valuable in combat than lesser men.

Yet lesser men were not really the object. In most armies the chariot evolved basically to fight other chariots, or at least to bring heroes into contact so they could duel on foot.[28] Here was the key to this kind of combat—find and kill the leadership. Thus, military historians miss the point when they provide detailed tactical descriptions of such actions, imputing motives which did not exist and labeling as maneuver what really only amounted to crazed looting.[29] Such engagements turned on one encounter only, the melee around the headmen. Should the king and his prime retainers fall, the battle was lost.

This exposes the weakness of the entire system. It was powerful and intimidating, but utterly brittle and vulnerable to decapitation. Great empires could and did melt away in an afternoon. Thus, after generations of expansion and conquest, Sargon's grandson Naram-Sin had only to meet one defeat (ca. 2230 B.C.) before the barbarous mountain dwellers to the east, the Gutians, and the Akkadian Empire became no more than a pale memory in the minds of a Sumerian poet centuries later: "In not five days, not ten days . . . The herald could not proceed on his journey; the sea-rider could not sail his boat . . . brigands dwelt on the roads; the doors of the gates of the land turned to clay."[30]

Almost nine hundred years would pass before history gave birth to an imperial beast with an appetite of the same magnitude. The history of Assyria is the history of war. Thus, A. T. Olmstead notes that from 890 to 640 B.C., the great age of Assyrian imperialism, the records listed wars for 180 of the 250 years.[31]

More than any other, this state epitomized the character of the transnational tyranny. Ruthless, endlessly aggressive, and hated by practically all with whom they came into contact, the Assyrians built one of the great empires of all time. A dominion welded together by an administrative structure of unprecedented dynamism and fed by an army remarkable for its versatility, inventiveness, and efficiency, the Assyrian Empire was destined to survive for some seven centuries. Yet in the end it would meet the same shattering fate as its Akkadian predecessor.

Though longtime residents of upper Mesopotamia, the Assyrians were slow to assert themselves. Until about 1360 B.C. they remained the vassals of the kingdom of Mitanni, which at its height straddled the upper reaches of the Tigris and the Euphrates.[32] A combination of Hittite pressure and internal dissension severely weakened the Mitanni, allowing Ashuruballit, the first of the great Assyrian warrior-kings, to take the offensive against his former masters, beginning an up-and-down succession of wars and conquests destined to claim as victims all of Mesopotamia, Syria, Palestine, and finally Egypt. Assyrian history was not without its reverses, and more than once the empire shrank practically to the gates of Nineveh. But always it would reassert itself.

To a great degree this resilience was based on an army which remained by and large much better organized and equipped than those which resisted it. Built on multiples of a basic tactical unit of ten, there are indications that discipline and control within the force were of a distinctly higher order than anything that had come before.[33] Moreover, the Assyrians' attitude toward weaponry, rather than being traditional, was experimental. Indeed, there is evidence that this was a conscious policy pursued with considerable energy, if somewhat sporadically. Thus, Assyria stands as a major exception to the tranquil course of weapons development and a prime example of the congruence between arms innovation and political voracity.

At the center of the Assyrian arsenal was the bow, an exceedingly powerful composite weapon with its ends characteristically curled forward like the bill of a duck.[34] Yet more significant than the bow's form and performance was the versatility with which it was used. As in other armies of this sort, the basic tactical unit consisted of foot archers, either employed as skirmishers or massed in groups. The Assyrians, however, departed from their rivals in the unprecedented lengths to which they went not only to protect the latter category of bowmen but to integrate them with other capabilities. After the reign of Ashurnasir-pal (885–860 B.C.), ranks of archers are depicted as not only screened by shield bearers and heavily armed spearmen, but themselves dressed in long coats of mail and conical helmets.[35] Such measures were extraordinarily costly in metal, especially iron, which the Assyrians pioneered using on a large scale. Yet they achieved an important result—the stability in these formations necessary to exploit other tactical possibilities. For the Assyrian army was history's first embodiment of the principle of combined arms, capitalizing with ruthless pragmatism on all known weapons and introducing new ones when the opportunity presented itself.

Not unexpectedly, the chariot, now a two-wheeled vehicle made heavier and more stable during the reign of Tiglath-pileser III (747–727 B.C.), retained a prominent place as a mobile platform for nobles armed for close combat but relying on the bow.[36] More significant, though, was the introduction, sometime around 875 B.C.—likely in emulation of the nomad or possible the Sumerians— of troops actually mounted on horseback.[37] Faster than the chariot and incomparably more agile on rough terrain, mounted troops were an immediate success. Indeed, the Assyrian grafting of archer to horse not only interjected a vital element of tactical flexibility, but in fact constituted a first cut at what would come to be the deadliest weapon combination prior to the introduction of firearms.

Yet there was one catch. Carvings indicate that the Assyrians never learned to ride very well, certainly not well enough to take full advantage of the man-horse synergy. For one thing, they did not have saddles.[38] Realistically, the effective wielding of a composite bow at a full gallop while riding bareback required a level of skill obtained only through a lifetime on a horse. Nomads might manage such acrobatics, but the precarious perch of Assyrian horse archers in relief provides a graphic illustration of the sociological limitations on ancient weapons innovation. You could put a man on a horse, but there was no guarantee that he would stay there.

Nevertheless, mounted troops, even relative tenderfeet, proved extremely useful to the Assyrians in functions extrinsic to the central action, namely reconnaissance and pursuit. Now an enemy might be kept under observation and assaulted at exactly the moment when conditions were most propitious. Still more important, once his formations were broken, survivors could be effectively pursued and prevented from rallying, thus rendering Assyrian battle tactics considerably more deadly and decisive.

Yet in a larger sense the fundamentally predatory nature of these functions— seeking out the victim and then running him down for slaughter—provides a deeper insight into the Assyrian martial ethic, or lack of it. Here, again, the absolute ruthlessness of the hunt has come to transcend the mitigating influence inherent in intraspecific combat. This is characteristic of the Assyrian approach to war, a perspective nowhere more evident than in their devotion to siegecraft.

It is probably safe to assume that up to A.D. 1650 more resources were invested in defensive walls than in all other public works combined. Regardless of culture or politics, virtually every urban center above hamlet size in the temperate band of Europe, Asia, and North Africa would come to have its surrounding ramparts.[39] So strong was the urge to fortify that imperial entities would eventually attempt to seal off entire regions in this manner. (It is a singular fact that the Great Wall of China remains the sole object of human endeavor visible to the naked eye from near-space orbit.) Considering the means available, the magnitude of the effort expended on walls of all sorts is staggering.

Yet in a violent world they were the ultimate insurance policy, the final refuge in times of danger. While walled strongholds were never an absolute guarantee of safety, their prevalence argues convincingly for their basic soundness. Prior to 880 B.C., walled towns sometimes fell to starvation, treachery, undermining, or direct assault with scaling ladders.[40] But in general, attacking armies lacked a reliable means of reducing stone and masonry fortifications and consequently tended to avoid them. War, then, was largely a pragmatically circumscribed activity— intraspecific inhibitions reinforced by the obduracy of brick and rubble. Armies of young males might fight in the field to their hearts' content, but larger populations (the old, women, and children) remained relatively immune to their depredations.

Figure 4. Assyrian battering ram, one of the most fearsome and effective weapons in history, in relief from the northwest palace of Ashurnasirapal Kalakh (Nimrud) Chamber B. c. 870 B.C. Reproduced by courtesy of the trustees of the British Museum.

Yet the Assyrians would have none of these limitations. They descended upon safe havens, in Byron's words, "like a wolf on the fold," carrying with them siege engines capable of beating down the defenses which had frustrated others.

The Assyrian battering ram was one of the most ruthlessly successful weapons in history. Introduced during the reign of Ashurnasir-pal, the same military wizard who fostered mounted troops, these rams appear in relief as already extraordinarily well developed mechanisms, again illustrating the suddenness and precocity of ancient weapons innovation.[41]

Built on a six-wheeled wooden frame and covered with protective plates of leather and wicker, the engine's projecting beam was suspended in such a way that it might be directed either horizontally or upward as the tactical situation demanded. Different bits were provided for brick or conglomerate. There was even a turret for observation or defensive fire.

Visually the machine is startling, an acute prophecy of an early-twentieth-century armored vehicle. Yet functionally there was a major difference. Tanks have evolved largely to fight other tanks. Battering rams were aimed at walls; the developmental action was strictly asymmetrical, as is almost always the case with siegecraft and weapons employed primarily against civilian populations.

For the battering ram implied what amounted to total war, calculated and frequently merciless. After taking one town Ashurnasir-pal bragged: "I cut off their heads. I burned them with fire, a pile of living men and of heads over against the city gate I set up. Men I impaled on stakes. The city I destroyed, devastated. I turned it into mounds and ruin heaps, the young men and maidens in the fire I burned.''[42]

This sort of ritual slaughter is particularly endemic to siege warfare, though it also occurred after field actions. Clearly separate from the tactical confrontation itself, it appears more closely akin to experiences surrounding the hunt. Quite literally, the victor casts aside any feeling of common humanity and indulges in killing for its own sake. Whether this was because man lacked the inhibitory mechanisms of a natural predator or was instead purely a cultural adjustment is impossible to say at this point. But humankind, and particularly the Assyrians, had enlisted a terrible capacity in the cause of war and politics—a capacity that would lead one day to the death camps of Auschwitz and the targeting of urban populations with nuclear weapons.

But, as always, beneath the bloodlust was the calculating hand of self-interest. Once the killing stopped, the robbery and economic exploitation began.

For the instruments of conquest must have been expensive beyond all precedent. Metal-based armor protection for thousands; a massive stock of war horses to be cared for and fed; siege engines weighing in the tons to be either transported or constructed on the spot—all the innovations the Assyrians sprung on their victims translated into what must have been an order-of-magnitude leap in the cost of waging war. Moreover, as military specialties increased in complexity, the force structure became, by necessity, more professional. Though the national levy was still called, by the time of Sargon II (a usurper whose taste in nomenclature testifies to an acute sense of history) in about 720 B.C., the core was an actual standing army.[43]

Seen from a cost-benefit standpoint, such a force was entirely inappropriate for a primitive economy based mostly on subsistence agriculture unless it largely paid for itself. To maintain its own sophistication the Assyrian military machine had to fight and keep on fighting. The enormous hauls of metal and slaves from the cities taken were the fuels which fed the economic fires of the military leviathan. As costs rose, so did the pulse of Assyrian history, which after 745 B.C. comes to resemble a vortex of destruction. The sack of Damascus (732), the sack of Samaria (722), the sack of Musasir (714), the sack of Thebes (671), the sack of Susa (639)—each was a military victory but also a monument to the insatiable hunger that drove the beast.

Inevitably, as the empire grew beyond the limitations of its communications and administrative network, revolt spread among conquered nationalities. The Assyrians responded with characteristic harshness, going so far as deporting entire populations as a means of pacification.[44] Yet they could not extinguish the spark of disobedience, and gradually more and more resources were consumed in putting down new conflagrations. Worse yet, the increasing difficulty of the task bears witness to the growing military capabilities of Assyria's foes.

Generally in the ancient world, geographical isolation and tradition-based weapons choice combined to foster a relatively high degree of arms asymmetry. In the case of the Assyrians, however, success over several centuries inevitably led to imitation. As metal production, especially of ferrous ores, grew, mail, helmets, and particularly iron-bladed swords became increasingly more common throughout the region. Organizations also improved, with hierarchies of ten becoming the basis for command structures in a number of armies besides the Assyrian. Specialist troops also proliferated, and new forms of arms were consciously assimilated. Thus Samuel, upon establishment of the central kingdom of Israel, declared a chariot squadron might be set up for the first time.[45] It must have happened again and again as the rule of symmetry silently asserted itself and the Assyrian military advantage gradually slipped away. True enough, this took place over several centuries, and the Assyrian army continued to win battles right up to the end.

Yet in the last analysis, innovation and hegemony based solely on superiority of arms proved largely self-defeating. The Assyrians raised the level of expertise within their army to the limits of technological and sociological possibility. But in doing so they merely provided a standard to be equaled.

After the death of Ashurbani-pal (626 B.C.), the leadership faltered, and nothing remained to hold the empire together. All of Mesopotamia rose in revolt. Whether Arnold Toynbee is correct in assuming that depopulation was the ultimate price of militarism, Assyria, at this point, was indeed "a corpse in armor."

Finally, in 612 B.C., surrounded by enemies, Nineveh would fall, her walls breached, no doubt, by the siege engines her rulers had so confidently introduced centuries before. "Desolate Nineveh," sneered Nahum, prophet of Yaweh. "Who shall bewail her?"[46]

Chapter 4

THE GREEKS

I

Nahum was right. In 401 B.C., barely two hundred years after the fall of Nineveh, Xenophon the Athenian, one of ten thousand fugitive Greek mercenaries, would pass the ruins and speculate as to their origin. Yet it seems none of the locals could provide anything of substance, and he would leave no better informed than when he arrived.[1]

This sojourn did not simply epitomize Nineveh's dismal fate; it pointed to a profound change in military history. The fact that this Greek was alive and sight-seeing, and not taking his place in a pile of severed heads at the foot of the Persian great king, signified better than anything else could the geographical shift of military power out and away from its traditional home, the Middle East. A few weeks earlier at Cunaxa, Xenophon and his companions—bunched together and fighting with spears—had cut like a knife through the traditional bow-based, aristocrat-dominated mass army of the East.[2] The days of the Persian Empire and the style of fighting upon which it was founded were numbered.

Actually, the seed of this transition had been planted earlier, 450 years before, in the fertile imagination of a blind Greek poet, recounting the deeds of heroes still four centuries further back in the past who had fought in a manner which the Greeks would one day cast aside.[3] But the genius of this man Homer was such that the images of combat he created would never fade from memory. His greatest poem, was called the *Iliad,* and it was destined to become the most influential tale of war ever composed.

To say the *Iliad* was the Greeks' favorite story vastly understates the case. In their eyes it epitomized everything that was Greek. It was the foundation of their religion. It defined in many ways their conception of reality. It set the standard for social behavior and etiquette. And above all, it told men how to act when they fought one another.[4]

The action of the *Iliad* spins out over several weeks or months (Homer is vague on time) of the ninth year of a war between an invading confederation of mainland Achaean Greeks and the allies and residents of the city of Troy—mostly Greek too, but inhabitants of the northwestern coast of Asia Minor.

To say that the invaders have laid siege to the city is technically correct but stretches the point entirely. Not only do the Achaeans lack siege engines, but the obvious good health and energetic conduct of the defenders indicates that the attackers have not even attempted to separate the city from its food supply. History indicates, and the characters are frank to admit, that raiding and plunder were economically viable activities. Yet in this case the campaign has stretched far beyond its potential for profit.

Rather, the *causus beli* is to be found with a woman, Helen, the beautiful wife of one of the leading invaders, Menelaos, stolen years before by the Trojan prince Paris, or Alexandros as he is alternately called. It is the redress of this insult and the sheer love of fighting which has kept the Greek heroes on the plains of Ilion for so long.

This is war. Yet its issues have been reduced largely to personal terms. Basically, the central characters of both armies are collections of individuals striving for above all, personal glory and a chance to be remembered. In this regard the Homeric conception of warfare, unlike the Assyrian, seems fundamentally in consonance with the characteristics of intraspecific combat. Conversely, predatory values are less apparent. Homer's characters are among the most violent in literature. But they do their killing under controlled circumstances, on neutral ground away from women and children, and according to a prescribed code of conduct.

The world Homer describes is also an aristocratic one; armies are led and dominated by the same figures who hold what normally amounts to hereditary political power. Not surprisingly, the action in the *Iliad* reflects what is essentially a hierarchical worldview. There are instances of martial insubordination (both the god Ares and the goddess Aphrodite are wounded by mortals), but in no case is a significant character killed by a member of the lower strata.

Combat, then, is mainly a matter of major figures, and it is almost inevitably individualized in stylized duels between warriors of approximately equal status.

Significantly, this form is carried to its logical conclusion when everyone agrees to lay aside their arms while Paris and Menelaos "fight alone for the sake of Helen and all her possessions."[5] Thus, intraspecific fighting in its purest form comes to serve as an equivalent for war.

Nor was this necessarily an isolated occurrence. From the staged duel between Sinuhe, the Egyptian chamberlain of the Twelfth Dynasty, and the "mighty man of Retenu" to the combat between David and Goliath of Gath, history has provided a number of examples of duels taking place under similar circumstances.[6] Unfortunately, as a means of settling larger issues, single combat had decided shortcomings, especially from the perspective of the loser. Thus, rather than accept the consequences of Goliath's defeat (slavery), the Philistines fled and had to be run down by the Israelites.[7] Similarly, Menelaos, at the point of victory, has

Paris snatched away to safety by Aphrodite, and the fighting among the others continues unabated.[8]

Nonetheless, even under these more promiscuous circumstances, combat remains highly formalized. Generally, major combatants ride into combat in chariots but choose to fight on foot. Here, as a preliminary, they often slaughter a few underlings. Significantly, all such victims are named even if they are mere spear fodder. Since the birth and prowess of an opponent are directly proportional to the glory gained from fighting him, the necessity for identification is a critical element, not just in the *Iliad* but in heroic warfare in general. Thus, once major combatants pair off, Glaukos and Diomedes, for example,[9] they frequently resort to elaborate introductions in order to determine relative status. Combatants also engage in considerable bluff and posturing, usually hurling insults back and forth before moving to more lethal activities.

Actual fighting, once begun, merely continues the normalized sequence of events. First the opponents take turns casting spears at each other from relatively long range. Should this prove inconclusive, one or the other might throw a large rock (optional). At this point the antagonists close and attempt to stab with their extra spears. This failing, they move in still further and finish the fight with their swords.

What emerges is as rhythmic and formal as a sword dance, with blows struck alternately and martial conventions observed scrupulously. Yet it is also deadly, the direction of combat steadily diminishing the range between opponents. Here, as is characteristic of epic poems, the violence is clinically, almost pornographically, described, with limbs lopped off, necks slashed through, and faces cleaved to the teeth with sanguinary regularity. In spite of its danger this is clearly the preferred means of combat, with he "who fights at close quarters" being a frequent and positive Homeric epithet.[10]

It is also true that heroes generally embody certain stereotyped physical characteristics. They are big, for example, size being equated with power in the Homeric scheme of things. Thus, Achilleus, though probably smaller than Aias, is nevertheless described as "gigantic" and at one point remarks to a doomed foe, "Do you not see what a man I am, how huge, how splendid?"[11] In addition, major characters tend to be fast, frequently running down fleeing opponents and on occasion engaging in races among themselves. Finally, they are loud, indulging in horrific war cries calculated to terrify and thoroughly in keeping with the intimidating image the hero seeks to project. Yet it is worth noting that these criteria of size, speed, and resonance, though impressive in their own right, are also the same ones which usually differentiate antagonists within other species. Nor were they solely applicable to heroic warfare. Rather, they were destined, for a number of reasons (not the least of which is the brilliance of Homer's language), to play a lasting role in the phenomenology surrounding military thought in general.

As might be expected, weapons choice in the *Iliad* is very much in keeping with the outlook outlined above. Thus, major combatants normally take the field armed for close combat. Weaponry is highly symmetrical, with Greek and Trojan basically armed alike on most occasions. Thus, during one of the few mass encounters in the poem, the two sides are described as "locking spear-by-spear, shield against shield at the base, so that buckler leaned on buckler, helmet on helmet." [12]

But if the basic panoply is largely universalized in function, it is nonetheless individualized in terms of worth, craftsmanship, and psychological significance. Even though the *Iliad* is filled with metallic imagery such as "bronze-clad Achaeans," it is clear that the substance is in short supply and only the heroic minority can afford a full set of equipment. Thus, arms and armor are highly prized, being not only major items of personal property but also quite literally totems of combat since the ultimate object is to strip an opponent of his accouterments.

Also, it is apparent that the appeal of arms is not simply honorific and utilitarian but aesthetic. Some of Homer's most lyrical passages are reserved for descriptions of weaponry, the most famous being the 140 lines at the end of book 18 depicting the armor Hephaistos has forged for Achilleus. [13] (This relationship is also significant. It is clear here and at several other points in the poem that the men making the weapons are not the ones using them. Hephaistos, though a god, is nonetheless a cripple and hardly a warlike figure. Moreover, it is apparent that although the embellishments are his, the actual form of the armor is dictated by his heroic customer. This is typical of preindustrial arms making, a symbiosis destined to determine, as much as anything, the pace and direction of weapons technology.)

Yet for all their value and appeal, no character in the *Iliad* would subscribe to the notion that arms make the man. The status of a combatant is determined by his courage and prowess. Weapons are certainly an important element, but largely as a reflection of the men using them.

A case in point is the bow, the sole exception to the favorable portrayal of arms in the *Iliad*. Diomedes speaks the mind of the Homeric warrior when he addresses Paris:

You archer, foul fighter, lovely in your locks, eyer of young girls
If you were to make trial of me in strong combat with weapons, your bow would do you
　　no good at all. [14]

It hardly seems coincidental that Paris the adulterer is the only major character in the poem to place principle reliance on the bow. For it is strongly implied that he who breaks the vows of marriage also transgresses the rules of war.

Yet it does not necessarily do him or his fellow bowmen any good. Archers are portrayed as basically ineffectual, especially against major combatants. If their hands do not shake or a goddess does not brush the arrow away, the wounds they inflict on the principals are almost always minor.

Yet this is obviously more than just a matter of utility. Idomeneus hits on the major failing of the bow when he notes, "My way is not to fight my battles standing far away from my enemies." [15] The bow simply does not fit the confrontational image which is the essence of heroic warfare as far as Homer is concerned. Consequently, it is relegated to a subordinate status, while the primacy of armored close combat was crystallized, first in the *Iliad* and then on the battle-fields of Europe for the next twenty-six hundred years.

The relationship between these two events, the literary and the historical, needs to be clarified, however. The veracity of Homer has been subjected to endless debate. Yet modern scholarship, beginning with the discovery of Troy by Heinrich Schliemann in 1871, has tended to support the accuracy of the information in the poem. Obviously, there are inconsistencies and literary conventions. Homer's troops, unlike those of real literary generals such as Caesar or Xenophon, seldom eat. Yet overall the match between archeology and the details of the poem has been suffi-ciently demonstrated to lead even so careful a scholar as N. L. G. Hammond to conclude that the "general situation and the civilization portrayed in the poem are historical."[16] The power of the oral tradition to transmit accurately through a period of centuries has been established repeatedly. Under the circumstances it is logical to assume that the ideas and attitudes reflected by the characters are not merely Homer's, but that they represent actual values of Achaean warriors around 1100 B.C.

But if these concepts can be shown to be historical, they also transcend time and place. There is much about Homer which is archetypical. One of the reasons his work has lived is that he wrote about war as men thought it should be. Heroic warfare developed repeatedly in cultures largely isolated from the Middle East and Europe. Moreover, in India, China, Southeast Asia, and Japan it would remain the dominant form of combat long after it was subordinated in the West. Plainly, this type of war gave vent to some very basic attitudes and beliefs. In the sphere of weaponry this was reflected in several nearly universal themes: the fascination with the horse, the emphasis on elaborate body armor, and the general symmetry of arms.

Yet it is also important to realize that there are certain elements which are parochial, peculiar to Homer and the world of the *Iliad*. In particular, the disre-gard of the bow, the sequential orchestration of combat, and its very confronta-tional nature were elements not necessarily found elsewhere. Sun Tzu, a Chinese general of the sixth century B.C., would write an extremely influential treatise which, by taking full cognizance of the bow, would set his culture's military history off in an entirely different and more subtle direction.[17] Yet it is Homer's prejudices, not Sun Tzu's, which lie at the base of our own conceptions of war and weapons. And it is the West, not the East, which is responsible for the military-technical revolution which now confronts us. This is why Homer is so important, and why the Western military tradition, in particular, must be understood before we can plumb the depths of our dilemma.

There can be no doubt that the Greeks placed great stock in the accuracy of the *Iliad,* with even the scrupulous Thucydides citing Homer as fact.[18] Yet they were not literalists. They realized that it described times long past. It was the story, not its details, which captivated them. This and the magic of the poetry were the mechanisms of transmission, the means by which Homeric archetypes etched themselves into first Greek, then Roman, conceptions of war—and finally into our own. Yvon Garlan notes the degree to which the Homeric model has retrospectively imposed itself on our ideas of combat among other ancient European Archaic societies.[19] He is right, but he might have wondered at the precision of the fit. The ancient world was not all that insular a place. These groups, too, were susceptible to Homer's influence, if not directly through hearing or reading the poem then at least through the behavior of adversaries on the battlefield. Tactics were not critical. Both the Greeks and the Romans would change tactics as the political situation dictated. But ancient warfare would never lose its Homeric spirit and also its prejudices. Even today, though rationality and technology have captured the tangibles of battle, Homer still marks its beat.

II

Great change began around 1100 B.C. when Greece was plunged into darkness with the collapse of the palace economies that were the political base of the Achaean warriors who fought at Troy.[20] Although the society which emerged after the so-called Dorian invasion remained aristocratic, the Mycenaean state structure had been replaced by other principles of social solidarity, still nascent but destined to assert themselves.[21]

It took different forms in different localities. Yet in all of them the gradual crystallization of the city-state structure brought with it an increasing self-consciousness and self-respect among larger populations. While there were other manifestations, these changes were most tangibly represented in a proliferation of military equipment and a change in tactics.

The subject has been hotly debated, but anecdotal evidence seems to indicate that through most of the Archaic period aristocratic power was based on heavy cavalry.[22] Between 675 and 650 B.C., however, a new type of fighting appeared.[23] (This is quite literally true since the best evidence of the change can be found in the figures depicted on certain proto-Corinthian vases of the period.) Massed heavy infantry, known as hoplites and armed primarily with spears, overturned the cavalry, which without stirrups could not hope to generate the power to attack even small formations of foot soldiers so long as they stuck together.

This was the key. It is generally assumed that hoplite armament (shield, or *hoplon;* torso armor, at first a "bell" cuirass and later a metal-reinforced corslet; helmet; greaves; short iron sword; and a six-foot thrusting spear) and phalanx tactics are logically inseparable. This is not the case. They were discrete phenomena—simultaneous, perhaps, but separate.

For one thing, the heavy panoply of the hoplite was not necessary for spear-based, close-formation tactics. The consistent success of both the later version of the Macedonian grand phalanx and the Swiss pike formations, neither of which used much body armor, proved this.[24] Moreover, there is a tendency to label hoplite equipment as something new and revolutionary when in fact it was a close approximation of the accouterments of the *Iliad*.

What was taking place amounted to a classic act of upward mobility. The increasing availability of metal and the skill to work it were making it possible for nonaristocrats to acquire the traditional arms of the aristocracy. Yet they did not need them to defy their former masters, nor would such equipment help them very much if they stood alone. Only cohesion, the willingness to fight together knowing that everything depended on the skill and fortitude of one's neighbor, prevented them from being ridden down like fleeing hares. F. E. Adcock is essentially correct when he says no form of combat could so plainly illustrate the social solidarity of the Greek city-state.[25]

Yet in the beginning it must have been more a matter of class. This was the origin and essence of the characteristic Greek neglect of cavalry. What had once been the arm of the overlords would seldom be allowed to exceed one part in ten in a normalized military levy of the classical period.[26] Peltasts, or "light troops," presumably lacking the wherewithal to fully equip themselves, were similarly subordinated.[27] On the other hand, the large middle group of *zeugitai,* or "men of the line," dominated ancient Greek military history, just as they rode astride Hellenic politics.

In this regard it is important to realize that military considerations often lay at the root of Greek governmental innovation. Questions of who would do the fighting, how, and under what circumstances were perceived as vital ones and a natural focal point for political creativity. Since a standing army was considered an instrument of tyranny in almost every city-state save Sparta, the solution which emerged took the form of an army of amateurs, a middle- and upper-middle-class militia, participation in which was defined by wealth.[28]

This is the true significance of hoplite armament. Its possession was the prime qualification for full political participation. It became, in effect, the talisman of the political revolution which had taken place.

Yet direct-participation politics, which was at the core of this revolution in most communities, could be practiced only at a local level. Thus, Greece emerged and remained a patchwork of states, each one fiercely dedicated to its own self-determination and all engaged in an eternal soap opera of war, diplomacy, alliance, and betrayal. The obvious political analogue is that of Sumer, where the city-state system also spawned the heavy-armed phalanx. Indeed, the emergence of two so similar systems in two societies so widely separated in time and culture would seem to be a rather clear affirmation of the intimate relationship between weaponry and politics.

In the case of the Greeks, phalanx tactics and hoplite equipment, as well as direct-participation politics, reinforced the city-state system and the localization of power. For in practice the heaviness of the hoplite's accouterments, along with a tendency to drift to the right or unshielded side, insured that phalanxes had to meet on level ground under fairly contrived circumstances, minimizing maneuver and turning the contest into a giant shoving match. Everything was reduced to one supreme effort. The team whose line finally crumpled was routed, and the battle was over. For to get away, the vanquished party had only to cast aside some or all of his protection and his pursuers, unless they were willing to do the same, could not catch him. The poet Archilochus was the most famous advocate of this tactic:

> My shield I left beside a bush, because I must.
> It's not the poor thing's fault—some Saian now
> Has joy of it, but I have saved my life.
> What care I for that shield
> A parting curse on it
> Another day I'll buy one just as good.[29]

Nor was cavalry numerous or skillful enough for sustained and ruthless pursuit.

The object of battle was territorial, to drive the enemy from the field, not destroy him. This in itself was a significant change and one that would have some impact on the future of Western warfare. In the *Iliad,* territory was primarily neutral, the combat itself being the major objective. This was also largely true in regard to the transnational tyranny, where the killing of the leadership generally meant victory. Now it seems one of the most common and ancient imperatives of intraspecific aggression, the physical possession of the field, had reasserted itself to define the ends of engagement.

After the fight was over the rights of the dead were inevitably respected, with the losers sending a herald to ask formally for permission to return to dispose of the bodies. Finally, a trophy was erected, usually a simple piece of armor representing a collective exorcism, and the chapter was declared closed.

One battle usually sufficed to end a war. Campaigns normally began in the summer and ended at harvest time. If nothing had happened by then, everybody went home content to have trampled the enemy's fields and perhaps cut down a few of his olive trees. Land, unless it was close enough to the city walls to permit full political participation, was seldom annexed. Finally, the city walls themselves were largely sacrosanct. While towns were taken at times through treachery, sustained investment or use of siege engines were not a major part of Greek warfare until the rise of Macedon.[30]

Yet the highly contrived and ritualized nature of warfare among the Hellenes, its tendency to narrow the scope and variety of combat down to one climactic act, should not be allowed to leave the impression that it was drained of violence. On the contrary, the Greeks' national form of combat frequently struck others as quite frightening. Thus, Herodotus has Mardonius, the malign counselor of Xerxes the Great King of Persia, speak of the Greeks as waging war "irrationally" and fighting in such a manner that "even the victors come off with great loss."[31] Three hundred years later Polybius cites the Roman General Lucius Aemilius Paulus as confessing to his friends at home "that the Macedonian phalanx was the most formidable and terrifying sight that had ever met his eyes."[32]

Probably these critics had a point. The phalanx was too deadly for the purposes of its users. Localization of power, which was a function of direct-participation politics, insured that war was a regular, even necessary, feature of life. (Athens, for example, was at war two out of every three years during the 150 years separating the Persian Wars [490 B.C.] and the Battle of Chaeronea [338 B.C.]. Yet the Homeric tradition of confrontation, along with the development of a very effective killing machine in the phalanx, insured that combat, when it came, was inevitably costly in lives. The insistence on Homeric panoplies, along with the prevalence of spear-induced puncture wounds, turned battles into lethal slugfests, which to be endured on a regular basis had to be encased in ritual and psychological buffers against what must have been a frightening and bloody reality.

Adcock is probably correct in stating that, except for the Spartans, the Greeks fought the way they did largely because they lacked the quality—some call it discipline—which shuts the mind to fear. The liveliness of the Greek imagination made panic a constant possibility. Therefore, battles had to be approached carefully, through a series of familiar conventions.[33]

Although the participants had changed, the Homeric sequence of events was maintained. Javelin-throwing light troops, or peltasts, engaged first at longer ranges; then the phalanxes ceremoniously assumed the order of battle and rushed together to finish the issue at close quarters.

Not unexpectedly, armament was almost exclusively symmetrical, though there were some local differences. The Boeotians and the Thessalians placed somewhat more emphasis on cavalry. Yet in general the Greek infantryman went into battle knowing the weapons he would face were matched to his own. Indeed, what often proved to be the major tactical feature of hoplite battles, the tendency to drift to the unprotected right, was a direct result of carrying the same arms in exactly the same manner.[34]

It seems that in historic times the Greeks did not resort to the expedient of individual combat. Yet in the so-called ritual wars (institutionalized conflicts fought again and again over a disputed piece of territory), they appear to have adopted the custom to their mass mentality, conducting staged battles with matched bodies of men. Thus, Herodotus writes of a combat between three hundred Spartans and an equal number of Argives over Thyreae, which ended at darkness with the sole surviving Spartiate stripping the armor from the dead and claiming the field.[35] Strabo cities a similar instance of a continuing fight between Chalcis and Eretria over possession of the small Lelantine plain in which the contending parties inscribed on a pillar the exact conditions under which the fight would take place, including a provision explicitly forbidding long-range missiles.[36]

Such a prohibition illustrates not only the subordination of the bow but also the lingering grasp of Homer on the Greek military mind. The conventions the Greeks chose to apply to warfare tended to be those favored by the fighters at Troy, which in turn were related to an earlier tradition of intraspecific combat. Nor had weapons changed much, the basic elements of the Achaean panoply all being represented in those of the hoplite. This is significant because the Greeks, possibly foreshadowed by the Sumerians, were pioneers in what the modern world knows as mass-participation warfare, using armies of highly motivated troops belonging to nonaristocratic social orders. Yet this group, when the opportunity arose, did not reject the already ancient conventions and instrumentalities of war. Rather, they sought to adapt their new way of fighting, as best they could, to what had come before.

For our purposes this is worth noting since one day it would no longer be the case. Eventually, those who would come to be known as the bourgeoisie, would begin to apply their considerable energies and technical skill to making armaments more suited to what they perceived as their own interests. It was an experiment destined to end in our own peculiar dilemma as possessors of arsenals, in large part, too powerful to use.

But for the Greeks, the dawn of that day would remain two thousand years in the future. The rise of Macedon and the successor monarchies would bring on an outburst of arms innovation, but the causes of this outburst would be different and its momentum not sustained. Meanwhile, in the Greek city-state the alliances between weapons technology and the middle class would remain unconsummated, stayed by the admonition of a blind poet.

III

It is, of course, more than a little ridiculous to treat Greek warfare as if it were solely a terrestrial matter. For the Greeks were a maritime people, more dependent on the sea than any ancient culture save that of the Cartho-Phoenician.

Hellenic civilization after 650 B.C. can no longer be thought of as primarily a phenomenon of the mainland. The previous three centuries had orchestrated a steady migration, causing group after group to spill off overseas—never inland, but choosing instead to island-hop and work their way along the coast, both east and west, until their colonies stretched from what is today Marseilles to the interior coast of the Black Sea. They were, as Aristotle described them, "frogs"—an amphibious people joined together solely by their ability to sail the seas. Such vital and tenuous links naturally called forth their own defenses. This is why the Greeks, above all ancient peoples, were pioneers in naval warfare.

It is difficult to establish when men began extending their quarrels to the liquid medium. Probably it happened quite early, most likely in one of the rivers which were the lifeblood of the most ancient civilizations. Yet the first saltwater naval battles for which there is any substantial information took place quite late, around 1200 B.C.[37]—an epic struggle between the invading "sea people" (probably Philistines) and the Egyptians depicted in the magnificent relief at Medinet Habu. The vessels on both sides were lightly built and not apparently specialized for warfare (the Philistine craft lacked even oars vital to maneuver under battle conditions). Hostile action was accomplished essentially through an extension of terrestrial techniques, the Egyptians being armed with composite bows and intent on keeping their range and the sea people relying on spears and swords, useful only if they were able to close and board. While hardly sophisticated, such natural versions of land battles probably represented the state of the art for other seafaring peoples of the time.

Yet it also seems probable that piratical raiding, rather than set-piece battles, was the most prevalent form of naval combat.[38] And it is clear that by this time it was the Greeks who were the masters of this form. If the *Iliad* was the bible of land warfare, it was the *Odyssey* which would define the lives of the Greeks who plied the seas, or rather skirted them. Following the coastline and landing at night to sleep and forage for food, they by necessity came into contact with a variety of people, some of them hostile. Life at sea must literally have been a series of

Figure 5. Reconstruction of the Medinet Habu relief depicting the first saltwater sea battle between the "sea people" (probably Philistines) and the Egyptians, Twentieth Dynasty, Rameses III (1192–1160 B.C.). Biblical Heritage International Publishers, Tel Aviv, Israel.

adventures, and to survive, the Greeks, like Odysseus, had to be skillful and wily and at times bloody-minded. Thus, the ships described in the *Iliad* and the *Odyssey*—lithe, slender sailing galleys similar in most respects to the Norse longboats of A.D. 1000—were specialized for the lives and activities of their occupants. Fast rather than stalwart, they were designed for transport and pursuit rather than actual fighting. They were warships. But they remained light enough to drag up on the beach while the actual fighting took place on solid ground.[39]

During the obscure period after 1000 B.C., a significant change took place, however. Geometric vases began depicting a feature Homer never described—the ram.[40] While it is impossible to say with certainty that it was the Greeks rather than their major naval competitors, the cities of Byblus, Sidon, and Tyre—known collectively as Phoenicia—which were responsible for this innovation, it was the Hellenes who chose to record it in their ceramics. Whatever its origins, the ram was of major significance, comparable in the eyes of ancient naval historian Lionel Casson to the introduction of the naval gun twenty-five hundred years later.[41]

Certainly, it had a similarly fundamental effect on the means of combat. What had been simply an instrument of transport became a weapon in and of itself, an oar-driven projectile specialized for inflicting puncture wounds on enemy hulls. Actual fighting at sea now had a single real rationale behind it. Whole ships might be sunk with one well-placed blow.

More subtle but of some significance was the individualization of combat which the ram implied. Rather than acting as a base for a mass of individual combatants, ships became integral fighting units to be deployed and maneuvered as such. Not only was it natural for combat to develop as a series of individual actions—single ship versus single ship—but the necessity to close dictated by the ram's operating principles also tended to impart a confrontational, even Homeric, flavor to naval combat.

These tendencies were intensified by subsequent developments. It is important to remember that ancient warships were oar-driven craft relying primarily on speed, sort of lethal racing shells. Yet the addition of bronze-clad rams, along with the timber reinforcement necessary to withstand the impact of collision, meant a considerable penalty in weight. To compensate, ancient naval architects took to increasing the number of oars to the greatest degree possible. The most obvious way to do this was simply to lengthen the boat. Yet too many rowers working in single file, each requiring about three feet of water line, created a craft that was overlong and dangerously frail amidships. The practical maximum seems to have been reached with the single-banked penteconter, which ran about 125 feet in length (75 feet to accommodate the twenty-five oarsmen on either side and an additional 50 feet for ram, foredeck, and poop).[42]

Yet this limit was circumvented sometime between 750 and 700 B.C. through the addition of a second bank of oars, essentially above the first, nearly doubling the rowers without substantially increasing the length.[43] To do this required reinforcement, making these biremes by necessity heavier, a trend intensified by the further addition of a raised fighting deck. Growth, however, did not stop here.

Rather, the movement reached a plateau sometime around 600 B.C. when the shipwrights of Corinth succeeded in adding a third level of oarsmen, probably by means of a low outrigger, to create the so-called trireme (three-fitted). While the exact configuration of these vessels has been the subject of controversy,[44] they were clearly a success and became, in essence, the standard ship-of-the-line for the next two hundred years.[45] But perhaps more important than these technical advances for the future of warship design was the conceptual hierarchy they created in men's minds. Although the trireme was clearly dominant in terms of numbers, the important principle of differentiation by class and the perceived superiority of size had been firmly established. Thus, the lightest, single-banked triaconters were relegated to scouting duties, while the trireme assumed the mantle of capital ship, its services being reserved for serious engagements. This was no artificial contrivance. In general, triaconters remained light and maneuverable enough to avoid all but their own kind. On the other hand, only triremes were capable of standing up against triremes. So compelling was the logical basis for a hierarchy of ships that it would remain the central premise of military naval architecture until the middle of the twentieth century. Bigger is better, and like must fight like. In this regard ships themselves became analogues of heroic warriors, brooking no opposition from below, certain of their inherent superiority, and determined to fight one another.

Yet Greek naval warfare, like the phalanx, was also a corporate activity. Triremes were rowed not by the proverbial galley slave but by citizens. In Athens, for example, each ship formed the nucleus of what amounted to a boat club. With a wealthy patron or trierarch as sponsor, the crew practiced together on a regular basis. Keeping 170 oarsmen working in unison, in what was still more of a racing shell than a battleship, was no easy trick, and cities such as Athens and Corinth, which emphasized their navies, had an inherent advantage which they compounded through the development of an increasingly complex set of tactics.[46]

This, rather than weaponry, was the key to Greek naval supremacy. For as is true of so many ancient weapons, the development of the trireme took place rapidly and basically stabilized with subsequent modification surrounding the periodic addition and removal of a fighting deck for marines.[47]

Military naval architecture was also extremely symmetrical. Indeed, so quickly did the Phoenicians and even the Egyptians adopt these rowing innovations that there is some question, just as with the ram, whether they were of Greek origin at all.[48] Whoever was first, it is clear that the liquid medium encouraged a faster transfer of ideas, thereby intensifying naval symmetry and minimizing the isolation-induced weapons variations characteristic of ancient land combat. Thus, J. S. Morrison and J. F. Coates, probably the most reliable sources on the technical details of ancient warships, note that the Greek and Persian fleets at Artemisium in 480 B.C. must have been very similar, even indistinguishable when seen from a distance.[49] This had not changed by the battle of Cnidus in 394 B.C., nor would it change significantly for another half century. Just as with land arms, the Hellenistic age would usher in a period of technical development, but from roughly 550 B.C. down to the death of Philip of Macedon, naval warfare in the eastern Mediterranean basin was stable and symmetrically focused almost entirely on one class of ship.

IV

The ancient Greeks were among the most creative races in history, and it is reasonable to ask why it was that they did not place greater reliance on technological innovation. In the civilian sphere the prevalence of slaves has often been used to account for the lack of interest in laborsaving devices. But this explanation is not sufficient in the case of armaments since it was almost always citizens who did the fighting. Rather, it seems the Greeks developed weapons and tactics suited to their own political, sociological, and psychological paradigms and, having done so, were essentially satisfied with them. Better weapons might have meant victory in certain instances. Yet winning outside the accepted military conventions implied the sacrifice of more deeply held values. But if the Greeks placed emphasis on the rules of war and frowned on those, such as the Aetolians, who habitually broke them, they were not great moralizers on the subject. Rather, from the evidence, or lack of it, it is possible to conclude that they hardly thought about constraints on the way they fought. Similarly, weapons down to 400 B.C. appear to have been taken pretty much as a given. There were some refinements, but a conscious strategy to improve killing efficiency was entirely missing.

This unselfconscious state seems reflective of the entire Greek outlook toward war. For a people noted for their analytic turn of mind, the Greeks devoted remarkably little thought to the phenomenon of armed conflict. Even Plato and Aristotle, who did consider the nature of persistent city-state rivalries, refused to treat war as a subject in and of itself.[50] Wars were important; war was not. Aristophanes's *Lysistrata,* frequently cited today as a landmark in antiwar thinking, in fact contains no impassioned protest against the bloodshed but only a ribald female remonstration against its time-consuming nature and the women's resulting loneliness. Even Pericles's "Funeral Oration" contains little that could be called true remorse. To be sure, there must have been much individual suffering and grief, but in the main the Greeks seem to have viewed war as a natural part of life not subject to internal reform.

Certainly, from one perspective they had every reason to be complacent about their style of fighting. Developed basically for intramural combat, it proved extremely effective against other races, particularly the bow-based infantry of the Persian Empire, the greatest transnational tyranny of the day. Twice invaded within a decade, the Greeks on each occasion beat back the Persians in a most decisive fashion. Indeed, it is safe to say that their greatest difficulty in the campaigns of 490 and 480 B.C. was the need to unite temporarily in order to field forces large enough to face the mass of Persians, which, in the latter invasion of Xerxes, may have numbered anywhere from sixty thousand to several hundred thousand (Herodotus put the figure at five million), along with 1,207 triremes.[51]

On land the Persian cavalry was unable to keep the Greek phalanx off the immobile mass of foot archers whose arrows were largely ineffective against a heavily armored foe intent on keeping out of range until the final charge. When this occurred, first at Marathon and later at Plataea, battle degenerated into slaughter. The Persian navy, reinforced with Ionian Greeks, fared somewhat better but eventually fell apart at Salamis.

By the end of these campaigns the Greeks had every reason to believe themselves capable of standing up against any armed force they might encounter, particularly if it was Persian. Nor was the dream of revenge and conquest lost upon the collective Hellenic imagination. Isocrates was only the most articulate in arguing for an invasion of Persia as a means to national unity.[52] But at this point in history direct-participation politics basically precluded larger amalgams. Rather than unite, the Hellenic world chose to cluster around the antipodes of Sparta and Athens, eventually fighting one of the most disastrous wars in history.

Tactically, if any conflict was ever preordained for frustration it was the thirty-year Peloponnesian double war, beginning in 431 B.C. It was a passion play of asymmetric arms—the Athenians with their navy commanding the sea and the Peloponnesian League, led by Sparta, utterly dominant on land, and neither side really able to get at the other. Year after year the Spartan alliance invaded the Attican peninsula at will, ravaging crops and ripping up vineyards. Yet they could not induce the Athenian hoplites, outnumbered by approximately fifty thousand to thirteen thousand, to come out from behind their walls and fight. Nor did they have the siege engines to breach these fortifications. So they had to content themselves with agricultural mayhem and an occasional curse in the direction of the long walls connecting Athens to her seaport, the Piraeus.

The sea was the key to Athenian survival. Her maritime empire fed the city with grain from the Black Sea and contributed revenues greatly superior to those of her enemies.[53] Moreover, a navy of three hundred triremes provided the mobility to raid the Peloponnese at points of her own choosing, thereby avoiding numerical disadvantages. Yet raids did not amount to decisive land battles, and nothing short of this could break the will of Sparta and her allies.

For their own part the Peloponnesians were hardly more successful in coming to grips with Athens at sea. Short on timber and trained oarsmen, the league, on several occasions during the first portion of the war, launched modest flotillas intended to probe for weak points in the Athenian thalassocracy. Timorously led and tactically inept, the collective fate of these ventures was epitomized in an action off Rhium in which the Athenian admiral Phormio literally ran circles around the Lacedaemon squadron until its ships ran afoul of one another and fell victim to ramming attack.[54]

So the war dragged on, a senseless string of ups and downs for both sides, until after ten years, more out of exhaustion than anything else, they agreed to a truce. Within five years, though, the fight was on again, pursued with a growing sense of desperation. The corrosive effect of the Peloponnesian War on Greek political morality and the gradual decline into brutality and excess were brilliantly chronicled by Thucydides. Yet, perhaps because he was a man of his times, he seems to have largely missed the connection between the more general phenomenon and weaponry. Desperation was overturning the balance of arms. In an agony of frustration, men began experimenting with new ways of killing one another.

Plainly, siege warfare was becoming more frequent and more bitterly contested, with primitive battering rams being employed against Plataea in 427 B.C. and elsewhere.[55] Fire also was a more frequent feature of such attacks, with the Boeotians taking Delium with the aid of a bellows-powered flamethrower in 423.[56] By 398 the tyrant Dionysius of Syracuse, the Ashurnasir-pal of his day, was able to deploy a full array of siege engines against the city of Motya, including massive rams, towers, and sophisticated arrow-firing catapults.[57]

Nor was the spirit of innovation limited to the reduction of strong points. At sea the Syracusans defeated the Athenians in the Battle of the Great Harbor (413 B.C.) in part because they had cut down and reinforced the bows of their triremes to allow them to ram head-on rather than just amidships.[58] Fifteen years later the same Dionysius was engaged in a naval competition with the Carthaginians, which resulted in ships rowed in combinations of four and five, a pattern of growth which would eventually spell the end of the trireme's dominance.[59]

Not even the hoplite remained unaffected. In 425 B.C. the Athenians, using primarily lightly armed peltasts, succeeded in trapping and then capturing a force of 290 Peloponnesian hoplites, 120 of them Spartiates. "Nothing which happened during the war caused greater amazement in Hellas," remarked Thucydides.[60] In part this must have been due to a sudden awareness that the penalties paid in weight and mobility for Homeric accouterments were heavy indeed. As J. K. Anderson notes, this lesson was reflected in the gradual scaling down of the phalangites' protection during the late fifth and early fourth centuries, along with the increasing importance of the light-armed *peltasts* under innovative commanders such as Iphicrates of Athens.[61]

Yet the Greek city-state would not reap the benefits of these martial advances. They were a product of, and came to signify, not strength but political weakness and futility. Both Athens and Sparta were important military-political archetypes—the commercially oriented, liberally inclined, naval-based state versus the conservative, totalitarian, agriculturally dominated land power, a stereotypical match destined to be repeated throughout the history of the West, right up to the present. But for the time being the future of Hellenism belonged elsewhere. It was the transnational tyranny and the outlanders of Macedon who would inherit the military possibilities of the fourth century.

V

These judgments would have struck any Greek prior to 360 B.C. as ridiculous. Macedon was the land of the bumpkin, a place about which jokes were made. Neither in their own eyes nor in the eyes of Hellas proper were Macedonians considered Greeks. They worshipped the same gods and participated in the Olympics, but they spoke, in addition to Greek, Macedonian, an archaic tongue which reflected their considerably divergent ethnic makeup.[62] More important, they were worlds apart politically, the revolution which shaped the greater part of Greece having missed them entirely. Rather than city-states, Macedon was organized around a tribal structure and ruled by a hereditary line of monarchs, the Argeadae.[63] Yet, historically, the unity implied by such a system was continually belied by a string of squabbles over succession, petty revolts, and hereditary quarrels of one sort or another. Macedon might have continued to limp along, an obscure backwater place preyed upon by Greek and barbarian alike, had not fortune intervened and infused her ruling class with the stuff of genius.

First two of them, father and son, followed by a host of successors, some only a few degrees less talented—these Macedonians would project themselves over time and space, coming to rule half the known world and dominating the eastern Mediterranean for most of two centuries. It was they who would Hellenize the East. Yet the mechanism they would employ bore little resemblance to the politico-military institutions of the Greeks. Instead, they resurrected the transnational tyranny and propped it up with, among other things, a weapons technology which for sheer creativity surpassed any in the ancient world. In this respect Macedon owed more to the rulers of Assyria than they did to Themistocles or Pericles.

It all began with Philip II. Elected regent in 359 B.C. at the age of twenty-one, he was already a young man of considerable experience and no little determination. Having spent three years as a hostage at Thebes in the house of Epaminondas, the most famous general of his day, Philip was thoroughly familiar with the elder man's oblique order and massed left wing, and sought almost immediately to adapt them to Macedonian circumstances.[64] Fortuitously, the native phalanx was a new institution, barely a decade old and therefore pliable.[65] When Philip finished his modifications, it was almost unrecognizably changed.

Designed around a basic building block, or *syntagma,* of 256 men, lined 16 across and 16 deep, the Macedonian phalanx was not only uniformly thicker but projected a good deal farther ahead than its Greek counterparts. For Philip had replaced the conventional spear with a sixteen- to eighteen-foot-long *sarissa* and trained his men to wield it with both hands, thereby precluding any shield beyond a wicker target strapped to the forearm.[66] Although helmets and greaves were worn, body armor was omitted, apparently on the theory that the phalangite's best defense was the hedgehog of spearheads extending from four rows back. This worked remarkably well, not only providing a tremendous advantage in reach over the traditional hoplite phalanx but also thoroughly intimidating the bow-based Persian infantry. In the latter case, however, the phalanx was often held in reserve.

In this regard, it is important to realize that the Macedonian phalanx, although it did possess the one necessary qualification for such a force—men sufficiently motivated to fight at close range—was not the product of a natural political evolution, but was instead the conscious creation of Philip and his immediate predecessors.

The national arm of Macedon remained heavy cavalry, or the king's "Companions," similar in most respects to the aristocratic horsemen which preceded the phalanx in Greece.[67] Despite its archaic origins it was the "Companion" cavalry which would provide the major strike force in Macedon's Asian conquests. Against the Greeks, however, the phalanx remained critical.

Versatility was the key to Macedonian military success, that and the ruthless application of force as the situation demanded. Thus, when Philip appeared before Amphipolis in 357 B.C. still early in his career, he arrived with a full complement of siege engines and promptly sacked the town. Against the brigand Prince Bardylis the Illyrian, and later the Thracians and the Scythians, he made good use of light cavalry and peltasts in waging what amounted to a guerrilla campaign.[68]

In essence, it was Philip's will to power which transcended the political parochialism and narrow military conceptions of the Greeks. Using whatever weapons were necessary, he did what he had to in order to win. Thus, after the Battle of Chaeronea in 338 B.C., he would have the Theban Sacred Band, the best infantry in Greece, systematically slaughtered.[69] It was a brutal act, yet it served a political purpose. For the first time, one man was undisputed master of the Greek peninsula. Later, after Philip's assassination, Thebes would revolt. His successor, Alexander, would waste no time in utterly destroying the city, and selling its population into slavery—like father, like son.[70]

It has been said that Alexander was the greatest soldier in history. There can be no doubt that he was a tactical genius and a charismatic leader of the first order. Yet his success against the Persian Empire was based largely on political insight, an instinctive understanding of the transnational tyranny's power base and the possibilities of its destruction.

Seventy-five years before, in 401, Cyrus, the renegade brother of Artaxerxes the great king, had hired thirteen thousand Greek hoplites (among them the same Xenophon who wondered at the ruins of Nineveh) in an attempt to seize power. In the showdown at Cunaxa, Cyrus had been killed, but the Greek elements of his army retained their integrity, having plowed through the entire Persian left wing without suffering a single casualty.[71] Despite the treacherous seizure and execution of their leaders, they managed to fight their way across nearly a thousand miles of hostile territory to the Black Sea, where they sailed again to Greece. At the time it was considered a great feat, a trek brilliantly publicized by Xenophon in his *Anabasis*. But it was really a study in lost opportunities. With some cavalry and a truly audacious leadership, the Greeks might have marched on Persepolis and set themselves up as rulers. Such was the nature of their military superiority.

These possibilities were not lost on Alexander, who was nothing if not audacious. The nature of the army he sent to Asia reflected an instinctive understanding of the military problems he would face. It was a chameleon force, capable of adapting to practically any situation. About one-ninth of the combined force of thirty-five thousand was heavy cavalry ("Companions" or Thessalians) aimed at bringing the Persian nobility to bear. Another 70 percent were phalangites (half Macedonian, half Greek) targeted against the great king's mercenary Greek hoplites. To deal with the survivors there were Paeonian and Thessalian light cavalry armed with lances and javelins. Unlike among the Greeks, considerable attention was payed to missile troops: Cretan archers, Rhodian slingers, Agrianian javelin throwers were all included. Finally, there was an extremely elaborate siege train under the Thessalian Diades, the developer of the Greek version of those Assyrian standbys, the wheeled battering ram and the portable siege tower.[72] All and all it was the most elaborately differentiated army yet assembled, heterogeneous not only in function but also, significantly, in nationality.

For Alexander had turned the campaign into a crusade. His visit to Ilion and his sacrifices in honor of Achilleus were no hollow gestures. It was the Homeric spirit of the West which constituted the major advantage of his army.

Yet it was Alexander's instinctive understanding of whom to close in on which brought him victory so precipitously. In all his major field battles—Granicus, Issus, and Gaugamela—Alexander personally led his "Companion" cavalry directly at the Persian leadership, seeking to kill or scatter them as quickly as possible.[73] The Persians, for their part, also made every effort to eliminate the young Macedonian invader.[74] For both realized the nature of what was at stake—that power in the transnational state was completely concentrated in the hands of the king and his retinue. Conquest simply meant their elimination and, subsequently, replacement.

Alexander was personally an extremely attractive figure, a virtual incarnation of the youthful dream of transcendence. For this reason he became the center of a romantic myth which, in a sense, endures today. But the modern cult of Alexander, rather than emphasizing his magical or godlike qualities, has tended to read into his character a more contemporary set of virtues. This Alexander emerges as student and follower of Aristotle, the restorer of democracy to the Ionian and mainland Greeks and a conqueror more out of emotional longing then calculation.[75] Characteristically, his career is portrayed as a gradual descent from this political state of grace to the degenerate status of oriental monarch, living proof of the dictum "power corrupts." Whatever responsive chords this image may strike, there is reason to believe it is exaggerated, that the real Alexander was ruthless and opportunistic from the beginning.

At age eighteen he personally supervised the slaughter of the Sacred Band.[76] At twenty-one he would sell the women and children of Thebes into slavery.[77] Three years later he would do the same to the inhabitants of Tyre.[78] After Granicus he would have almost twenty thousand trapped mercenary Greek hoplites systematically put to the sword.[79] All this before he turned twenty-five. Certainly, he was capable of magnanimous gestures. Yet these, like his acts of brutality, generally had a practical purpose.

The political settlement reached first by Alexander and elaborated upon by his Successors was representative of a mind steeped in the politics of reality. Alexander found an empire held together by a pyramid of power and he simply replaced the capstones. Indeed, much to the chagrin of the Macedonians, he seemed willing to let even the subject nobilities participate in the process of ruling, an experiment quickly halted after his death.[80] But what was seen as despotism, the forms and ceremonies necessary to legitimize the new order, was merely a reaction to the inevitable. Alexander may have come to think of himself as a god, but he was never a fool. And the fundamentals of the political arrangements he made were practical enough to persist for almost two centuries. Westerners might rule, but the transnational tyranny remained.

Alexander was primarily a leader and tactician, not an innovator. Yet his openness to military invention was at once very Macedonian and in congruence with the image presented above.

The attack on Tyre was his technological extravaganza, a textbook demonstration of how far Western siegecraft had come in just seven decades. The centerpiece was a half-mile mole built out to the island city, one of the two pieces of ancient military engineering to endure to the present (the other being the Roman's ramp to Masada). When this came under attack, Alexander, probably at the instigation of Diades, introduced both shipborne battering rams and finally the marine boarding bridges which finally took the city. Heavy use was also made of the arrow-firing torsion catapult and, for the first time, the stone-throwing *parabolos*.[81]

Alexander's interest in projectile-firing engines also carried over to his field campaigns. The concept of field artillery appears to have struck him first, and he went to extraordinary lengths to transport his catapults across Asia, using them ultimately to clear the farther bank of the Jaxartes.[82] Finally, there were the elephants he met on the Hydaspes in his epic battle with the Indian prince Porus. It has been said his troops were never the same afterward. Yet Alexander was quick to grasp the significance of these warlike pachyderms (untrained horses would not charge them, nor could the phalanx keep them at bay) and arranged for substantial numbers to be returned to the West, where his Successors would eagerly compete for them.[83]

There is a tendency to believe that the three major Successor states which would spring up at Alexander's passing (Antigonid Greece, Seleucid Syria, and Ptolemaic Egypt) were other than he had intended, parasitic perversions of his political intentions.[84] In one sense they were. Alexander was a conqueror and probably would not have stood for the reversion to the Greek practice of factionalism and balance-of-power politics. Other than this, however, the major political and military dynamics of the Hellenistic world appear to stem directly from Alexander and the Macedonian environment which produced him.

Intellectually and economically, the Successor states contributed a great deal, injecting the energizing force of Hellenism into a variety of more traditional cultures. Yet their gratitude is nowhere apparent. The Successor states perpetuated themselves by naked force. Only Macedonian military dominance stood between the Successors and oblivion.[85]

But that dominance was no stable thing. Rather, it continued to adapt to changing circumstances. For one thing, Macedonian males could not be kept at arms forever; the economic and personal burden was too great. The Antigonid dynasts would continue to call up the national levy in emergencies, and both the Seleucids and the Ptolemids would plant Greek agricultural settlements in hopes of achieving the same capability. But, in large part, military affairs became a matter of mercenaries. Yet the inherent lethality of the phalanx did not mix well with the psychology of such troops. As W. W. Tarn notes, mercenaries often fought well enough so long as it was worth fighting, but there was nothing to die for.[86] Hence, the natural tendency, particularly in Egypt and Syria, was to find alternatives to phalanx warfare.

One direction which this would lead was toward an increasing reliance on cavalry. Not only did the numbers of Seleucid and Ptolemaic horse increase steadily, but tactics came to be dominated by this arm. Significantly, cavalry was less and less used to charge through gaps which might form in the phalanx, being concentrated instead against itself in the classic symmetrical fashion.[87] Horses, particularly the Nesaean stallions of the Seleucids, were also being bred larger. This was a good indication that the Successors were already experimenting with heavier and more comprehensive armor for their riders (and perhaps the horses themselves),[88] a first step leading eventually to the juggernaut Parthian cataphracts, the ancient analogues for the medieval knights.

This process points in the direction of the second Hellenistic detour around the phalanx—weapons technology. In truth, Hellenistic weapons technology was a good deal more audacious in conception than it was useful in battle. But what is truly suggestive about the process is that it appears to have been a conscious strategy and one aimed at a perceived reluctance or inability of troops to fight in a more traditional fashion—a situation not so very different from the one to be found at the roots of our own weapons revolution. Consequently when someone asked Antigonus Gonatus, "How should one fight the enemy?" his reply had a peculiarly modern ring: "Any way it seems useful."[89]

Not a great deal of historical work has been done in this area. But is seems clear that the mechanisms of innovation were spurred from above, driven by the requirements of the monarchs themselves rather than "bottom-up," as was the case in the Industrial Revolution, when the middle class moved into arms technology, also as a way around traditional means of combat.

The fitting out of men by the thousands in Homeric accouterments presupposes a significant industrial base in Greece from the sixth century B.C. on. Like Greek politics, however, it was fragmented, ranging from cottage-scale establishments in small city-states to impressive factory-based enterprises in places like Athens. One major effect of the Hellenistic monarchies was to centralize weapons manufacture in state-owned arsenals and shipyards, a compression of effort which likely had a catalytic effect on the imaginations of those working there.[90]

Probably the most significant example of Hellenistic military technology was provided by the evolution of the torsion catapult. The first arrow-shooting catapult is said to have been developed at Syracuse for the tyrant Dionysius around 400 B.C. But this machine, which probably grew out of the *gastrophetes,* or crossbow, was limited by the resilience of its flexing wooden bow. Shortly before 300 B.C., however, this element was replaced by two vertical cylinders of twisted material (women's hair was best) which attached to the bowstring by means of inserted wooden arms.[91] This so-called torsion catapult was vastly more powerful, being able to shoot down a man at several hundred yards.

Despite the catapult's sophistication (from a physics perspective it was probably the most advanced weapon yet perfected), the technologists of Ptolemaic Alexandria continued to strive for basic improvements. In an effort to correct the major failing, a slow rate of fire, Dionysius of Alexandria fashioned a repeating catapult in which the release of the string loaded a new arrow.[92] But the projectiles carried only a short distance. Ctesibius, after briefly attempting to replace the organic skeins with metal springs, sought to construct a catapult based on compressed air.[93] Yet it, like the other experiments, would not find practical application. Nevertheless, all are significant since the men who conducted them were deliberately exploring physical and mechanical principles in order to improve what was already a satisfactory weapon. Rather than politics, something approaching science was driving the process.

Moreover, it is important to note that these technologists were not necessarily military men. For the first time there are signs that the armorer was no longer an utterly subordinate figure, that the complexity of weaponry was beginning to cause his own design ingenuity to play a larger role in the end product. Hence, the example of a genius like Archimedes of Syracuse being drawn away from geometry to build war engines becomes, if not exactly common, then at least not entirely extraordinary in the Hellenistic world.

No doubt this set some precedent for the future. Nevertheless, it did not imply total freedom of thought, as the fate of the catapult's progenitor, the man-portable *gastrophetes,* illustrates. Clearly, it was suppressed, a significant act since the roughly simultaneous appearance of the crossbow in China[94] would revolutionize infantry tactics in the direction of deception and avoidance as exemplified in the writings of Sun Tzu. Crossbows are slow-shooting, but their bolts pack enough punch to prevent even heavily armored infantry from closing in on their users.

Apparently, this was a step even the Hellenistic monarchies were unwilling to take.

Naval developments followed an analogous though somewhat more bizarre path, accelerating steadily toward a veritable crescendo of gigantism. As noted earlier, the process began around 400 B.C. when the Carthaginians and Dionysius of Syracuse began building first "fours" *(tetrereis)* and then "fives" *(pentereis)*. These innovative craft, possibly inspired by Carthaginian example, seem to have been based on placing two men at an oar. Thus a "four" was a simple two-banked vessel, while a "five" was a trireme with only the top bank rowed by a single oarsman. Down to 315 B.C. only one new craft was added—the "six," to complete the cycle—and all remained relatively rare.

From this date, however, the pace quickened, with the "five" replacing the trireme as the standard ship of the line and a host of new vessels proliferating in a tit-for-tat sequence which constituted at once the greatest naval arms race in ancient history and a sort of caricature of all such endeavors.

The basis for these vessels was the multiman sweep (three men or more), at once more powerful and vastly less demanding in skill—a necessary consideration given the political environment and the resultant deterioration of crews.[95] Appropriately enough, the sponsor of this scheme was Demetrius the Besieger, the profligate son of Antigonus the One-Eyed and Hellenistic prince par excellence. His first venture into naval architecture was a "seven," but Diodorus indicates that he quickly moved to "nines" and a "ten."[96] As his enemies followed suit, Demetrius continued to up the ante, which by 301 B.C. included an "eleven" and a "thirteen." Thirteen years later he was up to a "fifteen" and a "sixteen" when his bitter enemy Lysimachus countered with the *leontophorus,* a ship described by Memnon as "remarkable for its size and beauty"[97] and probably built on the lines of a catamaran.

Not to be outdone, Ptolemy II, backed by the wealth of Egypt, entered into a shipbuilding program which dwarfed those of his rivals. At its bloated peak (around 246 B.C.), his fleet consisted of 17 "fives," 5 "sixes," 37 "sevens," 30 "nines," 14 "elevens," 2 "twelves," 4 "thirteens," and, to absolutely crush the competition, three gargantuan ships, a "twenty" and two "thirties."[98] The size of some of these vessels can be judged by the vital statistics of the quintessential giant, Ptolemy V's "forty." Four hundred fifty feet long, fifty-seven feet abeam, accommodating four thousand oarsmen, four hundred deckhands, and twenty-eight hundred marines, she was not only the largest vessel in antiquity but also virtually worthless militarily, a mere showpiece.[99]

Indeed, the general effect of the naval arms race, particularly in vessels larger than "fives," must have been a diminution in tactical potential. For even more than speed, ramming requires maneuverability, certainly not the strong suit of galleys ponderously rowed by five or more men at a sweep. With the adoption of a catamaran form, even limited use of the ram became impossible. These were floating citadels, and naval tactics with such ships became again a matter of boarding and perhaps catapult fire, a sort of siege warfare at sea.

Nor was this an isolated phenomenon. Virtually the entire array of Hellenistic military innovations—catapult field artillery (seldom used), elephants (basically tropical animals and prone to a variety of ailments in other climates), even heavier cavalry (lacking the stirrup, it still could not hope to break up massed pikemen)—was overrated. Doubtless, the level of technical sophistication and the spirit of inquiry implied in a number of advanced prototypes were startling in their modernity. But until man was ready to exploit the power latent in the substances around him, there simply were limits on the destructiveness which could be achieved by mechanical means alone.

In lieu of this, design ingenuity was largely directed toward predictable ends, primarily those having to do with size. Ships grew mindlessly, and the catapult, rather than the crossbow, found its way into Hellenistic arsenals. If not exactly translatable in reality, the equation of size with power clearly held sway psychologically. Thus, Demetrius's enormous "city taker," a siege tower nearly one hundred feet tall and crammed with all manner of military engines, never took a city, but was remembered nonetheless and immortalized by Plutarch.[100] But here, again, the attraction of large and elaborate weapons and their contrast physically to the real killers, the spear and the sword, appears to touch on some older and more universal themes, particularly the analogous contrast between the elaborate but relatively harmless tusks and antlers of intraspecific combat and the lethal but unobtrusive fangs of the predator.

But, in fact, not even the *sarissa* was immune to growth. In an effort to get five spearheads projecting from an advancing line, the Macedonian spear was increased first to twenty-one feet, then to twenty-five. While the Greeks customarily followed Macedonian arms symmetrically, the latter figure was obviously excessive and, after an unfortunate encounter with a Spartan force under Cleonymus, was reduced again to twenty-one feet.[101] Even this was too long.

In spite of these problems, however, the phalanx continued to assert itself. Rather too deadly and difficult to man, it was nevertheless decisive. Thus, at Raphia in 217 B.C., after the cavalries of Ptolemy IV and Antiochus III had canceled each other out, the heavy infantry settled the issue.

Closer to home, the pikemen of Macedon were once again on the ascendancy, led by their energetic ruler, Philip V. Through a combination of soldiering, diplomacy, and treachery, he had gained control of the entire Peloponnese and seemed on the point of dominating, once again, all of Greece. His only real obstacle was an Italic people of somewhat obscure origins but growing power, the Romans. They had crossed over to Hellas to aid, among others, the Athenians, who were friends of Rome's trusted ally Ptolemy IV. But it was a pretext.

Fifteen years before, Philip had allied himself with the archenemy Hannibal as the Roman Republic fought for its very life.[102] Most probably the Macedonian king had done so offhandedly, simply another maneuver in a career which amounted to little else. But it was not the kind of thing the Romans forgot—or forgave.

No matter that eighty years before Pyrrhus, the Epirote condottieri, had fought the Romans in Italy and had thrashed them in two out of three battles. True, his victories were costly (proverbially so, in fact), but they had nevertheless clearly established Hellenistic tactical superiority. Moreover, this time they would be fighting real Macedonians and on their own territory.

The war began well enough for Philip, if rather more slowly than he might have hoped. There had been but one engagement, a cavalry clash in which the Macedonians had fought well enough to at least hold their own. In an attempt to whip up enthusiasm for the war, Philip decided to hold a mass funeral for those who had fallen. It proved to be one of the least successful pep rallies in history. The Macedonians, used as they were to the neat wounds inflicted by javelin and *sarissa,* were unprepared for what they beheld. Livy writes: "When they had seen bodies chopped to pieces by the Spanish sword, arms torn away, shoulders and all, or heads separated from bodies . . . or vitals laid open . . . they realized in a general panic with what weapons, and what men they had to fight."[103] Philip's army was never the same.

Three years later, while marching through the foggy hills of Cynoscephalae, he would blunder into battle with Titus Quinctius Flaminius, gradually committing his entire army. For a while the phalanx held, fighting with the advantage of the uphill slope. But then the Romans, whose tactical formations allowed them to break into small units, moved in from all sides. Spears pointing in every direction, the phalanx could no longer hold them off. At one point Philip ordered those near him to drop their *sarissa* and fight with swords. But it was no use. Those who did not run were hacked apart like the corpses at the ill-fated funeral. Macedon would fight again (meeting utter destruction at Pydna in 168 B.C.), but Cynoscephalae marked the end of its military supremacy. Power had once again shifted west.

Chapter 5

ROME

I

The Roman army of 200 B.C. was already the product of four centuries of evolution. At Cynoscephalae it was not quite a finished product, but was close enough to already constitute the most reliable killing machine in the entire era of muscle-powered warfare. To provide an indication of relative lethality, it is probable that the *gladius,* or Spanish short sword (still quite a recent innovation at this point), would eventually account for more deaths than any other weapon prior to the advent of firearms. Literally millions would fall to this vicious little meat cleaver.[1] Yet its deadliness was not so much a function of the weapon as it was the result of the men using it.

The Romans were not necessarily an innovative race. They were adept organizers and engineers, looking at certain questions with a realism which is striking even today. Yet they were also bound by a web of superstition and tradition, of which war and weapons were very much a part.

Nevertheless, political will and the experience of fighting practically every military power in the Mediterranean basin at one time or another continually prodded Rome to experiment until a formula was found which allowed maximum utilization of her major military asset, the incredible bravery and aggressiveness of her troops. Rome did not always win. For the most part her generals fought by the rules and could be fooled. But at the level of the individual soldier, the system never failed.

The symbol of Rome was a she-wolf—the legendary adoptive mother of the eponymous founders, Remus and Romulus. Militarily, this could not be more appropriate. For the Roman infantryman not only killed as expertly as any soldier in history, he killed with the calm precision of a carnivore dispatching its prey. Firsthand Roman combat reports, particularly Caesar's *Commentaries,* are striking in their blandness of tone, the absolutely matter-of-fact way the carnage is described. For the Greeks, combat was a terrifying if exhilarating experience. For the Romans, it was largely in a day's work.

It stands to reason that the unmatched political will of the Roman state lay at the root of this outlook. Just as the she-wolf hunts to eat, Rome waged war, ultimately, to consume her opponents. Yet the means by which this essentially predatory end was transmitted to the individual soldier was paradoxical in that it expressed itself primarily through the exaltation of the intraspecific medium of individual combat. Indeed, the Homeric ethic was taken to its logical extreme by Rome in the creation of an army in which each soldier fought in the heroic manner and at the closest possible range.

The unprecedented intensification of both predatory ends and intraspecific means was not something achieved without a conscious effort, nor could it be sustained in the absence of careful psychological accommodations. Thus, the third element in the Roman military formula—and the essential prop for the other two—was a commitment that troops, up until the moment of battle, would be as well trained, armed, fed, and rested as careful planning and logistics could possible make them.[2] The Romans, more than most, realized that bravery was a short-lived and unpredictable quality. Consequently, they set about to maximize the chances that it would appear at the right time.

It was with this triad of ferocity, skill, and logistics that Rome came to conquer most of the world known to her. This done, the same combination held together what was one of the largest empires in history for half-a-millennium. Its evolution is worth examining.

II

While the evidence is slender, Garlan and others agree that Roman military institutions began their development, like those of so many other races, with aristocratic heavy-armed cavalry.[3] However, contact and possibly conquest by the Etruscans, a thoroughly Hellenized people, seems to have acquainted the Romans with the military institutions of the Greeks and caused them, indirectly at least, to adopt the heavy-armored phalanx. These changes were recorded in the so-called Servian reforms (after the semimythic Servius Tullius) around 550 B.C.[4] Livy has left us a detailed description of these reforms,[5] and it is apparent that their central thrust was to base political participation on the possession of arms and to designate those wealthy enough to afford a full Homeric panoply as the prime fighting element. The remainder was either light-armed troops or exempt. (As an indication of their status and relationship to war making, it is worth noting that armorers came from this last category.)[6]

This situation persisted until around 400 B.C., when several important developments took place. The first was associated with the ten-year siege and capture of the Etruscan city of Veii. Because of the length of the operation, dictator M. Furius Camillus introduced regular pay for those serving, thus taking the first step, as H. H. Scullard notes, in the transformation of the citizen militia into a professional army.[7]

Then in 390 B.C. a truly shattering event occurred. A band of thirty thousand Gauls crossed the Apennines in search of plunder. A wild race given to drunkenness, human sacrifice, and oratory, they rushed into battle naked and screaming, wielding long iron swords with frantic abandon. Physically much larger than the Romans (they may have held as much as a five- to seven-inch height advantage) and outnumbering them by approximately two to one, they literally engulfed the phalanx at the River Allia.[8]

The marauders then swept on to Rome, which they thoroughly sacked. Livy portrays the Romans, now refugees from their own homes, watching the havoc from atop a nearby hill "as if Fortune had placed them there to witness the pageant of a dying country." Yet their resolve remained unbroken, and with all else lost they looked "solely to their shields and the swords in their right hands as their only remaining hope."[9]

This episode may have been apocryphal, but the sentiment was not. Rome would not soon forget the Gauls. Never again would she fight unprepared or without taking advantage of every human resource available to her. Over the course of the next century (the exact dates are very much in dispute), Rome would engage in a series of basic reforms which would transform her army from a massive pincushion into a buzz saw of individual warriors, a sort of human equivalent to a school of piranha.

The trend established by formalizing pay for military service was continued in a complex process, known as the Union of the Orders, which, by opening the political system to greater participation by plebians, made this group much more readily available and effective for military service.[10] Thus, through political accommodation, Rome broadened the formerly narrow base for the phalanx to incorporate the entire body politic.

Much the same thing was happening externally. Rome was muddling toward an alternative to the city-state and the transnational tyranny—an entity at once larger in area and still capable of commanding the kind of loyalty necessary for aggressive fighting forces. Politically, this search would fail, but militarily it would not. For it was the peculiar genius of Rome that she was willing to share her citizenship, or a reasonable facsimile therof, with those she had conquered.[11] Thinking themselves Romans, they would fight as Romans. While revolts among "allies" were not unknown, by and large they remained remarkably loyal. The days of being outnumbered were over. Fair treatment opened to Rome a pool of manpower which allowed her to face defeat after defeat and still take the field with full levies.

It also raised important tactical possibilities. If the phalanx had broken in the face of the Gauls, it was due more to corporate brittleness than to the shortcomings of the individual components. Roman troops had always been steady and brave, and the reforms which followed catered to these instincts.

First and foremost, the thrusting spear was largely abandoned in favor of the sword. Two-thirds of the dominant heavy infantry—the first two lines of a basic three-line formation—were equipped with two weighted throwing javelins (pila) to momentarily break the enemy's cohesion, while the Romans weighed in with swords (at this point about two feet long and optimized for stabbing). Only the third line, older men used as a screen for the others, retained the spear.[12] Pay now made it possible for all men to be well equipped defensively, with a helmet, breastplate, a single greave, and quite probably the best shield in ancient warfare, a stout, rectilinear affair with iron around the edges.[13] So, just as Livy would write, Rome staked her future on the shields and swords in the right hands of her men.

The verified existence of the *spolia opima* (literally, the "richest spoil," granted only when a Roman commander personally killed his opposite number in single combat) as far back as 435 B.C.[14] indicates that individual fighting had long been a Roman preoccupation. But the conditions of war in the fourth century, particularly during the Samnite Wars (343–290 B.C.), served to increase this emphasis still further. Samnium was rugged, hilly country. In order to maneuver effectively, the Romans had to open their formations, a strategem workable only if the legionary was left free to roam his designated area of approximately thirty-six square feet.[15] Unlike the phalanx, where a single spear meant nothing without others, the legionary was essentially on his own when confronting the enemy.

Beyond his area of responsibility, however, he was hardly a free agent. As part of the tactical reform, the basic three-line grouping was further split vertically to create rectilinear maniples of 120 men, each capable of individual maneuver.[16] Normally a Roman legion of thirty maniples lined up in a checkerboard pattern, but if the opportunity arose maniples could shift position or even change form as the situation demanded. It gave the Roman legion unparalleled flexibility. Again and again, enemy forces would break when confronted with a few spare maniples coming at them from an unexpected direction. Further developments would lead to an even more supple tactical instrument. But for the time being, there was nothing like it in Italy or anywhere else.

Of course, the skills implied in both the complexity of maneuver and the reliance on the most deadly form of hand-to-hand combat meant another step in the direction of professionalism. Roman legions practiced incessantly. They had to or the formula would not have worked. Fighting like this demanded that the individual be thoroughly conditioned, trained through repetition to react in patterns so predictable that fear and revulsion could not break them down. Roman soldiers were not automatons. Caesar makes it clear that even for the best-trained troops panic was a possibility. Yet it was minimized in every way possible.

Flavius Vegetius Renatus, the chief recorder of the Roman military system, notes that particular attention was placed on not only marching and tactical formations but swordplay. Recruits were first provided with wooden staves and shields (double the weight of real weapons), which they employed pummelling wooden posts in extended practice sessions twice a day. Gradually, more advanced techniques were introduced—aiming for the vital points of the body, the ability to deliver a blow without opening for a counter, the emphasis on more lethal thrusting strokes whenever possible. "Every means of taking advantage of an adversary" was drummed into the legionary's head, until he emerged virtually a professional swordsman.[17]

Figure 6. This detail from a sarcophagus illustrating legionnaires fighting barbarians depicts the very close and brutal nature of Roman combat. Reproduced by permission of the Bettmann Archive.

This brings up a more controversial point. Gladiatorial contests were first recorded in Rome in 264 B.C., shortly after the major reforms, held originally by private individuals as part of funerals for famous relatives.[18] Whatever the games later became, the initial intent appears to have been instructive. Besides celebrating individual combat, these contests performed a function that training could not. They showed men death, hardened them to its sight. For besides skill the other essential element of the Roman style of fighting was absolute cold-bloodedness. The callousness of Rome, the casual attitude toward death epitomized in the games, is seen today as a barbaric aberration. Yet viewed from a Roman perspective, the games were probably a good deal more serious and less depraved than we might imagine. For a state built on military power and dedicated to the sword and the shield, the act of combat would seem to have been a natural object of fascination. Rome needed men who killed easily and killed individually, and the games served both ends.

While the importance of individual combat to the Roman military system can be readily demonstrated, its ultimate origins are more open to question. Yet it remains true that the sequence of combat established by the reforms—from the casting of the pila to the closing encounter with swords—duplicates exactly that which is practiced in the *Iliad*. The nature and means by which the latter came to be superimposed upon the former will probably never be established with any degree of precision. But it does not seem unreasonable that the epic would have been heard in Rome by 400 B.C., perhaps as an impromptu translation from the lips of some Etruscan bard.

Since the floodgates of Hellenism did not open in Rome until the First Punic War, it does not seem likely that the military reformers consciously adopted Aias and Achilleus as models. Rather, it was the universality of these characters and the degree to which they epitomized warlike virtues which seems to have caused them to be ingested by the culture and to subtly condition its martial preferences. After the sack of 390 B.C., Romans felt the need to reform militarily and apparently fell back on the style of fighting which struck them as bravest and most decisive. In this respect the legionary stands in a line stretching back beyond Homer to the close-in hunters of the Pleistocene.

On the other hand, the prejudices of an earlier era were also perpetuated. In particular, the possibilities of the bow were disregarded. Although Vegetius recommends archer training and cites several instances in which such troops had been useful, he does so offhandedly, obviously aware that these are exceptions.[19] The Romans themselves fielded few if any archers, normally relying on allied units when they used them at all. Rather than the bow, *velites,* or "light troops," were armed with the javelin.[20]

This does not seem accidental. The Roman army was by its nature confrontational; its central aim was to close with the enemy and chew through his formations. Under the circumstances, the bow must have been rejected as much for what it symbolized as for its actual tactical qualities. In this regard the Roman army scorned the bow institutionally for exactly the same reasons Homer's heroes did so individually. One day legionaries would pay for this contempt at the hands of the Parthians, but even then they would not change.

Something similar seems to have happened in the case of cavalry. Roman armies were proverbially weak in this arm, again relying heavily on allied forces. And Hannibal, among others, would capitalize on this shortcoming with disastrous results.[21] Here, again, the actual source of this condition is hard to pinpoint. Yet it seems likely that the political changes implied in the Servian reforms and militarily represented in the shift in emphasis from aristocratic horse to middle-class and well-to-do heavy infantry had something to do with it. As with the Greeks, these attitudes, once established, may have simply perpetuated themselves. The Romans don't seem to have had any particular prejudice against horses per se. But like the Assyrians, neither were they known as great riders, naturally preferring to fight on foot when they could. Thus, Roman cavalry had a decided tendency to devolve into infantry as horsemen dismounted, like Homeric warriors, to join the melee. The problem was that cavalry should act as the eyes of the army, constantly probing for the enemy's main concentration. Confrontational tactics like these, on the other hand, simply allowed Roman horses to be pinned down. Thus, much as with the bow, the central martial ethic impinged upon a fighting arm in a manner that was counterproductive.

But if the Romans lacked an appreciation for the true nature and uses of cavalry, they cannot be accused of ignoring the virtues of mobility, especially strategic mobility. To this end they would turn their army into the fastest-moving force in the entire era of muscle-powered warfare. The Romans were great marchers, capable of a consistent twenty miles a day while laden with as much as sixty pounds of supplies and equipment. But, frequently, physical endurance was secondary.

For an army's speed was a function largely of its route, which in the case of the Romans was a highway system destined one day to surpass in quality and extent anything constructed prior to the great American interstate network. Begun in 311 B.C. during the Samnite Wars, the essential prototype, the Via Appia, was constructed for the sole purpose of rushing troops and supplies from Rome to the war zone.[22] It would be followed by the great northern route, the Via Flaminia, to speed the military passage into turbulent Cisalpine Gaul. To these would be added the vias Latina, Salaria, Clodia, and Aurelia, until the Italian peninsula was bound in a web of paving stones. One day the web would extend far beyond Italy, knitting together the entire Mediterranean basin and enabling it to be held and defended by an army which frequently did not exceed 175,000 regulars.[23] But in the Republican era, particularly prior to Hannibal, the highway system was less an accomplished fact than a state of mind, a symptom of the determination of Rome to support her troops with any means at her disposal.

The resurrection of the Homeric ethic succeeded in large part because of an institutional commitment to deliver troops to the battlefield in absolutely the best condition possible. At the core of the support structure was the practice of castrametation, or the habitual construction of elaborate fortified camps at the end of each day's march. "The camps of the barbarians are not barbarian," exclaimed Pyrrhus the Epirote in 280 B.C.[24] Already normal procedure prior to 218 B.C., castrametation would be transformed into an obligatory part of Roman military life by the depredations of Hannibal. Precisely laid out in a rectilinear pattern which seldom varied, the camps provided the legionary not only with tangibles such as shelter and a place to store food and valuables but also with a psychologically familiar retreat from what was often a very hostile and dangerous outer environment. Livy makes the point that Roman generals customarily accepted battle only if they were within a short distance of their camps.[25] Since troops on the run are at their most vulnerable, the availability of a safe haven probably saved countless Roman lives, in addition to providing a rallying point from which a defeat might be reversed. For castrametation implied a sophisticated awareness of the psychology of territoriality and the relative advantage of defenders over invaders. Thus, by transporting a bit of home into enemy territory, the Roman invaders in effect reversed roles and were able to assume the mantle of protector.[26]

This concern with defense is typical. What Rome won she would protect. After the sack of 390 B.C., her first step, even before the reform of the army, was to reconstruct the city walls in stone twelve feet thick, twenty-four feet tall, and 5.5 miles in circumference.[27] One day under Hadrian she would gird the entire northern tier of the empire in a string of fortifications dwarfing anything yet attempted by a military power. Relative to the work forces and resources available, the effort involved in both cases was tremendous, illustrative of not only the Romans' continuing commitment to permanence but also a realistic awareness that one day they would be subject to attack.

Certainly, Rome had never refrained from assaulting the strong points of her enemies. For if the Romans were among the greatest military builders in history, they were also among the most adept at tearing down fortifications. Unlike Greece, siege warfare had existed practically from the beginning of the Republic. As far back as 502 B.C., consuls Opiter Verginius and Spurious Cassius were said to have assaulted Pometia with mantlets (portable shelters) and other machinery, probably including the battering ram.[28] A hundred years later Veii would fall after a siege of ten years which, according to Livy, included extensive earthworks, towers, mantlets, penthouses, and eventually a tunnel drives into the heart of the city.[29] After the experience of the Hannibalic War and later during Caesar's campaigns, the Romans would refine siege warfare into an ordered series of steps, a methodical process by which a noose of men and machines was drawn around a town until it submitted or fell. Mechanically, the Romans were not great innovators in this area. In large part they employed siege engines inherited from others, particularly the Hellenistic world. Yet they were used with a ruthlessness and an organizational mastery that were unprecedented, except perhaps by the Assyrians.

This was characteristic. Weapons and their development were strictly subordinated to the larger system. Whereas the arms industries of the Successor states had taken on a life of their own, feeding off the spirit of innovation, this never happened with Rome in either the late Republic or the Empire. Armorers remained anonymous and their arsenals strictly dedicated to the overall formula. There were innovations, but they were inevitably answers to specific problems rather than being undertaken for their own sake. Perhaps illustrative of this divergent orientation is the Hellenistic tendency to name weapons after their operating principles and characteristics (*euthytonon* and *palintonon* for arrow- or stone-throwing torsion catapults, *aerotonon* for the pneumatic-powered engines of Ctesibius), as opposed to the Roman practice of using analogous animal names (onager, corvus [crow], testudo [tortoise], *muscli* [little mouse]).

Indeed, the larger fascination with predatory imagery—the wolf and the eagle—probably epitomizes Roman intent as well as anything. The state had an open mind toward new weaponry, but no more so than it was attracted to the anachronistic virtues of individual combat. Just as the predator kills with any means available, so did Rome. All were merely components to an end defined by political ambition. And it was this ambition that would prove Rome's salvation when all else failed in the great duel with Carthage.

III

Just as Rome represented a new stage in the political development of the West, so was Carthage an updated derivative of the East. Founded by Tyre around 815 B.C. on the northwestern coast of Africa, the colony, rather than appoint her own kings, which would have smacked of disloyalty, developed an extremely stable constitutional oligarchy with its power rooted in the mercantile and manufacturing nobility.[30] For Carthage's wealth and her empire were based more on trade than despotism, and her bases, or "factories," came to line the North African and Spanish coasts like so many branch offices. By necessity, transit and communications for such a network had to come by sea, and the Carthaginian navy, having met and defeated the Greek Phocaeans, came to dominate the western Mediterranean.[31] Rowed by citizens (unlike the army, which was normally a mercenary force), the navy was renowned for both its tactical excellence and the quality of its ships.[32] Clearly, it was no force to be taken lightly.

Yet a clash was predestined. East versus West, commercial versus agrarian, army versus navy, each facing the other from opposite sides of the Mediterranean—Rome and Carthage were natural enemies, and when both became embroiled in the vicious internal politics of Sicily, war was only a matter of time. It came in 264 B.C.

Rome's problem in the First Punic War was essentially the same as Sparta's in the showdown with Athens. How does a land power come to grips with an enemy whose strength is based at sea? Whereas Sparta temporized, Rome immediately built a navy.[33]

Having only a very few of their own triremes, individually no match for the Carthaginian "fives," the Romans resorted to what would one day become the characteristic weapons acquisition strategy of the determined underdog—reverse engineering on a massive scale. As the story goes, a wrecked Punic "five" was recovered and used as a model for a fleet of a hundred duplicates, built in sixty days from the hewing of the timber while crews were taught to row on great stages erected on land.[34]

Yet the Romans, realists if nothing else, apparently had few illusions about the tactical capabilities of their ready-made, mirror-image fleet. To counteract its collective lack of skill they equipped its vessel with grapnel-based boarding bridges (corvuses) thereby turning loose on the Carthaginians the major Roman military asset—swordsmen.

In the navy's first real test, consul C. Dulius in 260 B.C. successfully turned a sea battle into a land battle off Mylae using the corvus, and in the process sank or captured fifty Punic warships. Rome would win five consecutive victories before her beginner's luck ran out.

In 255, returning home from an abortive invasion of Africa, the fleet encountered a terrific storm off Cape Pachynus which sank 170 ships and drowned over sixty-eight thousand of the crew, a figure with T. Frank suggests accounted for 15 percent of the able-bodied men in Italy.[35] Undaunted, the Romans simply raised taxes and built a replacement fleet of 220 ships the next year. It too would be largely destroyed in a storm off Cape Palinurus two years later. Again it was rebuilt, only to be defeated in 249 by the Carthaginians, who were learning to avoid the corvus. To compound matters, the rest of the Roman ships ran into still another storm off Cape Pachynus and were virtually obliterated, leaving only 20 of the original 220 ships which had begun the year.[36]

Its treasury exhausted and manpower depleted, but with no thought of giving up, Rome required almost seven years to build another fleet, this time financed through private loans to the state. Composed of 220 "fives," all lightly built without the corvus, this iteration of Roman sea power was at last ready to meet the Punic navy on its own tactical terms—maneuver and ram. Only with the greatest difficulty did Carthage respond, putting to sea a poorly manned, poorly equipped flotilla of 170 vessels, which was quickly defeated off the Aegates Islands in 242 B.C. After twenty-two years the war was over.

Rome showed amazing determination. Strictly a land power, she had not hesitated to fight at sea and had suffered repeated disasters in doing so. It is quite possible that Roman and allied war dead approached four hundred thousand, a figure unprecedented in prior military history.[37] It is apparent that Rome at this point had created a societal structure of sufficient resilience to wage something approaching total war in the modern sense, a capability unique for its time.

But if Rome's perseverance was extraordinary, the instruments she employed were not. True, the corvus was a significant innovation. But its central aim, boarding to avoid maneuver, was actually a retrogression. Moreover, Rome's final victory in the Aegates was won without the corvus, using ships and tactics virtually identical to her adversary's. Yet the triumph of symmetry at sea would be followed by an unexpected and entirely ironic sequel, the triumph of symmetry on land.

Rome had not heard the last of Carthage. Like the Peloponnesian War and a number of other decisive conflicts in the future, the duel with Carthage would be a compound affair, destined to resume when both parties were sufficiently recovered. Only this time Rome would find herself challenged on Italian soil— invaded and befuddled by one of the greatest generals of all time.

After Hannibal crossed the Alps, his original army of thirty-eight thousand reduced to nineteen thousand bedraggled, half-frozen survivors, he did an interesting thing. Polybus tells us he held a gladiatorial combat between some captured Gauls, the winner to go free. The pair, picked by lot from among their fellows, was overjoyed and fought bravely to the death. "Fortune has brought you to a like pass," Hannibal told his troops after the contest was over. "She has shut you in on a like field of battle, and [now] you must either conquer or die." [38] Since none of the troops was fool enough to contemplate seriously a retreat back over the Alps, the message took hold, and they fought accordingly.

The incident was typical of both the war and the man. The second Punic conflict was waged with utter desperation and fueled by the hatred of Hannibal. Unfortunately for Rome, he was a tactical genius.

Perfectly aware of Roman aggressiveness and weakness in cavalry, again and again Hannibal would first strip the Romans of their reconnaissance capability with his own excellent Numidian horse and then lead them into elaborate traps. Here, however, the superbly trained Roman swordsmen might have fought their way out had it not been for one much-overlooked factor. Hannibal had taken the core of his army and reequipped it with captured Roman weapons.[39] Symmetrically armed and suitably motivated, it was able to capitalize on Hannibal's tactical feats and destroy the trapped Romans in close combat.

In just three battles—at the River Trebia, at Lake Thrasymene, and finally the crushing defeat at Cannae—Rome would lose perhaps 150,000 of her best soldiers. Finally, under the leadership of Fabius Maximus, known as the Cunctator, or Delayer, they backed off and dogged Hannibal for thirteen years as he marched around southern Italy trying to break up the Roman confederacy. Yet political will and perseverance would win out when arms could not. There were some defections—Capua, the second city on the peninsula, being the most notable. But Rome's alliances held, and in the end Hannibal retreated to Africa to be defeated by Scipio Africanus at Zama in 202.

Arnold Toynbee, in his book *Hannibal's Legacy*, maintains that the Carthaginian general ruined Rome—that coming on top of the strain of the First Punic War, his depredations overstressed the Republic and set loose forces which would eventually lead to its collapse.[40] From a politico-economic standpoint this argument has some merit, but militarily it is difficult to support. Rather than weaker, the armed forces of Rome emerged from the double war (the Third Punic War was little more than a coup de grace) considerably stronger. Whereas before Rome had no navy, now she had one of the best. Meanwhile, the legionaries, some of whom had been in the field for close to two decades, were now virtually professional soldiers. No doubt this caused great dislocation in an agrarian society. Yet the continued evolution of the infantry was at the heart of Rome's future, the nursery of empire.

Legionaries now fought with the *gladius,* introduced by Scipio Africanus during his campaigns in Spain. Rather than bronze or iron, these blades were forged of tough steel from Toledo, rendering them virtually unbreakable—not an inconsiderable psychological advantage in the heat of battle. Short (no more than twenty inches), relatively heavy, and sharpened on both edges, the *gladius* was equally suited for slashing or thrusting and therefore ideal for the close-in style of fighting. Here again, the adoption of what amounted to a foreign-made weapon illustrates the acute Roman perception of what constituted appropriate armament and a willingness to so equip her troops.

Around 100 B.C. the process of improvement was continued by Gaius Marius, a man of his times, both an unscrupulous politician and an excellent soldier. As such he understood the main lines of development and moved accordingly. *Velites,* or light troops, became an allied responsibility, while the Romans concentrated solely on heavy infantry, now organized in cohorts of six hundred men. Within these formations, armaments were also standardized, with the thrusting spear of the third line replaced by the pila of the first two.[41] (Marius's pilum was a clever device, its metal head being attached to the wooden shaft with a dowel designed to break on impact, to prevent it being thrown back.) Around this time the familiar rectangular, semicylindrical shape of the Roman shield also reached its final form, while the cumbersome breastplate was replaced by more flexible armor made from chain or small plates sewn to a leather tunic. Training was further improved, not illogically, with arms drills adapted from the gladiatorial schools. Marius also increased self-sufficiency by requiring his troops to carry entrenching tools and several days' rations. "Marius's mules," they may have called themselves, staggering under the load by day, but at night they slept secure and well fed.[42]

It can be said that, both tactically and in terms of equipment, Marius gave final shape to the system. But in doing so, he had opened the recruiting rolls to landless volunteers who were now not only professional soldiers but more dependent on their commanders than on the state for a future after demobilization. As a result, the legionary would become a tool of faction, and Rome would be plunged into a revolution which would not end until Augustus Caesar emerged supreme and redefined the army's role in the state.

IV

He was the all-time master of political obfuscation and constitutional ambiguity. Whereas his adopted father, the great Caesar, would have made himself king, the son cloaked one-man rule in the fiction of the Republican restoration, and in so doing preserved the state and the Empire.[43] For without the Augustan settlement, Rome would have torn itself apart.

Militarily, the situation was impossible. Asking legionaries to practice their lethal craft against each other was simply untenable. Troops grew sullen and mutinous, at times avoiding combat altogether. In the end the decisive victory at Actium was achieved more through desertion than bloodshed.[44] Next to reconstituting the government, Augustus realized the necessity of restoring the army.

For the reputation of Rome's legions was all. As Edward Luttwak correctly notes, after the wars with Carthage, Rome had conquered the entire Hellenistic East virtually without fighting, relying instead on bluff and coercive diplomacy.[45] No soldier himself, this was the kind of victory Augustus preferred. Whether by instinct or analysis, he understood the full measure of deterrence implied in the possession of a military tool like the Roman heavy infantryman. Thus, he was able to reduce the number of legions to twenty-eight, from a total of nearly seventy fielded by both sides during the civil war. These he used sparingly, fighting largely to attain shorter, more "scientific" borders, as Ronald Syme and others have pointed out.[46]

Yet relative inaction did not imply a diminution in quality. And this was critical, for the Roman army at this point was nakedly professional. But its style of fighting demanded motivation exceeding that of pure monetary gain—the same contradiction which the Hellenistic monarchs failed to resolve. This is why the fiction of the restoration was so important. Augustus recreated a Rome worth believing in and therefore worth fighting for.

It is true that through most of the first two hundred years of empire the great majority of barbarian incursions were on a small scale, extended raids best dealt with by auxiliary troops and light cavalry. Yet always in the background was the heavy infantry, ready to deal with any larger threat and thereby maintaining the escalation dominance essential for long-term stability.

This is why such elaborate measures were taken to insure that the requisite level of quality was maintained. Recruitment was careful and normally highly selective, requiring a certificate of full Roman citizenship and a medical examination, along with optional letters of recommendation.[47] Pay was good, and medical treatment and standards of housing and hygiene were on a level not again exceeded until the nineteenth century, if then. Yet comfort did not mean laxity. The Jewish historian Josephus would write, perhaps as an admonition, "Each [Roman] soldier daily throws all his energy into his drill, as though he were in action. . . . Indeed it would not be wrong to describe their maneuvers as bloodless combats and their combats as sanguinary maneuvers."[48] Occasionally, legionaries were allowed to go soft, but over the course of hundreds of years this was remarkably infrequent. If Rome's soldiers fought less frequently than their

Republican predecessors, they were prepared all the more meticulously lest the impression of power fade.

Not surprisingly, defeat, though infrequent, brought forth an exaggerated reaction. This is why Augustus went to such trouble to recover the eagle standards lost by Crassus to Parthia fully fifty years before, and why, after the annihilation of three legions in the Teutoburg Forest, he would wander his palace muttering, *"Quinctili Vare, legiones redde."* (Quinctictius Varus, give me back my legions).[49] More to the point, it was why, in A.D. 70, after suffering a series of humiliating defeats at the hands of the Jews, Rome would occupy three full years and one entire legion reducing the stronghold of a few hundred Zealots at Masada, and in the process build the huge ramp referred to previously. Such a project has no explanation beyond the realm of the psychological. Rome had to appear implacable, and her legionaries invincible.

And in doing so she brought a new phenomenon into man's historical existence—peace. For the first time an agglomeration of nationalities, many of whom had been imperial peoples at one time or another, managed to live together on a long-term basis, largely free of war. True, from time to time there was intramural violence concerning the succession (Cremona, for example, was brutally sacked by the followers of Vespasian in A.D. 69). Yet in large part the first three hundred years of the empire, particularly the eighty-two years between the accession of Trajan and the death of Marcus Aurelius (the period Gibbon called the most felicitous in human history),[50] were remarkable for their pacific nature. But if the Pax Romana was unique in European history, it nonetheless provides a convincing demonstration that war is not inherent in human nature. Rather, it is about economics and politics, and when those become moot, the most natural state of humankind is one largely devoid of organized violence. Peace in this case was based on overwhelming strength and domination. Rome ruled a tranquil world primarily because she had cowed her enemies, both internal and external.

V

Militarily, the causes of degeneration and collapse are many. Clearly, legionary involvement in politics and the mechanisms of the succession had a destabilizing effect. Rome's territory lay astride natural migration corridors which, during the late Empire, increasingly subjected it to wave after wave of westward-moving barbarians.[51] Moreover, sustained exposure to the Roman military system acted symmetrically to sharpen barbarian fighting skills. Naturally, as the threat grew, protection became more expensive. It has been estimated that during the early principate the cost of the army accounted for no more than one-half of revenues.[52] However, costs steadily accelerated throughout the second and third centuries until, as Rostovtzeff theorized, the burden of defense began to strangle the larger economy and society.[53]

Yet when all of these factors are considered, Rome's military disintegration in the fourth century can still be traced to one essential: her legions were no longer invincible, nor were they perceived to be so by her enemies. And this boils down to a matter of personnel.

Strategically, one of the keys to Rome's defense was the mobility of her major units. But beginning with Hadrian, legions were deployed at fixed bases, which in most cases they never left again. Soldiers grew attached to localities and acquired unofficial families, and the legions gradually became fixed, rather than mobile, assets.[54] *Vexillaliones,* or the practice of combining unattached men from multiple legions, provided for a field army, but not one necessarily united by long training and tradition. To make matters worse, autochthonous troops began to be supplemented by ethnically unassimilated *numeri,* fighting in their own style with native weaponry. From here it was a short step to turning the Empire's defense over to a variety of thinly disguised outsiders—our barbarians versus their barbarians.

It has been said that Rome's growing emphasis and eventual reliance on cavalry—some bowmen, but primarily heavy lancers or cataphracts—was necessitated by the need to deal with adversaries who themselves were increasingly mounted lancers likely to appear at any quarter.[55] While such an explanation is in consonance with the logic of weapons symmetry, it obscures the degeneration of Rome's once-lethal swordsmen. In the words of Jomini: "Those formidable soldiers who had borne the casque and buckler and cuirass at the time of the Scipios under the burning sun of Africa found them too heavy in the cold climate of Germany and Gaul and the Empire was lost."[56]

As darkness fell, two voices were heard offering possible solutions, which themselves epitomized the dilemma. The first was the anonymous author of *De Rebus Bellicus,* who in A.D. 370 became the first Roman military thinker in over half a millennium to propose major technical change, suggesting, among other things, a paddle-wheel ship driven by oxen, an inflatable pontoon bridge, three types of frameless chariots with scythes, and two new ballista which did not employ torsion. In all, his object was plain—to save manpower: "Invincible Emperor, you will double the strength of your invincible army . . . countering the raids of your enemies, not by sheer strength alone, but also by mechanical ingenuity."[57] So once again, just as in the case of the Hellenistic monarchs, science and innovation were conceived of as an alternative to willing and aggressive soldiers.

Such an option was undoubtedly an anathema to Flavius Vegetius Renatus. Writing in the same decade, presumably after the debacle of Adrianople, he proposed the opposite tack, a return to the original system.

We know so many of the details of Roman military practice precisely because Vegetius saw it slipping beyond recollection and committed it to writing in an effort to resurrect it. "Victory in war," he wrote to Valentinian II, "does not depend entirely upon numbers or mere courage; only skill and discipline will insure it."[58] But his advice would go unheeded, as of course it had to. For the political and corporate will which had engendered the legionary system had long since departed. Nor was mechanical invention any real option since destructive power remained tied to human- and animal-generated force.

Yet there is some irony in the alternative Rome did choose, the armored lancer, since at the very beginning of the empire her legions had been exposed to a more deadly weapon system—in fact, the most deadly of the entire era, the mounted archer.

Chapter 6

EQUES

I

Crassus needed a military reputation. As the third member of a triumvirate that included two great soldiers, Pompey and Caesar, he had only wealth and ambition to his credit. Therefore, he jumped at the chance to lead a punitive expedition against the upstart Parthians, a feudal nobility of nomadic origins who had carved an empire out of the former dominion of the great king of Persia. In the spring of 53 B.C., he crossed the Euphrates at the 37th degree latitude and headed inland with seven legions and four thousand Gallic cavalry.

After a four-day march, he reached the vicinity of the town of Carrhae, where he encountered the Parthian force. It was a unique deployment, the first of its kind among organized states in that its normal infantry contingent was missing, leaving only cavalry—a minority of heavily armored lancers (the nobles) and a much more numerous group of light horsemen using the composite bow.[1] It was to this element that the battle would belong.

At first contact, Crassus formed a hollow square, with his cavalry on either flank awaiting the Parthian attack which would bring the armies to close quarters. It never came. Instead, the Parthian archers halted within effective bow range and began subjecting the legions to a withering barrage of arrows. Crassus did nothing until he realized his tormentors were being resupplied by camel train. He then sent out offensive detachments, first of cavalry, then infantry. In each case the mounted archers feigned retreat and then surrounded and annihilated Crassus's men—firing accurately at full gallop, even out over the hindquarters (the origin of the term *Parthian shot*). Over the next two days the slaughter continued until, out of an army of over forty-three thousand, only ten thousand were left to escape.[2]

Weapons-wise, Rome and the legion had met their match. In over 250 years of trying, the Empire would never really succeed in eradicating Parthian military

power, relying primarily on diplomacy to hold it in check.[3] This is symptomatic.

As we noted earlier, politics and empire were primarily functions of agriculture—"hydraulic societies," as Wittfogel calls them. But the Parthians represented nomad rule, lineal descendents of the first desert raiders. The reign of the Arcadids was reasonably long but strangely vaporous. When they became masters of the Seleucid kingdom, they took over Greek methods of administration and made use of Greek secretaries, Greek science, and the Greek language for trading. But unlike others, they were not deeply affected by Greek culture. They continued to speak their own tongue (Pahlavi), but left no written literature—or art or architecture, for that matter.[4] When their time came, they passed from the scene virtually unnoticed by history, their heritage no more substantial than the desert wind.

Militarily, they were just as elusive. They would feign retreat only to attack. They would engulf rather than confront. Tactically, they cared nothing for territory, scorning the agrarian conception of battle, concentrating on killing instead. And above all, they could not be caught.

The Eastern composite bow was a tremendously powerful weapon, with a man-killing range of well over 200 yards (verified by tests performed in the nineteenth century at the behest of Napoleon III).[5] Nonetheless, a body of foot archers could still be run down by determined infantry on good terrain from this distance in something under a minute—normally not enough time to do decisive damage. Yet mount these archers on horseback, giving them adequate means of retreat, and they become practically invincible at this level of technology. This had become apparent as far back as the Assyrians, who adopted horse archers, though without a great deal of success. For as we have already seen, riding and shooting a composite bow simultaneously requires a lifetime of training, for the common man an opportunity afforded only by an occupation on horseback. Given the basic Homeric and Western animus against the bow, this additional difficulty was sufficient to cause the Romans—in the past so quick to pick up on foreign weapons developments—to largely ignore this one for 350 years.

When cavalry was at last embraced by Rome, the bow would be used, but the lance preferred, a decision made practically unanimous by the feudal nobility of Europe. So it became one of the supreme ironies of Western military history that a culture in which all political power ostensibly rested upon coercion should come to disregard the deadliest weapon system available. For the bow just did not fit, either culturally or economically. And that, apparently, was paramount—although it could not preclude the likes of Genghis Khan.

II

It could be said without exaggerating overmuch that the entire Middle Ages was built on a few bits of leather and metal. For without the stirrup, the medieval lancer, to which the entire economic system was dedicated, would not have constituted a fully credible weapon system.

To a remarkable degree, the type had been anticipated long before in the de-

velopment of the Parthian cataphract. Nomads had long padded their ponies against arrow wounds, and the Parthian nobility extended the practice to covering both their chargers and themselves with a thick layer of mail and even plate.[6] This, of course, was heavy, causing them to further enlarge the sturdy products of the Nesaean stud captured from the Seleucids in order to produce a truly monumental breed of equines, fine of foot unlike plow horses but barrel-chested and heavily boned and muscled enough to carry their now considerable burden.[7] Yet the power and weight inherent in such a combination was in most ways antithetical to the agility and maneuverability required for mounted archers. Rather than the bow, the natural weapon of the cataphract was the lance.

So it came to pass that the swirling mass of Parthian horse archers would be led by an elite of iron men astride huge chargers and so heavily protected that, as Tacitus notes, such warriors could barely stand if unhorsed.[8] This must have occurred frequently, for if the lumbering cataphract generated the requisite momentum, balance and shock absorption were other matters entirely.

Though he probably had a rigid-frame saddle to help prevent being knocked out over the horse's rump, a Parthian cataphract had absolutely no means of lateral stability, clinging to his mount solely through the pressure exerted by foot and thigh. Thus, any blow delivered even slightly to the left or right was likely to unhorse him. Given these conditions, the lance had to be employed primarily as a thrusting weapon operated with two hands rather than being held at rest, further eroding the viability of the man-horse synergy by precluding a firm grip on the reins and the use of an adequate shield on the opposite side.[9] Thus, heavy cavalry remained technically deficient and still unable to break up formations of resolute infantry. Moreover, they were expensive, requiring not only a significant investment in arms and armor but a considerable establishment to breed and care for war-horses. Therefore, although the Sassanians and the Sarmatians took them over after the Parthians, they remained primarily weapons of the East and eventually faded out of existence.[10]

This is not meant to imply that the cataphract was an unattractive option. Quite the contrary, from a preferential perspective it was close to ideal. All cavalry, particularly this kind, have certain clear psychological advantages in combat. The act of putting a man on a horse, preferably a large horse, raises him above other men. While others must walk, he rides, elevated physically and forcing those below, quite literally, to look up to him. In this respect it is an aristocratic weapon par excellence, and the equestrian predilections of practically every ancient nobility, including even the Iron Age Greeks and pre-Republican Romans, bears this out in fact as well as theory.

Also, size itself must have been an important intimidating factor. Faced with something like a cataphract bearing down on him, an infantryman is unlikely to have perceived simply a man riding a horse, but rather an armored juggernaut, at once larger and more terrifying than any one of its constituent parts. Speed also must have had a telling effect. Under most conditions an armed man riding a horse in good condition can move at between two and two-and-a-half times the rate of a similarly equipped man either walking or running.[11] Not only does this insure tangible benefits in the ability to initiate and break off combat with slower adver-

saries, but, as has been noted before, speed appears to have a value in and of itself. Much the same thing can be said of noise. Indeed, the frequent references to the "thunder of horses' hooves" in descriptions of cavalry charges would seem to indicate that this was a significant element in the psychology of equestrian warfare.

Cavalry, in particular the armored lancer, was a confrontational device. As with other analogous forms, the object was to close with the enemy, to run him down and impale him. It was therefore very much in the tradition which had begun with the hunting of large herbivores and had been codified and transmuted by Homer into what is now referred to as the Western military tradition. Thus, the fact that cavalry was not more of a factor in the early Middle Ages, as the historical record shows it was not, seems logically to have turned on technical considerations. This is why the introduction of the stirrup was of such significance.

The so-called Ross-Brunner-White thesis, which traces the politico-economic essentials of feudalism to Charles Martel's sudden emphasis on heavy cavalry around A.D. 740, and this to the availability of stirrups,[12] has been challenged on a number of grounds. Granted, it can be argued that feudalism was a more gradual process, its antecedents existing long before, and its final form not taking shape until fifty years after Charlemagne's death. Similarly, it can be maintained that the spread of the stirrup and the kind of fighting it made possible was irregular in terms of both time and geography.[13] Yet such critiques seem, if even unconsciously, to underestimate the true significance of purely military contingencies at this point. Whenever it came, the lateral stability provided by the stirrup was real and injected a vital and heretofore missing element into shock cavalry, thereby catalyzing the characteristically rapid sequence of ancillary developments which is typical in the evolution of dominant weapon systems.

When combined with a saddle built up at the pommell and cantle for longitudinal support, the stirrup welded rider and horse together sufficiently well to open up an entirely new means of attack. Rather than thrusting out himself, the lancer could now hold his weapon at rest in the crook of his arm, using the combined weight of his body and his charging stallion to deliver a blow of unprecedented violence, a fact attested to by the sudden appearance of baffles on lances to prevent them from penetrating too far and getting stuck.[14] This arrangement also had the additional benefit of freeing the opposite arm to control the reins and carry the kite-shaped shield which was the rider's major means of turning aside equivalent blows. For the balance between offense and defense was also essential to the stability of the system.

Not surprisingly, the distinctive Frankish throwing ax, the *francisca,* would disappear in favor of a forty-four-inch long sword, useful on foot but primarily aimed at providing extra reach from the back of a horse. Helmet design also improved, with the ancient crested form replaced by a highly functional conical iron headpiece with attached nose protector. The length of the mail shirt, universally the basic item of armor, was increased to cover the knees of the rider. Over time this protection would gradually spread, with the addition of the hauberk to cover the area between helmet and shirt, gloves, and eventually mail breeches.[15]

But the essential elements of knightly equipment were in place by A.D. 950.[16] So in a period as short as a century, this developmental sequence deposited an extraordinary durable and effective weapon system on the stage of European history, and its effect was bound to be felt both politically and economically.

The exact nature of the causal relationship between the appearance of shock cavalry and feudalism is a controversial subject. Yet it seems indisputable that such a relationship did exist, and that each element reinforced the other.

Given the reduced levels of economic productivity at this point in history, shock cavalry was bound to be extraordinarily costly and therefore selective. It has been estimated that the equipment to outfit one knight amounted to the cost of about twenty oxen or the plow teams of at least ten peasant families.[17] Moreover, fighting in this manner was extremely demanding, requiring an extended training period and virtually constant practice. Plainly, to be successful the participants required steady, though not necessarily intensive, economic support and the leisure time to indulge their martial proclivities. With the exception of the metal used in arms, all the necessary elements (feed, war-horses, livelihood, etc.) could be supplied in an agrarian setting, either nonmonetary or minimally so. Yet, quite plainly, only a very few could participate, living essentially off the slender but growing surpluses such a system could offer. In return they provided but one service, although a necessary one—protection.

For beginning around A.D. 750, western Europe was beset by a plague of seaborne vultures, known collectively as the Vikings and sailing shallow-draft, single-sail, square-rigged galleys not unlike those of the Mycenaean Greeks two millennia before. Tactically, the Vikings were ideally suited to the political ecology of the time. For the world they found in their first great series of raids into Northumbria and Aquitaine was analogous to the hair and fingernails growing on a corpse. As Georges Duby has noted, what passed for a governmental structure in Europe, and in particular the Carolingian Empire, at this point was "no more than a glorified village blown up. . . . A political edifice based on the remnants of Roman culture which turned out to be in fact no more than a re-assembly of the debris of the old."[18]

Sailing from Norway and Denmark out of the fog of the North Sea, the Vikings descended first on the coastal towns and later traversed the major riverine arteries, spreading havoc and inevitably disappearing before the ponderous mechanisms of Saxon and Carolingian retribution could be applied. Indeed, by camping on estuarial islets and maintaining a water barrier between themselves and their victims whenever possible, the Vikings were virtually invulnerable to political entities whose power was inversely proportional to the distance from the center of government and imperfectly linked by a chain of personal obeisance.

Such a situation could only exaggerate trends already extant. Thus, in an effort to increase the mobility of his army, Charles the Bald, in A.D. 864, issued the Edict of Pitres, ordering all free Franks who owned a horse or could afford to keep one to serve mounted.[19] More and more, initiative was left to the local level, the most tangible effect being the growth of fortifications, first in towns and later throughout rural France, primarily in the form of earthwork-based motte-and-bailey castles.[20] The sole refuge for a people terrorized by the latest wave of marauders, such fortifications enabled their masters to exact a still-larger share of the constantly increasing agricultural product, and in doing so, to further formalize the manorial system and the domination of the peasantry which it implied.[21]

For the significance of the castle was both symbolic and real. At once the perfect architectural expression of the military aristocracy, castles also could and did control the land against raiders, their range being that of the heavy cavalry within them—about ten miles if you wanted to be home by dark.[22]

Yet, in fact, the results of the odd confrontation between the Vikings with their generalized longboats and the terrestrials with their specialized cavalry and castles were somewhat ironic. The Viking longboats, though fast and magnificently seaworthy, were essentially without offensive capability.[23] They were means of transport only; raiding was accomplished through forays inland. Here, especially as marauding faded into actual conquest, the Vikings reacted symmetrically to the weapons of the defenders, learning to fight from horseback, building fortifications, and, like the Normans, beginning to live and act remarkably like those they sought to replace.[24]

But if the Vikings could be assimilated, the measures taken against them did not quickly fade away. The combination of heavy cavalry and castles had the effect of diffusing power and spreading it throughout the countryside. For if charging horses ruled the field, they could not reduce a castle. Thus, a defeated, outnumbered, or simply recalcitrant vassal could often take refuge behind his walls and wait out external authority. Politically, it spelled the collapse of centralized government, the atomization of power. For cavalry and castles formed a closed system at once supporting and cancelling out each other, but normally immune or at least highly resistant to large political groupings.

III

Throughout the preceding chapters, it has been argued that the relationship between weapons, styles of warfare, and political systems is intimate and self-reinforcing. The feudal age which emerged after A.D. 1000 is a prime example. In the absence of large, centralized, politically ambitious states, warfare lost much of its predatorial cast and took on more of the characteristics of intraspecific combat.

As befit the age, war and fighting became a matter of class. For the aristocracy which emerged at the point when the term *miles* ceased to mean soldier and began to mean knight bore the exclusive right to bear arms.[25] Membership, though increasingly hereditary—especially at the upper reaches of the nobility—was primarily defined by the ability to fight, specifically as shock cavalry.

From the greatest of lords to the most minor henchman, all shared the socialization process surrounding this most demanding means of combat. F. M. Stenton has called "the apprenticeship preceding knighthood the most significant fact in the organization of feudal society."[26] Beginning at puberty and frequently requiring long residence and training among peers in the households of the great lords, it created a corporate self-consciousness, a cosmopolitan fraternity of arms, confident in its solidarity and reveling in its traditions.

It is frequently said that the self-image of the knight was delineated chiefly by two ideal virtues: loyalty to one's liege or overlord and prowess in combat. In the case of the former, although it remained vigorous locally, there was always room for treachery and rebellion regionally and beyond. In the second instance, however, there can be no doubt as to the importance of fighting well. As Lynn White, Jr., notes, "The new mode of combat, with its high mobility and fearful impact opened fresh fields for individual prowess."[27]

Certainly, there are instances of large-scale battles and disciplined maneuvers by squadrons of knights, but the emotional focus of combat had drawn down again to the level of the individual. As a motive for belligerence, politics never entirely disappeared. But its impact was fragmented and therefore subject to usurpation by other values. Gradually, fighting became a formalized ritual for attaining dominance, remarkable in its similarities to those of certain other mammals.

Archetypical of this turn of events was the development of tournaments—those elaborate, deadly, and completely realistic games of war to which the knightly class became hopelessly addicted—beginning in the early twelfth century.

It has frequently been noted that the circumstances of vassalage, and later primogeniture, created a class of surplus males, the younger sons of the knightly aristocracy for whom the choices were reduced to the priesthood or a life of adventure among wandering bands of peers, the so-called knights-errant.[28] Genetic strategies being what they are, many chose or were thrust into the latter category. For, as Duby notes: "These adventures were also revealed as quests for wives, perhaps first and foremost. . . . All *jeuvenes* were on the lookout for an heiress."[29] Such a union was the quickest and safest means of gaining land and support. This being the case, however, there was bound to be competition, and, given the importance attached to prowess at arms, the development of something like the tournaments seems entirely logical.

It can, of course, be argued, as did Sidney Painter in his biography of William Marshal, that women were neither present at early tournaments (though they later became assiduous spectators) nor the prime aim of participation, that being ransom or the capture of horses and weapons.[30] Yet this misses a larger point. Tournaments were from the beginning an opportunity to identify and rank dominant males. Indeed, Painter's own hero, the redoubtable William Marshal, was quite literally a product of the tourney. The younger son of a minor vassal but a formidable fighter, he wandered from event to event for fifteen years, building a near-legendary reputation which earned him an heiress, great estates, and ultimately the regency of England[31]—the medieval dream.

Of course, war provided similar though less observable opportunities for such displays. And in many instances even the participants might have had trouble telling the two apart. For both were so laden with the stuff of biological ritual that it is possible to wonder whether this had not become the major intent.

The very nature of the joust—high-speed, head-on collision with protruding, tusklike lances—invites comparison with the spectacular ceremonial combats of a

Figure 7. The Joust 'of war' from the Mittelalterliches Haubuch, c. A.D. 1300. Reprinted by permission of the Bodleian Library.

variety of ungulates—significantly, perhaps, nonpredators. As with all such contests, combat was individualized and hemmed in by an elaborate web of submission-related rules. The essence of what has come to be known as military chivalry was illustrated when William Marshal, vassal of the warring Henry Plantagenet, happened upon the ostensible enemy, Richard *Coeur de Lion,* with neither hauberk nor mail and therefore very vulnerable. "By the legs of God Marshal do not kill me. That would not be right for I am unarmed."[32] Grumbling, Marshal shifted his lance and merely ran through Richard's horse. Although it would not be hard to cite similar examples, this is not meant to imply that fighting had become nonlethal. This was a violent age. Genealogical evidence and knowledge of contemporary medical practice indicate that the life of a knight was both dangerous and prone to be short. Nonetheless, when compared with something like the Roman legion, it is fair to say that killing itself had become a secondary objective.

Furthermore, the state of arms appears to have reinforced this situation. Although the mounted lancer possessed extraordinary offensive power, he was also extremely well protected, his kite-shaped shield being optimized to turn aside a lance. Thus, symmetrically armed opponents frequently neutralized each other.

Certainly, knights occasionally turned on the lightly armed infantry of the day with deadly effect. Yet, as befit the intraspecific image, real combat—the combat that mattered in the eyes of the participants—was necessarily fought between equals in arms as well as class, and as such often produced few casualties. Thus, Marshal did not so much spare Richard's life as refuse to fight him without the proper accouterments.

Given these conditions, the weaponry of shock cavalry proved highly durable, dominating Europe until well into the fourteenth century. Deadly to outsiders and those below, it was nevertheless eminently usable among the ruling classes—the ideal instrument of the status quo. As is common of weapons in nature specialized to enforce dominance, the vestments of heavy cavalry were extremely formidable visually, relying on a heavy measure of implied threat. The Middle Ages was a time overlaid with symbolism, and the charging armored juggernaut and the crenellated battlements of the medieval castle took their places as the prime archetypes of coercive power, images of such potency that they would endure long past their tactical demise, to condition weapons choice right into the industrial era.

There was but one exception to the ideal match between knightly arms and heroic warfare. Yet even it enriched the symbolism. For one knight encased in full battle array was virtually indistinguishable from another, a situation which tended to defeat the whole purpose of combat. In response, individual warriors took to adorning their shields with specific insignia (coats of arms). Genetic advertising, it was in one respect analogous to the decorative coloration of competing males in numerous species. Yet it was utterly functional in another regard, for if brave deeds were to be remembered, their perpetrators had to be identifiable.

And so there grew up a sort of international corporation of heralds, the regulators of civilized warfare, who hung like scavengers about the battlefields and tourney grounds, their designated function being to ascertain brave deeds, assign credit, and name names to be later recorded by a corps of chroniclers dedicated to embellishing these bare facts. Thus, chivalry gave birth to a philosophy of history which, as Lynn White, Jr., notes, proclaimed the immortalization of brave deeds to be the principle duty of Clio.[33]

A similar urge gave rise to the primary secular literary manifestation of the age, the chanson de geste. One has only to peruse the meticulously detailed blow-by-blow accounts in the *Chanson de Roland* or encounter the adulterous arrogance of a Tristan to realize that these tales are in fact the analogues to Homer and, still earlier, the epic of Gilgamesh. The same confrontational values and worship of close combat had been accurately transmitted to these medieval literary bruisers, further reinforcing their primacy and insuring they would be passed on.

Just as in the *Iliad,* horses and arms specialized for close combat were inevitably singled out as items of great worth. Swords, in particular, were treated with extreme, at times almost unbelievable, reverence. Thus, Zoe Oldenburg notes with wonderment that Roland, who through the entire poem has only a few words of praise for his betrothed, breaks into a regular soliloquy when, at the point of death, he realizes that his sword, Durendal (epic blades were inevitably named), might fall into the hands of the hated Saracens. "Ah Durendal, good sword, your unlucky day, for I am lost and cannot keep you in my care. . . . Ah Durendal, how beautiful and bright, so full of light, all on fire in the sun.''[34] While most protagonists were less bathetic, they would have readily agreed with El Cid the Campeador: ''Lances and swords must be our shelter, or else on this meagre earth we cannot live.''[35]

For weapons in the chansons, as in life, were clearly and premeditatedly instruments of class, tailored to the needs of the aristocracy. Armorers, on the other hand, are lower-class figures and barely mentioned. Only their creations matter.

Nor does the bow play a significant literary role. While not necessarily treated with the disdain of a Homer, it is, when in the hands of the hero, preeminently a weapon of the hunt, not of battle.

Combat, when it comes, is formalized, honorific, and inevitably fought with the traditional instruments matched symmetrically, even against the Moors. It could hardly be otherwise. Just as with the *Iliad,* these gore-encrusted passages formed the archetypes of combat which fixed military stereotypes in men's minds. Almost by definition, they had to be fought according to the rules. Combat was simply too important to have it any other way. For although heroes nominally subscribed to other values, it was prowess, not truth or justice or piety, which was the ultimate measure of behavior. Thus, Tristan could offer himself for combat to prove he had not slept with the king's wife although it was obvious he had.[36]

In this and other respects, life followed art. The values of combat did in fact spill over into a number of societal functions from which they are strictly segregated today. As one consequence, in most feudal societies some form of trial by combat was incorporated into the judicial structure, particularly for high crimes. While such practices were probably more honored in the breach than the observance, we nevertheless see William Marshal, at the ripe age of sixty-six, offering to defend himself by force of arms against the charge of harboring a traitor.[37] (In fact, by giving shelter to his renegade friend William de Briouse, he had done just that.)

But clearly more remarkable than these judicial encroachments was the effect of fighting values upon the medieval Church and, it should be added, vice versa. For if this was a time of rampant, almost anarchistic bellicosity, it was also a period suffused with piety. Under the circumstances it was nearly inevitable that one would affect the other. Fighting being the major educational preoccupation of aristocratic youth, and the Church being the key repository for the younger sons of the nobility, it is not surprising that among the ranks of the ordained were those who joined in the interminable brawling of the age. In fact as well as fiction, we find individual clergy battling side by side, and with much the same gusto as, their secular peers. Yet organizationally, intellectually, and morally the Church increasingly came to oppose the climate of intramural violence and did what it could to mitigate its consequences.

IV

Commencing around A.D. 990, basically coincidental with the collapse of royal authority in France, the movement known as the Peace of God began as an attempt to protect "sacred things," that is, the servants and sanctuaries of Christianity, from the depredations of local strongmen. Backed by meaningful threats of excommunication, the effort was basically a success and was quickly expanded to include the protection of all the "unarmed"—women, children, the old, and the poor.[38] Yet these first councils did not deny the aristocracy the right to fight. They sought only to isolate the violence to men-at-arms, even if these did include certain of the clergy. By the end of the tenth century, however, bearing and using arms began to seem evil in the same way as greed and the sexual act did to those in the forefront of the movement to reform the Church. Consequently, knights were urged to abstain from battle, much as everyone else was urged to abstain from other pleasures of the flesh, for the good of the soul. Thus, peace was to reign from Wednesday evening to Monday morning.[39] By extending the areas from which war was forbidden, first to certain places then to particular classes and finally to a specific time frame, the Church was moving in the direction of prohibiting bloodshed among Christians. But if this was to be the case in an age seething with violence, there had to be some outlet. Thus was born the idea of the Crusades.

The train of events set in motion by the Council of Clermont in 1095 was unique in a number of respects. Yet the military dimension was as astonishing as any. As noted earlier, the fragmentation of European politics appears to have left the institution of war open for co-option by other sources of motivation. And it was into this void that the Church had moved. The pugnacity of the warrior class would be turned outward against the hated Muslims and dedicated to the sacred mission of recovering the Holy Lands. Yet those forces, once unleashed, proved not so easy to control.

Certainly, in terms of military organization, the expeditions which resulted were only minimally imprinted with Christian influence. They were instead thoroughly representative of what war had become in western Europe. If the Roman legion—so thorough in its organization and subordination that it seems almost genetically controlled—can be compared to an army of insects, then the original Crusader contingents can be likened to a wandering herd of male ungulates, its constituents jostling constantly for control, periodically breaking apart and moving off in different directions, but all driven by a larger force at once compelling and evanescent.

Nonetheless, tactically they were not to be taken lightly. Both of the major military powers in the Near East at the time, the Seljuk Turks (the Crusaders' main adversaries) and the empire of Byzantium, were capable of fielding forces of a high order. While the Turks relied on more traditional but still very formidable Asian horse archers, the Byzantines carried on the Hellenistic tradition of diversified forces and the Roman legacy of professionalism to create a combined-arms force remarkable even today for its complexity and sophistication.[40] Yet the man-for-man superiority of the European shock cavalry was such that it not only negated its own manifest organizational deficiencies but also allowed for what amounted to a military miracle, the capture of Jerusalem in 1099.

Yet the first Crusades also began a sequence of developments, the consequences of which neither Christian authority nor the European aristocracy could possible foresee. In particular, the Church was finding its involvement with war and weapons less temporary and controllable than it might have expected.

For conquest required protection. Yet the temporal rulers of what were known as the Latin States were dramatically short of manpower and funds. So the Church came to countenance the formation of military orders, the Knights Templars, Knights Hospitallers, and the Teutonic Order, initially to protect pilgrims but shortly to take a major role in the defense. But if the orders could not ultimately save the Latin States, the idea of God's own heavy cavalry battling heathen in the land of Christ had enormous appeal, and they would quickly grow rich and fiercely independent, each destined for a remarkable, if not necessarily pious, future.[41]

The Church not only had trouble controlling its Christian soldiers; the technical course of war would also take a new and unexpected turn. As military confrontations go, the three Crusades were unusually asymmetric in tactics and weaponry since the powers involved had long been separated both geographically and culturally. Under the circumstances, a premium was placed on experimentation and the exploitation of weakness.

Thus, after suffering several drubbings in close combat with knights, the Seljuk horse archers took to avoiding pitched battle and concentrated instead on harassment with their fine composite bows. For their part, the Crusaders gradually discovered the uses of infantry and firepower (more accurately, quarrel power) to hold ground and bring the enemy to bear at long range.

Now foot soldiers had certainly never disappeared from European warfare. But in an environment where heavy cavalry was both extremely aggressive and symmetrically oriented, they were seldom decisive. Yet the tactical situation was entirely different in the Middle East, and besides, the Christian infantry had a new weapon.

Though the crossbow had been rediscovered and available in Europe since the early eleventh century, it is probable that it was brought to the Holy Lands primarily as a novelty, perhaps mainly for hunting. Yet the weapon had two characteristics which made it an instant winner in this arena: unlike a reflex bow, it could be shot accurately with very little training and, more important, it packed the power to knock a man out of the saddle at ranges of up to one hundred yards.[42] In a climate of sporadic attack, where its slow rate of fire made little difference, the crossbow, by the Third Crusade, became a key element in a sophisticated infantry-cavalry combined-arms team crafted by Richard *Coeur de Lion* to fight on the march.[43]

But its implications went far beyond the Latin States. By A.D. 1100 the square-headed, armor-piercing quarrel had become commonly available and the crossbow was being used in Europe to shoot down knights.[44] To a political and social structure welded together with chivalric fighting skills acquired at great cost, such a development could only prove ominous.

Once again the Church stepped into the breach, with the second Ecumenical Lateran Council outlawing the use of the crossbow among Christians in 1139. As perhaps man's first overt attempt at arms control, the edict deserves more attention than it usually receives. In particular, its effort to enforce weapons symmetry and what amounted to the technological status quo would prove characteristic of arms control in the future. There was also an element of implied cynicism, or at least situational ethics, here that would tend to be true of other efforts in this direction. For the Church in no way discouraged the use of the crossbow against Muslims.[45] This was symptomatic of European Christianity's entire involvement with war during this period. Having failed to deal with the root causes of violence, the Church sought to turn it outward against those seen as alien.

Indeed, this also appears to be the key to the feudal aristocracy's tactical flexibility and open-mindedness toward new weaponry while in the the Holy Lands. As might be expected from anthropological precedent, the decorum of war and the aversion to weapons deemed less than honorific were sharply reduced in fighting against those seen as alien, even if conceded to be fellow humans.

Yet such a breakdown was bound to reverberate back across Europe as Crusaders returned with these lessons fresh in their minds. Feudalism and knightly supremacy would last well into the fourteenth century, but they would never be the same after the experience in the Holy Lands.

In fact, the crossbow's slow rate of fire and proneness to break in wet weather limited its actual effectiveness in Europe, especially in pitched battle. Yet its psychological impact cannot be dismissed. The ancient prejudices against personal missile weapons had been compromised, if not totally dispelled. Military prepotency was no longer exclusively a matter of one class, an event dramatized by the death of Richard *Coeur de Lion* in 1199, shot down by a quarrel as he rode gaily before a besieged castle.[46]

Like all armored vehicles when threatened, knights took refuge in more protection. Mail would gradually be replaced by plate, and armor would be extended, with limited success, to the horse. Knights would grow steadily slower and still less maneuverable until they could hardly move unaided. Yet never again would they feel immune to all but other knights.

Something analogous happened to the castle. As might be expected in an era of fortified places, the siege played a major role in medieval warfare.[47] Rather than a series of pitched battles, war was often a matter of creeping advances from one fortified place to another. But, as befit the general encroachment of intraspecific values during this period, the inherent ruthlessness of this type of combat was mitigated by a number of factors.

Perhaps more frequently than actual investment, castles were simply bargained for and exchanged through a transfer of allegiance. Otherwise, the siege was primarily passive. While starvation was the obvious threat, it too was softened by common resort to truces and a variety of safe conducts.[48] Prior to the Crusades, in cases where fortresses were actually overwhelmed, the technical means brought to bear were not impressive, consisting primarily of traditional battering rams, scaling ladders, and undermining techniques effective primarily because of the fairly primitive state of the defenses.

Yet contact with the East changed much of this. The elaborate Byzantine city defenses, consisting of double and triple lines of massive turreted walls, particularly impressed the Europeans. Nothing like this existed in the West, and it resulted in a virtual revolution in castle construction during the twelfth century.[49]

However, as Oman notes, the Byzantines also retained all the major engines of Roman siegecraft—the vinea and testudo, the torsion catapult, onager, and ballista. While the sources are unclear as to the mechanisms of transmission, it seems hardly coincidental that large stonethrowers made their appearance in the West by 1147. This, in turn, set off a rapid sequence of improvements, leading ultimately to the counterweight-powered trebuchet, a machine which modern experiments have shown to be capable of casting rocks of three hundred pounds for distances of up to three hundred yards.[50] Walls now actually could be shattered and broken down from long range, and residences subjected to bombardment.

Yet it would be difficult to demonstrate that the balance between defense and offense was in any fundamental sense upset. Fortifications were greatly improved in design and solidity, while instruments such as the torsion catapult were often extremely useful in fending off attack. Rather, the real effect of the techniques brought back from the East was to raise the level of violence and the cost of waging war, the logic of which pointed to larger political amalgams and more centralized control. This, like the crossbow, did not result in immediate change. Yet the diffusion of power had been reversed, and it was only a matter of time until the military system which had enforced it would be broken down.

V

There was an analogue at sea. While commerce and piracy never exactly ceased in northern waters prior to the Crusades, the Vikings' inability to tell the difference between the two and the overwhelmingly agrarian nature of European society insured that the focus of combat and weapons development would be in a non-maritime direction.

The Viking type (itself innovative structurally, with its compact internal frame and flexible, clinker-built shell) did undergo some further development, but in a very predictable direction. By the year 1000 the craft had been gradually lengthened to produce an elite of first longships, then dragon ships—a rudimentary hierarchy of ships prematurely abbreviated by the tendency of such elongated hulls to bend, or hog, amidships.[51] British and northern European warships added fore and aft fighting castles. Yet they remained, like their Scandinavian cousins, basically square-rigged, oar-assisted longboats without fundamental means of offense.[52]

The Crusades exposed the western Europeans to a much more sophisticated naval world. Since A.D. 600, naval warfare in the eastern Mediterranean had been dominated by the various iterations of a basic ram-based bireme developed by the Byzantines and known as the *dromon,* or "runner." Though similar in conception to the galleys of the ancient world, it carried two significant innovations: a triangular, or lateen, rig which allowed it to sail as close as sixty degrees to the wind, and Greek fire, an incendiary liquid (probably a mixture of saltpeter, sulphur, and petroleum) shot at short ranges from a hydraulic siphon in the bow.[53] An interesting anticipation of the application of chemical energy to warfare, Greek fire was premature in that it capitalized solely on the combustive, not propulsive, possibilities of such mixtures. Yet the *dromon* itself would be adopted, basically without change, by the Muslims and the Italian commercial states.

In spite of its static design, the *dromon*'s continued existence testified to a level of naval organization, shipbuilding skill, and commerce unknown in northern Europe. Western Europeans such as Richard *Coeur de Lion,* who was forced to give battle to a particularly large *dromon* while approaching Palestine, could not have failed to be impressed. By the same token, the influx of Crusaders and the opportunity to transport them not only increased commerce in the eastern Mediterranean but exposed the ambitious maritime states of Italy to the possibilities of trade with northern Europe.[54]

While direct commercial and technical interaction would come somewhat later, the Crusades' effect of raising the general level of trade and transport in northern Europe, would also lead to a renewed interest in ship design, the most noteworthy product of which was the development of the large, oceangoing cog. Basically a very beamy sailing transport, the cog revealed considerable military potential in her sheer size, height, and ability to carry fighting men.[55] A sort of castle at sea— one might almost say a bridge between the medieval fortress and the battleship— only the cog's lack of speed and maneuverability allowed the Scandinavian type to persist lingeringly until the fourteenth century. But if the cog could not catch those who might harass her, neither could her opponents successfully attack. And it was this defensive capability which proved critical to the cog's success as a trader. Within confines set by slowly improving navigational tools, well-manned cogs, like those of the Hanseatic League, might now ply the high seas with relative impunity, carrying volumes of cargo undreamed of just a few generations before. Thus by 1250, as Richard Unger notes, more people, both northern and southern, were engaged in seaborne commerce, than at any time since the late Roman Empire.[56]

The need to protect and extend this trade would soon lead to more formalized navies and specialized weaponry. But these were expensive and therefore in consonance with land-borne trends favoring larger political entities, which would in turn create the conditions to foster an acceleration in creative naval architecture.

VI

But before this could take place, something entirely unexpected came on the scene. It was as if the desert wind had whispered to the nomad horse archers that their time was growing short, that soon great change would forever remove their chance to rule. So they burst out of the Gobi, swallowing whole nations in their path— the terrifying possibilities of the desert raider disciplined and brought to fruition in the invincible armies of Genghis Khan.

For if the stirrup had made the knight possible, it had been taken up considerably earlier (ca. A.D. 500–600) in central Asia, enabling horse archers to ride and shoot with unprecedented effectiveness.[57] In a tier extending from Afghanistan to Mongolia, an environment harsh beyond all measure of European experience, men learned to use these tools to the absolute limits of human skill and endurance. Here there was no margin for error. The sparseness of the land and the ferocity of the climate worked on man and horse and equipment to remove all that was not essential, to produce a warrior as cruel and free from ceremonialism as he was self-sufficient. And of these, none was harder and more ruthless than the nomadic Mongolian tribesmen living in and around the Gobi desert, where in an endless combat among themselves and their neighbors, they perfected the sweeping tactics of ruse and lightning attack.[58] Clothed in sheepskin and light armor of boiled hides, requiring only powdered millet and the milk of the mares they rode (small, agile ponies almost immune to cold, and feeding on pasturage, not fodder), and armed with a superb composite bow of up to 165 pounds draw that could be shot with devastating power and accuracy[59] these crusty specimens were the raw material for what would become perhaps the most voracious fighting force ever assembled. Yet this required organization and direction, a catalyst to transform what was before no more than a swirling mass of convoluted violence.

In 1167, the Year of the Pig, it was Mongolia's fate to be visited by a genius, born on that date, according to legend, with a clot of blood in his fist the size of a knucklebone.[60] Temujin, they called him, after a Tartar captive, as was the custom. He was the son of a minor chieftain, but spent his youth in extreme privation, having been cast adrift with his mother and six other children after the father succumbed to poison. In an environment normally fatal to those without tribal protection, the family survived, doubtless due in part to the growing skill and cunning of the oldest son. For Temujin's name was soon spoken around the camps with increasing frequency as a bold and enterprising young man. He married well, made astute alliances, and was soon at the head of a band of twenty thousand horsemen. Yet as he moved from battle to battle, eliminating his enemies one by one, he would never forget an insult or leave a grudge unanswered. "They are the soldiers of the Uruds and Manguds," warned one nomad who had seen Temujin's army fight before. "They pursue men like game. . . . They slay them and take from them everything."[61]

By 1206 he was proclaimed supreme khan (*Genghis Khan* is one of several corruptions of the title) of "all who dwell in tents of felt."[62] This was important. For Genghis Khan was not simply a leader of the Mongols. In his time he would recruit commanders of twenty nations. His was to be an army of nomads, and his train of conquest an outbreak of a way of life.

It was in his first imperial campaign against the Chin, an invasion provoked by a fifty-year-old murder, that he first revealed himself.[63] For he had the mind of a herdsman, a keeper of goats and sheep. And now he would collect nations in the same manner.

The army which he set upon the inhabitants south of the Great Wall was totally cavalry yet utterly disciplined. Organized pyramidally according to the ancient formula of multiples of ten, it maneuvered its more numerous adversaries like a pack of well-trained sheepdogs. The horse archer remained dominant, but appropriate weapons were adopted as the situation demanded. Having encountered heavy infantry and cataphracts, shock cavalry was quickly added, armed with lances and captured mail. Similarly, when frustrated by the walled cities of northern China, the Mongols seized upon the full range of Chinese siege engines and methodically recruited a corps of captured technicians to work them.[64]

This was typical. Subjugated populations were viewed as chattel to be exploited for their skills—or killed. The cruelty of Genghis Khan's armies is, of course, legendary. Yet his was the callousness of the shepherd—thinning the flock and then setting it up for future shearing. The nomad's contempt for the sedentary way of life was proverbial, and in this context the agriculturalist became virtually a separate species—to be preyed upon and exploited rather than fought with as an equal according to intraspecific custom. The record is full of ghastly tactical tricks played upon the nomads' opponents with horrific effect, and all are united by a uniform Mongol disregard of any shared humanity between themselves and those they attacked.

The theme was continued and intensified when the khan turned westward against the Khwarizmian kingdom of Persia, again on the pretext of a murdered ambassador. Proclaiming himself the "flail of God" to the citizens of the captured Bukhara,[65] he waged a war that in three years left the entire region blighted. Terror-induced passivity was the intent, and atrocity and rapid movement the major means of accomplishment. There is an oft-repeated story in Ibn al-Athīr telling of a Mongol soldier who, having taken a captive but lacking a sword to dispatch him, simply told the man to lie down and wait until he returned, which of course the prisoner did.[66] Collectively, this was exactly the intended effect of an encounter with the khan's so-called horde—ironically named since in reality the invaders were almost invariably outnumbered by their victims.

Fear and exaggeration radiate outward like ripples in a pond. And it is probable that Western Christendom first heard of the terrible scourge from the East shortly after the nomad captain Subedie led a raiding column into the lush pastures of Azerbaijan, crushing first the armies of Georgia in 1221 and then a heterogeneous assemblage of Russian princes.[67] But at this point the territory stretching beyond the Holy Lands was virtually a vacuum, and word of an attack from this quarter must have been greeted with incomprehension and disbelief. Yet the great raid of Subedie proved invaluable to the Mongols in terms of military intelligence, and it was at this point, most sources agree, that a general invasion of Europe was first conceived.[68] Characteristically, it did not come for fifteen years, put off until 1237 by the death of Genghis Khan and the choice of his successor.

Yet delay in no way diminished the fury of the onslaught or enhanced Christendom's ability to deal with it. The contrasts between the adversaries could not have been more stark. European armies were, at this point, basically crowds of individuals, the key members fighting in a manner heavily laden with intraspecific features. The Mongols, on the other hand, were meticulously disciplined and governed by only the stark logic of predation. Perhaps equally detrimental was the agriculturalist's view of territory. Battle among sedentary peoples almost always boils down to a matter of physical displacement. Yet the occupation of space meant little to the nomad. Their swirling tactics, feigned retreat, and sudden assault were the warlike evolcations of a spirit which knew no fixed domicile. The object was to kill and subjugate.

Thus, in three years of intermittent fighting, most of what then constituted Russia was utterly cowed, and its richest city, Kiev, destroyed. The invaders then moved into Poland, where they sacked the lovely city of Cracow on Palm Sunday 1241. Bypassing Breslau, they converged on Liegnitz, where Duke Henry of Silesia and the Teutonic Order had collected a heterogeneous force of between twenty and thirty thousand Poles and German knights to bar the way into the Holy Roman Empire. The day ended with Henry's head on a pike and nine bags of ears being collected from the European dead.[69] Hungary was next, invaded from at least four directions. Once again Christendom and chivalry took a stand under King Béla at Mohi, only to be virtually annihilated by the loss of sixty-five thousand men.[70] On Christmas Day, 1241, the invaders crossed the frozen Danube and appeared to be heading toward Vienna. There was nothing to stop them from plunging deep into Germany or the rich commercial states of Italy. Yet as Europe watched in disorganized horror, the Mongols did something very much in character: they began to retreat as unexpectedly as they had come. Whether because Hungary marked the western terminus of the steppes or because of growing dynastic quarrels, the nomad thrust into Europe melted away with the snow in the spring of 1242, never to return.

True enough, nomad imperialism did form lasting tyrannies in primitive Russia and central Asia. Yet those in advanced Persia and China lasted less than a hundred years.[71] The horse archer was, at this point in history, the deadliest weapon system known to man. This had long been true. But it was an arm resting on a way of life incapable of assimilating advanced political and economic forms. As J. J. Saunders notes, Mongol culture was without architecture or even the concept of settled towns. It lacked manufactures or writing; the *Secret History of the Mongols,* from which so much knowledge of the khan is derived is the sole historical document of an otherwise illiterate race.[72] Their power rested solely on their military skill and the deadly combination of bow and horse.

VII

Yet the future of weaponry lay in Europe—first in social change, then in a technological revolution which would relegate even the horse archer to the status of an anachronism.

By the year 1300 the winds of change could be felt blowing from a number of quarters. Over the previous century the crossbow had been joined by several other new infantry weapons such as the Lucerne hammer and the halberd, a combination pike and battle-ax which, according to Oman, could cleave a helmet or a shield like pasteboard.[73] Foot soldiers were now also better equipped defensively, armor protection being no longer the sole prerogative of the mounted knight. All of this, moreover, was indicative of the growing sophistication and productivity of medieval ferrous metallurgy, which, after the year 1225, began to take off. Ultimately, this factor, when combined with the invention of firearms, would change weapon design fundamentally. Yet in the beginning the transition would take place according to more conventional means.

At the end of the thirteenth century, in the mountain fastness of Switzerland, the urge for independence combined with a strong egalitarian streak to produce a nascent confederation of independent cantons and the beginnings of a national army. Poor but independent, not serfs but free peasants and burghers, the Swiss naturally gravitated toward one another, fighting in close formation from the beginning. In their early battles with the Habsburgs and Burgundian nobility, they favored the relatively short (six to ten feet) halberd.[74] But as the need to repel cavalry charges became more apparent, the primary arm gradually shifted to a nineteen-foot-long, iron-tipped pike that was a virtual reincarnation of the Macedonian *sarissa*.[75] The tactical formation which emerged—a human hedgehog fronted by four rows of spears—was a familiar one. The Swiss, like the Sumerians and the Hellenes, reacted to analogous socioeconomic conditions by introducing the phalanx to the battlefields of Europe.

The politico-military parallels with the past are remarkable. As before, near-total reliance was placed on the foot soldier, with cavalry or missile weaponry being virtually ignored.[76] Moreover, as with earlier phalanxes, the spirit of equal participation, more than obedience, drove the Swiss formations into battle. Before La Bicocca the cry went up: "Where are the officers, the pensioners, the double-pay men? Let them come out and earn their money fairly for once: they shall all fight in the front rank today."[77] And so they did, taking the head of the leading column and dying almost to a man.[78] Here, again, the inherent lethality of phalanx warfare stood in marked contrast to the armored roughhouse of the knightly joust. The Swiss fought with a ferocity that appalled contemporaries, making a particular point of neither giving nor receiving quarter.[79] Rather than courtly surrender and elaborate ransoming procedures, battle for the Swiss was reduced to stark life-or-death terms.

Like the Greeks, the Swiss would also recognize the monetary possibilities of tactical ascendancy and become great mercenaries. Indeed, *pas d'argent, pas de Swisses* (no money, no Swiss) would become a sort of national motto. Yet, gradually, exposure to the Swiss formations brought forth predictable reactions. In Germany, Emperor Maximilian raised a corps of pikemen and halberdiers, the landsknecht, trained to fight in exactly the manner of the Swiss.[80] But if they suffered heavily in symmetrical confrontations with the Germans, the Swiss fared even less well against the Spanish, who, as Machiavelli noted, took a leaf out of the Roman text, "having no other difficulty except that of getting near enough to the Swiss to reach them with the sword."[81] Swiss battle formations would remain viable until the early years of the sixteenth century. But they would do so as one of several competing styles of warfare, neither unique nor invincible.

Meanwhile, something analogous but in other ways entirely new had transpired across the English Channel. Since the Norman Conquest of 1066, Britain had been ruled by a feudal nobility which, though in the process of assimilation, remained arrogant and perceptibly alien. Their weapons, as might be expected, were the classic instruments of shock cavalry, and came to symbolize their domination. On the other hand, military archery, though it had no previous particular significance among Anglo-Saxons, began to grow in popularity among the lower classes, borrowed from the still-independent Welsh.[82] Thus, the semilegendary figure of Robin Hood takes on particular significance, at once a symbol of national resistance and an archetype of the men now taking up the bow. Yet in a larger sense the inherent prejudices against the bow and its ability to kill at long range were being further broken down. Rather than the instrument of Paris the adulterer, the bow became, in the English context, the arm of the patriotic underdog.

The weapon itself is of some interest. The crossbow was certainly known in England during this period, being banned by the aristocracy in the Magna Carta in 1215.[83] Yet the device was also spurned by the yeomanry, who chose instead the longbow, a weapon so simple that it was known as far back as the late Mesolithic period.[84]

Instead of being pieced together from several disparate materials, the longbow was formed from a single carefully shaped piece of wood. Yet its simplicity belied its sophistication and awesome capabilities.

The key to the longbow was the type and placement of its material. Though they could be and were shaped out of elm, hazel, ash, and other secondary timbers, none could touch yew for power and durability. Yet the true bow lay well inside, embedded in the heart of these sacred and poisonous trees. As Robert Hardy, a contemporary expert on the bows, notes: "It has been discovered again, or perhaps it was a knowledge never quite lost, that within a yew log, rightly cut from the tree, are the natural components of a 'self-composite' weapon, the perfect natural material to resist tension, the sapwood, lying next to the perfect natural material to resist compression, the heartwood."[85] The emergent bow was not flat-bellied as is common today, but rather more in the shape of a long, tapered cylinder or oblate. The thicker the section, the greater the power, but also the more brittle. So increments in girth had to be accompanied by proportional increases in length; ergo the terminology. They were indeed long bows, the most powerful used at Agincourt probably measuring six feet four inches and achieving a draw of 120 pounds (54 kilograms).

Obviously, the strength and coordination required to shoot such an instrument with any degree of accuracy was not trivial. In fact, it was a skill which not only required considerable instruction but was easily lost, thereby necessitating constant practice. Yet a fully trained longbowman was a formidable military asset, capable of piercing mail consistently and plate at short ranges, and attaining a rate of fire of up to twelve arrows per minute, far faster than a crossbow.[86]

Capabilities like these were not likely to be missed by those interested in power. Such a man was Edward I, intent as he was on bringing his rowdy nobility to heel and creating what amounted to a national army under his control. Having seen firsthand the effectiveness of Welsh archers, he set about recruiting skilled units from places like Gwent and Macclesfield and using them to train his own levies, gradually building numbers sufficient for massed formations.[87] But these were not the passive arrow lofters of the transnational tyranny. They were highly motivated free men, armed and ready for close combat should their primary weapon fail or ammunition run short. True, elements were recruited from pardoned criminals, but in general they constituted a disciplined and stable fighting force, the heart of the professionalized field army with which the English monarchy sought to enforce its hereditary claims in France during the Hundred Years' War.

As John Keegan explains, the key to British tactics was the establishment of a narrow-fronted killing zone around two hundred yards deep, into which several thousand arrows could be launched in sheets at approximately ten-second intervals.[88] Such a deployment took utter, some might say unfair, advantage of the confrontational ethos of the feudal warrior. And on three separate occasions—Crécy-en-Ponthieu (1346), Poitiers (1356), and Agincourt (1415)—the flower of French knighthood insisted on charging like lemmings into this lethal space with disastrous results, losing fifteen hundred, two thousand, and six thousand of their number, respectively.

In all cases it was the asymmetric nature of the confrontations which was responsible for their lopsided deadliness. The French urge to close and the inability to inflict damage at other than point-blank range sealed their fate. The English longbow was too powerful and could take effect at too long a range. The time-to-target–casualty ratio which had previously doomed the foot archer now had been reversed in his favor.

In an effort to compensate, the knights sent their chargers, which could not be armored effectively against the galling waves of arrows, to the rear. Yet, dismounted, the knights not only prolonged their time in the killing zone but discarded their major military virtue, momentum.[89]

Besides, compensation could only go so far. The obvious solution, adopting the longbow himself and fighting symmetrically, was really no option at all. The knight could no more turn away from the sword and lance than he could take up the pike and join the newly resurgent phalanx. Skill with these traditional weapons, along with the horses he temporarily eschewed to fight the English, defined his whole existence. They were the basis of his education, the heart of his identity, and the prime means by which he measured himself against other men—to say nothing of largely determining his economic status. For the knight there would be no turning back. He was the human equivalent of some overspecialized reptile. As conditions changed he was locked into a response pattern which could only exaggerate what had once made him invincible. Yet the future would not countenance such sanctuaries, though the dream would persist in other weapon systems.

And what of the longbowman? Ultimately, he would prove to be only a transitional figure. Yet his existence was in a number of ways a portent of things to come. First the English yeoman archer, along with his cousins the crossbow-toting Genoese and Pisan mercenaries, had succeeded in significantly undermining the basic Western animus against killing at long range. While these prejudices would never quite be extinguished, this constituted the decline of a tradition which stretched back to Homer and beyond, and its partial replacement by an ethic which would in large part make modern war possible. Furthermore, the premeditated establishment of a killing zone introduced in a major way the element of total impersonality into European warfare, a feature which has become characteristic of our own military experience. Individualized combat would also persist. Yet chance and the faceless agents of death would more and more come to rule the battlefield.

In the near term the longbowman's fate was similar to that of other weapons practitioners. Rather than suicidal charges of the French nobility, he would come to feel the sting of his own cloth yard shafts. For at home in England, symmetry reasserted itself, and battle became increasingly a matter of withering arrow barrages. Though it is probable that many filled the ranks of Wat Tyler's rebel forces, by and large the longbowman remained the pawn of the competing noble factions struggling to unite the country. Thus, at Shrewsbury in 1403 and later in the great battles of the Wars of the Roses, opposing formations of longbowmen volleyed thousands of arrows into each other's lines until the projectiles became intolerable and the issue was settled at close quarters.[90] The results were appalling. On Palm Sunday, 1461, a daylong battle fought in a blizzard on Towton Heath resulted in something like twenty-five thousand killed or wounded, a slaughter so great that the waters of the little River Cock ran red for miles.[91]

As contemporary illustrations show, more and more the archer sought refuge behind plate, half armor, or even full armor.[92] Yet it was no more of a refuge for him than for the nobility. For there was a new weapon abroad which would prove consistently capable of penetrating any armor.

In 1346, as Edward III moved toward Crécy-en-Ponthieu, the evidence indicates that he carried with him not one but two military surprises. The first, of course, was the longbow, not yet seen on the Continent and destined for stunning success. But the second, a curious fire tube made and supplied by the armorers in the Tower of London, had practically no effect on the battle, though it does seem to have been fired.[93] Two hundred forty years later, in 1588, when Britain mustered her forces to face the expected Spanish invasion, not a single longbow would remain among the trained troops. In the interim the odd fire tube had replaced them all, and the age of man-powered warfare had drawn to a close.

VIII

Much the same sequence of events took place in military naval architecture—political consolidation, accelerated development, a reexploration of prior initiatives, and then great change. As in the Hellenistic era, the key institutional change appears to have been the establishment of naval arsenals consciously dedicated to improving ship types. While France, England, Portugal, and Spain would all set up government-operated wharves, the model for all, and the most seminal influence in naval architecture during the period from 1300 to 1550, was the Arsenal at Venice.[94]

Its success was almost immediate, with the yard's first experiments in galley design resulting in radical improvement over the *dromon* shortly before 1300.[95] By placing three rowers on the same level seated in echelon, all using sweeps of different lengths, the Venetian designers kept the center of gravity as low as possible and produced probably the optimal propulsion system for the oared ram. Shortly thereafter, as part of the naval program prompted by the Second Genoese War, the innovative shipwrights at the Arsenal would begin to explore the possibilities of much larger galleys—so enthusiastically, in fact, that the government quickly clapped limits on the size of war vessels.[96]

This was a rare occurrence. Having drifted into a policy of a shipyard owned and operated by the state, the authorities thereupon sought to optimize conditions, enlarging the area in 1305 and again in 1325 and consciously attracting engineering talent with the opportunity to exercise it with a minimum of outside interference as to technical matters.

Once together in the Arsenal, however, designers and artisans alike were faced with the problem of communicating their ideas and, since the yard was a continuing endeavor, preserving them for the future. This led directly to the first treatises on shipbuilding and the beginnings of standardized naval design.[97] This was of particular significance since hull construction was undergoing major changes in both northern and southern Europe, with heavy, largely unsupported outer planking systems giving way to a light external shell and extensive reliance on internal framing—thereby gaining strength and saving wood.

Yet the Arsenal's influence in these matters was not solely a function of warship design. This is an important distinction. Unlike the Hellenistic monarchs, the dominant political element in Venice owed its power and wealth primarily to commerce. And the larger galleys produced in the Arsenal were a significant component of their success. For these vessels were at the heart of the south-north alum-wool trade and the pilgrim-spice shuttle to the Levant.[98] In order to further encourage their construction, private shipbuilders were supplied with certain parts by the Arsenal and offered inducements to work there. Thus, rather than being a sterile hybrid devoted to purely military ends, the Arsenal fueled and was fueled by the fires of commerce which were taking hold of Europe's future.

Indeed, it was the design of trading galleys, not the development of pure warships, which revealed most definitively the limits of oared ships. For the desire to carry more cargo and build bigger ships was innately at odds with efficient propulsion since beyond a certain point extra oarsmen could be added only at great sacrifice to valuable cargo space. Coincidentally with the oarsman's burden growing heavier and more hopeless was a general diminution in his status. Very soon only slaves, criminals, and the unwilling would serve in the galleys, and coupled with the general depopulation engendered by the Black Death, the problem of filling the benches would become chronic after 1350.[99]

Yet it was the introduction of the gun that would finish the ancient oared warship as a prime naval weapon. Besides largely invalidating its primary armament, the ram, guns were heavy and required a broad, stable platform not easily satisfied by a galley. Rather, it made more sense to place them on a sailing vessel. Not only could such ships be built beamier, but, as T. C. Lethbridge notes, they were undergoing a revolution in sail design and rigging during the early fifteen century which would remove most of their shortcomings in speed and maneuverability.[100] Not illogically, it was the Arsenal at Venice which would first combine the heavily reinforced internal construction, full ship's rigging, and a low hull configuration dedicated to optimal placement of guns to produce, during the early years of the sixteenth century, the galleon, the first truly successful warship based on firearms and the archetype of all that would follow over the next three hundred years.

The transition from mechanical- to chemical-powered warfare was one of the major watersheds in man's history, a transformation that would change forever the rhythms of war and weapons development. For it is a singular fact that at the twilight of the former era, all the traditional martial components—at sea the oared ram, and on land the nomad horse archer, the cataphract, the foot archer, the phalangite, even the Spanish reincarnation of the Roman legionary—remained to a greater or lesser degree viable. After four thousand years of more or less constant warfare, none had been completely wiped off the field of battle, a fact which says something very fundamental about weapons development at this level of technology.

Not only did the course of arms appear cyclic, but it is reasonable to assume that, had it not been for the imposition of chemistry, all these basic types would have persisted indefinitely.

Plainly, this was more than a matter of technical factors. From an objective standpoint, some weapon types were clearly dominant—the horse archer, for example. Yet within reasonable limits, the choice of arms during this period seems to have been determined more by considerations of politics, sociology, anthropology, and tradition than by effectiveness. This would change dramatically over the era stretching from approximately 1500 to 1945. Yet in no case would military technology proliferate in an atmosphere devoid of military culture. New weapons would always have to be integrated with, and made relevant to, the ethos surrounding military organizations. Yet this matrix was largely a function of the era of man-powered weapons, just as its own course was deeply influenced by attitudes developed in a time dominated by hunting, not war.

Thus, free-floating fantasies of heroic combat and armored archetypes, sweeping nomadic attack, and staunch phalanxes would tint the vision of weapons developers and users right up to modern times. The logic of weapons symmetry, the fondness for the horse, the penchant for size, the love of speed, the urge to make noise, and the yearning to identify and confront are not merely of antiquarian interest. They are the progenitors of our own death machinery, frequently metamorphosed by time and technology but nonetheless driven by the same logic, serving the same ends. This is why it is worth knowing about the history of these weapons.

Chapter 7

GUNS

I

Charles VIII had no idea that history's gears were shifting. As he sauntered into Italy with his cannon-laden army in 1494, this feckless ruler of France could have no way of knowing that he was initiating a new era in war and politics, a 450-year search for dominance in a militarily preeminent Europe. He wouldn't have even called it an invasion. He was, in fact, on his way to a crusade, hoping to embark from Naples to reconquer Jerusalem.[1]

Yet fantasies of the past were not to be served. The unlikely Charles was marked instead as a new kind of prince. And, more importantly, his army became a prototype for a new kind of warfare, a test-bed upon which the military lessons of half a millennium would begin to be worked out with startling rapidity. At the root of this revolution in martial affairs, as commentators as far back as the chemist Robert Boyle in 1660 came to realize, was gunpowder.[2] Yet this was not apparent in 1494 and would only gradually become so as the Italian Wars ground along their inconclusive course.

The gun at this point was not new but nearly two centuries old. The idea that powder, if suitably confined, might be made to cast a projectile with unprecedented force and velocity apparently occurred almost simultaneously to European and Chinese craftsmen sometime between 1290 and 1320.[3]

Why it was that the possibility of firearms largely bypassed the Chinese, while causing European rulers and artisans to invest entirely more energy in their development than pure efficiency would seem to have warranted, remains controversial. Social historians, specifically William McNeill, tend to emphasize factors of organization and capital incentives.[4] Certainly, the uniquely close relationship between business enterprise and weapons development existing in Europe during the entire period at hand must be accorded a major role in the subsequent course of arms. Yet an approach which emphasizes the impact of more fluid and pluralistic organizational models on martial innovation tends to obscure other important aspects of the question.

Why was it, for example, that the Turks, organized along Asiatic and noncapitalistic lines but very much a part of the European political network, were so quick to adopt the cannon and arquebus? Was it possible that history and politics had simply rendered the participants in this particular political network more warlike and therefore more inclined to countenance and even sponsor new methods of killing?

Alternately, the causal impact of the purely technical should not be underestimated. Ultimately, it was the fortuitous confluence of technologies which allowed European artisans to capitalize on the possibilities of firearms. Hence, the first major improvements in these devices—the replacement of the dartlike projectiles pictured in the earliest firearms with spherical stone shot and the resulting elongation of the barrel from a vaselike form, to the familiar tube optimized for maximum acceleration from the expanding gases—dovetailed neatly with other European strengths.[5] For the resultant higher velocities, enhanced still further by the introduction of corned powder in the mid–fifteenth century, caused gunsmiths to strive for still longer and larger caliber tubes, a thrust necessarily foreshadowed by the perfection of the bell caster's art during the twelfth and thirteenth centuries.[6]

But if the cause of Christianity was to provide the method, the warrior's ancient companion, bronze, would provide the material. For it was this Homeric metal, expensive but rust-free and tougher than cast iron, which would prove the artillerist's favorite for all but the largest pieces until even the nineteenth century.[7] Yet here again, new methods of extraction, along with mining techniques (among them the use of gunpowder for blasting) first developed in the Harz Mountains, would open the rich argentiferous copper deposits of central Europe to systematic exploitation, insuring by 1450 an adequate supply of the metal to fuel this second martial Bronze Age.[8]

Ultimately, however, technique is merely a reflection of the minds of the participants. Hence, if we are searching for clues to explain the differential acceptance of firearms, we must also look inward, if possible. In this regard it is worth remembering that although kings and princes spawned and paid for ballistic developments, it was the dynamic class of European artisans and technologists who pursued them.

The mythical creator of the *gonne,* Bertholdus Schwartz, was no noble gendarme but a Faustian tinkerer of obscure origins,[9] as was, on a less fanciful note, Pedro Navarro, born humbly in 1460 and fated to become the most famous military innovator of his time.[10] Such men, although involved with weapons and things military, were less inclined to hold to the ancient preconceptions surrounding arms with the same degree of tenacity. Conversely, the obvious relationship between their own skills and the great and growing power of their creations must have had an intoxicating effect on these innovators. Picture, for example, one of the huge stone-throwing bombards of the mid–fourteenth century, casting projectiles with a thunderous roar—probably the loudest artificial sounds yet generated—with masonry-shattering impact. Purely mechanical engines, the trebuchet, for example, might approximate these primitive fire-belching monsters statistically, but without the drama, the infernal overtones. Those who wonder at the gunsmith's persistence fail to consider the fascination of power made manifest. Certainly, other areas in which Europe took the lead, science and heavy industry, for instance, were similarly attractive. Yet arms development was the most direct outlet for such feelings. As much as anything, these men were driven by the illusion of armipotence, and since the gun was at the beginning of its development, their technical skills were frequently rewarded with spectacular gains in performance. From the beginning, cannon, because they were so well suited to reducing stone fortifications, were favored and, with the introduction of cast-iron balls around 1450 became truly formidable weapons.[11]

Yet there was also the handgun. At first it was little more than an iron tube stuck in a wooden board and fired through a touchhole. Yet the matchlock-triggered arquebus, as it came to be known, would be developed into an effective, if slow-firing, man-killer by the time of Charles VIII's invasion.

So it was that virtually under the noses of an aristocracy which had long monopolized war and weapons these middling types, exhibiting the proverbial virtues of their class—industry, persistence, and ingenuity—came to change forever the basic conditions of an environment essentially alien to them.

Yet they did so unconsciously, blinded by the pursuit of power and largely oblivious of its human consequences. Technically clairvoyant they were. For as we shall see, by 1550 virtually every possibility of chemical-energy warfare had at least been conceived of. Yet it would require a century-and-a-half cycle of war and a mountain of maimed flesh to reveal fully, in its grim magnificence, what they truly had wrought.

II

Europe was spoiling for a fight—itching for it. Political forces which had been gathering for centuries were about to crystallize into a swollen update of ancient Greece, a shifting patchwork of regional powers at once locked in internecine combat and brimming with political energy for vast overseas expansion.

The essence of this dynamic relationship has come to be known as the "balance of power." Yet viewed from a slightly different perspective, the period stretching from 1494 to 1945 could well be called the "search for hegemony." For the old urge for transnational tyranny and the even stronger desire to prevent it remained very strong themes of European politics throughout. Undeniably, the emphasis and context would shift with time, but in its essence this was an age of princes, the ultimate agents in the pyramid of power characteristic of such a social order. Historians who wonder at the stupidity of Charles VIII's and the later Valois's attempts to conquer Italy, or at Hitler's invasion of Russia, miss an obvious point. Feasibility and vital interest were secondary. Conquest was the objective. It was often that simple. Of course, not every power sought transnational dominion, nor did every period sanction it. But it remains an underlying theme to everything else.

As might be expected from the previous chapters, it will be maintained here that the nature and subsequent history of politics was deeply conditioned by the development and use of firearms. But if the simultaneous emergence of the gun and modern European history was not accidental, neither was the relationship exclusive or direct. The new order required several other key preconditions. Hence, in practical terms, the gun's potential deadliness was perhaps no more important than the availability of manpower to shoot them and the basic compatibility of firearms with the needs and capabilities of these troops.

For a number of reasons, including primogeniture, a sharply rising rural population, and the prevalence of local wars, Europe in the last decades of the fifteenth century was full of fighting men. Swiss pike troops, German landsknecht, Irish and English adventurers, displaced French gendarmes, tough Castilian foot soldiers—they would come from every corner of the Continent to join the fighting.[12] Ultimately, though, it was not numbers or variety of supply but terms of service which were primarily responsible for filling the military rosters and populating the battlefields of the coming 150 years.

Every age has its metaphors, master concepts which because of their spectacular success in one area, tend to be applied in all directions. In our own time it is the logic of the computer. In our grandfather's day it was evolution. In the time of the gun it was the dictates of commerce and capital formation—mechanisms which provided the generalized framework for a host of endeavors, among them war. It was no coincidence that *condottiere* meant literally "contractors," or that the mercenary bands of the period were known as "companies." They were exactly that, corporate entities dedicated to making a profit. If the historic disarmament of all but the nobility left a void in terms of civil experience with mass military participation, paid soldiers and armies for hire would quickly fill the vacuum, solving military manpower requirements admirably. But, as inappropriate metaphors are inclined to do, this one created a monster in the process. Armies would grow dramatically and, in doing so, would draw in new elements destined to play roles of increasing importance. More to the point, these were to be parts intimately related to firearms.

One of these was massed infantry. The European peasant, though suitably conditioned to bloodshed through the annual slaughter of livestock, was largely without military tradition or skill with weapons. Experiments (noted in the previous chapter) with the pike, crossbow, and longbow had presaged his reemergence on the battlefield. But it was with the handgun that the infantryman was destined to march through the age of chemical-energy weapons. Like the crossbow, the handgun was complex and relatively difficult to fabricate. But it was also capable of effective use by neophytes, after a fairly short period of training. Moreover, the need for powder, ammunition, and the expense of the guns themselves added a new dimension to the field of logistics. Yet these complications were anticipated and met by the mechanisms of capitalism, while at the same time serving to further the ends of commerce and industry. And it was this synergy and the free transfer of goods which allowed what amounted to an inter-European small-arms industry to flourish by the end of the fifteenth century, easily keeping pace with the expansion of armies and providing the foot soldier with levels of physical equipment and deadliness that were without precedent.[13] But more to the point, the gunsmith brought fourth a weapon innately well suited to the mercenary mentality—a device that did not necessitate hand-to-hand combat. So it was that the concept of long-range killing won itself a permanent place in an arm which in European tradition had been almost exclusively dedicated to close combat. Certainly, the urge to close would not vanish from the thoughts of infantrymen (or at least their commanders), but it would be permanently compromised.

Meanwhile, in the other sphere of long-range killing, artillery, the same set of forces was at work with similar results. As is well known, the bureaucratic integration of fundamentally new weapons and those who service them poses a very basic challenge to military organizations. In the case of the cannon, this chasm was largely bridged by the hearty girders of capitalism. For at the dawn of chemical-energy artillery, as A. R. Hall notes, it was expected that those who cast the cannon would also serve them in battle, procuring powder and shot as well.[14] While this tradition did not persist, throughout the sixteenth century artillerists remained highly specialized, retaining an intimate knowledge of all phases of manufacture, testing, and use. They were not soldiers but more akin to alchemists, members of a guild which, disdaining military discipline, passed its secrets to apprentices only, jealously and under oath.[15] So it was that gunners came to be grafted onto the armies until the time of Gustav Adolph, not as subordinate arms but as craftsmen and independent contractors working for a profit.

While no longer cast by their users, cannon themselves remained similarly entwined within the cash nexus. The extreme size of the earliest guns (the Hungarian-made pieces used by the Turks to reduce the walls of Constantinople were so big as to necessitate fabrication on the site)[16] insured that, from the beginning, cannon manufacture would be a reasonably large-scale enterprise. While the introduction of the iron ball led directly to much smaller individual pieces, the process remained highly metal-consumptive, difficult, and expensive. For at least two centuries, each cannon was the product of an individual mold, virtually a piece of sculpture which, once founded, still had to be laboriously bored and finished, a process made somewhat easier by the application of waterpower.

Opportunity and expense further multiplied with the French and Burgundian introduction of viable two- and four-wheel gun carriages in the last decade of the fifteenth century.[17] Now heavy artillery might travel at the speed of an advancing army, but doing so required great numbers of horses to pull not only the pieces themselves but wagon trains filled with the requisite powder, shot, and supplies. Plainly, even before the first first great conflict of the era was fought, this new tool of war had rather decisively upped the ante necessary to play the game. Available technology and fiscal mechanisms were equal to the strain, but only a very few could still pay the bills.

In large part this was why the era of firearms was destined to be an age of princes. Geopolitically, Europe at this point was far from complete. Yet by the year 1500 several of the key cultural-territorial amalgams were sufficiently coalesced to provide their rulers with the military resources and political energy to play a major role in transcontinental affairs. Areas of fragmentation would persist—Italy and Germany, for instance. Yet plucky minor players like Wallenstein and the Hohenzollerns would remain the exception, not the rule. From this point it was the major princes, those of France, Spain, England, the Holy Roman Empire/ Austria, Turkey, and later Russia and Prussia, who would dominate the action. Most were periodically constrained by internal concerns and practically all were chronically underfinanced. Yet only they controlled the populations of multiple millions and the economies of sufficient complexity and energy to man and finance the new style of warfare on a sustained basis.

So it came to pass that European history was even further personalized, cast in a great melodrama of family feuds and idiosyncratic disputes. If Continental political thinkers had difficulty seeing beyond monarchy, this was one major reason why. The unitary actor was key, the very touchstone of the system. As before, the aristocracy and the other social orders maintained themselves, but less as self-directed forces than as components of a hierarchy capped by the prince himself, preoccupied with his own calculations and pursuing his own interests. If today the phenomenon of personal whim deciding the fate of millions—Ferdinand II fretting over Imperial protocol while his subjects were ravished by war and starvation— strikes us as obscene, we might remember that all schemes of government are ultimately run by men. Nonetheless, it is equally true that for the period at hand the nature of war, weaponry, and politics did tend to exaggerate even further the importance of a very few individuals, creating what amounted to a historical star system. Kings could rule wisely or they could rule unwisely, but it was by their hands that the future would be shaped.

In 1513 a disgraced Florentine diplomat, seeking to curry favor with a man he had every reason to hate, saw this and began writing what was to be the greatest political "how-to" manual in the history of Western thought. Niccolò Machiavelli, though a republican by sympathy, was no man to turn a blind eye to the facts. His text was about princes, for princes, addressed to a prince, and, so no one should miss the point, entitled *The Prince*.

Though generally considered the quintessential guide to the balance of power, it is also true that *The Prince* aims at and recommends political transcendence whenever possible. Hence, Machiavelli's analysis extends to Alexander's decapitation of Darius's empire as well as contemporary Italian peninsular affairs.[18]

Also, though obviously concerned with all political means at hand, Machiavilli left little doubt as to which he considered most important. With such a system, he realized, when the test of battle came, it was the ruler who must personally take the lead. "A Prince should therefore have no other aim or thought, or take up any other thing for his study, but war and its organization and discipline, for that is the only art that is necessary to one who commands."[19]

Machiavelli was acutely aware that the nature of war had changed both rapidly and fundamentally, and in his later misconceived work, *The Art of War*, sought to accommodate this transformation. No soldier himself, he missed the significance of firearms entirely.[20] Yet he did perceive the limitations and dangers of the international bands of mercenaries who were coming to do the fighting, and accurately foresaw that no prince could ever fully control and utilize his military resources until he had a national army at his back.[21]

It should be remembered that Machiavelli wrote amid the political ruins of a land ravaged by wars fought badly and by blundering outsiders. He wrote so that such a thing might not happen again, so that rulers and conquerors might learn to do their work well. Thus, if Machiavelli has come down to us as a consummate realist, he was also, from the perspective of 1513, a rather hopeless idealist.

III

For the age of princes had not begun auspiciously—not auspiciously at all. Rather than an exercise in power politics, the Italian Wars, the first of the era's great pan-European conflicts, resembled a lingering fight provoked among rival species over a particularly fat carcass. For sixty-four years, from 1495 to the Peace of Cateau-Cambrésis in 1559, the French and Habsburg dynasts would engage in almost continuous fighting with, as Charles Oman notes, little profit to either.[22] Meanwhile, soldiers from a dozen European states marched back and forth over prostrate Italy, and sated themselves with each other's blood.

Yet the bloodletting was not simple a function of strategic incompetence and muddleheaded leadership. From the beginning, the dramatically higher level of violence was directly attributable to the introduction of firearms on a large scale. Cannon capable of killing seven hundred men in three minutes (Novara, 1513) or cutting down thirty-three men-at-arms with one ball (Ravenna, 1512) shocked Italian condottieri, among whom casualty lists of three dead (Zagonara) or no dead (Molinella) were previously not unknown.[23] In the heat of anger they reacted by denying quarter and, in the case of one Paolo Vitelli, by plucking out the eyes and cutting off the hands of those caught with arquebuses.[24]

In the long run, however, the major response was symmetrical, with most participants acquiring similar arms for themselves. So it was, as casualties mounted still further, that French men-at-arms such as Blaise de Montluc were heard to complain: "Would to God that this unhappy weapon had never been devised, and that so many brave and valiant men had never died by the hands of those . . . who would not dare to look in the face of those whom they lay low with their wretched bullets. They are tools invented by the devil to make it easier to kill each other."[25]

And as death dealing was facilitated, so were the ancient predatory instincts for slaughter stimulated. Thus, Europe would be plunged into an increasingly violent cycle of wars lasting until 1648, great brawls whose motives and strategic objectives were frequently obscured by the very ubiquity of the killing. Exorbitant deadliness had been a problem with weapons since the introduction of the phalanx by the Sumerians. But never before had it reached such a pitch. C. V. Wedgewood, the great historian of the Thirty Years' War, notes that during the course of the conflict the population of Germany plunged from 21 million in 1618 to around 13.5 million in 1648.[26] Truly, man had reached a new stage in his evolution. For the first time death dealing would achieve the level of ecological blight.

Politically disastrous, the period of the Italian Wars nevertheless was an extraordinarily interesting and fertile time both technically and tactically. For the precocity of arms reasserted itself, not only sketching in the major outlines of fire fighting but in large part defining the possibilities of weapons employing chemical energy.

This was not done easily but only through a process of groping and reluctant experimentation. Not surprisingly, the participants clung to the past, referring whenever possible to the great body of military writing preserved from the Greeks and Romans. Yet answers to tactical questions surrounding the growing complexity of arms were not easily derived from ancients. It was not simply a matter of two traditional branches, cavalry and infantry, being joined by a third, artillery. Firearms, by virtue of their operation, raised a host of use-related issues resolvable only through direct experience. In this case direct experience took the form of a series of set-piece battles, beginning with Cerignola in 1503 and ending in 1525 with Pavia, the last major European field engagement for almost a generation.

While much remained to be worked out, certain things became clear beyond doubt. The relative helplessness of cannoneers and arquebusiers when loading, for example, injected an element of tactical instability exploitable through maneuver, the use of reserves, and close cooperation of separate arms—all of which took on increased importance during the period and naturally rendered command a good deal more cerebral than it had been in the past. While not entirely shorn of his Homeric trappings until the eighteenth century, the military leader was increasingly cast in the role of battle manager. Hence, the cannonball's ability to penetrate body after body, given terrible vent at Ravenna, was henceforth respected by commanders who took care to avoid massing deep formations of infantry within easy range of field pieces. Similarly, Gonsalvo de Córdoba's extraordinarily effective use of arquebusiers packed in elaborate field fortifications such as at Cerignola demonstrated rather definitively the basic advantages of the defense in engagements featuring infantry armed with muzzle-loading small arms.[27]

Cavalry, on the other hand, was primarily victimized by firearms in the Italian Wars and would not be positively affected by them until the wholesale adoption of the newly invented (ca. 1520) wheel-lock pistol. Capable of one-handed fire and possessing a windproof triggering mechanism, the small guns were an immediate success among horsemen. Once adopted, however, the weapon quickly caused tactics to shift dramatically from the headlong charge to the ponderous caracole, an ill-conceived maneuver aimed at blowing a hole in a pike formation through the discharges of successive waves of pistol-laden horsemen.[28]

So it was that, by the end of the Italian Wars, all three operational components—two traditional and one new—not only had been deeply influenced by firearms but had developed a general, if incomplete, doctrine for their use.

Certainly, it would not be true to say that the gun had driven, or would soon drive, all other weapons from the field of battle. Though two of the most ancient—the sword-shield combination and the bow—were among the first to go, several members of the previous era's arsenals found relatively secure futures.

Indeed, the eventual success of the arquebus and later the musket would be predicated for a time on a symbiotic relationship with the pike phalanx, which could keep off attackers and break opposing lines discomposed by firepower. So too did cavalry eventually cast aside their pistols and return to lance and saber. Yet it is equally true that these accommodations were inspired by firearms, provoked by either the peculiarities of their use or the formations they demanded.

In the latter instance, particularly, the tactical implications of the handgun were at odds with prior military experience. For in order to maximize firepower and avoid being slaughtered in clumps by cannon, optimal deployment of small-arms infantry, maneuvering out in the open, demanded that clear limits be placed on the depth of troop dispositions, and that they be stretched as far as possible. On the other hand, Renaissance military thinkers found only thick, compact formations in Vegetius and the Greeks. This simply reinforced common sense. One didn't have to be an antiquarian to realize that stringing out men all over the battlefield would lead to dangerous instability, especially if these lines were taken in the flank by cavalry.

Thus, subsequent formations were deeply affected by a fundamental tension between the necessities of firepower (steadily squeezing troops into a linear order) and the exigencies of military experience (seeking to add solidity through mass and depth). While this conflict would persist to the time of Napoleon and beyond, infantry dispositions would generally follow the dictates of the gun.

Thus, as early as 1516, Spaniards began experimenting with the countermarch, an internal maneuver in which successive ranks of arquebusiers, or later musketeers, each fires a volley and then retires between the files to reload.[29] At the time of its introduction, a minimum of ten ranks was necessary to keep up a steady rolling fire, but this would be reduced. The countermarch was extremely intricate, requiring steady practice. Yet as infantry trained, rates of fire improved, allowing more men to be removed from the files to further elongate the line until, at the end of the seventeenth century, it reached a standard of three ranks.[30] Although the more elaborate forms invariably worked better in training than in battle, the effect of the countermarch was nonetheless very significant and lasting since it established the original conditions for loading drill, which was to be at the heart of small-arms infantry tactics until the middle of the nineteenth century.

It is commonly said the period of the Italian Wars marked the reemergence of infantry as the predominant element in field warfare, yet this is probably overdrawn. Until perhaps 1870 each of the three basic components—infantry, artillery, and cavalry—had strengths and weaknesses capable of exploitation by the other. Thus, without field fortifications, which mercenaries were proverbially unwilling to dig, infantry in their elongated disposition were brittle and prone to opportunistic attack. So too was the relatively stationary and slow-firing artillery of the day. Cavalry, on the other hand, possessed the mobility and potential to intimidate those on foot, but was terribly vulnerable to firepower. Tactics, then, resulted from the complex balance among these three elements. Most battles did eventually turn on the symmetrical match between rival lines, but seldom in isolation from the dangers and possibilities of the other two. This condition emerged during and shortly after the Italian Wars and would remain characteristic of much of the entire era.

Yet change is a relative matter, and for those in the midst of it, especially if they are concentrating on other things, often imperceptible. Despite all the bloodshed, the new weaponry, and the tactical ferment, it is probable that relatively few participants would have been willing to concede that field warfare had changed in any fundamental way.

It was symptomatic that artillerists were commercially grafted onto the armed forces rather than being bureaucratically integrated. So was it characteristic that the ranks of arquebusiers were attached to the fringes of blocky field formations like tactical cummerbunds. Guns were certainly a force to be reckoned with on the battlefield, but they were held at arm's length whenever possible.

On an intellectual plane this was registered by an almost compulsive reference to the ancient military authorities on questions of tactics and dispositions. It would seem that virtually every thoughtful captain in the era of chemical energy read and studied Homer and Vegetius, and quite possibly Thucydides, Tacitus, Polybius, and Aelian.[31] In part this was a matter of availability, Renaissance scholarship having liberated in these Greek and Roman texts such a large body of rationally analyzed military experience. Be that as it may, classical writings probably have had a more lasting influence on military thinking than on any comparably significant field of endeavor.

Thus, the lessons of firearms were largely perceived through minds conditioned by the military beliefs and expectations of the previous era. This was the framework upon which new weapons would be hung if at all possible—the persistent conceptual anachronisms which make the military past worthy of careful consideration.

On a more personal level, the rituals and preconceptions surrounding war and weapons had always served to define the individual identities of the trans-European aristocracy. Sandwiched between resurgent monarchy and the mercenary rabble, men-at-arms clung to as much of the past as was possible under difficult circumstances.

Thus, before Ravenna, the first field action to be decided by an artillery barrage, the rival commanders exchanged formal defiances by trumpet.[32] Similarly, the institution of individualized combat lived on in the face of massive encroachments of capricious killing. In 1503, for example, during an arranged truce, thirteen French men-at-arms staged a ritual fight with an equal number of picked Spanish knights before the town of Barletta.[33]

As late as 1536, Emperor Charles V saw nothing peculiar in challenging the king of France to single combat. Moreover, as Michael Howard notes, the latter accepted, and an actual fight was prevented only by the intercession of the pope.[34] Such bravado was also evidenced by the persistent urge to close. For not only mounted knights but infantry commanders (though not necessarily their mercenary troops) continued to hold the hand-to-hand melee to be the ultimate object of battle and seldom missed an opportunity to join in. Hence, in 1525, Francis I, finding his army thoroughly surprised and misaligned at the battle of Pavia, would lead charge after charge into the Imperialist lines in a desperate attempt to hold off the enemy. Eventually, the king's horse would be shot out from under him and he would be captured, provoking the greatest slaughter of French noblesse since Agincourt 110 years prior. Fate was even less kind to young Gaston de Foix, duke of Nemours and commander of the victorious French army at Ravenna. Having already won the day, he and twenty gentlemen gaily charged a retreating column of desperate Spanish arquebusiers and pikemen, who, being in no mood for chivalry, gunned them down to a man.[35]

Such anecdotes seem largely paralleled by casualty figures among subordinate command elements. At Ravenna, for example, eleven of twelve colonels commanding units for the losing Spaniards were killed, while among the winners virtually all the officers of the German mercenaries died fighting.[36] Similarly, at Marignano (1515) and particularly La Bicocca (1522), where officers were coerced into fighting in the front ranks, the Swiss command was nearly wiped out. At Pavia almost all those in charge of units on the French side perished around the king.[37] Indeed, by this time the ancient urge to fight at close quarters began to take on suicidal overtones.

Yet so basic an element of the warrior ethic could not be lightly cast aside. For a while men-at-arms took refuge behind thicker and more complete plate armor. By 1530, however, the introduction of the musket, a heavier small arm capable of piercing any personal armor at two hundred meters, revealed this as largely futile.[38] To a degree, the rapid adoption of the pistol can be attributed to the fact that it was a short-range weapon allowing horsemen the firearms equivalent of hand-to-hand combat. But if the pistol provided a suitable outlet in some respects, it was altogether more deadly and capricious than the devices which preceded it. In a melee anyone—noble or common, skilled or unskilled—might shoot you down. Indeed, it is safe to say that most warriors of the period would have agreed with Cervantes's Don Quixote when he cursed:

> Blessed be those happy ages, that were strangers to the dreadful fury of these devilish instruments . . . which is the cause that very often a cowardly base hand takes away the life of the bravest gentlemen, and that in the midst of that vigour and resolution which animates and inflames the bold.[39]

Although in many ways the warlike conventions of the previous era would persist, the emergence of the gun required a basic redefinition of what constituted courage in battle. This would take time, but a foreshadowing of the direction it was to take was provided by an incident which took place during the siege of Oudenaarde, near Brussels, in 1582. As J. L. Motley, the historian of Dutch independence, recounts it, one afternoon in early spring Phillip II's famous general Alexander Farnese, the duke of Parma, had a table set near the trench works so he and his staff could dine in the open air.

> Hardly had the repast commenced, when a ball came flying over the table, taking off the head of a young Walloon officer who was sitting near Parma. . . . A portion of his skull struck out the eye of another gentleman present. A second ball . . . destroyed two more of the guests as they sat at the banquet. . . . The blood and the brains of these unfortunate individuals were strewn over the festive

board, and the others all started to their feet, having little appetite left for their dinner. Alexander alone remained in his seat. . . . Quietly ordering the attendants to remove the dead bodies, and to bring a clean tablecloth, he insisted that his guest should resume their places.[40]

Roland might have drawn the sword Durendal and charged the offending cannon, but not Parma. His response was one of passive disdain. If flesh and bone were unequal to flying lead and iron, the spirit still was. Parma's defiant hospitality was a prototype, still a rarity among his peers. But one day men of courage would be inclined to stand fast and take it. Rather than ferocious aggressiveness, not flinching became the sine qua non of the warrior class.

IV

It is perhaps symptomatic that this premonitory incident took place during a siege. For in this sphere of land warfare the impact of firearms was immediate and revolutionary. In an era in which the ancient rituals of war were themselves under attack and the traits of predatory aggression were coming to predominate, it is not illogical that the siege should play a central role in the fighting. Yet the gun's shattering impact on age-old masonry curtain walls and the manifest prosperity of key urban centers added a new dimension of inventiveness and intensity to this brutal art.[41] So sieges, particularly in the period before 1648, came to be frequent and prolonged. In this regard they paralleled recent military experience, subjecting civilian populations to extremes of privation and violence while revealing the utmost peril of municipalities lacking adequate defenses.

Virtually as the era began, Charles VIII had sprung one of the more notable technological surprises in history on the walled Italian cities he confronted in 1494. Overawed, Naples and the pope surrendered almost without a shot being fired. The sole resister that year, the Neapolitan border fortress of Monte San Giovanni, made famous by withstanding a prior investment of seven years, was reduced to rubble within eight hours.[42] But if Charles and the French thought they had gained a permanent advantage, they had not reckoned on the velocity of military technology when confronted with a major disequilibrium. Italy's best minds, including Leonardo da Vinci and Michelangelo, immediately began a frantic search for a solution.[43]

Their efforts did not long go unrewarded. As F. L. Taylor explains in his study of the Italian Wars, the fourteen years between 1494 and the siege of Padua in 1509 were ones of intense and fruitful experimentation, culminating in a startling redress in the imbalance between the offense and the defense.[44]

As early as 1500, the Pisans, besieged by the Florentines, discovered that, unlike stone, loosely packed earth was capable of absorbing cannonballs with little damage.[45] Rather than high, vertical curtain walls, defenders took to building low, sloping dirt ramparts fronted by ditches, presenting attackers with very difficult obstacles which were both small targets and largely cannon-proof. Should a breach be threatened, there was generally time to construct a second interior line of emergency earthworks covering the first and confronting the assaulter with still further obstructions.[46]

Yet it should be emphasized that such structures were not simply a passive reaction to cannon but were largely predicated on their use. For it was quickly discovered that the best means to fight gunfire was symmetrically, with gunfire. At first defenders improvised, installing the weapons so as to shoot through ports along the linear face of curtain walls. With time, however, Italian military engineers learned the virtues of irregular placement and mutually supporting bastions projecting outward so as to provide diagonal flanking fire against assaults from all directions. Gradually, moats and other outworks were added, including a smooth, bare glacis upon which attackers would have to pass under fire without benefit of cover.[47]

By 1520 fortifications on the Italian model were fully developed and, although extraordinarily expensive and labor-consumptive, were spreading throughout Italy's major cities. Indeed, if sources such as the Chronicles of Cremona can be taken as typical, the entire peninsula must have begun to resemble a gigantic public works project. A decade later, spurred by the likes of artist Albrecht Dürer, publisher of the first book on fortifications ever printed, cannon-proof defenses began to diffuse through Europe, or at least those portions, such as Holland, which could afford them.

The proliferation of the so-called *trace italienne* was, as William McNeill astutely concludes, an extremely significant factor in European history in that it placed a very tangible impediment in the way of a single transnational polity at the very time the possibility of such an entity loomed up in the form of the Habsburg dynasty.[48]

Yet to participants the rise of the *trace italienne* probably had a more immediate significance. In some instances it bought safety but hardly immunity. Faced with gun-based defenses, besiegers took to the pick and shovel, burrowing below ground with trench works (hired laborers, and not mercenaries, did the digging) that first surrounded the fortifications and then closed in with zigzag slits and concealed batteries. Once the earthworks reached the glacis, sappers then drove mines underneath, which they filled with explosives, thereby marking the spread of gunpowder to this ancient tactic. At the climax, charges might be blown and batteries unmasked for a final bloody assault.

Defenders, for their part, might dig equally tedious and dangerous countermines and trenches, seeking to thwart this objective.[49] Thus, siege warfare settled down to a nasty, laborious equilibrium, the rapid development of defenses having served only to further prolong and brutalize what had always been a particularly harsh form of warfare. Sieges came to last years, and, if successful, victorious troops increasingly vented their frustrations on defeated urbanites in orgies of rapine and killing. Even towns which successfully resisted were at times reduced to such extremes of privation that law and morality broke down completely. So it was that the fruits of man's genius, this remarkable and precipitous cycle of innovation, should have brought forth only a veil of tears and man's terrible capacity to apply the logic of predation to conflicts with his fellows.

It is important to emphasize that genius is not too strong a word to use with respect to certain participants in the development of the *trace italienne* and the arms revolution in general. Just as occurred at the very beginning of the atomic age, the period of the Italian Wars marked one of the rare points at which men of towering intellect became involved with weapons development. These were not warlike men, quite the contrary. Like Einstein, Bohr, and Kapitsa, it appears that Leonardo, Michelangelo, and Dürer were simply swept up by the events of the day, convinced, despite reservations, that their importance warranted direct participation. What was accomplished was quite remarkable, literally the delineation of the weapons types made possible by chemical energy, along with many of the components necessary to carry these applications to their logical conclusions.

But it was not just the geniuses. As John Nef noted almost half a century ago, these men were not solely responsible for what amounted to a corporate experience in technical clairvoyance, a trans-European eruption of death-dealing ingenuity. As far back as the 1430s, the blind visionary Jan Žižka and his embattled Bohemian Hussites anticipated amazingly the armored column with their *Wagenburgen,* caravans of horse-drawn, armor-plated carts equipped with firing ports, small portable bombards, and a variety of primitive small arms.[50] Screw-based breech-loading and exploding shot, two prime factors in the artillery convulsion of the nineteenth century, were known before 1500.[51] In terms of small arms, the shoulder stock, the wheel lock (the basis for the pistol), and rifling were all in use by 1525. By this date or shortly after, there also had been numerous experiments with multiple barrels and, in one case, a true attempt at a Gatling.[52] Hand grenades, land mines, and a variety of incendiaries were also developed during this same time frame. Indeed, it is possible to say that by 1530 the essence of the modern battlefield had been sketched in one form or another. Yet as impressive as this corporate body of work might seem, even more significant was that which did not materialize, but continued to exist only in the mind's eye.

This is the realm of genius, and it is why the participation of a man like Leonardo da Vinci was so important. He did not like war, which he stigmatized as *"bestialissima pazzia"* (the most bestial madness). Nor do his ruminations on weaponry occupy more than a small portion of his voluminous manuscripts. Yet Leonardo, perhaps more than any other major scientific thinker, was blessed with the talent he defined as "pre-imagining—the imagining of things that are to be," and it was this gift which proved so valuable when applied to military affairs.

Unlike other key marital thinkers—Machiavelli, Jomini, or Clausewitz—Leonardo was largely unconcerned with formations, tactics, and doctrine, turning instead to the artifacts of battle: weapons, "the things that are to be." Characteristically, Leonardo's specualtions on the future of arms were not the enigmatic utterances of the seer but precise and mechanically credible postulations, at once natural for one who had worked as a military engineer and yet destined to serve as archetypes in the Western technical imagination. Taken as a whole, Leonardo's commentary on weaponry reads a bit like a Renaissance version of the slick "wish lists" our own military establishment periodically floats through Congress, catalogues of weapons both real and imagined, presented in a context largely divorced from their use. Drawing on history, the speculations of contemporaries, and his own protean imagination, Leonardo describes at one point or another caltrops, fireballs, poison arrows, torsion catapults, scythed chariots, Greek fire, mortars, cartridges for small arms, air guns, steam catapults, a Gatling-type gun, rocket launchers, armored vehicles, submarines, and chemical warfare.[53] Though scattered through his notebooks, this body of suggestions, along with his speculations on flight, indicates strongly that Leonardo caught with one sweeping glance the future of weaponry until the mid–twentieth century.

While insights of genius defy exact attribution, we need not retreat into mysticism to account for them. In the case of Leonardo, it seems possible that his extreme technical and scientific aptitude allowed him to grasp the multiple destructive possibilities of chemical energy and project them accurately out across the future. Nor was he alone. Based on a number of similar, if less-inspired, writings and the spate of invention before 1530, it would seem that the future of chemical-based weaponry is best conceived as having hung latent over mankind almost from the inception, accessible to only a few but there nonetheless.

Yet if this were the case, at whatever level of imagination, the question naturally arises: Why didn't the armaments revolution go further toward fulfillment? Obviously, there were technical and metallurgical limitations in the sixteenth century, the most critical being a portable, self-contained power source. But if Western man would have to wait 350 years for advanced heat engines, there remained other avenues of potential advancement, such as ballistics or military chemistry, which might have been explored further. Why weren't they?

In one sense the question cannot fairly be separated from the larger issues surrounding the march of technology in general. Yet it would also seem that the manifest intent and obvious effects of arms innovation during the period of the Italian Wars should have exerted some rather specific influences on those involved.

Here, again, the character of Leonardo is particularly revealing. John Nef, seeking to explain the apparent success of inhibitors on military technology during the Renaissance, fastened upon a "widely expressed horror for the invention of the gun" and a "wholeness" in man's technological pursuits which prevented easy escape from the moral and religious ramifications of death-dealing devices.[54] These are points well taken. There is evidence of such mechanisms at work. But in the case of Leonardo, there seems to have been something else, a budding dichotomy of the spirit which forecast great change. Clearly, Leonardo was horrified by what he had seen of contemporary warfare, and it has been suggested that his military innovations were offered solely in the context of defensive preparation. Yet this is neither strictly true nor convincing in a larger sense. There is an implied enthusiasm to his destructive creativity, an obvious braggadocio in his letter to Ludovic Sforza seeking employment as a military engineer which does not square well with a totally benign interpretation of his motives.[55]

Unlike previous military technologists, there are strong indications that Leonardo consciously applied his reasoning power and understanding of nature to systematically explore the possibilities of destroying human life. Moreover, he did so with a singular concentration on the deadly mechanism itself, largely ignoring the tactical and strategic implications. Yet he also appears to have approached weaponry with much the same ambivalence of modern technologists—spewing forth destructive ingenuity while at the same time infected with a Faustian sense of foreboding. Thus, in one famous passage Leonardo could propose the submarine and decry its possibility in literally the same breath.[56]

For the time being, religious and humanitarian restraints would hold, and Leonardo would refuse to reveal further details of his submersible on "account of the evil nature of man." Yet one day his intellectual heirs would find themselves free of the web of guilt and responsibility which joined the two halves of Leonardo's nature, and would rather quickly create not simply models and ideas for slaughter but its reality. This day would not dawn for more than three centuries, but the necessary concepts and psychological adjustments emerged much earlier.

Chapter 8

HARVEST OF BLOOD

I

Gradually, the flames of war had sputtered out in the scorched Italian peninsula, and by 1560 fighting had largely ceased there. Yet in no way did this preface general peace. Rather, the participants—pools of French, Spanish, and German fighting men—spilled back northward, carrying with them the sparks that would ignite and gradually envelop Western and central Europe in a fire storm that would not come under control until 1648. At the core of this inferno were the Habsburg dynasty and the emergent kingdom of Spain, successors to the abortive Valois reach for hegemony and the first of the major claimants to trans-European dominion.

Here at the rarified level of international politics, cool and well insulated from the flames, the confusing mass of violence and political turmoil can be explained fairly well as a manifestation of the balance of power or, alternately, as J. V. Polisensky has concluded, a fundamental conflict between two rival social and economic models, one centralized and hierarchical, the other pluralistic.[1]

Yet it was particularly telling of the times that these wars were fought, overtly and in the minds of the participants, largely along religious grounds, life-and-death struggles between Protestantism and Catholicism. It does not seem coincidental that of all motives for mass violence except perhaps race, religious differences are most effective in undermining a sense of shared humanity and allowing men to behave as if enemies are actually of another species. So the crossbow was countenanced against Muslims. And now, under alternate banners of Christ, did men struggle for and against transnational hegemony over Europe, in the process allowing war to be overrun by all manner of predatory excess: the brutal sacking of civilian population centers and the attendant abuse of women and children; the refusal of quarter and the ritual slaughter of prisoners; the startling growth of mass armies themselves. Indeed, from the brutalized perspective of the hapless peasant or townsman, the entire cycle of wars might best be understood as a massive and savage people hunt, with themselves as quarry. For beyond politics and religion there was the specter of mercenary bands living in a predatory symbiosis that spelled permanent social and economic change.

Given the coincidence in time between the shift to a more predatory form of warfare and the appearance and growing use of firearms, it is hard to escape the conclusion that the two were intimately related. Yet the nature of the interaction is difficult to define precisely. For example, although it is suggestive that a number of small-arms innovations (rifling, the flintlock, and the bayonet) were first developed for hunting during this time frame, it would be stretching things to propose a clearly delineated relationship. Similarly, it is probable that any direct feedback loop (gun causing brutality and vice versa) oversimplifies what is likely to be a complex phenomenon.

Yet it is also quite apparent that firearms made death dealing decidedly easier, and in doing so greatly aided the cause of slaughter. John Nef has stressed the psychological attractions of long-range killing, particularly its removal of the perpetrator from the consequences of violence.[2] While it seems reasonable that the destruction of human life should be more abstract and agreeable at a distance, it is also true that many battles in the sixteenth and seventeenth centuries ended in swirling melees followed by a slaughter of the defeated which was anything but antiseptic.

On the other hand, it seems indisputable that fire fighting at long ranges was less dependent on the traditional warrior virtues of physical prowess and raw courage, and therefore more suited to mass participation. Rather than requiring immersion in the martial arts, killing was reduced to a fairly abstract mechanical act. The mathematically inclined could mow down a file of infantry with a single well-aimed cannonball, while the mercenary rabble could be taught to load and fire small arms with a reasonable assurance that, should a hit be scored, the resulting wound probably would be incapacitating. So armies grew and casualties mounted, and with them came the climate of callousness which characterized the hunt.

II

But if Europe was primarily occupied with internal convulsions during the period between 1495 and 1648, it is also true that external sources played a role in the growing violence. The Continent was both under siege and in the process of exploding upon the world with a great spasm of conquest. In both cases, factors of race and religion would provoke a particularly virulent form of warfare which was not only related to adoption of the gun but reverberated back upon Europe to further brutalize the climate.

Consider the case of the Turk. The political effect of the gun upon the Muslim world was decidedly different from the European pattern of rapid and relatively homogeneous adoptions by a network of sovereign states. Instead, only one power, the Ottoman dynasty, took up firearms with real enthusiasm, and the gun in turn rewarded the Turk with conquest and dominion over the entire Muslim crescent.

A more typical response to firearms was that of the Mamluks, who were aware of the gun perhaps only fifty years after its introduction in Europe yet still had adopted it only on a very conditional basis when the Egyptian kingdom fell one-and-a-half centuries later in 1517. Quite symptomatically, as David Ayalon notes, the gun was seen as a weapon of the siege or to be used against Christians.[3] In the field, however, matched against other followers of the Prophet Muhammad, the Mamluks considered the gun beneath their dignity, an utter contradiction of the horse-based and close-combat-oriented *furusiya* exercises which formed the heart of the elite's military training rituals.[4]

The Turks, on the other hand, had no such scruples. It appears that the Ottoman dynasty first used guns somewhat later, when they were more effective, and employed them almost immediately against Christians according to one tradition cited by Stanford Shaw.[5] Certainly, the virtues of firepower were less likely to be lost on an extraordinarily ambitious power sandwiched between aggressive neighbors than on the relatively isolated and secure Mamluks.

Yet in the long run it was probably more factors of organization than military need which motivated and facilitated the Ottoman integration of firepower. At the core was the power of the sultan, until the seventeenth century an autocrat of the most rarified sort, presiding over a classic transnational tyranny. The system was not a traditional one, but had in fact been recently imposed upon the turbulent and previously nomadic Turks by a series of energetic rulers, the most significant being Mehmed II. Though culturally devised, the state bore more than a passing resemblance (particularly as it related to the sexuality of the ruler and his minions) to the genetically based organizational forms of the social insects.

Critical to enforcing the sultan's will was his corps of drones, the Janissaries, a paid slave army of soldiers, bureaucrats, and technicians who, though not eunuchs, were forbidden to marry and largely sequestered from women.[6] Created and developed as a deliberate counterweight to the rowdy horse archer nobility which had previously dominated Turkish forces, it is logical but still somewhat remarkable that the Janissaries should have constituted an infantry force of outsiders—Christian hostages brought to the sultan at a tender age and then subjected to the most meticulous discipline and training.[7]

Although Sultan Orphan armed the Janissaries with traditional weapons when he founded them in 1320, the mystique of the bow and lance had only a limited time to penetrate to the heart of the corps before the possibilities of firearms became apparent to Murad II around 1420. He and his two immediate successors, Mehmed II and Bayezid II, rapidly and efficiently grafted both cannon and small arms, manned by their personal slave troopers, onto the traditional Turkish military forms.[8] What emerged was probably the deadliest fighting mechanism yet created, a swirling Asiatic horde with a lethal nucleus of firepower. The key was the superb discipline of the relatively small Janissary units, whose training enabled them to operate both classes of fire weapons with an effect out of all proportion to their numbers.

While the Turks had previously accumulated a modicum of success against Christian and Muslim alike, after 1453 and the fall of Constantinople to Turkish siege guns, they began to become much more formidable. Conquest, however, only whet their appetite for world dominion. Like Rome, the archetypical predatory land power, the Turks took to the sea unnaturally but with determination, at first allying themselves with piratical North African corsairs and eventually challenging Christendom for the entire Mediterranean basin in a series of naval battles and amphibious operations of monumental brutality. But if the legendary defense of Rhodes and Malta by the Knights of Saint John and the climactic battle of Lepanto caught the imagination of the age, it was the reality of Turkey as a land power which seemed to be tilting history in the direction of the Sublime Porte.

In the twelve years following 1514, Ottoman armies dealt Safavid Persia a crippling blow, conquered the Mamluks, and then invaded Hungary, annihilating the defending army at Mohács and taking over the country. In all cases superior firepower was directly responsible for Turkish success.[9] A thrill of dread spread through Christendom as the Habsburgs under Charles V and Süleyman I, the greatest of the Ottoman sultans, became locked in a mortal struggle that would find Vienna itself twice under siege. The legions of Christ would gradually come to prevail, but this was in no way seen as inevitable at the time.[10]

While the limitations of transport and communications served at times to muffle the immediate sense of emergency, war with the Turks had a significant impact on the European military psyche. In particular, factors of race and religion led to an exaggeratedly predatory form of fighting in which the ritual killing of prisoners and the brutalization and enslavement of women and children became particularly pronounced. In both siege and slaughter the gun's role was a major one, with both sides endorsing the weapon as eminently suited to an adversary largely represented in subhuman terms.

If, however, the gun's place in the mayhem and the impact of the Turkish Wars on later European callousness are at least recognized, other historical lessons posed by the Ottomans have been all but ignored. Since firearms are normally considered a European phenomenon, it is usually assumed that the Turks adopted them because they were somehow European. This does not seem to be true. The Ottoman dynasty was thoroughly Asiatic in origins and outlook. Instead, it appears that the Turks, like the Romans, aopted new arms primarily as a result of political ambition, attaching them to existing military institutions with a cold-blooded pragmatism. They were not innovative in this regard so much as they were exploitative. Turkish weapons technology was an exercise in political opportunism which, as the sultanate retreated into the harem and the Janissary ethic was ruined by dilution, vanished with the will of the state.[11] What remained was a parasitic imperial entity which, though it ruled its polyglot constituents with a relatively lighter hand than Christian equivalents, still had more in common with Sargon's Akkadian Empire than a modern nation-state. Yet such a polity had, at the very dawn of the age of firepower, managed not only to arm itself with the most modern weapons but to take particular advantage of their capabilities through superior discipline and training. If the future of weaponry belonged to Europe and the West, the example of the Turk should have provided sufficient indication that it was not necessarily an exclusive possession. Given sufficient will, arms would be had—if not exactly created, then at least reverse engineered.

A more congenial and therefore more memorable military encounter with what we today describe as the Third World was provided by the discovery and conquest of the Americas. Here was a suitable tableau on which to establish the legend of absolute and innate European military superiority, a great orgy of plunder and power politics featuring the simultaneous fall of two great empires to tiny bands of conquerors and, ultimately, two continents for the taking. The political and economic influence of the New World is generally credited with having the utmost significance for the subsequent course of world history. Yet the role of the gun in this acquisition, though tacitly conceded, is seldom emphasized. It is generally recognized that the collapse of both the mezzo-American empire of the Aztecs and the hegemony of the Inca was brought about by a combination of factors: extreme political opportunism, an insatiable lust for gold, and the ruthless pursuit of technological advantage being the most frequently noted. Yet the degree to which firearms alone drew these elements together and exaggerated their impact on traditional and ritualistically oriented societies is seldom alluded to.

Eighteen hundred years earlier Alexander, too, had correctly perceived that he had only to decapitate the Persian Empire to rule it. Yet he required the army of Macedon to do so. In the case of Cortés and Pizarro a similar end demanded a relative handful of Spaniards. In a very real sense the gun accounted for the difference. Strictly speaking, it was European arms and not just firearms which proved so devastating against native Americans. Cavalry overawed them, while iron swords and armor confounded their obsidian-tipped arrows and blades. Nevertheless, there are numerous indications that it was the gun, at critical junctures, which utterly demoralized the Indian warriors and robbed them of their power to resist. The *Codex Florentine,* Fray Bernardino de Sahagún's remarkable compilation of contemporary sources, repeatedly notes Aztec fighters fainting away at the reports of discharging cannon.[12] William Prescott, too, in his narrative of the surprise and capture of the Inca, places heavy emphasis on the auditory impact of gunfire in pacifying his bodyguard.[13] Without doubt, the great majority of Indian casualties did not fall prey to guns. Yet firearms served to epitomize the conquistador's military advantage, imparting to it a magical quality which made resistance so much more manifestly hopeless. Culturally and technically overwhelmed, the Indians had no recourse to the traditional responses of the underarmed, either symmetrical weaponry or, for the more desperate, counters. Instead, they had only to submit.

Yet in submission there was a sort of revenge. Among other things, the legacy of the conquistadors was more bloodshed at home and the ultimate exhaustion of the Spanish branch of the Habsburg dynasty.

The syndrome of political variables which would subsequently dominate European politics—extreme Machiavellian expediency, capitalism, and the new military technology—made it not only possible but inevitable that the Americas would be drawn into the European sphere. The process was only accelerated by the subsequent discovery and exploitation of huge gold and silver deposits in Peru and

Mexico, a cache destined to be the line of credit for the endless war in the Netherlands. Soon the new roomy, wind-powered warships, themselves made possible by the gun, were plying the Atlantic in fleets, either transporting bullion or hunting for those that did. Huge sections of the globe were suddenly annexed to the European political system and cash nexus, creating the basis for further expansion and ultimately a migration without precedent in modern history.

Yet European contact with the Americas also had a decidedly negative aspect. As the writings and work of Bartolomé de Las Casas demonstrate, the conquistadors were insatiably greedy men who conceded the Indians' humanity only grudgingly, if at all, in their relentless search for plunder.[14] Even more than with the Turk, the differentiating forces of race, religion, and culture conspired to encourage the Europeans to exaggerate the predatory elements in warfare and kill wantonly, practically from beginning to end. That the Aztecs subjected Spanish prisoners to human sacrifice and fought largely with the aim of gaining captives only served to intensify the European bloodlust. Taking full advantage of the weapons asymmetry, they engaged in frequent and unprovoked massacres in both Mexico and Peru. In the former instance, Cortés fittingly sealed the doom of the Aztecs with a final, almost genocidal, siege of Tenochtitlán (Mexico City today), for which Prescott cites casualty figures of from 120,000 to 240,000.[15]

Unlike the collision with the Turk, however, it would be hard to make the case that the fighting style of a few soldiers of fortune, thousands of miles removed from the center of action, was directly influential in brutalizing the great series of European wars which broke out after 1562.

But neither should the example of the conquistadors be ignored. These were entirely representative soldiers of their age, mercenaries who in many instances had learned their trade in the Italian Wars under Gonsalvo de Córdoba. They had been trained to use technology's bounty to kill with impunity for pay, and when the opportunity arose they did so. The phenomenon of denied humanity, so necessary to the predatory side of warfare, would ultimately be played out primarily in religious terms within Europe. Yet the model for internal combat was not fundamentally different from that which was established against the Turk and the American Indians. Furthermore, the concept of race, arising to a significant degree from these contacts, would continue to color European attitudes toward not only war with those perceived as alien but their very right to freedom. Thus, sixteenth-century European conceptions of slavery, as Winthrop Jordan notes in his book *White over Black*, arose primarily from the Turk, whose galleys came to be filled with Christian captives, and were subsequently exported to the Americas.[16]

III

But, ultimately, it was the inhumanity which Europeans applied to themselves which caused the period from 1562 to 1648 to be such a horrific one. Just why it was that predation and technology were turned inward with such willful malevolence is hard to pin down. It is generally agreed that the pressures exerted by fundamental economic, cultural, and spiritual change played a significant role in agitating the political climate. Nonetheless, historic example seems to indicate a definite relationship between the drive for transnational dominion, the promiscuous use of weaponry, and very brutal and costly wars. We, forty years into the nuclear era and confronted by a Soviet empire which has established its rule over numerous nonassimilated nationalities, can take little solace from those events which began to unfold seventy-five years into the gunpowder revolution. Massively increased firepower, a greatly complicated logistics train, and the constant economic pressure exerted by mercenary troops turned the armies of the day into rapacious, ill-disciplined swarms whose ecological impact is best compared to the depredations of the species *Eciton burchelli,* nature's own army ants. For eighty years these armed bands were destined to stagger about the Netherlands, France, and Germany, destroying all before them and all too frequently accomplishing nothing of particular political value. Indeed, a contemporary blessed with neither blinding religious faith nor the facade of a historical explanation might well have wondered if northern Europe had not taken up killing largely for its own sake.

Fed by returning waves of veterans from Italy, war ignited during the 1560s almost simultaneously in France and the Netherlands and continued in parallel but very distinct courses for virtually the remainder of the century.

In the former instance the struggle enervated central government sufficiently to remove France as a major international player until well into the next century. For those with an interest, the fighting can be broken down into nine separate phases, the cumulative effect of which was military confusion interspersed with acts of random violence, the most famous of which is the massacre of Saint Bartholomew's Day Eve (24 August 1572).[17] Tactically, the action generally revolved around mercenary cavalry encounters in which short-range pistol firefights predominated and the defeated foot soldiers and horsemen were run down and killed.

Sieges were less evident than in the Netherlands, and there was considerable single combat and chivalrous display (Henry of Navarre was a sort of Tristan incarnate). Yet the tone of the fighting was probably better represented by the fate of Anne de Joyeuse, the defeated commander at Coutras, his brains blown out even as he reminded his captors that his ransom was one hundred thousand ecus.[18] This was typical everywhere. It continued to be a dangerous time for the military aristocracy, and many key figures—including two of the greatest, William the Silent and Gustav Adolph—would fall to pistol shots at close range before the new definition of courage made such encounters less likely.

Meanwhile, the French continued to learn little and suffer much, trapped in a cycle of violence, the causes of which were succinctly put by the Huguenot philosopher La Noue: "The young have been reading too many romances of reckless adventure . . . and objectless fighting. The old have been reading and re-reading Machiavelli. . . . It is hard for the nation to settle down after so many nerve wracking years."[19]

Peace would prove just as elusive in the Netherlands—though for other reasons and with strikingly different conclusions. Rather than civil war, the *causus beli* was a growing sense of nationhood and a concomitant awareness of being occupied by foreign troops. Rather than enervation, Dutch suffering was transmuted into commercial vigor and cultural greatness—a time of trial which gradually brought forth the first modern prototype of maritime democratic capitalism, a virtual reincarnation of the Athenian politico-economic model.

For a time wedded to ritual, it is fitting that this cycle of history should have begun with a great ceremony, the abdication of Emperor Charles V in Brussels on 25 October 1555. Into the great hall of the royal palace limped the ruler of much of Europe, his disease-wracked body supported by the young favorite, William of Orange, and his halting progress toward the throne marked intently by the great Flemish lords who were his subjects. Awaiting him was his son and heir, Philip, who in later years must have reflected on the singularity of this transfer of power, which not only brought together the two great protagonists of the subsequent generation but also marked a new stage in history. For besides an admission of age and infirmity, Charles's retirement was a tacit acknowledgment, at least on the part of its last unified ruler, that the Habsburg dynasty's dominions had grown too large and diverse to rule as a whole. Whereas Charles had been a transnational figure, his successor, Philip, was primarily the king of Spain. Yet this he would never accept, thereby plunging himself and his state into a series of wars which would be the ruin of them both.

Of course, as the theory went, this was what the prince was supposed to do: pursue power, seek to dominate. The fact that western Europe was congealing into self-consciously national entities which would effectively preclude a transnational structure was not clear, and therefore that fact only gradually modified the rules and motives of the game. Meanwhile, in the eyes of princes more constrained by circumstances, Philip was only seen as acting out his preordained role.

Perhaps the sole dissenter would have been William of Orange, the king of Spain's bête noir. As Philip left the Netherlands for Spain, never to return, he exploded at Orange: "It is you who have ruined all my plans. Not the Estates, but you, you, you."[20]

It was true. The cunning but affable Orange was the perfect foil to the secretive, misanthropic Habsburg. Yet the distinction went deeper. William would be a new kind of ruler, guiding the fate of a new kind of state, still only half-conscious of itself. A Catholic and an outsider ruling Protestants, William the Silent was sustained not by heredity and tradition but by the affection of his people. So it was that he reveled in the ambiguity of his title, stadholder. In a time of extreme religious bigotry and political rapacity, he remained tolerant and limited in his goals, wanting above all that the Netherlands become a place where Catholic and Protestant might live together in peace and prosperity.[21]

Yet Philip would have it otherwise, and his instrument was the Inquisition. Throughout the Netherlands, Protestants were subjected to increasing harassment and persecution. Though there was considerable indigenous Catholic support for the crackdown, the major impetus was Spanish. A great ziggurat of intolerance was constructed—a shadowy tower of foreign spies and inquisitors, administered by an artificially bloated Church hierarchy and buttressed by an occupying army made up of the toughest and most experienced troops in Europe. But as the weight of the edifice grew heavier and the lists of those proscribed longer, the spark of revolt spread among the industrious Netherlanders and the ironic cry *Vivent les Gueux!* (Long live the beggars!) was heard to echo through every town and city of the United Provinces. So Philip sent them the duke of Alva, probably the finest soldier of his day and certainly the cruelest.

The duke's intent and outlook were made instantly clear on 16 February 1568, when a sentence of death was passed down on the entire population of the Netherlands, subject only to specific exception.[22] Alva would have utter submission or genocide, and the veterans of Spain stood ready to enforce his will.

For the Netherlanders, confronting the tercio was not easy. The blocky Spanish formation had evolved out of a basic sword-pike square through the steady addition of firepower around the fringes. Though slow on the attack, the resulting unit had lost none of its solidity, while steadily increasing the rate of fire.[23] Facing up to such a force required similar steadiness and determination, qualities which the hastily assembled Netherlanders and German and Huguenot mercenaries they hired simply did not have in sufficient quantity. Before close combat could ensue, this sort of fighting—unlike Greek phalanx warfare—demanded an initial period of attrition, which in turn required that men perform fairly abstract but precise movements under extreme emotional stress. Not surprisingly, training and experience paid huge dividends for the Spanish, while the Netherlanders suffered disaster after disaster.

The fate of Orange's three-pronged attack of 1568 was typical. First, in mid-April de Villers's luckless force of three thousand was basically annihilated around Dalem by Sancho de Avila, who lost just twenty men.[24] Three months passed when Louis of Nassau, Orange's brother, seeking to get his troops to stand, took up strong but perilous positions on the Jemmingen peninsula, surrounded on three sides by the swiftly flowing Ems. The Spaniards simply ran them over, driving six to seven thousand into the river to drown, a disaster which the burghers of Emden first realized when several thousand broad-brimmed Dutch hats floated by.[25] A few days later at Saint-Valéry the third force under Cocqueville was reduced from twenty-five hundred to three hundred, again with minimal Spanish loss.[26]

Nor did the situation in the field improve quickly. Throughout the ensuing period, the Spaniards subjected the Netherlander forces to a variety of ruses, ambushes, and night attacks (*encamisadas,* named for the white shirts worn for recognition in the dark), which were not only extremely deadly but alarmingly predatory in their implications. The ferocity of the Spaniards was amazing; at times they waded for miles up to their necks in tidal estuaries (they were largely non-swimmers) simply to get at their prey who by now were thoroughly cowed and increasingly unwilling to take the field under any circumstances.[27] When they did, the results were the same. Thus, in 1576, eight years after Orange's initial campaign, a combined Netherlander force of burghers, aritsans, and peasants was routed by the Spanish at Tisnacq with a relative loss of two thousand to two.[28]

Under the circumstances, it is not surprising that sieges came to dominate the action. And indeed here was the beginning of the Netherlander's advantage. As a testimony to their wealth and the prior prevalence of dynastic warfare, the Low Countries in the sixteenth century were more thickly sown with fortifications than most places in Europe. The rapid and inevitable spread of the *trace italienne* only further strengthened what were already unusually strong positions. For, in most cases, prepared fortifications in the war zone were surrounded by elaborate water defenses, which not only precluded mining but provided a ready lifeline to the sea.

The very strength of the Dutch positions, as William McNeill has noted, had immediate economic consequences for the Spanish, necessitating sharply enlarged armies and ever-increasing quantities of powder and shot.[29] Even the infusion of American silver, which helped finance these massive investments, was a double-edged sword since it radically altered the European price structure, further impoverishing the commercially reactionary Spanish monarchy. Despite tripling taxes in Castile between 1556 and 1577, Philip had to repudiate his debts four times and never succeeded in paying his soldiers on time.[30]

This, in turn, undermined discipline and spread the spirit of mutiny through the Spanish troops, already frustrated by the Low Country defenses. Gradually, it came to be understood that should the Spanish succeed in taking a town, the population and its possessions would constitute, in essence, the rewards. So it was that, as the revolt dragged on, predatory behavior reinforced by economic self-interest came to assume a very pure form. Thus, in addition to plunder, not only did the slaughter of adult males and ritual rape of females increasingly become routine, but other more esoteric acts began to crop up. Repeatedly, according to John Motley, Spanish troops took to drinking the blood of their victims, while on the other side females increasingly came to assume an active role in the actual combat.[31]

The net effect of this unremitting bloodletting upon weapons development was certainly significant, if somewhat complicated and difficult to interpret. In one sense the initial period of inventive fecundity which characterized the dawn of the age of firearms had largely passed.

The three key weapons—the muzzle-loading musket, the cannon, and the pistol—were well established as the dominant man-killers, the technically unpretentious equivalents of the Roman short sword and the inconspicuous fangs of the predator. There would be further qualitative advances of significance: more reliable firing mechanisms, the incorporation of the integral bayonet, and more mobile cannon carriages. Yet in many ways the form and function of these devices were largely fixed, and with them the core armament of military forces until 1840.

Nevertheless, war in the Netherlands did bring major changes; its very scale and bitterness saw to that. Thus, in terms of quantity and utilization, the nature of these core arms and their role in land warfare would largely be finalized during the period between 1570 and 1609. Yet perhaps even more significant for the future was what took place at the outer fringes of weapons development—half-remembered occurrences which revealed, possibly for the first time, the true dimensions of man's willingness to unleash his technical skills in the cause of mass destruction.

As alluded to earlier, one of the major military phenomena of the period was the steady increase in the size of armies, a condition made possible in large part by the relative ease with which untrained men could be taught to use firearms with at least some degree of efficiency. Spain, the most ambitious power, led the way in this regard, with the total number of men under arms reaching around three hundred thousand at the height of the military effort in the 1630s.[32] Meanwhile, her enemies' forces, while smaller, had also expanded quickly. And, in fact, armies would continue to grow, leading eventually to the staggering, ecologically menacing juggernauts which the likes of Wallenstein and Gustav Adolph would field during the Thirty Years' War.

The manpower-gun relationship did not work in just one direction. It was a self-reinforcing feedback loop in which accretions in manpower created a steady and increasing demand for firearms, particularly small arms.

Significantly, it was the mechanisms of capitalism and the spirit of bourgeois enterprise which fulfilled the need. As an ambitious military power, Spain had armed itself early and well with firearms. But with the exception of military engineering, the Spaniards were never particularly innovative with war machinery. Nor were they very successful in encouraging arms manufacture at home, especially cannon. In the overtaxed, restrictive economic environment he had created, Philip's state-sponsored artillery foundries withered like parched grapes.[33] So Spain and her prince were forced to turn to the very Netherlands where they were fighting for not only military supplies but weaponry.

In particular, the bishopric of Liège, notably not under Spanish rule, became a major seat of arms production. This was especially ironic since it was only after 1492, when the bishopric disarmed and declared itself neutral, that the weapons industry really began to flourish. Repeated subsequent occupations proved counterproductive in that they inevitably interrupted gun manufacture.[34] So the Liègois won their independence on the paradoxical premise that only in an atmosphere of peace could the tools of war be steadily supplied to the firepower-hungry belligerents which surrounded them.

But here, as elsewhere, it was capitalism which provided the impetus. Left to their own resources, and allowing the market to come freely into play, the Liègeois came to produce the best and cheapest weapons in Europe, and grew rich in the process. Moreover, as efficiency climbed and supply increased, the problem of obtaining firearms, powder, and ammunition in sufficient quantities ceased to be a major limiting factor in military operations.[35] For the next 250 years, firearms would remain cheap and plentiful. Though there would be much starvation and depopulation among humans, guns continued to be fruitful and almost always well fed.

It is perhaps appropriate that not only the proliferation of muzzle-loading firearms but their feeding would have been perfected in the hedonistic Low Countries.

Though the Protestant inhabitants of the northern Netherlands also bought many of their own land arms from the Liègeois, they were in outlook and capacity for invention a great deal different than their Spanish adversaries. It is safe to say that at this time there was no more dynamic people on earth than the citizens of the emerging state of Holland. Though they frequently suffered atrociously at the hands of the Spaniards, their enterprise and business skill allowed them to turn the war to their own economic advantage. Rather than growing poorer over time like the Spanish, the Dutch waxed steadily richer.[36]

Yet their military problems persisted, and it was characteristic that they should turn their energies in the direction of weapons innovation in an effort to solve them. Therefore, while the new methods of fortification were largely introduced to the Low Countries by Italian military engineers, it was the Dutchman Simon Stevin who best adapted them for local conditions using water barriers and sharper bastions enabling mutual support with small arms.[37] Similarly, when the need arose for a fieldpiece that was lighter but retained much of the range and accuracy of cannon, the Dutch led the way with the introduction of the howitzer.[38] But, in fact, military innovation in Holland had less to do with tangible device technology than with the use of what was already available in new ways.

This was epitomized in the remarkable career of Maurice of Nassau, prince of Orange, the son of William the Silent. Made stadholder at age seventeen, immediately after his father's assassination in 1584, Maurice already showed extraordinary maturity and an almost innate understanding of the tactical implications of firepower.

As this was a war of siegecraft, Maurice naturally turned his energies to this form of combat. Through concentrating his artillery, Maurice learned to generate massive barrages capable of creating practicable breaches much more quickly than before. Using long approach trenches to shield his guns, he cut casualties and attrition among his own troops, while sharp enforcement of the articles of war and the liberal terms he offered induced those besieged to surrender more quickly.[39] Thus, at least by implication, an element of humanity was injected into this most brutal form of attack.

While these developments would prove to be of lasting significance, Maurice is far better known for his innovations in battle formations and infantry training. By 1590 it had become obvious that if the Dutch were to field armies which could stand up to the tercio, major changes would have to be made. Methodically, Maurice and his cousins William Louis and John of Nassau studied the problems and worked out solutions in war games played with lead soldiers, a convention which in itself indicated the direction of their work.[40] Characteristically, lessons learned were couched and interpreted in terms of Aelian, Vegetius, and the military classics of the mechanical era. Yet the solutions they reached, though superficially parallel to the Roman battle order, were headed in an entirely different direction, toward maximizing firepower through elongation of formations and rapidity of loading.

Seeing the advantages of smaller units and linear groupings, the reformers reduced company strength dramatically and then squeezed the tercio from into an oblong of but five deep in a front of fifty. Trevor Dupuy rates the increase in firepower on the order of 100 percent,[41] but the resulting formation was also potentially very brittle.

By the time of the reforms, Maurice was an experienced soldier and realized that the implications of these new formations demanded an entire reconstruction of his forces. For at the center of his ideas was the necessity for absolute discipline and control. In a very real sense, his men would have to be turned into automata. To do this the Dutch came to rely almost totally on mercenary troops, taking care to insure that they were paid with absolute regularity, thereby eliminating the major cause of endemic mutiny so instrumental in brutalizing war. But if compensation was steady, Maurice's troops certainly worked for it. Not only were they required to dig siege works and the fortified encampments Vegetius praised so highly, but they were subjected unremittingly to a new kind of drill which would revolutionize military tactics.

With very considerable insight, the historian William McNeill has fastened upon these routines as the core institution of the firepower armies which would dominate European politico-military affairs until at least 1840.[42] Contemporary armies did, of course, train recruits. Maurice differed in being a great deal more systematic and orienting the regimen around weapons drill. Thus, he broke apart the complicated set of movements needed to load and fire a matchlock gun into a series of forty-two successive motions, giving each a name and an appropriate command. Soldiers were relentlessly conditioned to perform each movement in unison, the net effect of which made volley fire easy and natural, thus further enhancing the shock effect on enemy lines. Finally, Maurice took up and meticulously dissected the Spanish countermarch, teaching his men, after firing, to retire precisely between files to reload.

The resulting maneuver was an archetypical blend of ritual dance and mechanistic discipline, at one atavistic and pointed toward the technological future. McNeill writes:

> Such drill, repeated day in day out, had . . . [a] . . . dimension which the Prince of Orange and his fellows probably understood very dimly if at all. For when a group of men move their arm and leg muscles in unison for prolonged periods of time, a primitive and very powerful social bond wells up among them. . . . Perhaps even before our prehuman ancestors could talk, they danced around camp fires, rehearsing what they had done in the hunt and what they were going to do the next time.[43]

Yet in another sense there was nothing at all primitive or recessive about Maurice's drills. They were a mélange of highly abstract gestures, largely alien to the heroic standards of the previous era. Rather than intimate physical contact and direct infliction of injury, everything turned on the repetition of second-order movements performed on a killing instrument optimized for long range. To a degree, this had been true of the bow. Yet the motions involved were so much simpler and more direct, and, with the exception of the British longbowman, the probability of lethality so much lower as to constitute a difference in kind. Besides, the bow had only once been the prime arm of a major European infantry force. The musket was and would be the dominant infantry weapon for the next two-and-a-half centuries.

And in this there was much that was hopeful. The reforms of Maurice and his fellows would provide a palliative to a great deal that had gone wrong, or rather wild, in this period of military history. The extremely close control of troops, the regularization of their existence, and the abstraction of aggression all implied a ritualization of combat much more in consonance with the characteristics of intraspecific aggression. If, in the long run, it did not prove to be a foolproof system, it did at least provide a metastable means of using firearms without totally brutalizing warfare.

Yet Maurice and his well-trained mercenaries never really won a decisive victory in the field. They simply learned to hold their own against the heretofore invincible tercio. Thus, the reforms spread only slowly to Protestant Germany and hardly at all to Catholic Europe.[44] Nowhere were they followed to their logical conclusion.

Even granting the humane implications of close-order musket drill, there was an entirely darker side to the armaments developed and brought into play by the Dutch in their struggle for independence.

The most spectacular was in the form of an infernal engine, built by the Dutch to the specifications supplied by the Italian military engineer Giambelli. Disguised as a fire ship, it was in reality an enormous floating time bomb, its hull lined with bricks, studded with scrap iron and gunpowder, and fused by clockworks. On 5 April 1585, the ironically named *Hope* drifted on the tide against a densely manned pontoon bridge which the duke of Parma had laboriously constructed to lay siege to Antwerp. As some Spanish pikemen attempted to extinguish what appeared to be a sulky blaze, the entire ship blew up, strewing wreckage in a circle a mile in diameter.[45]

While no exact figures were reported by the mortified Spaniards, the number of killed and wounded may have exceeded two thousand. Even if considerably lower, this would still constitute far and away the greatest number of casualties ever to have been inflicted by the discharge of a single weapon. The instantaneous extinction of thousands was something new in death dealing, and the *Hope* was a monument to ponder. Although now only barely remembered, the ''Hell-burner of Antwerp'' was the conceptual progenitor of the devices which today so threaten our existence, demonstrating almost four hundred years before the fact the technical aptitude and appetite for mass annihilation.

To further reinforce the point, the Dutch engaged in still more wanton acts of destructiveness, waging war, when all else failed, on the very land itself. For, even at this point, Holland and Zeeland were composed of lands won largely from the North Sea and protected from its waves by a unique network of dikes, pumps, and windmills. Thus, the will to oblivion first manifested itself in the prince of Orange's order in 1573 to open the sea dikes and flood the land around Alkmaar rather then give the town up to the Spanish.[46] On this occasion the Spaniards lifted the siege before the land was totally drowned. Yet Orange's desperation did not abate, and three years later, when the war seemed all but lost, he unveiled a scheme to flood the entire country and embark the population aboard ship in an attempt at transoceanic migration.[47] The political situation improved, and the plan was never carried out, yet few doubt its sincerity. War had reached such a point that, given the requisite technical capability, literally nothing was exempt from the possibilities of violence. Despite the mitigating influence of Maurice's reforms, this was probably the most enduring lesson of the Dutch wars of independence.

The fact that the Dutch, in extremis, chose to take refuge with the sea raises one final and vital point. Ultimately, the sea was the basis for survival. The Dutch were a nation of mariners, and it was the wealth generated by far-flung commerce which provided the basic counterweight against the hegemonic Spaniard.

IV

The naval world of 1588 was a far different place than it had been just a few years prior. A fundamental shift from south to north, from Mediterranean to Atlantic had occurred which not only would have far-reaching effects on subsequent economic and demographic history but was to a great extent based on military innovation.

As noted earlier, the Arsenal at Venice was primarily responsible for the development of the first truly successful warship based on firearms, the galleon. By combining full ship's rigging, heavily reinforced internal construction, and a low hull aspect optimized for gun placement, the Venetians had created a military archetype destined to last for three hundred years. Yet there would be no immediate military advantage since in 1570 the Arsenal, by this time a major ammunition storage facility, blew up, with catastrophic results.[48] In a moment the republic became a naval power of the second order. As a testimony to her resilience, the city did form the Holy League and the next year participated in the great naval triumph over the Turks at Lepanto. Yet it was a sterile victory, lacking in political significance and fought with galleys, a doomed class of ships.

The naval future would be contested by the states facing the North Atlantic— Catholic Spain on one side and the Protestant Dutch and English on the other. And it was here on the high seas that the sail-powered warships would prove so spectacularly successful, enabling their owners to project firepower unheard of distances and in the process create world-girding empires.

Spain, however, took to the sea with the motives and inclinations of an imperial land power. As with Rome, the ocean was simply a means of coming to grips with her enemies and a conduit to obtain colonial tribute. Therefore, although commerce was involved, Spanish naval power was primarily a state enterprise aimed at strategic integration.

Meanwhile, as Motley noted 130 years ago, "Driven forth from their narrow isthmus by tyranny, the exiled Hollanders took to the ocean . . . transforming a peaceful seafaring people into a nation of corsairs."[49] Sailing their armed fishing smacks and coastal traders in and among the channels and shoals of their half-submerged land, the Dutch were virtually invincible and dealt with Spaniards who came after them accordingly. Perhaps because they had always earned their living from the sea, these lethal "sea beggars" were quick to put their military advantage on a paying basis by directly attacking Spanish lines of communications and shipping. As early as 1569, the prince of Orange was commissioning privateers to this purpose, and three years later the great Lisbon fleet was intercepted off Walcheren, yielding a net of five hundred thousand gold crowns, enough to keep the war effort going for at least two years.[50] Such windfall profits not only made further Dutch depredations inevitable but also drew in their even more aggressive fellow Protestants and naval collaborators, the English.

The career of Sir Francis Drake serves to epitomize the Spanish naval predicament. A driven man, dedicated practically from adolescence to wreaking personal havoc on Philip's empire, "El Draque" became virtually the devil incarnate to Spaniards who plied the seas, intercepting plate ship after plate ship and even further disrupting the staggering Iberian economy. By 1586 not a single bar of

Peruvian or Mexican silver safely crossed the Atlantic.[51] Humiliation followed the next year when the indefatigable Englishman attacked the Spaniards in their naval base at the Bay of Cádiz, demonstrating, in the process, the complete superiority of gun-based sailing warships over galleys even in sheltered waters.[52]

Yet Philip still hoped for revenge. In the early 1580s, shortly after acquiring Portugal with its extended Atlantic frontage and seafaring population, the king asked the Marquis of Santa Cruz, his Captain General of the Ocean Seas (the very title is revealing), what naval forces would be necessary to support an invasion of England. From that moment the Armada began to take shape.

Like most modern pretender navies, the Armada was largely the creation of a single outstanding individual, in this case Santa Cruz, the Spanish Tirpitz, the Iberian Gorshkov. With limited resources, he did a rather good job. While it is probably true that the grizzled veteran of Lepanto let his experience with galleys cloud his appreciation for firepower, the fleet he assembled was nevertheless a modern one whose core was made up of stoutly built galleons. As Michael Lewis points out, the common conception that the Spaniards had huge ships and the British tiny ones had little basis in fact.[53] The fleets were largely symmetrical.

The British did hold certain significant advantages. The prime architect of the anti-Armada was John Hawkins, outside of Drake the most renowned of the privateers and also the first major innovator in galleon design since the introduction of the class.[54] Like his naval reincarnation, Sir John Fisher, the father of the dreadnought battleship, Hawkins was fascinated with speed and big guns. So he lengthened and narrowed his galleons, at once allowing them to sail closer to the wind and mount more broadside firepower. Fore and aft castles were radically reduced, again not simply adding stability in heavy winds but also because they could mount only light, secondary batteries. Big guns belonged at or near the waterline, fired through hinged ports. Here, Hawkins's collaborator and rival, William Wynter, increasingly replaced the stubby-barreled, point-blank weapons with bronze culverins, long guns capable of casting an eight- or nine-pound shot more than one thousand yards with some pretense of accuracy. Moreover, these guns were mounted on mobile four-wheeled carriages, allowing them to be retracted and loaded inboard fairly rapidly.[55]

The ship which emerged was theoretically invincible—not only faster and able to outsail its Spanish rivals in all weather but capable of engaging them at ranges from which they could not retaliate. Three-and-a-quarter centuries later, this very same proposition would bring forth the HMS *Dreadnought*. It did not work well then, nor would it prove effective against the Armada. Neither were the Spanish successful with their close-in strategy and plethora of short-range man-killers. For, as Geoffrey Parker notes, recent archeological evidence indicates that all the large Spanish guns capable of inflicting significant structural damage at short ranges were mounted on cumbersome two-wheeled, non-retractable carriages that could not be loaded more than twice a day.

In fact, as the two fleets moved together off Plymouth, it was impossible to be sure what would happen. As Garrett Mattingly explains:

Fleets like these were a new thing in the world. . . . Nobody knew what the new weapons would do, or what tactics would make them most effective. This was the beginning of a new era of naval warfare, of the long day in which the ship-of-the-line, wooden-walled, sail driven, and armed with smooth bore cannon, was to be queen of battles, a day for which the armor-plated steam-powered battleship with rifled cannon merely marked the evening.[56]

In the series of running engagements that sputtered and crackled up the Channel, the Spanish alone would fire nearly 125,000 rounds,[57] testifying to the scale of the campaign and the acceptance of firepower aboard ship. Yet neither side could make their plan work. The Spaniards proved utterly unable to close and board, while the nimble British galleons sorely lacked the accuracy to inflict serious structural damage at long ranges. Only when the Homeric urge to move in overcame gunnery theory were the English able to do significant damage, and only because their big guns could fire rapidly, not accurately. But in the end it was the stormy North Atlantic and sheer privation that humbled Philip's Armada.[58]

Nevertheless, the defeat of the Spanish fleet remains a major milestone. The era of the battleship began with an indecisive campaign, yet the English held their ground and retained command of the sea. It was a grip which would not loosen until nearly the middle of the twentieth century. In a very real sense the Armada campaign brought the Royal Navy into being. It had existed before, but this fused its self-consciousness in the white heat of combat and provided the first milestone in an amazing string of victories. Though she would be challenged again, from this point Britannia ruled the waves, and she did so largely with battleships.

The sailing warship was uniquely adapted to stand the test of time. Powered by inexhaustible supplies of wind and guided by precision navigation instruments which were among the hallmarks of European technical supremacy, the range of these vessels was limited only by the availability of water deep enough to float their hulls. Virtually overnight, northern Europe had acquired a unique and formidable instrument of coercion which might be brought practically anywhere with a coastline, carrying very considerable quantities of men and equipment. From a political perspective, one could hardly ask for a more useful device. And, indeed, the great ships became the cartilage of empire, a key factor in the expansion and transcendence of European economics and technology.

Purely as a fighting mechanism, the sailing battleship also had very definite implications for the future of warfare. Like Maurice's automata infantry, tactically they were most naturally used in a formalized and artificial manner, very much in consonance with the major characteristics of intraspecific aggression. Although tactical formations gravitated toward multiple-unit lines of battle, combat within the line was individualized ship versus ship. Moreover, the physical characteristics of wood, wind, and water tended to enforce symmetrical engagement by class. In effect, large ships (those mounting more guns) could always defeat smaller ships but, due to their greater bulk, could not catch them. Hence, like tended to fight like. But this was part of a future as yet to be revealed.

In 1588, men were in no mood for moderation. It was understood that this was a fight to the death, and the ruthless, methodical slaughter of Spaniards shipwrecked on the coast of Ireland by agents of the Elizabethan government was very much in the spirit of the campaign.[59] Whatever the technical implications of the weaponry, the predatory urge had not yet been assuaged.

V

So it was that on land and at sea human ingenuity had come up with tactical solutions which, by the beginning of the seventeenth century, offered the possibility of containing the most destructive implications of firepower technology. Yet in large part the opportunity was not grasped. Northern and central Europe chose instead another half century of bloodletting, a suicidal last stand for the Habsburg dream of hegemony in the face of the inevitable forces of nationalism, and a time when relatively minor differences in Christian doctrine were allowed to blot out any shared sense of humanity among adversaries. In such an environment the gun was naturally used promiscuously and, in doing so, became a major factor in the mayhem.

Although it is a subjective judgment, there is a real sense that the Western way of doing things was brought to the brink during the Thirty Years' War, that the political anarchy and population collapse inflicted on Germany and Bohemia as a result of this conflict were the products of forces intrinsic to the politico-economic system itself. In the end the war would provide a stark example of what might happen should these forces not be tightly controlled. It was a terrible price to pay for a lesson that would eventually be forgotten.

There have been numerous historical explanations for the Thirty Years' War, and no wonder. This was a conflict of practically endless causal ambiguity, a war for all reasons. Looking back at the record, Marxist and religious historians, those emphasizing the role of free will and the prepotent individual, political theorists, and even astrologers have found ample cause to construct a chain of motivation at least roughly in consonance with their particular way of viewing the past.

But, besides a failure to account for each other, all of these explanations share a reluctance to assign a central role to violence itself. The idea that something deep within the developing economic and political structure demanded a great bloodletting is profoundly alien to most conceptions of European history. Yet hegemonism and the singular violence it provokes are the threads which remain most consistent up to and beyond 1648. Like a wandering epidemic, the bloodlust which had beset first Italy, then France and Holland, now engulfed Germany, festering as it never had before and drawing to it soldiers from every corner of Europe.

From the beginning, the course of the war showed itself to be heavily weighted in the direction of predatory aggression. Although individual combat persisted, this was definitely mass warfare, with the size of field armies creeping up to a theoretical preindustrial limit of one hundred thousand.[60] Not unexpectedly, pistol-wielding heavy cavalry assumed an enhanced importance, due in large part to its ability to run down troops seeking to escape combat. Increasingly, the refusal of quarter and the ritual execution of prisoners became the norm after battles. More-

Figure 8. Mass hangings during the Thirty Years' War, depicted in an engraving by Jacques Callot. BBC Hulton Picture Library/Bettmann Archive.

over, the cynicism with which this was accomplished tends to bely all motives beyond those of bloodlust. Depending on personnel needs, captives were either rerecruited by the winners or shot.[61] Repeatedly, Catholic mercenaries serving in Protestant armies were dispatched by their coreligionist conquerors, and vice versa. As befits the cynical motif, the element of sport came to be injected into these mass executions, with prisoners at times carefully lined up in order to determine how many could be felled with a single shot.[62]

To compound matters, the growing size of military forces and the increased logistical support necessitated by their guns insured that the violence was not to be limited to service participants, but would instead be shared by a wide range of noncombatants. With an insectlike rapacity these military juggernauts crept back and forth over Germany and what is now Czechoslovakia, cutting swathes of destruction, burning and looting and eating the countryside into chronic poverty and desolation.

Yet the sieges were worse. Though clearly less dominant than in the Netherlands campaigns, this form of action nevertheless reached new levels of brutality in the Thirty Years' War, escalating the same pattern of looting, mass rape, and indiscriminate killing into a frenzy of violence that was the grotesque fate of Magdeburg. History has seldom witnessed a scene so twisted as the victorious Te Deum sung in the redeemed cathedral amid the twenty thousand shallow graves and blackened ruins of the formerly Lutheran city. In order to save the town, it seems, it was necessary to destroy it.

There is, however, another school of thought on the Thirty Years' War, one which argues that this cataclysmic interpretation is an exaggeration. Strategic points certainly suffered, concedes S. H. Steinberg, but "the majority of towns never saw an enemy within their walls." Traditional estimates of a 30 to 50 percent population decline are similarly rejected as "purely imaginary," reflecting "an ignorance of scientific demography."[63] Even Geoffrey Parker, no sympathizer with this point of view, notes that the plague and war-related food shortages were much greater killers than the actual battles.[64]

Yet such a perspective largely ignores the centrality of the war in interrupting normal economic and hygienic functions, thereby creating the necessary conditions for major population collapse. Further, revisionists do not adequately account for the opinions of contemporaries that this was truly a time of horror and devastation. Arguing away such sources (letters, diaries, and chronicles) as the product of the bourgeois who lost the most does not remove illiteracy as a factor preventing the peasantry from recording their own suffering. Similarly, maintaining that rural depopulation was simply part of a migration to the city does not blot out its reality or the misery and starvation it engendered. Charles Wilson has labeled the revisionist case as "too neat and insouciant," [65] and it would seem that most contemporary authorities agree. Thus, the Belgium demographer Father Roger Mols, whose study of the period is considered the most sophisticated and reliable, supports traditional estimates of a 30 to 40 percent decline in habitation of those areas directly affected. [66] In short, the war really was a catastrophe.

In weighing the factors leading up to this conclusion, it is hard to dismiss the role of the gun. Whether serving as ready-made thumbscrews for peasants intent on hiding their food or women, shooting prisoners before a firing squad, or impelling Tilly's officers to melt down church spires for ammunition, firearms technology contributed both directly and indirectly to the burden which the war imposed. [67] Yet as all other forms of logistics collapsed, guns and powder remained plentiful, holding out the promise of turning peasants into soldiers with just a few weeks' training and thereby artificially enlarging the force structure and prolonging its ability to fight. So the war staggered on, orchestrated by the staccato crackle of gunfire. Yet the dance it produced was increasingly characterized by exhaustion, a lumbering shuffle to nowhere whose only real purpose, it seemed, was to grind the lives of innocents underfoot.

Nor was the realm of princes immune. In more than a few ways, Wallenstein and Gustav Adolph, the war's two outstanding personalities, were made by the gun. Like personal magnets, they became focal points for all of the military trends which had surrounded the early history of firepower technology, and in the crucible of their lives there emerged a new way of fighting. But not before it destroyed them both.

The dark figure of Wallenstein, violent, passionate, and insatiable, emerged out of the obscurity of the minor Bohemian nobility to become the war's greatest *condottiere,* master of a sprawling military enterprise whose ultimate purpose was as much to make money as it was to dominate. He was military capitalism personified, not a great general but a great businessman. In this capacity he turned his huge and semiautonomous estates in Friedland into a vast magazine capable of arming and equipping a personal army which numbered five hundred thousand at its peak. C. W. Wedgewood suggests that Wallenstein was the first European ruler to "conceive of a state organized exclusively for war." [68] She misses the point. He was no statesman. Wallenstein was and always would be a military contractor, albeit on a heroic scale. This is why his duchy of Friedland was turned to supplying his army with such ruthless efficiency. It was simply cost-effective.

Yet it was this pragmatism which also beckoned his doom. With continued exposure to the power structure, he would come to be perceived as pernicious.

His flamboyant disregard for the older standards of morality and propriety was no affectation, but went instead to the roots of his utilitarian soul. Birth and piety meant nothing to him in his choice of associates; only personal effectiveness mattered.[69] To an age steeped in ascribed status, this was revolutionary and dangerous. Yet blinded by astrologers and peculation, Wallenstein allowed himself to forget that the essence of war was military and political, not capitalistic. So he ran afoul of the power structure, which simply fired him, and then turned to an army meticulously prepared to fight, not turn a profit.

In the end, rampant capitalism and war did not mix well. The endless depredations of mercenaries, the cynicism and ruthlessness of politics, the very desultory nature of the campaigns were testimonies to the mismatch. As military contractor writ large, Wallenstein came to personify all these contradictions, and for this he was destroyed—the first and last of his breed.

The future belonged instead to armies chained ineluctably to the will of the state. And it was Gustav Adolph of Sweden who made such forces possible by taking up the reforms of Maurice and forging them into a coherent and battle-worthy system.

In this mangled segment of time, politics were never kinder to anyone than Gustav Adolph. Like Alexander of Macedon, it was his personal good fortune to be blessed with an evangelical cause in perfect consonance with his own and his nation's self-interest. Each had inherited, at an early age, a kingdom rife with internal dissension, the energy from which was successfully channeled outward in the form of a crusade. So it was that Sweden, though palpably threatened by the Imperialists, invaded Germany to save Protestantism. Master propagandists, Alexander and Gustav both justified themselves brilliantly in terms of contemporary ideals while plotting each move with the care of a diamond cutter. Like Alexander, Gustav characteristically wrapped himself in the mantle of transnational hero, yet beneath it remained the ruthless practicality of the military opportunist. For all was based on coercive power and its skillful exercise. Thus, just as the young king of Macedon had displayed a notable receptivity to military invention and combined-arms techniques, Gustav set about to equip and integrate his forces so that one might support the other. He succeeded so well that his system would last for 170 years.

Though Gustav Adolph cannot be accused of avoiding mercenaries while in Germany, it remains true that the core of his forces continued to be a conscript army established by his royal predecessor, Gustav Vasa, around 1550.[70] Not only were they impeccably loyal, but so long as Gustav Adolph lived, Swedish troops proved decidedly less brutal than their purely mercenary counterparts. Certainly, they were better trained and drilled.

Gustav Adolph's instructor Jacob De la Gardie had been a student at Siegen, the military academy set up by Maurice for Protestant noblesse.[71] Yet the lessons he faithfully transmitted to his royal pupil emerged much changed, metamorphosed into something a great deal more complete and systematic. In the fertile imagination of the young Swedish king, Europe's military future was taking shape.

The centerpiece of Gustav's battlefield was the infantry. Although he reintroduced the pike to stabilize the formation, his primary emphasis was on firepower.[72] Not unexpectedly, Swedish troops were subjected to continuous loading and marching drill, practically from the time of entering the service to the moment of battle. Discipline was rigidly enforced; most notably, every regimental commander was required to read the articles of war to his troops once a month. Even small infractions were severely punished. Yet uniformity of behavior was merely one element of the total process of homogenization.

Soldiers would not only move and act alike, they would look alike. So Gustav became the first major prince of the age to begin dressing his troops in similar garb.[73] And there was more to this than just visual uniformity. Whereas Wallenstein's infantry had a certain vested interest in wearing only an easily removable armband or other similar identifier, the proverbial loyalty of Swedish troops necessitated no such need to change appearances quickly.

As might be expected, the theme carried over to the weapons Gustav gave his foot soldiers to fight with. Not only was the arquebus dropped completely, but its hard-hitting if unwieldy successor, the musket, was standardized in caliber and significantly lightened—though not enough to remove the need for the cumbersome stabilizing fork. To further insure rapidity of loading and an even distribution of fire, paper cartridges with an equal charge and a properly sized ball, the first of their kind, appear to have been introduced.[74] Yet the system did not maximize hitting power until Gustav, having learned from experience, began emphasizing salvo fire, with two, then three, ranks shooting simultaneously.

This technique, however, raised, or rather exaggerated, a fundamental problem with gun-based troops—their almost total vulnerability while loading. This is why Gustav resurrected the pike. But its presence, though helpful, could not overcome the basic fragility of infantry formations dedicated primarily to muzzle-loading guns. Indeed, no amount of internal tinkering could change the ratio by which every concession to stability meant an equivalent diminution in killing capacity.

So Gustav, like Alexander's Macedonians two thousand years prior, turned to the concept of mutual support through combined arms. As in the past, the shock potential of heavy cavalry was not overlooked. Gustav worked hard to get the most out of his small Swedish horse, dropping the pistol caracole in favor of the more intimidating saber charge.[75] Yet a horse formation used in this manner was very much a one-shot proposition, an all-or-nothing weapon both difficult to control and best employed against a demoralized foe. Besides, this was the era of the gun, not the horse, and Gustav, being a man of his times, instinctively sought to protect his firepower with more firepower.

We have seen that, prior to this, artillery tended to be an institutional appendage, joined to armies solely through the contractual bond between civilian specialist and military customer. Gustav sought to change this, forming first a company, then a regiment of integral artillery organized as a distinct and regular branch of the service and manned almost entirely by Swedes.[76] Such a force was not only more aggressive but much more inclined to come to the aid of beleaguered countrymen in the infantry ranks.

Yet it was their weapons which made this possible. For Gustav realized that infantry support meant greatly enhanced mobility, which in turn demanded new fieldpieces. Fortunately, Sweden was blessed with a rapidly expanding metallurgical industry which, as Michael Roberts notes in his masterful biography, could be bent to the royal will.[77] Thus, by careful patronage and close supervision, the Swedish king achieved not only self-sufficiency in armaments but successful innovation in the desired direction. Calibers were reduced, charges premeasured, tubes shortened, and carriages redesigned in a concerted effort aimed at creating truly mobile fieldpieces. Probably most famous was Melkior Wurmbrandt's extremely light, composite-barrelled three-pounder, known to history as Gustav Adolph's "leather gun." Technically a failure, it nevertheless pointed the way to somewhat more robust Swedish regimental pieces which could easily be drawn by a single horse and were largely responsible for the Swedes' military success in Germany. Firing canister and grape out to about three hundred meters, these man shredders, if well deployed and in sufficient numbers, could effectively mask a vulnerable body of infantry and preclude a destabilizing charge by opposing foot soldiers.[78] Yet cavalry moved faster, often fast enough to surprise and overrun artillery batteries, a fact which completed the logical interrelationship of Gustav's battlefield.

The system which emerged was remarkably self-contained and interdependent. The use and defense of each component (infantry, artillery, and cavalry) required cooperation with all the others. Only in concert could such an army survive and fight successfully. A force structure like this was not only conducive to brilliant and cerebral commanders capable of juggling all elements at once, but also was so specialized as to constitute a separate form of existence which might effectively be segregated from everyday life and normal economic functions. This was the great promise of Gustav's reforms—this and the manner in which firearms were captured and accommodated.

Gustav Adolph was unquestionably a weapons innovator, a man with a clear understanding that increasing the deadliness of arms was directly related to tactical success. Nevertheless, his innovative path was that of the opportunistic commander. Primarily, he exploited what was available. Even the "leather gun" was an adaptation, having been seen in Zurich as early as 1623.[79] The experimental approach encouraged by Gustav left no particular tradition in the Swedish arms industry or anywhere else.

Quite the contrary, the major effect on weaponry was conservative. Henceforth, cavalry would rely primarily on the saber, not the pistol; artillery would form an integral tactical and institutional element of the fighting force; and infantry, the keystone of the battlefield, would be made up of highly trained and disciplined units using identical weapons whose performance characteristics were largely dependent on that training and discipline. If Gustav Adolph had any significant effect on the course of arms, it was to reconcile one to the other and place them in a state of equilibrium which would discourage further tinkering.

Yet at the time this was unclear. What was apparent after Gustav smashed Tilly's forces at Breitenfeld in 1631 was firepower, and Wallenstein, in the frenzy of activity which was his second administration, raced to remodel his artillery park to include a variety of light, mobile fieldpieces.[80] But symmetrical arms alone could not transform the basic nature and shortcomings of his force. Meanwhile, Gustav appears to have realized, as had Alexander under similar circumstances, that the war could be ended only by striking at the heart of Habsburg power, through Bavaria and on to Austria and Vienna.[81] So it was that he fell upon Wallenstein, already in winter quarters, and forced him to fight the climactic battle of Lützen in November 1632. Here Swedish infantry took full advantage of their training and discipline to root the Imperialists out of field fortifications and deliver what appeared to be a shattering blow to their cause. As Wallenstein was carried from the field, raging and wounded, he left only scattered remains of an army, "without artillery, without colors, and almost without arms," as Schiller put it.[82]

But Gustav did not live to enjoy the win. In the heat of battle the Homeric spirit overcame the cooler logic of firepower, and the Swedish king rushed off, practically alone, to rally the beleaguered right wing of his army. Almost immediately, he was hit by Imperialist musketeers, first in the arm, then in the back, and finally finished off with a pistol shot to the head. But as his bloody charger, running wild and riderless across the field, carried the tidings of his death to his troops, Gustav's disciplined Swedes only fought the harder, in a final tribute to the system he had taught them.

Politically, the death of Gustav Adolph was a disaster. In a time without guns, Alexander might survive his own heroics to sketch out the basis for a settlement. But now nothing would be settled, and much of Europe would suffer for Gustav's heroic self-indulgence. But few of his fellow princes would have blamed him at the time since the new etiquette of combat spread only slowly among them.

Nevertheless, Gustav's demise removed from the scene the only man capable of imposing an end to the fighting. Instead, the war would drag on for another sixteen years, politically little more than a mordant epilogue to the transnational saga of the Habsburgs. Fought under increasingly disorganized and impoverished circumstances, it revealed completely the inherent contradictions of the military-political model as it had come to exist. Armies increasingly devoid of intelligible political objectives, to say nothing of regular logistics, tended to degenerate into traveling mobs living in a symbiotic relationship with the countryside. Provoked to the point of suicidal rage, the peasantry frequently ran amuck in great, boiling rebellions whose pointlessness was as obvious as their cruelty. Living in the midst of this nightmare, thoughtful men witnessed what was happening with growing disbelief and horror, epitomized in the words of the peripatetic Dutch legal philosopher, Hugo Grotius: "I saw prevailing throughout Europe a licence in making war of which even barbarous nations would have been ashamed."[83] It was true. Europe was tearing itself apart, and in the process was edging toward a moral and intellectual abyss from which there might be no redemption. Yet men like Grotius were not lemmings. If nothing else, their instincts for survival willed them to make rules and stop the madness. And this they did.

Chapter 9

WHEN TIME STOOD STILL

I

Recently, a number of evolutionary biologists have cast doubt upon the conventional view of the development of life as virtually an endless progression of minute and nearly imperceptible modifications. Rather, a new understanding of genetic transmission, the mechanism of extinction, and the possibility of very rapid and all-encompassing environmental change has led to the suggestion that species formation took place in bursts, interspersed with long periods of virtual inertia.

While this hypothesis remains controversial, it is interesting that the course of arms is also best described as intermittent and clustering around major changes in fundamental technology. Yet the normal condition was stability, an equilibrium enforced by the logic of symmetrical arms, among other things.

The period between 1648 and 1850 was such a time, a span of two centuries during which European civilization managed to conduct its martial affairs largely without recourse to more deadly weaponry. That this stasis was supported by an increasingly anachronistic conception of social and political reality only serves to emphasize its robustness.

We, the inheritors of its eventual collapse, tend to view this period of military history as quaint and in large part irrelevant, a foppish aberration. True enough, it was based on a confluence of cultural, political, and technological forces, the resurrection of which cannot be expected.

Yet men of that time, like ourselves, faced the fundamental problem of controlling weapons a great deal more lethal than those which had come before, and in large part they did so successfully. For this they deserve our attention.

The key was moderation, a studied and rigidly enforced limitation of ends which would pervade the European political economic system until 1789 and again for some time after. A good deal has been written about the natural affinity between this system and the political absolutism which flourished contemporaneously. Undeniably, large standing armies and their accompanying tax and support structures were unpopular and therefore most decisively administered by an absolute monarch working, not coincidentally, through his standing army.[1] Similarly, the international officer corps used to manage such forces served admirably as a repository for aristocrats displaced by centralized bureaucracies. But if, in relations between states, the unitary ruler retained the flexibility to operate within such a fluid system, he was also thwarted by it. Absolutism was as old as Sargon. Yet the balance of power confounded what heretofore had been its profoundest tendency, inevitable and insatiable expansion. Rather than transnational tyranny, monarchs of the age were willing to settle for considerably less, a stable position on the European chessboard. Yet this was in no way a natural or inevitable accommodation, as the career of the wild man Charles XII of Sweden illustrates. These were men sorely constrained by the lessons of history, held in check by the recent memory of a century-and-a-half bloodbath. Reluctantly, it came to be accepted that over the long term only moderate ends could promote a moderation of means.

So, rather than manifest the political tendencies of transnational tyranny, the behavior of absolute monarchies came to resemble the multipolar dimensions of city-state-dominated polities such as Sumer or, more importantly, Greece. They too had to grapple with a particularly deadly instrument of war, the phalanx. And their solution was based on a profound ritualization of combat, a series of mitigating procedures which found their roots in the traditions of intraspecific aggression transmitted through the stirring battle images of Homer. Control of the gun demanded an equivalent resort to the rules, a redefinition of what constituted the limits of organized violence.

II

Huigh de Groot, or Grotius as he came to be called, knew war well. He had grown up amid the Dutch rebellion and never forgot its cruelty. Quite possibly this was why his masterpiece, *The Law of War and Peace,* came to be the official practitioner's guide. Like Homer's epics, Grotius's rules were hard rules, taking full measure of the realities and possibilities of mass violence. Yet they were still rules, limits to acceptable conduct which might reasonably be expected to be followed during hostilities.

This was why he was listened to. Though pompous and ineffectual as a diplomat, Grotius was no idealogue. He was a practically oriented jurist intent on circumscribing an institution, the inevitability of which he fully conceded. The question was not whether war would, or should, take place, but how and under what circumstances. In this he was emphatic. War consisted of a special state, the declaration of which had to be clearly stipulated in order for it to be considered "just."[2] Not for humanitarian reasons or to avoid the appearance of treachery, he was quick to add, but so "that it should be known for CERTAIN, that a war is not a PRIVATE undertaking of bold ADVENTURERS, but made and sanctioned by the PUBLIC and SOVEREIGN on both sides" (Grotius's emphasis).[3] This was the first condition of control—establishing who might fight. Henceforth, the lines would be clearly drawn. Only sovereigns and their direct agents had the right to conduct hostilities. All others were freebooters.

But if his conditions for participation were strict, Grotius's rules of conduct were in large part permissive. War remained war, and force, terror, and strategy its "proper agents."[4] Not only was killing in combat sanctioned, but the execution of prisoners, though not justifiable, was granted with impunity to "those who availed themselves of this barbarous custom."[5] A prisoner's vested rights consisted of the privilege of not being sold into slavery. On the other hand, Grotius left no doubt as to where he stood morally. Indeed, he becomes lyrical: "Forbearance in war is not only a tribute to justice . . . it is a tribute to the greatness of the soul."[6] Yet is was ultimately voluntary and impossible to enforce.

So were the rights of property. In theory the conqueror's dominion was absolute, entitling him to virtually free reign over what he took in the process. Yet, in practice, Grotius drew attention to a variety of restraints which had traditionally caused belligerents to exercise moderation in despoiling items such as fruit trees, works of art, and churches.[7] Such temperate behavior, however, had its basis in practical or moral considerations, not in the law of war.

The fact that Grotius's work came to be accepted as canon for the age's martial affairs is suggestive. For the contradictions present in *The Law of War and Peace* were also evident in the actual conduct of military affairs. Civility and moderation were ultimately a matter of choice, not necessity. In the absence of a single source of coercion, Grotius's laws, indeed all laws, were simply codes of conduct rendered workable by mutual cooperation. And war, beneath the puppet uniforms and beau geste, remained a brutal business. But if its black heart beat strong, it did so obscurely, cloaked in a mass of consciously maintained ritual and ceremony. Grotius's successors took considerable pride in their handiwork. If the reality of martial affairs did not exactly match their rhetoric and expectations, the significance of their achievement should not be underestimated. The transition to firearms had proved a major unsettling factor in European history. For two centuries these men succeeded in capturing and integrating the gun into a workable political system, while in large part forestalling the further evolution of the technology upon which it was based. Unfortunately, the arrangement could not survive massive social and economic change. Like Newton's physics, which was at the root of so many Enlightenment conceptions, the politico-military mechanism was a closed system whose precise equilibrium was based on limited inputs, the special nature of which became increasingly apparent with time.

Theoretically, a balance of power might accommodate any political hue. But just as the nature of the phalanx predisposed the Greeks toward a certain type of political participation, the gun and the kind of armies it created imparted a bias toward privilege and inequality in this version of the balance. When the social and economic foundations shifted, the edifice became unstable.

Yet viewed as a static entity, much as a contemporary observer might have done, the system gave every impression of stability and was in fact self-reinforcing along several dimensions. Certainly, the psychological adjustments made to European armies were thoroughly compatible with the maintenance of peace and order in societies rife with class differences. Professional, overwhelming force tightly bound to the bureaucratic will of the prince had the immediate effect of encouraging a level of domestic peace previously unattainable. This, in turn, had a salutary impact on economic conditions, facilitating increases in wealth which made still larger armies feasible as time went on.[8] Indeed, the state of Prussia was literally built on this truism. But if the very prosperity of the age came to be a prime determinant in unbalancing the ancien régime, this was hardly apparent to contemporaries who tended instead to equate wealth and tranquility with the status quo.

Perhaps best of all in the eyes of the ambitious monarch was the way in which the system accommodated what had always been the major obstacle to centralized royal power, the aristocracy. Not only did it remove them, but it did so in a manner that enabled them to be put to good use, doing what they liked to do best—fight.

And by this bit of serendipity, a remarkable scenario came to fruition. The very aristocracy which had been blown out of the saddle by firepower now came to be its chief inheritors. If the aim was to control the gun and forestall further technical evolution, then it could not have been placed in more responsible hands.

Operationally, this conclusion was reinforced by the necessities of the military system. For the training and discipline required by the preferred style of fighting created a particularly heavy demand for supervision, an officer class which the petty nobility, imbued with the habit of command, filled naturally and well.[9] Yet in doing so they imparted a distinctive and reactionary cast to the system. Control and stability came to be virtually ends in themselves—so much so that in an era of growing nationalism the officer class could remain virtually international (the sole prohibition was serving against one's sovereign) since all representatives could be sure of sharing the same authoritarian values.[10]

As much as anything else, these cosmopolitan loyalties enforced the homogenization of military opinion and insured that technical change, when it came, would be judged in largely political, not utilitarian, terms. There was a time when the reactionary machinations of such officers, beset by a host of new weapons, were held up for ridicule. Now, in the face of our own burgeoning arsenals, perhaps the opposite is coming to be true.

It can be argued that there was little of the humanitarian in the fighting prejudices of these officer-aristocrats, that it was simply a matter of self-interest and self-satisfaction. Perhaps, but statements by participants seem to argue the contrary. Soldiers of the age consistently refer to the more humane nature of contemporary warfare and the necessity of keeping it so. Thus, Count Wilhelm von Schaumburg could write with perfect sincerity: "To wage war on the offensive means to serve the evil passions, whilst to dedicate oneself to the defensive means to consecrate oneself to the welfare of mankind."[11] Overstated, perhaps, but there was also a tone of pride which would be hard to muster in the twentieth century.

Certainly, when viewed from an anthropological perspective, the tight rein of the officer-aristocrat led to a reassertion of those patterns of aggression characteristic within the species. Thus, the prevalence of maneuver and proverbial reluctance to give battle can be seen as a form of posturing and threat behavior, as

Figure 9. Formalized nature of eighteenth-century land warfare. Anonymous paint-ing of the Battle for the Crossing of the Dvina, 1701. Royal Palace, Dotringholm, Sweden/Bridgeman Art Library.

well as representing a pragmatic respect for the weaponry and the consequences of engagement. Similarly, the brightly colored uniforms and the precisely metered deployment of troops not only served a certain military purpose, but also reflected common paradigms of intraspecific aggression. So did the phenomenon of a pre-ferred battleground, a "duelling field," as John Childs calls it, in the Spanish Netherlands.[12] Scene of countless engagements, it was at once a measure of polit-ical reality (almost everybody wanted it) and harkened back to the ritual battle-fields of the Greeks, and the leks which certain animals habitually employ to determine dominance. Here, too, the prevalence of set-piece battles and the ten-dency to restrict siege warfare to purely military fortifications had the effect of eliminating all but grown males from the roster of combatants.

Once again, sexuality became associated with the warrior class, the concupis-cent young officer becoming an almost archetypical swain in both literature and reality. In the case of the hussars, a form of light cavalry descended from Hun-garian irregulars, this was not even limited to officers. Resplendent in fur caps, tight britches, bright tunics with horizontal frogging across the chest, even fur-trimmed jackets slung over the shoulder, these swaggering examples of genetic advertising earned a reputation as lovers far more devastating than any perfor-mance they gave on the battlefield.[13] Nonetheless, hussars were merely exagger-ations of trends evident elsewhere in the military establishment.

The rigid symmetry of arms maintained throughout the period also was in consonance with intraspecific aggression, and was the key determinant of the static ritual nature of combat when it did take place. While individual models and dimensions differed slightly, all armies in the eighteenth century were armed basically alike.[14] To be sure, the fact of identical weaponry was not dwelled upon. In those few cases in which innovations of significance appeared—the flintlock and the bayonet, for instance—they were quickly adopted by all, stabilizing the situation but provoking little impetus for further change.[15] As we shall see, talk of arms development, when it existed, was rather studiously ignored. And, in general, there can be little doubt that weapons symmetry was viewed as the natural order of things.

As with the Greeks, armament was highly lethal. But the central aim of combat was not to kill. Rather, it was to persevere. Therefore, pursuit of the defeated was almost always perfunctory, prisoners were generally well treated, and acts of slaughter became a rarity.

Combat, of course, was a massed affair. Indeed, the identical nature of force structures made pure numbers very important and undoubtedly contributed to the steady growth of armies over time.[16] Nevertheless, the phenomenon of individual combat persisted, even thrived, though not exactly on the battlefield.

This was the day of the duel. While private fighting was certainly nothing new, evidence, such as the frequency of admonitions against duelling, seems to indicate that it reached its apex in the late seventeenth and early eighteenth centuries.[17] As might be expected, the contests tended to take place under strict conditions (there were several attempts at codification, the most famous being the Galway code duello of 1777) and were generally concerned with matters of protocol or sexual access to females. Participation was scrupulously limited to those perceived to be of the upper classes, with officers, constituting by far the largest occupational group.[18]

But if the aristocracy controlled the field of honor, much as it controlled the battlefield, here too it was necessary to make concessions to weaponry. As the period began, duels were typically fought with one of a variety of specialized swords. With time, however, individual combatants increasingly switched to pistols—this in spite of their replacement as cavalry weapons by sabers.[19] Quite apparently, the new definition of courage had taken hold, with the impassive fortitude of the unflinching pistoleer coming to be preferred over the aggressive, point-blank orientation of the swordsman.

The lessons of the duke of Parma's spoilt luncheon served admirably in this new context. Yet further accommodation proved largely unnecessary. To a great degree, the aristocracy remained able to define the actual conduct of military affairs according to its own whims and preconceptions. Thus, armies came to epitomize social relationships as the warrior class had always seen them. In the words of Saint-Germain: "As things are, the army must inevitably consist of the scum of the people. . . . We must therefore rely on military discipline to purify and mold the mass of corruption and turn it into something useful."[20]

Depending on the metaphorical orientation of those involved, foot soldiers became, under such a regime, either superbly trained animals or automata. In either case, they were relegated to the state of an operational abstraction: "units of fire."

The prevalence of small tin soldiers, not only in the toy chests of future commanders but also on the game boards of actual field marshals and princes, is suggestive. So too are the cadet regiments of playmates bestowed upon both little Frederick the Great and young Peter the Great (he was never little), or the most flagrant example of all, the Potsdam regiment of giants so passionately collected by Frederick's father, Frederick William.[21] Real soldiers became, by an extension of this logic, things to be dressed up, marched around, and shot. In this respect they were toys, and are perhaps best viewed as such. For one central theme of the age was the determination that war not degenerate into a manhunt but remain instead a game.

A deadly and vicious game it was, however. And for the most part, as John Childs has pointed out, the common soldier bore the brunt of it.[22] For, at the critical moment, the system required him to stand imperturbably at point-blank range, disdaining all cover, and fire methodically into the enemy ranks until either small arms, cannonball, or cavalry saber cut him down. Not unexpectedly, battle casualties, as a ratio of those engaged, remained high and, when combined with attrition through sickness, left the actuarial prospects of the average infantryman decidedly dim.[23] This was the dark side of the Enlightenment conception of war. It was a system built on the back of a large sacrificial beast whose participation was always based on compulsion more than self-interest. As Frederick the Great would write, the infantrymen "must be made to fear their officers more than the perils to which they are exposed."[24]

Granted, the prospect of shelter, steady pay (in most cases it was scrupulously so), and access to some of the flashiest clothes available was not to be overlooked by the displaced agricultural laborers who made up the major portion of infantry. Nevertheless, the conditions of battle and the unpleasantness of training were sufficiently notorious to make the prospect of military life an anathema to all but the most desperate. Consequently, compulsion and trickery played a major role in recruitment throughout the period.[25] Conversely, all the major European armies suffered continuous attrition through desertion. More than once, overextended armies simply melted away.

Obviously, such troops could not be allowed to forage on their own. While on campaign they had to be fed regularly, a logistical task of truly monumental proportions. This was not only complex and expensive, it had the effect of tying organized forces to enormous, slow-moving wagon trains running into the thousands of vehicles and carrying not only provisions but the very ovens used to bake bread. Further laden with guns and ammunition, armies became effectively shackled entities, capable of only the most ponderous strategic maneuver.[26] Yet there were certainly stabilizing compensations. Not only was the ability to strike at the heart of another state effectively curbed, but even more important, armies were largely removed from the circumstances under which the worst depredations of the Thirty Years War had taken place. Regular nutrition, then, became a prime mechanism in the system of control to which the soldier and his weapon were to be subjected.

Yet in the eyes of his masters, the officer-aristocrats, the preferred solution remained the stick rather than the carrot—constant observation and supervision accompanied by heavy doses of brain-numbing drill. In the British army the ratio of officers to men grew to one to nineteen, and in the Prussian army, one to twenty-nine.[27] But if noncommissioned officers are counted, total supervisory personnel must have fallen not far short of 10 percent. By most accounts they stayed busy. For it was generally agreed that it required at least one year to teach a man the rudiments of soldiering and five or more to make a full-fledged veteran of him.[28] Among other things, this presupposed a large initial investment of time and resources, the value which it imparted to its recipients being among the sole mitigating factors in his existence. Trained troops were simply too valuable to be wasted.

The sheer complexity of turning a man into a soldier should not be underestimated. Consider, for example, this typical sequence of battalion training described by de Guignard in his *Ecole de Mars* in 1725.[29] Responding to a distinctive series of drum calls (*"Au Champs," "Generale,"* and *"Drapeau"*), the men initially formed up in close order and marched off under arms to the parade ground. Here the sergeants formed them up into five ranks and prepared for weapons drill. Officers took positions front and rear to supervise the evolutions, which in this case were governed by the "ordinance" of 2 March 1703 stipulating sixty-seven separate movements. Arms drill was then followed by "evolutions at the halt," concerned with countermarching by ranks and files, opening and closing files, and reducing the ranks. Next came firing practice, usually divided into fire by single ranks, fire by successive ranks to the rear, fire to the flanks, and general discharge of three or even four ranks simultaneously. The men also practiced forming squares by divisions and hollow squares facing inward to witness that most ubiquitous of eighteenth-century military motivators, punishment.

Soldiers were beaten, whipped, or hanged with more or less frequency by the various armies of Europe. Prussia was the most flagrant in this regard, but even under milder regimes the discipline was exceedingly harsh by today's standards. It was no accident that the name of the French itinerant inspector of training, Lieutenant Colonel Martinet, passed into our language as a symbol of authoritarian insistence on obedience down to the last detail.[30] His intent, and that of his colleagues, was total submission to an utterly contrived and counterintuitive behavior sequence. The means adopted, as befit the agricultural origins of those involved, were based primarily on the time-honored rites of animal training—breaking the spirit through a healthy measure of negative reinforcement and, above all, repetition.

Describing the complexity of training or its enforcement does not get at its essence, which was endless iteration. As noted earlier, the psychological state engendered by countless hours of repeating precisely the same motions, marching along at exactly seventy-five paces per minute each seventy-four centimeters in length, is not to be ignored. If Frederick the Great could write: "I come from drill. I drill. I will drill—that is all the news I can give you."[31] Think of how his troops must have felt. Gradually, the monumental boredom and commitment to activities having no meaning except in relation to the group had the effect of blotting out or at least dimming the individual consciousness sufficiently so that even the gore and chaos of combat could not interrupt the precision of the desired motions.

It worked. Troops trained in this manner consistently exhibited great discipline and fortitude under the most appalling circumstances, stoically performing their mechanical ballet while literally being blown apart. This attitude was at once the system's greatest strength and its ultimate failing. Unlike the methods of the Romans, whose *gladius* demanded a more activist mentality, the training procedures of the eighteenth century required and got little more than passive acceptance. For all the talk of bayonet charges, these were not particularly spirited or loyal troops. In most instances their behavior proved sufficient for its intended purpose, but in the face of a major crisis, endurance proved no match for enthusiasm.

It could be argued that conditions were a good deal better, and loyalties stronger, in the two other elements of the eighteenth-century armies—cavalry and artillery. Clearly, horsemen and gunners were recruited from more prosperous elements of society, and pay was inevitably better for both.[32] Not only did they escape the harshest aspects of discipline enforcement, but the risks of combat were significantly lower. Logically enough, espirit de corps among these elements did tend to be higher, and desertion rates correspondingly lower.[33] Nevertheless, neither horsemen nor gunners were immune to the mind-numbing tedium of training, each suffering under their own specialized drill routines in most armies. More to the point, these elements were very much in the minority numerically, constituting between 20 and 30 percent for cavalry and perhaps 2.5 percent for artillery.[34]

In almost every way the foot soldier was the centerpiece of the battlefield. Though other components played a vital and frequently decisive tactical role, it was the infantry around which all revolved. And, more than anything else, it was the nature of these troops and their use which imparted a distinctive cast to eighteenth-century warfare.

As noted earlier, the necessity of deploying men in very elongated formations to maximize their firepower also rendered them terribly vulnerable. Once a line like this was cut or started to fall apart at one point, the whole was very likely to crumble. Even orderly retreat under fire was difficult and dangerous. All too often panic and flight were the infantryman's only viable means of getting off the battlefield.

Or he could stand and fight. In essence, it was a psychological proposition, a thin line of men staking everything on their ability to perform a prescribed ritual while being subjected to the most horrifying possibilities—opposing infantry blasting away, cannonballs whizzing by, and the ever-present danger of cavalry, their thundering horses and their razor-sharp sabers—all really aimed at pushing the foot soldier over the edge. Quite naturally, the use of reserves also took on an increasing importance. For in an environment in which steadiness and precise movement under extreme stress were critical, fresh troops had an enormous advantage.

Yet if infantry were sufficiently well trained and numerous enough to maintain a steady rate of fire and execute the proper defensive evolutions, they could hold off virtually any foe. For reserves really only constituted more of the same fire to be endured, while cavalry generally could not charge a well-deployed defensive square with success. Nor could cannon, except at very close range with case shot, really do that much damage to a stretched-out line of men. So infantry remained the key, and tactics found their proper home at the juncture between fight and flight.

Yet in another sense the infantryman was little more than an extension of his own weapon. For ultimately the reality of the gun stood behind the contrived nature of military training and engagement. Looked at from this perspective, tactics became a prime means of arms control, or at least one of its major evocations. In the firepower equation, men were assigned most of the variables; weapons remained largely the constants. Thus, infantry might learn to fire fast (though aiming was not encouraged), but their weapons were not to be subject to conscious and sustained improvement.

This does not mean that there were no technical developments. There were several innovations of lasting significance, but their net effect was to reinforce the system, and adoption was based largely on compatibility with tactical preconceptions. In no sense was there commonly held to be a fundamental relationship between invention and military success.

The generic muzzle-loading musket, which would remain the basic European small arm until at least 1850, was finalized from a design perspective around the turn of the eighteenth century with several key innovations, the bayonet and the flintlock firing mechanism being the most important.[35] In the former instance, the need to protect musketeers while loading had led to the perpetuation of the pike, as noted earlier. Yet the elongated shape of small arms suggested an alternate solution, the attachment of a knife at or near the muzzle to create, in effect, an instant pike.

How exactly to join knife and gun remained a problem. After early attempts using flexible cord or plugging the barrel proved unsatisfactory, the socket bayonet, based on a sleeve which could be slid over the muzzle and secured with a lug and slot, provided a permanent solution.[36]

So the bayonet became a stable feature of the battlefield, a sort of last refuge of the infantryman shorn of his firepower. As would happen with a number of other weapons developments, the heroic definition of courage would seek to reassert itself, this time with the persistent fantasy of the bayonet charge. In reality, though, the bayonet's primary tactical significance was not offensive but defensive, as a means of protection.

The bayonet performed another function which was of significance for the working of the system: it homogenized infantry. Eliminating the pike insured perfect symmetry among foot soldiers, transforming them into standardized fighting modules capable of being plugged into any number of military combinations, a feature of no small import to a political mechanism whose primary balance wheel was coalition.

The replacement of the matchlock with a triggering device based on striker-generated flint sparks was also a marked advance, but a conservative one. Lowering misfires from 50 to 33 percent was both advantageous and acceptable in a regime permissive toward increases in the rate, though not necessarily the effectiveness, of fire. But perhaps more important, as David Chandler notes, was the simplification of loading procedures from the matchlock's forty-four steps to twenty-six for the flintlock.[37] Henceforth, more men could be trained in a shorter time to fire faster, a change which reinforced several acceptable variables while contradicting no important constants. This was also true of the iron ramrod, introduced in Prussia around 1720 and quickly copied elsewhere.[38] It offered nothing in the way of a gain in performance, simply a faster and more reliable means of loading.

Tactically, the resulting increased volume of fire from these innovations did have the effect of reducing the ranks from five to three.[39] Yet this simply further stretched what were already elongated formations. On the other hand, the fact that the iron ramrod and flintlock brought about basically no improvements in hitting power, range, or accuracy insured that the distances and conditions of engagement would remain stable.

Moreover, with the grafting of bayonet, iron ramrod, and flintlock onto the musket, small-arms development basically ceased. Archetypical was the case of "Brown Bess." First issued to English forces in 1703, this .76-caliber smooth-bore was perhaps the best general-issue firearm available in Europe during the eighteenth century. Destined to survive in slightly modified form for nearly 140 years, "Brown Bess" enjoyed a production run estimated at 7,800,000 with virtually worldwide distribution.[40]

The key to the gun's performance could be seen in the .71-caliber lead ball it fired. For the .05 windage left between ball and barrel was a concession to fast loading and insured that the musket's nominal range of 250 yards was actually reduced to not over 60 yards with any accuracy. But, of course, aiming was not encouraged. It was rate of fire which was judged to be critical, and in this category "Brown Bess" was impressive indeed, being capable of five shots per minute in the hands of an expert.[41] Theoretically, then, a fully trained force of two thousand might fire off ten thousand shots in sixty seconds, a fusillade sure to generate enough smoke to make all aim irrelevant after the first few volleys.

But if most shots were bound to miss, the infernal atmospherics, concussive sound, and obvious effects on those unlucky enough to be hit with almost an ounce of flying lead at point-blank range were sufficient to convince all but the most skeptical that this was truly a deadly and decisive means of combat. Used corporately, "Brown Bess" and her Continental equivalents gave every impression of being formidable weapons, their very ubiquity and similarity being prime indicators that they were not to be easily surpassed. If there already did exist relevant innovations such as rifling and revolver-based breech-loading mechanisms, their possibilities were easily enough ignored in an environment dedicated to the assumption that the variables of battle should not properly include weaponry.

While manifesting itself somewhat differently, the urge for control also played a major role in the development of artillery through most of the eighteenth century. Unlike the skills associated with other combat arms, gunnery was increasingly coming to be understood as a scientific and mathematical pursuit demanding advanced education and knowledge not ordinarily associated with the officer-aristocrat. Instead, the profession tended to draw the more technically oriented and frequently bourgeois types not easily assimilated into an army structure based on privilege and ascribed status. While the militarizing of artillery units, begun by Gustav Adolph, gained momentum slowly, the persistence of massive ordnance establishments, existing largely independent of the armies they served, tended to reinforce the trend toward separateness.[42]

But a want of lateral restraint did not preclude control from above. In fact, the survival of these ordnance establishments, whose authority extended from the manufacture, testing, and servicing of the cannon themselves to the education and training of their crews, was generally based on the direct patronage of the monarch. When Louis XIV had his cannon inscribed with the motto *Ultima Ratio Regis* (the last argument of the King), he probably meant it literally. For the special relationship between the prince and his artillery was based on important practical considerations. If infantry was the focal point of battle, it was cannon which were considered to be the most lethal individually. As such, they were hoarded by monarchs, prized as symbols of power. Yet a political condominium based on limited objectives also demanded that wanton deadliness be curbed and that weapons like the cannon grow no more destructive.

It seems more than coincidental that the course of artillery, at least until 1775, was largely retrograde. Numerically, this was represented by a diminution in the ratio of cannon to infantry from a high of four per thousand in the later armies of Gustav Adolph and Wallenstein to an average of 1.5 per thousand in twenty-one selected engagements between 1690 and 1745.[43] Moreover, tactically, artillery units were conceived of and used almost exclusively as defensive assets, primarily to protect the infantry. Such an orientation was obviously reinforced by considerations of mobility, or lack of it. Rather than follow up on Swedish success with very light fieldpieces, the majority of guns up to 1750 weighed in at a hefty three tons apiece if trails and carriages are included. This despite the discovery by one Antonio Gonzales, around 1680, that by refashioning the powder chamber from a cylindrical to a spherical shape, a great deal smaller charge could be used to generate the same range and penetration, thereby opening the way for dramatically lighter pieces.[44]

Yet the possibilities went largely unexploited. Consequently, when the Marquis de la Frezeliere, the French lieutenant general of artillery, promoted chamber designs based on the new concept, he not only met the most bitter opposition; but upon his death all his improved pieces were recast in the older manner.[45] Half a century later, when Joseph Florent de Valliere reduced the number of French pieces to four standardized calibers, he too chose to include only the older, heavier types.[46] Similarly, Louis XV is reputed to have refused to permit the use of a newly perfected gunpowder on the grounds that it was "too destructive to human life."[47]

Nor were the French alone in their conservatism. Fieldpieces used by all the major powers up to at least 1775 differed from one another only in detail; the archetype consisted of a bronze tube cast in a cored mold, a process which insured both excessive weight and considerable imprecision in dimensions and, therefore, accuracy. Even after 1740, when a Swiss perfected a method of boring out a solid billet, thereby producing a much truer barrel, the powers were slow to capitalize on the possibilities.[48]

As with the musket, it is clear that accuracy was not heavily emphasized.

Hence, the premeasured cartridges of Gustav Adolph were frequently overlooked in favor of the traditional powder ladle. Carriages and precise elevating mechanisms were similarly neglected until 1750. In part this was a reflection of the copious, target-obscuring smoke generated by black powder. Yet even under ideal atmospheric conditions, aiming simply consisted of squinting down the center line for direct fire or, alternately, raising the tube to forty-five degrees, which was widely and erroneously held to give maximum range.[49]

But perhaps of even greater importance in stabilizing the conditions of eighteenth-century warfare, at sea as well as on land, was the disinclination to employ anything but solid shot in strictly military engagements. Hollow, explosive-filled shells were certainly available, mortars being one of the prime means of bombardment during sieges, appropriately enough. Howitzers, too, fired a bursting shell.[50] Yet direct-fire pieces, clearly the dominant artillery weapon, would be fed no explosive shells. It was argued that the necessity of lighting the fuse before shooting was exceedingly dangerous. But after experiments around 1740 revealed that the initial blast of the cannon could be relied on to pass around the windage to ignite the shell fuse no matter what its position, this was no longer a tenable excuse.[51]

However, there was no corresponding rush to develop and employ ammunition which promised to blow apart stationary infantry formations as well as the thick oak sides of capital warships. Case shot, based on a variety of subprojectiles ranging from musket balls to nails, was employed against infantry and cavalry at close ranges but without secondary charges.[52] In fact, it is possible to say, until 1850, the application of chemical energy as a destructive agent rather than as a propellant was highly circumscribed. Since this does not appear ultimately to have been based on practical considerations, we are left to assume it was largely a matter of choice or, more precisely, a convenient disinclination to follow up on certain possibilities.

III

The great exception was siege warfare, where not only shell-firing mortars but large explosive mines were used as a matter of course. Here technology was anything but stagnant. Rather, it was applied with an increasingly scientific orientation to a variety of military problems facing both besieger and besieged. Yet this process was dominated by a single person, Sébastien Le Prestre de Vauban, and his ultimate commitment was to defend, not overcome.

Orphaned at ten and extremely poor, Vauben began his career as a private during the early campaigns of Louis XIV. Yet he had been carefully schooled in mathematics, and his knack for practical applications soon drew attention and later assignments of increasing responsibility.[53] France being in a period of expansion, Vauban was primarily directed to devise new forms of attack. To more effectively batter down defenses, he was the first to exploit the possibilities of ricochet, though he objected to the name, which he thought implied trickery. Yet more importantly, Vauban devised a systematic methodology for approaching forts by parallel trenches minutely calculated to provide the best firing angles and the most protection for his troops. Most decidedly, his emphasis was on the latter. Vauban's techniques were slow and required enormous labor, but his trenches provided cover right up to the point of attack and, if applied correctly, almost insured success.[54]

Vauban's true orientation became more apparent when French policy turned to defending acquisitions along the northeastern borders. To protect the natural line of river approaches into France, Vauban built a string of huge fortifications from Dunkirk on the North Sea through Lille, on to Valenciennes, Condé, Cambrai, and Douai. With these strongholds Vauban established his reputation as one of the great, perhaps the greatest, military architects of all times.

As John Childs explains, Vauban's designs were based on the application of simple geometry to insure that any attacker, no matter what his angle of approach, would be subjected to a withering cross fire. Not a square inch of cover or dead ground was tolerated within effective range of defending guns. Because of irregularities in topography and the shape of strong points, however, regular polygons—the classic star-shaped trace, for instance—were often either impossible to construct or insufficient in their coverage. Hence, separate bastions, themselves protected by outworks, were made necessary to close off extraneous angles.[55] Yet in doing so they raised still further the size and manning requirements of what became virtually military mazes. Although the profile of the construction was very low, the basic sequence of glacis, parapet, counterscarp, ditch, scarp, and rampart often occupied as much as three hundred yards in all directions and was a massive undertaking. But the strength of these fortifications, along with their positioning on key corridors into the Netherlands fighting ground, caused them to act like strategic magnets, drawing to them and pinning down huge attacking armies. As time went on, especially after 1750, the number of sieges increased dramatically, and it was possible to say that the science of fortifications had easily outstripped that of the gun.

Nevertheless, as Childs points out, we rarely hear of an unsuccessful siege.[56] Although some questioned the soundness of Vauban's designs, their usefulness as late as World War I argues the contrary. Rather than physical vulnerability, the proclivity to surrender seems clearly based on the psychology with which defenses were undertaken. Sieges, being traditionally the most brutal and predatory form of warfare, logically came under particularly close control in an age dedicated to military moderation. As befit the imposition of fighting values based on standards of intraspecific aggression, the precise conditions of submission were carefully stipulated and adhered to. Most influential in this regard was a letter dated 6 April 1705 in which Louis XIV ruled that henceforth a commander might surrender honorably after suffering one small breach and repulsing one assault.[57] Not only was this a significant departure from the previous standard of one large breach and several assaults, but the rule held firm until French revolutionaries guillotined a commander and his wife for such pro forma resistance.[58] "What was taught in the military schools," sneered Committee of Public Safety member Lazare Carnot, "was no longer the art of defending strong places, but that of surrendering them honorably after certain conventional formalities."[59] While strictly accurate, this statement misses the point entirely. To the eighteenth-century mind there was but one alternative to such contrived circumstances, and that was the wretched fate of cities like Magdeburg. So even in the face of technical developments which logically called for more die-hard resistance, a structure of moderation was developed and adhered to. Granted, there were instances when sieges were carried to their wanton conclusion. Yet these were rare and almost always provoked by stubbornness or atrocity.

It is also true that chemical energy–based weapons were used somewhat more promiscuously in sieges than in field actions, yet mines and exploding shells had been known for two hundred years by 1700. Moreover, solid shot fired from the standard bronze muzzle-loader remained easily the dominant projectile-gun combination during sieges as well as in the field.[60] Vauban and his mathematically oriented successors were essentially architects, not weapons developers; in fact, the net effect of their work was to further circumscribe the impact of the gun. This was entirely appropriate. More than small arms, the destructive potential of cannon was closer to the surface—if not obvious, then at least perceptible. Therefore, it was important that invention, if it was to be tolerated at all, should be enlisted to moderate destructive effects. For the unspoken theme of arms control was central to everything, the key to equilibrium.

IV

This was nowhere more apparent than at sea. Navies were the final component in the Enlightenment military mechanism, and undoubtedly the best balanced and most enduring. Here limitations of physics and materials conspired in moderation's behalf, so reinforcing the emergent naval order that certain of its key premises persist to this day. Yet, again, the great stabilizer was the imposition of the generic solid shot–firing smoothbore gun as the standard naval engine of destruction. So armed, all ships differed basically in degree rather than kind—the more guns, the more fighting power. Moreover, similarity in armament had direct repercussions for structure and propulsion. All sailing warships were built of wood, and in the vast majority of cases, one type of wood—oak. Yet this material had very definite strength limitations which prevented the construction of wooden ships measuring much more than two hundred feet in length, lest they be in danger of hogging, or drooping, at the ends. Since guns were mounted at regular intervals along each side of a ship, only a finite number could be carried per deck. If armament was to be increased further, it became necessary to pile gun decks one upon the other, a solution analogous to the stacking of oar decks in a galley. But in terms of propulsion, the consequences were reversed. Since all rates, or classes, of warships were square-riggers of the same basic configuration—each making use of a common power source, the wind—vessels with multiple layers of guns were by necessity slower than their more lightly armed cousins.

The upshot, as Julian Corbett notes, was an absolute segregation of function in naval warfare.[61] Smaller ships, inevitably outgunned, zealously avoided combat with bigger ones, while the very plenitude of guns which made larger vessels more powerful rendered them incapable of successfully pursuing the more dimin-

Figure 10. Formalized nature of eighteenth-century war at sea. The Action off Cuddalore, 1783, painting by August Louis de Rossi di Cerci. Compliments of the directors of the Musée de la Marine, Palais de Chaillot.

utive craft.[62] Hence, battles at sea unfolded with Homeric decorum, equals almost inevitably seeking out equals to engage symmetrically by class. In general the swifter, lighter rates made contact first and fought the opening rounds, with the more ponderous heavyweights being saved for the finale.

It was not only the sequence of battle but also its conditions which called forth an earlier heroic conception of fighting. "How much nearer, so much the better," observed Richard Hawkins in 1622.[63] English experiments with long-range gunnery were cast aside, and in their stead the urge to close would be given free rein for the next two hundred years, particularly among the ever-successful Royal Navy. So at sea, at least, the combat motifs of the previous mechanical era reasserted themselves.

And with good reason. The extreme inaccuracies imparted by the windage necessary for efficient loading of shipborne artillery, along with the natural rocking of the hull, insured that effective ranges did not exceed three hundred yards, a mere tenth of carry.[64] Further, the exclusive use of solid shot precluded serious structural damage being inflicted at any but these very short ranges where splintered oak had the additional effect of causing numerous secondary casualties. So it was that war at sea remained a gory rite of manhood, with combatants slugging it out "yardarm to yardarm," until one ship was so weakened that it could be taken by boarding or outmaneuvered and raked at the weak ends.

But as with land campaigns in this moderate time, pitched naval battles and decisive engagements remained relatively infrequent, the preferred tactic of the dominant Royal Navy being blockade. Blockade, as habitually employed by the English, encompassed a number of activities directed toward the military and economic injury of an adversary. Yet its basis was the physical interposition of the heaviest fleet units athwart the opponent's lines of trade and communication. While the maintenance of the blockade and, conversely, blockade-running, were left to smaller, swifter classes, in the long run only the physical removal of the battle line could end such a siege at sea. Therefore, engagements did take place and tactics did develop.

As might be expected, it was the Royal Navy which took the lead in working out the most advantageous deployment patterns. And as on land, this was determined largely by the configuration of the weaponry and placed heavy emphasis on control.

Since almost all firepower was located along the sides of the ship, it was critical that it face the enemy lengthwise whenever possible. Only one formation allowed multiple ships to satisfy this condition, and that was line ahead. This seems rather obvious now, but it required almost eighty years from the defeat of the Armada for the concept to sink in. Finally, it was perfected at the Four Days' Battle in 1666, where, as French observer de Guiche noted: "Nothing equalled the beautiful order of the English at sea. Never was a line drawn straighter than that formed by their ships; thus they bring all their fire to bear upon those who draw near them. . . . Whereas the Dutch advanced like cavalry whose squadron . . . come separately to the charge."[65] From this point, line ahead was established as the standard formation in all the capital ship navies of Europe.

Given this, the ultimate objective of an advancing file of sailing battleships became crossing an adversary's line of bearing. For as the ships proceeded past the opposing file, they could concentrate their entire broadside upon targets which could only reply with a few bow guns. Moreover, firing down a line of ships maximized the chances of hitting something. Yet such a maneuver ("crossing the T," it came to be called) required that all units follow the lead ship closely and exactly, a requirement which magnified the control and importance of the fleet commander.[66]

As much as anything, the centralization of command set the tone for subsequent naval engagements, or lack of them. For the necessity of maintaining the proper formation and the follow-the-leader mentality this engendered, stifled initiative and caused numerous opportunities for decisive action to be passed up, even among the audacious British.

Nonetheless, the structure of command and the degree of control which devolved from it were highly satisfactory in other respects. Of particular interest was the manner in which the structure was paralleled, and therefore reinforced, by the nature of the weaponry—a veritable hierarchy of ships dictated by the limitations of wood, wind, and a solid shot. Thus, an admiral aboard his flagship might command a line of battleships inhabited by captains, surrounded by a screen of progressively smaller craft controlled by a descending scale of officers. Under the circumstances, the idea of a smaller ship attacking a larger one was not just imprudent, it was fundamentally insubordinate.[67]

It was as if Homer had become a naval architect. Combat was parceled out among equals; power was precisely equated to size; and the ethic of close-in fighting was preserved. Indeed, the sailing battleship was a nearly perfect embodiment of intraspecific valuation—large (made to look larger by its sails), visually impressive, and capable of generating unprecedented sound and fury with its guns. So satisfactory was the state of naval architecture that it literally ground to a halt. Thus, the *Sovereign of the Seas,* launched in 1637, was similar in all but detail to every English capital ship built until 1860.[68] Even then sailing battleships remained impressive. John Ruskin would comment in 1830: "Taken all in all, a ship-of-the-line is the most honorable thing that man, as a gregarious animal, has produced."[69] He was close to the mark. It was honorable—a moderate weapon which nonetheless called forth the ancient virtues of combat.

Better still, it was durable. Properly maintained, a sailing warship might last for upward of a century and, considering the frozen state of naval technology, might well find some military use even at that advanced age. On a lesser scale, Nelson's *Victory,* the principal flagship at Trafalgar, was forty years old at the time of that battle.[70]

So the Royal Navy grew stronger and stronger, for the economics of the naval order were all in her favor. One seventy-four-gun ship-of-the-line required two thousand oak trees, each of which took at least one hundred years to mature.[71] In deforested western Europe an aspiring naval power had to manage its oaks carefully. Immediate and rapid construction of a fleet necessarily meant a shortage of trees later. On the other hand, a power such as England, which pursued a fairly steady construction policy, had a great advantage. During the period between 1689 and 1713, the Royal Navy emerged as clearly the strongest in the world; by 1727 it had eighty-four ships of the line on the books. By 1783 there were 174 battleships in the Royal Navy, though many were unfit for service. Finally, at the close of the Napoleonic Wars in 1814, an all-time peak was reached, with one hundred battleships actually in commission and a force of sixty fully seaworthy craft held in reserve.[72]

A preponderance of battleships—this was the essence of British naval power, at least as far as weapons were concerned. Power was a matter of counting. Like the homogenized infantry and artillery on land, ships and guns became the universal tokens of naval power. In a moderate time this only stimulated pretenders to possess ships of the line. Yet there was nothing preordained about this state of affairs. The battleship was really very vulnerable below the waterline, and the day would come when this weakness would be consciously exploited. But this day was far off, and for a while men could afford themselves the convenient forgetfulness which was the lifeblood of arms control in its most successful western manifestation.

V

Given our own more perilous condition, it would be reassuring if we could point to a prescriptive body of thought or a scrupulously executed plan by which weapons were to be curbed; instead, all that remains is a sort of somnolence. For us, living in a time used to probing the bounds of reality and possibility, self-imposed amnesia is not an easy concept to fathom. The idea that important areas might be shoved out of consciousness does not appeal to us. Nevertheless, it worked in other times. The Victorians did it with sex, and the eighteenth-century European ruling class did it with weapons.

The aristocratic guardians of the system, the officers, were men of action, not introspection—soldiers, not technologists. Weapons were an important part of their lives, but there was little incentive to tinker with them or even think speculatively about them. Psychologically, the tactical system worked to accommodate human nature to a specific level of violence. The idea of increasing this was profoundly alien, not only to the great bulk of less cerebral types but to military intellectuals as well. Thus, the anonymous late-eighteenth-century creator of the first fantasy of future warfare, *The Reign of George VI: 1900–1925,* foresaw no weapons developments at all, notes I. F. Clarke in his brilliant study of a genre destined to become remarkable for the accuracy of its postulated arms innovations.[73]

There were occasional exceptions, and the Marshal de Saxe, one of the age's most successful practitioners of the delicate art of avoiding battle, was one of them. First of 354 offspring of the aptly named Augustus the Strong of Saxony, Saxe apparently inherited some of his father's creative proclivities, and during a short period of illness began dictating his memoirs. Heavily dosed with opium, Saxe gave full vent to his military imagination, suggesting numerous arms improvements, the most notable being a very light infantry support piece, the amusette.[74] While the resulting *Reveries* reached print and enjoyed some readership, Saxe's hypothesized weapons were quickly forgotten. This was typical. In a time of military moderation, arms control was a passive activity, requiring only a short memory and the complacency to leave well enough alone.

Today arms control is presumed to be a rigorous pursuit, a quest whose goals are attainable only through carefully thought out and negotiated formulae. Everything is overt. Quite probably this is why the achievements of the Enlightenment in mitigating the consequences of weapons development have been overlooked. Because contemporaries wrote about it, the era is recognized as having succeeded, to a greater or lesser degree (depending on the historian), at limiting warfare. But since silence surrounds its counterpart, which was the tight control of weapons capabilities; this has not received similar attention. Even if it had, the results would not be encouraging to the literalist. For the conditions which made arms control workable, a series of shared but unspoken assumptions about the nature and limits of politics, do not exist today.

Nevertheless, there are still lessons to be learned from the eighteenth-century experience with weaponry. Whatever the conditions, we can point to this time as a period in which qualitative arms developments were curbed. Moreover, it was done in the face of external technical trends which continually raised new possibilities for weapons applications. By the 1830s armament, rather than being at or near the state of the art, was a technological backwater. The sanguinary promise of chemical energy had been arrested, its possibilities hedged in by solid shot, automaton soldiers, polygonal traces, decorous warships, and ritual. This was a major achievement. Firearms were in their own way as dangerous to that world as nuclear weapons are to our own. Yet men learned to live with them.

Chapter 10

A WORLD DESTROYED

I

The center could not hold. The ancien régime was a bulwark against change in a time of transition, a delicately balanced mechanism poised on a volcano. Given the forces to which it was subject, it proved remarkably tenacious. Yet in the end all would be swept away, including, ultimately, the Enlightenment commitment to arms control.

Historically, the key to the grand political mechanism was France and its first apostle, Louis XIV. For as the ambitious young French king reached his majority, he inherited a rich and industrious realm roughly three times more populous than England, Spain, or Austria, with access to both the Atlantic and the Mediterranean and possessing vast latent military potential. But although he centralized ruthlessly at home, building one of history's most absolute monarchies, he, unlike the Habsburgs, declined the mantle of transnational tyrant. Instead, he took up the Copernican imagery and became the Sun King. The analogy was an apt one. Europe was to revolve around Bourbon France, not be consumed by her.

Under Louis and directed by his war minister, Luvois, his architect, Vauban, and his generals, Condé and Turenne, France would come to adopt the military patterns which would characterize the era. His campaigns were undertaken with massive armies whose mobility was tightly bound to logistical support and field kitchens. Lines of advance were short and geographically predictable, normally being aimed at limited objectives. (It should be noted that in 1672 the French deliberately set out to destroy the United Provinces.) Battles, when fought at all, were usually waged on the traditional dueling grounds in the Spanish Netherlands. Inevitably, winter signaled the end of the campaigning season and the withdrawal of the French to winter quarters.[1] As Louis's fortunes swung and he became preoccupied with protecting his acquisitions, sieges and the conditions invoked by the king and his designer, Vauban, increasingly came to dominate the action.[2]

In all of this, Louis and his successors were opposed, and successfully so, by shifting coalitions of the remaining powers, their combination made easy by the homogeneity of military forces. Wars were frequent, and gains were modest and often temporary. Meanwhile, at sea, Louis's ambitious naval building program and plan for overseas expansion were consistently thwarted, first by the Dutch and English and finally by just the English. Thus, France came to be hemmed in on all sides, the pulsations of her borders marking the steady beat of European history.

II

So long as this central mechanism remained in proper alignment, the larger engine of European politics would retain its equilibrium. Yet there were strains almost from the beginning. For a system of absolute rule is vulnerable at all times to the eccentricities of absolute rulers.

And just as the eighteenth century began, the monarchs of Europe found themselves joined by what amounted to a juvenile delinquent. After three years of uneventful rule, few had stopped to consider the character of eighteen-year-old Charles XII of Sweden, least of all the amorous Augustus the Strong of Saxony and Poland, who rather thoughtlessly invaded Swedish Livonia without a declaration of war. He was soon joined by the king of Denmark and young Peter of Russia. They might have hesitated. Within a year Charles had driven Denmark from the war and destroyed a major Russian army of sixty-nine thousand at Narva.[3]

Yet even more thought-provoking was the manner in which this had been done. Charles had marched a vastly outnumbered force 150 miles through the autumn rains just to get at the Russians. Arriving at Narva in the midst of a snowstorm, he personally led his troops against their thoroughly entrenched opponents, stopping to fire but one volley. The rest was done with cold steel, bayonet, and cutlasses. Not only had Charles needlessly risked his person and broken all the rules of engagement, he had apparently transcended the new ethnic of firepower, ignoring the very system which his royal ancestor Gustav Adolph had helped to create.

But the war was far from over. While Charles chased the by now thoroughly frightened Augustus through the swamps and forests of Poland, Peter coolly created an army based on European standards of discipline and firepower. Also, to serve it he built an arms industry based on imported technology, which gradually grew capable of equipping his forces with the flintlocks, bayonets, and artillery they so desperately needed.

Meanwhile, in late 1707, Charles made the decision to strike out for Moscow, the first of those whose ambition led them to make this fatal error. As he began the invasion of this huge half-orientalized country, Charles must have seemed to some as Alexander incarnate. But he was merely violent, his political instincts being guided solely by an overdeveloped sense of honor.

Having drawn Charles away from Moscow, Peter let the terrible winter of 1708–9 and his scorched-earth policy enervate the Swedish army. Then in the early summer of the next year, thoroughly outnumbered and practically without cannon or even powder, the Swedes again attacked entrenched Russians at Poltava in the Ukraine. This time they were slaughtered, taking over 30 percent casualties and eventually surrendering their entire force.[4]

Yet the war dragged on, kept alive by Charles's intransigence. Finally, a decade later, still taking chances, he met the fate of Gustav—a bullet through the brain. It was a fitting end. His chief legacy, the twenty-one-year Great Northern War is generally considered to have been the most vicious of the era, resembling in many respects the Thirty Years' War which claimed Gustav.[5]

Times had changed, however. Peter had kept his head, adopted the weaponry of his enemies, and then lured them into a geographical trap. It was a strategy which would raise Russia to greatness, but as yet it merely announced the arrival of another player on the European chessboard. Sweden, on the other hand, would not be heard from again.

But it was not merely the gyrations of its aberrant types which preyed upon the stability of the general balance. It was ill served even by its stalwarts. For a commitment to moderation and the observation of certain warlike conventions in no way implied a common moral perspective. Indeed, the very nihilistic nature of the balance encouraged the most cynical sort of aggrandizement. In the end the system rewarded strength above all things, the sole condition being that it be used prudently. A realistic perspective, perhaps, but not one which encourages loyalty or cohesiveness.

A case in point was Prussia, particularly the Prussia of Frederick the Great. It is probably safe to say that the international system made Prussia possible, the twisted offspring of its militaristic tendencies. For, in the Compte de Mirabeau's words, "Most states have any army; the Prussian army is the only one that has a state."[6]

The Peace of Westphalia in 1648 left the electorate of Brandenburg in a very bedraggled state. Decimated by the Thirty Years' War, cut off from the sea, and scattered in unconnected fragments across the Northern Plain from the Rhine to the Vistula, this patchwork which would become modern Germany seemed to have very little with which to recommend itself to the future. Then, out of the blue, the ancient house of Hohenzollern, plodding rulers of Brandenburg since 1417, began producing extraordinary leaders. The prototype was Frederick William, subsequently known as the Great Elector. He set the pattern for much that was to follow, organizing an efficient centralized government operated by a disciplined civil service, a postal system, even a reformed tax structure. But in one way or another all was directed toward the greater end—the care and feeding of a massive standing army,[7] the sole state institution capable of knitting together the disparate patchwork that was Brandenburg and later Prussia. At his death the Great Elector left his dominions with an army which Michael Howard estimates to have been forty-five thousand strong.[8] Given a population of about two million, this worked out to 1 soldier for every 44 inhabitants, a very high ratio when compared with the equivalent French rate of 1 to 150. But it would climb higher.

The next major chapter in the saga of the Hohenzollerns began in 1713 when twenty-five year old Frederick William assumed the throne. For the next twenty-seven years, every bit of parsimony and good government he could muster was directed toward the expansion of the army to eighty thousand making it the fourth largest in Europe and accounting for one in every twenty-five Prussians.[9] Superbly trained and equipped, he used the army sparingly in battle, but took full advantage of its threat potential and the prestige it imparted to what was still a very small state.

But it is safe to say that Frederick William valued his army for its own sake, and that the origins of this attitude are best revealed in his greatest passion, the notorious Potsdam Regiment. Known all over Europe as the Blue Prussians or the Giants of Potsdam, they were twelve hundred men organized into two battalions, no member of which was less than six feet tall (a remarkable figure when one considers the average male of this time was less than five feet six inches.)[10] Perhaps the frankest example of intraspecific valuation in recent history, Frederick William's giants literally cost him millions (at one point he payed 8,800 taler for a single Irishman who measured seven feet two inches) and were virtually his only form of amusement.[11]

For Frederick William was a sick man, tortured by a metabolic derangement which manifested itself in a variety of bodily ills and a terrifying temper. And more and more it was vented at his son and heir, the lad who came to be known as Frederick the Great.

Young Frederick had been a frail, polite little boy whose first toys were lead soldiers and whose first lessons were the evolutions of Prussian drill. Yet as he moved into adolescence, Frederick developed a passion for France, music, literature, and a clique of effete carousers—all to the disapproval of his thoroughly Germanic father, who took to throwing fits at the very sight of his son. Finally, after Frederick attempted to flee the country, Frederick William decided to break the boy. He accused him of treason, imprisoned him, and then, before his very eyes, had his presumed lover, Katte, beheaded. Yet nothing seemed to hurt Frederick as much as kicking him out of the army and removing him from command of his boy regiment.[12] The Prince repented, masking his aesthete tendencies and subjecting himself to his father's Spartan regimen aimed at making him a capable ruler, Prussian style.

Frederick was an apt student. Immediately upon his father's death he attacked Austria, precipitating the War of Austrian Succession, and making off with the rich province of Silesia. This cynical commitment to aggression would, however, be paid back in spades eight years later when Austria, Russia, and France all declared war on Prussia, whose only support was far-off maritime England. Frederick found himself fighting for the life of his state. Reduced at times to casualty-depleted, ill-trained regiments, the beleaguered Prussian king was forced to fight again and again. For a time it seemed as if he might commit suicide. But in the end, remarkably, he prevailed, keeping all his ill-gotten posessions and ending the war on honorable terms.

Yet the costs of the Seven Years War were terrible. One hundred twenty Prussian generals, including virtually all of Frederick's friends, had been killed. Dresden was smashed, and the agricultural districts lay in ruins. Even under eighteenth-century conditions, the accumulated depredations of this prolonged war required that Frederick spend the remainder of his life putting his country back together.[13]

Nevertheless, he had also transformed Prussia into virtually the premier military power in Europe, supporting a standing army of 162,000—only 11,000 less than the army of France.[14] The lesson seemed unmistakable. Even under conditions of limited warfare, military power and large forces were the surest means to political success. States all over Europe, including some preposterously small ones, continued to expand their forces.

So, like the antlers of some of the largest ungulates, the growth of standing armies came to weigh down the body politic. As force structures swelled into the hundreds of thousands, they began to consume significant portions of the labor force. Taxes increased, billeted soldiers became more and more burdensome on civilian populations, and previously stable regimes grew ripe for revolution.[15] Meanwhile, the outcast armies with their aristocratic taskmasters remained profoundly alien to the class destined to inherit power. Though many stood to gain from victualage contracts and a prosperous arms industry, the turbulent, dynamic bourgeois generally perceived massive standing armies as expensive symbols of repression.[16] When the time came, they would discover a more efficient means to the same end. In an economic and demographic environment which could now tolerate the periodic absence of significant portions of the male population, one had only to convince them to fight for freedom, to die for a cause.

III

The American Revolution provided the first signs of what would happen. The North American colonies had been settled under conditions of more or less continuous violence. And as Daniel Boorstin reminds us, the Indians who lay in wait for the earliest colonists had not read Grotius.[17] They were hunters who responded to these hairy, white Europeans as if to another species. "The Indian kills indiscriminately," explained the Reverend Joseph Doddridge in the late eighteenth century. "His object is the total extermination of his enemies. Children are victims of his vengeance, because, if males they may hereafter become warriors, or if females they may become mothers."[18]

The colonists, in the tradition of the wronged imperialist, reacted from their own predatory tradition and began waging a war of annihilation against the Indians. And a significant component of this had to do with weapons.

Marking a milestone of sorts, certain colonists during the French and Indian Wars resorted to trading smallpox-contaminated blankets to local tribes with immediate and devastating results. While infected carcasses had long been catapulted into besieged cities, this seems to be the first time a known weakness in the immunity structure of an adversary population was deliberately exploited with a weapons response.[19]

Of much more significance, however, was the colonial proclivity to use what were essentially hunting guns against their Indian foes. By around 1750, the so-called Pennsylvania rifle, later famed as the Kentucky long rifle, was already considerably modified from its Alpine European prototype. Although slow load-ing—traditionally accomplished with a mallet and a short iron rod—did not dis-qualify the rifle for use in the backwoods, the nascent Americans came up with a quicker, easier means, utilizing a greased patch wrapped around the ball which could then be pushed smoothly down the bore. The resulting weapon was ideally suited to conditions of sporadic aboriginal violence, where targets were fleeting and every shot had to count. Hunting and war, the essential conditions were the same, and so the population came to arm itself like none in Europe. "Rifles infinitely better than those imported, are daily made in many places in Pennsyl-vania, and all the gunsmiths everywhere [are] constantly employed," warned an Anglican minister writing home in 1775. "In marching through the woods, one thousand of these riflemen would cut to pieces ten-thousand of your best English troops." [20]

So grew the legend of the omnipresent frontier marksman, hunting Indians or British regulars with the same deadly efficiency with which he stalked game. Playing upon the myth early in the Revolution, General George Washington is-sued an order in which he urged "the use of Hunting Shirts, with long Breeches . . . [as] it is a dress justly supposed to carry no small terror to the enemy, who thinks every such person a compleat Marksman." [21]

In fact, the Pennsylvania rifle, even using a greased patch, was too slow-loading for massed field actions, and, using muskets, Continental regulars proved decidedly inferior to the Hessian and British professionals sent up against them. Only when Europeans like von Steuben subjected them to traditional drill training did the colonists begin to gain a measure of consistency in formal combat.

But still the myth of the citizen-sharpshooter lived on. Using innovative tac-tics, amateur American officers learned to make the most of their troops, empha-sizing skirmish, ambush, and harassment with snipers. If colonial troops were quick to desert, they also continued to volunteer their services in reasonably large numbers, albeit on a short-term basis. As Boorstin notes: "The American center was everywhere and nowhere—in each man himself." [22] Boston, New York, Phil-adelphia, and Charleston—all the key colonial cities had been occupied, but al-ways without decisive results. And still the countryside remained rebellious, a dangerous morass where every tree hid a potential rebel sharpshooter.

The only key British advantage was sea power, which insured their lines of communication and support while enabling them to move troops up and down the eastern seaboard far faster than equivalent colonials. And this strategic edge in concentrating trained regulars kept them in the war.

The rebellious colonists responded by playing the classic role of the inferior naval power, practicing *guerre de course* by staging hit-and-run raids on British commerce with privateers and a small body of frigates, which persisted in ignor-ing the hierarchy of ships by attacking Royal Navy vessels much larger than them-selves. [23]

Yet this was a mere annoyance. David Bushnell had bigger things in mind. As an undergraduate at Yale College in 1773, he had designed and built the first successful submarine, the *Turtle,* a diving bell–like craft maneuvered with vertical and horizontal hand-cranked screw propellers based on theories advanced by the mathematician Bernoulli.[24] Now, during the Revolution, he proposed to use "Turtles" to attack British warships with large time-fused, zero-buoyancy charges of powder, clamped surreptitiously to their bottoms as they lay at anchor.

Through a combination of bad luck and poor equipment, Bushnell's "Turtles" never succeeded in sinking an English warship. Yet the concept was not only sound, but he had hit upon the true vulnerability of the battleship-based naval hierarchy: it could be attacked from below. Once again the colonists refused to play by the military rules. Ignoring the precepts of weapons symmetry, they sought to overturn established advantage through radical means. It was an ill omen for British sea power. And sea power Britain could not afford to lose.

The truth of this statement was demonstrated in the fall of 1781 when the French Admiral de Grasse arrived off Virginia with a squadron of ships-of-the-line to blockade the York and James rivers, thereby depriving General Cornwallis, camped on the York peninsula, of his seaborne lines of support. Rather than move inland immediately, he hesitated and soon found his way blocked by Washington and a strong Franco-American force. Within a month he had surrendered his entire force, effectively ending the war.

It has been asked why the British gave up so quickly after Yorktown. In part this can be explained by the hopelessness of the military situation, their inability to strike a decisive blow. Yet it also had to do with their own outlook. Cornwallis and his fellow officers were military men of the eighteenth century. When faced with unfavorable military prospects there was no terrible stigma attached to surrender. Soon, though, such men would meet an opponent whose rapacity was not to be curbed, against whom only die-hard resistance could succeed.

The eighteenth century was a time for generals. The degree of control which had to be exerted over this sort of firepower army logically demanded almost total centralization of command. While reality compromised this somewhat, it still remained true that enormous responsibilities devolved upon a very few individuals. It has been estimated that, without electronic communications, about eighty thousand troops is the maximum which could be effectively directed by a single commander under ideal conditions.[25] As armies steadily grew, the art of generalship came to exist at and beyond this ragged barrier. Moreover, it was done with force structures which were increasingly complicated and notoriously brittle.

Tactically, battle became an exercise in opportunism—seeking a vulnerability and exploiting it with devastating force, while at the same time avoiding a similar fate. Reserves were thus increasingly numerous, and their timing and use became critical. Indeed, so daunting was the task of juggling the many variables of battle while immersed in its confusion that the ability to do so came to be described in near-mystical terms. Coup d'oeil was the phrase used to characterize the rare gift of insight which enabled a commander to take in at a glance all tactical probability and project exactly the right moment to apply overwhelming pressure. In essence, the general became a cerebral figure, a condition doubtless fostered by the new ethic of courage under fire. Rather than flailing away with a broadsword or charging with a lance, the classic military pose now caught the commander peering over a map or snapping a spyglass shut with a decisive flick of the wrist.

Given the political and social structure of the day, only a very small number ever got the opportunity to command. Of those, even fewer had any talent for it, but those who did had an inordinate advantage. With the homogenization of armament and training, basically only numbers and leadership mattered. And given the difficulties of deployment, even numbers might be overcome by a clever general. Commanders of the caliber of a Turenne or a Marlborough were consequently extremely important figures with the futures of whole states and even coalitions at times resting on their shoulders. But they were not generally princes. Of those few who were, Frederick the Great basically accepted the limitations of the system, and Charles XII was half mad. Nevertheless, the possibilities remained for a supremely talented general, whose military skills were matched by equivalent political gifts and ambitions, to ride roughshod over the system. Thus, the opportunity for transnational tyranny was a latent, but always potential, threat to the grand political balancing mechanism.

It was a single man who was destined to deliver the crushing blow to the system. But it was the French Revolution which brought him into being. And it was this upheaval which finally undermined the military solution of the ancien régime.

IV

France had been for centuries the linchpin of the balance, its center of gravity. Her revolutionary destiny—the execution of the monarch and thousands of aristocrats—was bound to be interpreted as the gravest sort of challenge by the other key members of the European power structure. Perhaps equally threatening was the role played by the French military establishment. Its officer corps severely depleted by emigration, the standing army proved incapable of supporting the ancien régime, and in certain instances actually abetted its fall.[26] Nonetheless, early in the fighting which inevitably followed, the Revolution revealed a capacity for organized violence which exceeded all expectations.

Initially, the Prussians and Austrians had expected to sweep the hastefully assembled volunteer force away by their mere presence within French borders. Thus, rather than strike at Paris and the heart of the Revolution, the Prussian duke of Brunswick insisted on confronting the apparently disorganized French at Valmy. The latter, however, fought unexpectedly well, firing up to twenty thousand artillery rounds to keep the Prussian infantry at bay. Bewildered, but hardly mortally hurt, Brunswick withdrew.[27]

In the interim the French began organizing what Theodore Ropp calls the "first national army in modern European history."[28] Having run short of volunteers during the winter of 1792–93, the National Convention voted the conscription of three hundred thousand men. The first of many such call-ups, it roughly doubled the size of the army. From this point France would draw on a manpower pool vastly larger than those which fed the professional armies of her enemies.

Yet in the near term it hardly mattered, for the second season of war with the First Coalition was far worse than the first. Dumouriez's army in the Netherlands was defeated, at which time the general deserted to the allies. Four days later they invaded France, and nothing stood between them and Paris but a small, disorganized force. Nevertheless, the allied armies settled down to a three-month siege of two relatively unimportant positions and then wasted more time maneuvering the French forces away from the road to Paris. Still, when the way was clear, they hesitated,[29] for the Coalition generals remained prisoners of their own military background. Thrust into an environment that demanded decisive action, they could answer only with forbearance and moderation.

Meanwhile, great changes had taken place in Paris. In April the National Convention, hoping to deal decisively with the growing chaos surrounding it, had established several tribunals, including a twelve-man Committee of Public Safety with vast powers. It used them ruthlessly, establishing near-dictatorial rule but doing very little about the military emergency.

Then in August 1793, a forty-year-old engineer captain, Lazare Carnot, was elected to the Committee of Public Safety and put in charge of military affairs. Subsequently known as the "Organizer of Victory," Carnot surrounded himself with capable young innovators and set about rebuilding the French army. Troops were taught to mass quickly into columns, their movements masked by a loose order of sharpshooting skirmishers (introduced by Lafayette after observing their effectiveness in the American War of Independence) and heavy artillery barrages. Then, when the moment was right, they were to charge with the greatest speed and resolution into the enemy line.[30]

Casualties were bound to be high, but this was plainly a tactic designed to confound the brittle firepower formations of the day. It also said a good deal about the Revolution's willingness to accommodate itself to the military conventions of the ancien régime. Troops were also organized for the first time into divisions, developed with the idea of relatively small units (perhaps twelve thousand men) embracing all three arms (infantry, cavalry, and artillery) and thereby becoming capable of independent operation.[31]

To arm these forces, Carnot had the Committee of Public Safety undertake a remarkable program of economic mobilization. Labor and resources were drawn on a national scale, scientific talent was recruited, and great public weapons factories were established in the gardens and parks of Paris—all done within the space of months.[32] By 1794 Paris had become the largest small-arms producer in the world, turning out something like 750 muskets a day, when all of Europe had never produced more than a thousand. Artillery casting took longer to learn, yet it too benefited from mandatory technical courses, and production soon shot up. More important, perhaps, the designs used were those Gribeauval had tried to introduce before the Revolution, featuring standardized calibers and interchangeable parts.[33] Henceforth, French artillery was the best in Europe.

The remaining element was leadership. "Act of offensively and in masses," Carnot had instructed his generals. "Use the bayonet at every opportunity. Fight great battles and pursue the enemy until he is utterly destroyed."[34] Instead, Revolutionary commanders remained largely passive. Bullied by the firebrands in Paris (over three hundred of their number had been sacked and executed since 1789) and often harboring sympathies for the ancien régime, generals persistently fell back on the training of a lifetime and adopted the dilatory practices of their First Coalition adversaries.

With increasing frequency, then, the authorities in Paris turned to younger men. By the spring of 1794 they had promoted a class of generals which was to include eight future marshals of France, their average age at the time being under thirty-five.[35] Yet the emergence of this group was in no way the most significant outcome of this particular class. For it also included a twenty-three-year-old artillery brigadier who was destined to conquer most of Europe.

V

For a future ruler of France, Napoleon Bonaparte's origins could hardly have been more obscure. The son of minor Corsican nobility, he spent much of his youth away from his family sequestered in French military schools, eventually accepting a commission in the artillery, the sole branch in which his birth and poverty would not be held against him. Even as the Revolution engulfed France, young Bonaparte's military career remained notable only for long leaves of absence spent in Corsica trying to put his family's affairs in order.[36]

Finally, in the summer of 1793, with the entire South of France threatening to go over to the Bourbons, Napoleon wrote a pro-Jacobin political tract, *"Le Souper de Beaucaire,"* which pleased the brother of Robespierre. Consequently when Toulon, the most important naval base in the country, raised the standard of revolt, young Bonaparte was entrusted with the artillery of the Republican force laying siege to the city. Mostly due to Bonaparte's energy and clever placement of batteries, the English naval squadron under Lord Hood was forced to evacuate, and the city fell soon after.[37]

Once inside, Bonaparte made sure the resistance was broken, driving all the Royalists into the great square of Toulon, where he mowed them down point-blank with a salvo of artillery. "The vengeance of the French Republic is satisfied," he addressed his now-prostrate foes. "Rise and go to your homes." No sooner did the survivors attempt to obey than a second burst sent still more to their deaths.[38]

Admittedly, this was a British account, but the incident was very much in character. Toulon made Napoleon Bonaparte famous and caused him to be promoted to general. Less than two years later he would again turn his cannon on civilians, this time the Paris mob, breaking its power forever. The Republican authorities could not do enough for their your savior, promoting him to commander in chief of the Army of the Interior, by far the largest force in France.

Yet Bonaparte's eyes were fixed upon the ragged, half-starved army of Italy, strung out across the impoverished foothills of Piedmont. They were to be his sword, and would win him his first real military reputation. "Soldiers," he addressed them in the spring of 1796.

You are hungry and naked; the government owes you much but can give you nothing. The patience and courage which you have displayed among these rocks is admirable; but they bring you no glory. . . . I will lead you into the most fertile plains on earth. Rich provinces, opulent towns, all shall be at your disposal; there you will find honor, glory, and riches.[39]

Like the exhausted soldiers of Hannibal, they could hardly miss his point. It was during the Italian campaign that the Napoleonic war machine first revealed itself to a shocked Europe. Bonaparte was a new kind of general, and he led a new kind of soldier. Together they proved themselves virtually invincible. For, indeed, both played by a different set of rules.

The troops inherited by Napoleon were the children of revolution, far different in their basic motivation than the professionals who first faced them. The French were active rather than passive. They fought to kill, using swarms of elusive sharpshooters and very rapid movement of massed formations. They refused to expose themselves unnecessarily to fire, but they were nonetheless extremely aggressive when called upon.[40] All of this required intelligence and initiative. They took orders, but they could also improvise.

As good as French troops were tactically, they were better strategically, for they could move like no other troops in Europe. Both literally and figuratively, they traveled light. French soldiers did not desert in masses. So they could be trusted to forage, live off the land. Thus, the endless supply trains which had so shackled the armies of the eighteenth century could be cast aside, and, so disencumbered, the French were able to maneuver with ease around and behind their befuddled foes.[41] Yet this capability, originating in the breakdown of revolutionary logistics, remained basically latent until Napoleon discovered it and began racing around the peninsula of Italy.

He did not fight the Austrians there so much as he hunted them, running down their armies with a relentless logic that was almost inhuman. At times he was in danger, but he was never out of control. His grasp of detail and appetite for work certainly magnified his military talents, yet the essential ability to project himself and his opponent out into the future, running down all the combinations of circumstances that might befall them both, was a gift no amount of diligence could compensate for. During the early days of the Italian campaign of 1800, Bourienne, his secretary, found Napoleon sprawled full length, pushing colored pins into his ever-present maps. "Here! I will fight him here on the plain of Scrivia," he said, pointing at the village of San Guiliano three miles east of Marengo.[42] Two months later he would administer a crushing defeat against the Austrians at almost precisely this point.

Coup d'oeil raised nearly to the level of omnipotence and Bonaparte the endless and brilliant propagandist would make the most of it, doing everything in his power to cast himself in superhuman terms. He was his own masterpiece, the heir to an image so potent that his mere appearance on the battlefield could and did turn the tide. He seldom dabbled in tactics, letting his generals see to the specifics of the fighting. His role was "being there," the source of almost endless inspiration to his troops. Frenchmen by the thousands, perhaps hundreds of thousands, would have gladly cast away their lives for just a smile, a nod of appreciation. Such was his power over them. He was their soul, their essence. They had tied their fate irrevocably to his own. And knowing this, he took endless advantage of them.

For behind the facade of charisma was the expedience of a mind which knew only relative advantage. There can be no doubt that Napoleon was a military genius. Yet a good measure of his astonishing success, particularly in his early campaigns, was based on the calculated transgressions of what were universally held to be the norms of European military conduct. With utter disregard for the consequences, Bonaparte resorted to a range of activities heavy with predatory overtones. He fought to destroy his enemies, using every ruse and stratagem to force them into decisive combat when they least desired it. But victory on the field was perceived as merely an intermediate step. If possible he pursued survivors relentlessly, using Murat's cavalry like hunting dogs to track them and crush their will to resist further.[43] Once captured, prisoners' rights were generally respected. Yet there were incidents of slaughter, particularly at Jaffa in the Near East, where forty-four hundred Turk prisoners were cut down,[44] and the vicious Spanish and Russian campaigns. Finally, it is true that the French army's ability to live off the land found its origins in the Revolution, but it was Bonaparte who took ruthless advantage of it, frequently allowing his troops to rape, pillage, and kill wantonly as a reward for their perseverance. This was the darker side of France's new army. Once again war came to involve civilians suffering in large numbers, and once again mass armies brought a blight upon the land. Yet it served Bonaparte's purposes, as did his other transgressions. And by them he won victory after victory and destroyed army after army.

Yet it would be a mistake to assume that he transcended totally the structure of military moderation which he found and exploited. It was, after all, the context for all of his endeavors, and he accepted a number of its conventions apparently without question. For example, he scrupulously observed the ceremonial aspects of military life; reveling in parades and forever reviewing his troops. So, too, did he accept the decorum of military diplomacy, generally treating vanquished commanders with studious respect. He had none of the personal bloodthirstiness of a Sargon. Indeed, it is a measure of the new ethic of firepower that Napoleon appears never to have killed a man in close combat. Nonetheless, his own conduct in battle epitomized courage as it had evolved in the presence of the gun. He was fearless in its face, adopting the studious oblivion that had become de rigueur. Yet he was not personally aggressive in the traditional sense. He did not kill; he directed the killing.

His attitude toward weaponry was similarly orthodox. Like virtually all great Western generals since Ashurnasir-pal, Napoleon was more of an opportunist than an innovator, adopting the best of the changes that had resulted from experimentation during and slightly before the Revolution. Even so, he retained a distinctly atavistic taste for the traditional.

Trained as an artillery officer, he was at his most progressive here. Bonaparte was perhaps the first commander to fully understand the latent killing power of the cannon, and he would use it copiously to inflict over 50 percent of the battle casualties suffered by his opponents. Once again, the number of pieces reached the levels used in the Thirty Years War. "Experience has shown," he would write, "that it is necessary to have four guns to every thousand men."[45]

Technically, the quality of field guns improved also, with Gribeauval's designs proliferating throughout Napoleon's forces. Artillery pieces were lighter and much more precise, being bored out on the great lathes perfected by Jean Maritz around 1790. To these had been added less cumbersome and much better designed carriages, not only improving significantly the mobility of conventionally drawn pieces but allowing for a whole new type, the so-called horse artillery, consisting of a four-pounder pulled by enough steeds to keep up with true cavalry.[46] Sights were also better, and Gribeauval's introduction of the screw-based barrel elevator made ranging more precise—both indicating a renewed, and ultimately very significant, interest in aiming.

Still, in its essence, artillery was not greatly changed. Cartridges were used once again, and howitzers firing exploding shells were employed with increasing frequency, but the triumvirate of solid shot, smoothbores, and muzzle-loading still clearly held sway on Bonaparte's battlefields. Horse artillery, though useful, was simply too livestock-consumptive to ever constitute more than a fraction of the total, while improved sighting was still bound to run afoul of the smoke-generating capacity of black powder. Napoleonic artillery was certainly improved, but progress was ultimately confined to the refinement of what were very old and traditional designs. The fundamental limitations of the basic weapon were not attacked in any systematic way, nor was there any sense that Bonaparte thought they should be.

This outlook was even more pronounced in the arming of French infantry and cavalry. Despite a heavy reliance on skirmishers and sharpshooters, Bonaparte retained the musket as the primary weapon of light infantry, as well as troops of the line. Rather, it was the English, profiting from their North American experience, who began furnishing skirmishers with rifles, using, as Depuy notes, sub-caliber bullets when a high rate of fire was necessary and a full-sized round and greased patch when accuracy mattered.[47] If anything, Napoleon's favorite infantry weapon was the bayonet, the use of which, though still selective,[48] very effectively demonstrated the difference in motivation between French troops and their adversaries. This penchant for the archaic can also be seen in Bonaparte's resurrection of specific heavy cavalry units, the cuirassiers, equipped with body armor, steel helmets, and mounted on huge steeds trained to charge infantry even under heavy fire.[49]

Yet Napoleon's penchant for weapons representative of the prior era was secondary and intended mainly for psychological effect. Like his contemporaries, Bonaparte's ultimate reliance was on the gun, with the understanding that "it is by fire and not by shock that battles are decided today."[50]

And what was true on land was equally or perhaps more true on the water. Even at the height of his military fortunes, Bonaparte was tremendously frustrated by British sea power. Yet when it came to naval armament he showed little real inclination to look beyond the British-inspired hierarchy of ships. Thus, the French and English battleships which fought at Trafalgar were basically interchangeable, and none of them greatly changed from the *Sovereign of the Seas* launched nearly three centuries before.[51]

In the last analysis, the emperor of the French viewed weapons much as he viewed soldiers. They were simply means to a larger political end, and here he would show absolutely no moderation at all.

He was almost the perfect evocation of the transnational tyrant, harnessing the latent but titanic forces of this strain of government. Like a tsunami he crashed across Europe, shattering the superstructure of political and military moderation. But also like one of these giant waves, he was destined to pass quickly, leaving what is all too often the only legacy of tyranny, a path of desolation and a multitude of graves.

If the course of European military power has been irresistibly westward, it has been the peculiar destiny of its tyrants to head east. So it was that Napoleon took the first opportunity to invade the storied land of Egypt. It was 1798, France was besieged by the English, and he was still six years from becoming emperor, but Bonaparte was able to persuade his short-lived political masters, the Directory, that a blow in this direction would threaten India and draw off the British. More likely he was following the footsteps of Alexander and Caesar.

Barely escaping Horatio Nelson's net of British battleships, he arrived on the banks of the Nile to give a stunning demonstration of what disciplined firepower meant when confronting those without it. Mutinous, sweltering in woolen uniforms, and nearly crazy with thirst, the French goaded the Mamluk cavalry (apparently oblivious of their disastrous experience with Janissary firepower three centuries prior) into charging their howitzer-filled hollow infantry squares. When the slaughter was over, four thousand Egyptians lay dead, having managed to kill only twenty-nine French. The next morning, Cairo surrendered. The country was Bonaparte's, and his men celebrated by fishing in the Nile with bent bayonets for richly adorned Mamluk corpses.[52] It was the best luck they were to have on the water.

Less than two weeks later, at sunset, Horatio Nelson's battleships would sweep down on Admiral Breuys's fleet anchored in Aboukir Bay. In the nocturnal battle which ensued, the English admiral broke "decisively," in Ropp's words, "with eighteenth century naval routines" and, rather than fight in parallel line ahead, cut the French file in half, concentrating two ships on one. Before dawn on 2 August, the French admiral was dead, his flagship blown up and most of his other battleships disabled, aground, or captured.[53] Bonaparte and his army were trapped.

With true Napoleonic logic, Bonaparte chose to save what was most important, himself. Leaving his army to rot in the desert, he escaped aboard a small squadron with only his bodyguard and a few key marshals—Berthier, Murat, and Lannes.

There ensued a period of glory. Though the Egyptian campaign undoubtedly hastened the formation of the Second Coalition by revealing to Europe the extent of his ambitions, Napoleon's enemies continued to play into his hands by trying to fight him with armies best suited to eighteenth-century combat. Disaster followed disaster.

First came the Austrians. Blind to his opponent's speed and cunning, the "unhappy General Mack" found himself surrounded at Ulm in October 1805 and was forced to surrencer his entire army. Two months later Napoleon cut the combined Russian and Austrian army in half at Austerlitz, and, taking no prisoners until the last hour of the battle, inflicted gruesome casualties. Days later the Habsburg emperor sued for peace.

The next year it was Prussia's turn. At Jena-Auerstedt the static, exposed Prussians were first shot to pieces by concealed French skirmishers and then broken and driven off the field by a combined attack of almost forty thousand reserves. But it was the relentless pursuit of Murat's cavalry which proved most decisive. When it was over, 140,000 men had been captured, and the Prussian standing army, 140 years in the making, had ceased to exist in thirty-three days.

Still, total victory eluded Bonaparte. For, as Henry Kissinger has astutely remarked: "He had forgotten, if he ever knew, that his great victories had been due as much to the ease which his opponents had accepted defeat as to the success of his arms."[54] From this point he would face sterner foes.

The British were one such opponent. On the very same day he received General Mack's surrender at Ulm, a great naval action was being fought off Cape Trafalgar which would insure Napoleon's subjection to British sea power for the remainder of his career.

Bonaparte's understanding of economics was typically imperial. Finance meant taxes and requisition, and his Grand Army was kept fighting by huge indemnities inflicted on its victims: "Making war support war," as David Chandler notes he was fond of saying.[55] Like all such regimes, Bonaparte's sought to bring order to the marketplace through centralization and administrative fiat. Yet he succeeded only in disguising reality and the grim fact that the British navy was squeezing the economic life out of his young transnational empire. Therefore, his responses to the British blockade, the Continental System, and the later Milan Decrees, aimed at embargoing all trade with the island kingdom, were so delusional that everyone, including his own brother, Louis of Holland,[56] regularly ignored them.

So despite the burden of two decades of almost continuous war, Great Britain, like Holland two centuries before, grew steadily richer through trading with her foes. And the profits, in the form of large and regular subsidies, were used to bankroll Napoleon's enemies on land.[57] In essence, the blockade was forcing the emperor to pay for his own destruction.

Yet ingenuity and brilliance on the level of grand strategy translated into equal measures of tedium, danger, and suffering at the point of enforcement. As David Howarth notes, the maintenance of a continuous, close blockade of the French battle fleet at Brest and Toulon for upward of two years was arguably the greatest feat of seamanship in history.[58] Night and day, winter and summer, the British ships traversed the same stretches of water. Packed together almost one thousand to a ship, while cold, damp, and always eating the same maggot-infested food, their crews came to hate this duty and to long for the day of battle like no other. But, meanwhile, they stood a mile or two offshore, waiting, watching, always visible to their foes.

The French, for their part, grew soft in port, never really learning to sail their ships well. Consequently, on 20 October 1805, when Admiral Villeneuve led his thirty-three French and Spanish battleships out of Cádiz harbor toward the Mediterranean, it was with the enthusiasm of a condemned man on his way to execution.

Early the next morning, Nelson appeared, and there ensued a truly Homeric encounter. Disdaining all caution and deliberately allowing his T to be crossed, Nelson sailed directly into the long Franco-Spanish line with his twenty-seven capital ships in two parallel files. "We scrambled into battle as best we could," wrote one lieutenant, "each man to take his bird."[59] For the central British tactic was to close to within point-blank range and lay alongside any enemy hull which presented itself.

The resulting carnage was horrible on both sides. Yet the French, like the inhabitants of the Armada and so many naval pretenders before, emphasized what amounted to land tactics, making heavy use of small-arms fire, grenades, and even trying to board Nelson's *Victory* at a critical moment. They succeeded in killing the English admiral—shot through the spine by a musketeer in the mizzen top. But while they did so the *Victory*'s main guns and those of the other engaged British battleships worked grimly onward, literally shooting the French and Spanish ships out from under their crews. Trafalgar and the gale that followed left Napoleon's fleet shattered, twenty-two of its thirty-three capital ships either destroyed or captured.[60] Never again would France contest control of the sea. Yet it would also prove to be the last great victory of the English battleship.

Thwarted by sea, Bonaparte continued to nurture the delusion of sealing off the Continent from the English. The Portuguese, who had shown the temerity to refuse adherence to the Continental System, were first to draw his ire. "If Portugal does not do as I wish, the House of Braganza will not be reigning in Europe in two months time,"[61] he thundered at a reception attended by the ever-observant Prince Metternich. True to his word, he sent General Junot on a lightning campaign which ended in the sack of Lisbon and the infliction of a huge war indemnity. Yet his gains would prove transitory.

In 1808 Spain, a supposed ally, drew Bonaparte's attention. Again the emperor's motive was the enforcement of the Continental System, though this time the pretext was a dynastic quarrel between the decrepit Spanish king and his dimwitted heir apparent. Ever since the Spanish tercio had been humbled at Rocroy during the latter stages of the Thirty Years War, Spain's military power had continued to skid until its army was among the worst-trained and least-effective regular forces in Europe. Moreover, Napoleon had expropriated its fifteen thousand best troops for service in Germany.[62] Therefore, when he intervened with 118,000 French soldiers, it was with high confidence of success.

At first things went smoothly. But when Bonaparte attempted to install his brother Louis as king and sought to arrest part of the Spanish royal family, Madrid erupted. Within three weeks the entire nation was in revolt. Soon it would be joined by a British army led by the French emperor's nemesis, Sir Arthur Wellesley, the future duke of Wellington. But Napoleon was determined to prevail. "If I thought it would cost me eighty-thousand men I would not attempt it; but it will cost me no more than twelve-thousand."[63] A quarter of a million French would die in Spain, and still there would be no victory.

For, as David Chandler notes, the Spanish people themselves had declared war on the emperor. One by one he defeated the Spanish armies, yet the irregulars in the hills fought all the more ferociously, using terror and ambush whenever possible. The French responded with their own acts of atrocity until the conflict took on all the trappings of predatory aggression—indiscriminate killing, the involvement of women in the actual fighting, and the mutual denial of common humanity by opponents. This triumph of violence, visually captured by Francisco Goya's *Desastres de Guerra,* stands as a monument to the military future. For just as Napoleon had transcended the eighteenth-century concept of war, so the Spanish people found a way around conventional military power. They waged a war of national liberation, and everyone became a potential combatant, or guerrilla, as they called themselves.

But Napoleon was incapable of understanding the limits of his power, and therefore learned nothing. Meanwhile, his old enemies were coming to adopt new methods.

By 1809 Austria was back in the war, this time fighting with real national enthusiasm and an army based on conscription. Built by Count Stadion and Archduke Charles, this force was a far more rugged fighting instrument than that which Napoleon shattered at Austerlitz.[64] After a series of bloody battles culminating in Wagram, the emperor, using all his military talents, achieved a victory of sorts. But there would be no more Jenas. And the cumulative effect of battle after battle was seriously degrading the quality of French troops, particularly the cavalry.

Then there was Russia. Even in the early stages of the Napoleonic Wars, Russian troops proved particularly tough opponents, frequently preferring death to capture. At Tilsit the emperor had been wise to make peace with the talented but unstable Czar Alexander I. So Russia continued as it was before, a giant yet unconquered and, not incidentally, a center of opposition to the Continental System. But like the irresistible wail of the siren, Mother Russia called tyrants eastward. And as with Charles XII and Adolph Hitler, she would draw Napoleon to her ample breast only to crush him in an icy embrace.

Having gathered 614,000 troops of a dozen nationalities, Bonaparte expected victory within twenty days.[65] But Alexander knew better, having predicted to the French ambassador Caulaincourt almost a year in advance:

> If the Emperor Napoleon decides to make war, it is possible, even probable, that we shall be defeated, assuming that we fight. . . . The Spaniards have frequently been defeated; and they are not beaten. . . . We have plenty of space; and our standing army is well-organized. Your Frenchman is brave, but long suffering and a hard climate wear down his resistance.[66]

Napoleon's central army group, 450,000 combatants, would be destroyed in almost exactly this manner. Too big and unwieldy to force a decisive engagement with the elusive Russians, it was drawn farther and farther inland, losing men all the way. At Smolensk the central group was down to 156,000. The showdown at Borodino, which was probably unnecessary, claimed still more. And on 14 September, when the ancient city of Moscow was occupied, the French numbered under 100,000. Napoleon waited thirty-three days for Russians bearing terms of surrender. None came, and in the end there was nothing to do but retreat.

As the army recrossed the field at Borodino, it viewed a wasteland, described by Marbot as "covered with the debris of helmets, cuirasses, wheels, weapons, rags of uniforms—and 30,000 corpses, half-eaten by wolves."[67] It was a grim portent of their immediate future. Without winter clothes or provisions, and harassed by irregulars all the way, less than twenty-five thousand bedraggled survivors would pass out of Russia in mid-December 1812. Napoleon Bonaparte's days as a transnational tyrant were over.

Yet Prince Metternich, Bonaparte's inveterate enemy, would have had him as a ruler of France. As impossible as this transformation sounds, it had a certain basis in reality. For Metternich's Austria was a sort of political red giant, the as yet to be impacted remains of Europe's oldest transnational empire. Held together by concepts of feudal obligation, it was not a nation-state, nor did it dare to act like one. Austria's appeal to patriotism, her experimentation with a conscript army were desperate measures which could not be prolonged.[68] Bonaparte was an interloper who had smashed the Enlightenment balance mechanism which Metternich personified. Yet as emperor he sought to replace it with nothing more radical than the traditional transnational crown of power, a network of political dependencies overseen by a small body of relatives and trusted minions. As was Alexander willing to accommodate the Persian nobility, so was Napoleon ready to strike a deal with Europe's aristocrats if they would help him rule. Now, with Napoleon's star on the wane, Metternich sought to return the favor. He would transform the emperor into a monarch of limited pretensions and, more importantly, reintegrate France into the reemergent balance.

But the voracity of Bonaparte was not to be curbed, as his rejection of the prince's generous terms and his eventual return from Elba so amply demonstrated.[69] And Metternich the realist was quick enough to cast him aside. For Bonaparte was but an expedient by which the prince might achieve the rehabilitation of France operating within a newly balanced European system.

And at the level of high politics, at least, this is what Metternich succeeded in doing. The Europe which emerged after 1818 was made up solely of powers in repose, all firmly in the hands of conservatives united in their determination to maintain the status quo. Indeed, a map at the time hardly would have indicated that anything of particular significance had occurred since 1789.

But of course it had. And Metternich basically understood what it was. In 1820 he wrote what he called "a profession of faith" in which he traced the origins of the present crisis to the beginning of the sixteenth century and the cumulative impact of printing, the discovery of the New World, and the gun.[70] The chief products of these changes, the true harbingers of chaos, were, in Metternich's eyes, the middle class, previously held in check only by aristocratic restraints which now must be reasserted. This task he made his life's work. Yet he could have lasting impact only at the level of geopolitics. For, as Henry Kissinger recognized: "The war fought by the kings against Napoleon, was fought by the people in part against their own masters."[71]

This was Bonaparte's true legacy, however unintended. By so battering the institutions of the ancien régime, he created the conditions for middle-class transcendence. The international balance would live on as the only perceived alternative to transnational tyranny and because it sufficiently reflected cultural, economic, and technological reality. Yet its underpinnings were either radically changed or on their way to transformation. So it was with war and weapons. In several key respects, the Napoleonic Wars were the first of the modern societal conflicts. Essentially, this was a matter of scale.

Armies had been expanding through the eighteenth century until, by its later stages, the various European powers kept a combined total of almost half a million men on permanent service. Yet the high relative costs of professional forces put a very definite cap on their ultimate growth. Indeed, monarchs throughout the eighteenth century were increasingly hard-pressed to finance even moderate expansion of their standing armies.

Nor were there any obvious alternatives. Sweden had introduced conscription as far back as Gustav Adolph, and somewhat later Russia and Prussia followed suit, requiring landlords to furnish a certain number of men for extended service.[72] But in all cases the harshness of military life, the system's failure to generate more loyalty, and the impossibility of removing too many men from the agricultural sector of these relatively poor states precluded huge jumps in force structures.

But France in 1793 was different. This was an economic giant whose population, already the largest in Europe and expanding rapidly since the mid-eighteenth century, was caught up with political enthusiasm and ready to serve. Bonaparte would take full advantage of the situation, enrolling 1.3 million men by conscription and an even greater body of volunteers between 1800 and 1812.[73] In the end his enemies could only resort to similar methods, fielding armies numbering in excess of seven hundred thousand in 1812. Prosperity made these numbers possible, and political and patriotic zeal would transform them into reality. The demographics of war were revolutionized. Armies in the millions would soon be the norm.

Enrollment was but one dimension of this phenomenon; death was another. And here was the beginning of something very significant. A great many men were killed in the Napoleonic Wars, something like one million from battle wounds alone. French losses from all causes amounted to between 1.3 and 1.5 million; those of her combined enemies numbered at least that many.[74] These were primarily soldiers, not noncombatants. According to Houdaille, over 20 percent of all French males born between 1790 and 1795 died before 1816 from war-related causes.[75] Reproductively, this was bound to have an impact. And, indeed, the Napoleonic Wars not only brought to a halt the French population surge of the late eighteenth century, but began a long period of stability perpetuated deliberately through birth control methods introduced, possibly, through French soldiers' experiences with prostitutes.

The demographic impact of the Napoleonic Wars on France, and the subsequent effect of the two world wars on the habitation patterns of Central and Eastern Europe, has led William McNeill to assign to this class of warfare a primary role in relieving the pressures of excess population.[76] Although his approach is sophisticated and multidimensional, it seems extreme. Not only is it difficult to define what constitutes overpopulation, but it is also hard to believe that mass warfare would prove more attractive as a safety valve than emigration. Besides,

such an explanation dismisses too easily the personal aggressiveness of a Napoleon or a Hitler and the expansionistic tendencies of the kinds of states they both
personified.

Yet McNeill has nevertheless hit upon something. There was a lemminglike
quality to postrevolutionary French soldiers that foreshadows the mass acceptance
of death so characteristic of the great industrial wars of the twentieth century.
True, soldiers would no longer be required to stand in lines blasting away at one
another, but they remained all too willing to charge blindly into a maelstrom of
fire. Whether this thanatotic stupor resulted from some genetically transmitted
behavior pattern tripped, as McNeill hints, by overpopulation or was simply the
traditional acquiescence and obedience of those about to be slaughtered, played
out through a combination of the Homeric urge to close and the new ethic of
firepower (pretend the bullets aren't there), is obviously impossible to say. Yet
the fact that ordinary citizens, large segments of which had not been drawn into
the military since the days of the Roman Republic, would so willingly cast away
their lives on the battlefield was recognized and almost immediately exploited. In
particular, Napoleon's increasing reliance on direct assault of entrenched firepower was almost guaranteed to produce high casualties. Yet war's end brought
no concerted rejection of this approach. French military thinkers of the nineteenth
century were notable for lionizing the offensive spirit. This reassertion of the
ancient desire to close was particularly irrational in that the need to counter such
tactics was so amply served by steady and dramatic increases in firepower. Nevertheless, the offensive spirit and the automation of the gun were destined to collide,
with particularly deadly consequences.

From a societal perspective, however, it was also apparent that huge manpower losses and massive destruction could be much better endured by states
having undergone mercantile and industrial transformation. Thus, unlike in the
period after the Thirty Years' War, western Europe emerged from the Napoleonic
conflicts almost refreshed. This would certainly be less true of the two world
wars, but still the material recovery period remained remarkably short.

Indeed, on purely economic grounds, chemical energy–based societal warfare
had much to recommend it. Nevertheless, historians of the Industrial Revolution
have tended to either ignore the impact of the Napoleonic conflicts or assign to it
a negative role, as has, most notably, John Nef.[77]

This is peculiar. Not only did the wars draw off the underemployed masses
that commerce and industry were creating, but they generated huge markets for
the very metal-producing and machine-building sectors that were leading the economic revolution. Although individual weapons remained cheap, they were all
made of metal, and this factor, when multiplied by the massive force structure
involved, spelled an almost two-decade-long period of unprecedented demand on
Europe's ironmasters. This was particularly true in Great Britain, where the new
large-scale coke-fired blast furnaces of Wales and Scotland, hearths destined one
day to produce boilers and locomotives, were financed by the steady market for
smoothbore cannon.[78] Yet it was also apparent in France, where yearly production
of iron cannon shot up from nine hundred to thirteen thousand, and seventeen new
foundries produced up to fourteen thousand bronze tubes annually. In addition,
French fabricators turned out nearly four million small arms between 1804 and

1815, while, in England, Birmingham alone produced a similar number in the same time frame.[79]

True, war's end also brought an end to the demand for arms, and soon depression. Yet in England it also set off a mad scramble for new markets. And ultimately it was the largess of war which was primarily responsible for financing the key to future growth, the capacity to produce very large quantities of cheap, high-quality metal.

Meanwhile, the connection between huge profits and weapons had been firmly implanted in the entrepreneurial memory bank. These were really the same empirical, inventive types who had been creating weapons since the days of the Hellenistic monarchies. Basically, what had changed was an awareness that a great deal of money could be made doing it. Of course wars were known to be sporadic and based on conditions largely out of the control of weapons producers. Yet their interest and attention were really enough, for the design stagnation of available weaponry was bound to draw the attention of a group dedicated to making things work better.

VI

Actually, this process of improvement had begun during the last days of the ancien régime and appears to have been spurred somewhat by the coming of so desperate a series of wars. Gribeauval had refined, though not revolutionized, French artillery beginning in 1776, but wholesale adoption had to wait until Napoleon.

Meanwhile, there were other experiments of greater significance, if less immediate effect. During the siege of Gibraltar in 1779, the French introduced a 5.5-inch explosive projectile with a more rugged fuse, though it still had to be fired from a mortar and was never widely employed.[80] In 1784 General Henry Shrapnel developed the first explosive shell containing subprojectiles arranged to be scattered at high velocity upon detonation, thereby significantly increasing its kill radius. Notably, Shrapnel's invention was first used not in Europe but in Surinam in 1804, and was not to be proliferated during the Napoleonic conflicts despite some British use in Spain.[81]

In 1799 a British colonel, Sir William Congreve, took an interest in the primitive rockets he had observed in India and later produced an improved version with which he set the entire city of Boulogne afire in 1806. Obviously proud of himself he wrote: "The rocket is, in truth, an arm by which the whole system of military tactics is destined to change." He was premature, but for a time British ordnance makers shared his enthusiasm, developing an iron-headed version with a contact-fuse explosive charge and a two-mile range. But this was short-lived. Although Francis Scott Key would immortalize Congreve's "rockets' red glare," they failed in their main purpose (as the song's next line indicates) and were not used extensively again in the nineteenth century.[82]

Meanwhile, at sea Bushnell's submarine, as noted, had attacked surface vessels as far back as the American Revolution. Almost twenty-five years later, Robert Fulton briefly gained Napoleon's interest in a four-man submarine and a series of unpropelled, contact-activated, zero-buoyancy charges he called torpedoes. When the emperor turned to other things, William Pitt, in turn, encouraged Fulton to try out the devices against the French squadron at Boulogne, which he did the night of 2 October 1805, actually sinking a pinnace—the first such wartime casualty recorded. Yet in general the experiment was seen as a failure, and Fulton's torpedoes were quickly dropped. "Pitt was the greatest fool that ever existed," fulminated the earl of Saint Vincent, first lord of the Admiralty, "to encourage a mode of war which they who commanded the seas did not want, and which if successful, would deprive them of it."[83] Even in the air the infant balloon corps, founded in 1793 by French revolutionaries, was disbanded by Napoleon.

Quite plainly, the military establishment agreed with Admiral Saint Vincent. Weapons were to be taken as a given, not improved. What little enthusiasm there had been for martial invention within the military ranks evaporated at war's end, and in its place the convenient forgetfulness of Enlightenment arms control returned.

The profoundest example is Karl von Clausewitz, if only because he was the era's last and most brilliant student of war. Obviously a man of insight, his thoughts on the relationship between policy and coercion remain widely quoted, if not exactly followed or even studied. Yet as early as 1804 he clearly perceived the alternate poles of aggression—predatory and intraspecific—in describing two basic kinds of war, those "waged to exterminate the opponent" and those fought to "impose conditions at a peace conference."[84] But when it came to weapons, Clausewitz had virtually nothing to say. This was not characteristic. His unfinished masterpiece, *On War,* methodically sets out to examine, in excruciating detail, every aspect of tactics and strategy, and does so with a vengeance. But amid the hail of verbiage, the tools of the trade are hardly touched. Clearly, this was not a matter of ignorance since in asides Clausewitz reveals himself to be thoroughly conversant with the capabilities of contemporary weaponry.[85] Rather, it seems as if weapons were taken as a given, a sort of base condition which, like human nature, is so fundamental as to not require explanation. This, of course, was hardly the case, and it seems that a man of Clausewitz's intellect, writing as late as the 1830s, a time of rapidly increasing mechanical ingenuity, should have recognized the possibility that weapons might be improved decisively. Yet the thought apparently never fought its way into his consciousness.

This is highly understandable since this was one area in which aristocratic dominance had not been swept away. Indeed, the effective operation of Metternich's balance mechanism was highly dependent on the control of coercive instruments by those with what was essentially a reactionary worldview. So for a time military leadership remained in the hands of those who had always held it. But this was a temporary condition, dependent on peacekeeping armies, relatively small and well-insulated from the pervasion of middle-class values. But in the second half of the nineteenth century, large-scale conflicts would again erupt, and with them came the resurgent legacy of the Napoleonic era, the democratization of war and, not far behind, men anxious to make money improving its tools. Since then it has been one laborsaving device after another.

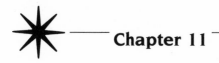

Chapter 11

DEATH MACHINE

I

Change would come at last. Near the midpoint of the nineteenth century a fundamental transformation overtook the course of arms in the West. Pressures had been building for almost a century, but it was not until approximately 1840 that they reached a sufficient intensity to overcome the psychological and institutional inertia which had been the essence of the previous era's accommodation to firearms.

By this time armaments had become a backwater, an exceptionally stagnant pool in an otherwise swiftly flowing current of technology. The sluices and barriers which isolated the military world and its tools were formidable, but so was the mainstream, and eventually the dams against change would begin to crumble.

Partially, this was a matter of neglect. In the Western world, the first half of the nineteenth century was a time of peace and optimism. As the years passed, the memory of Bonaparte grew dim, and subsequent wars proved mild and infrequent. Meanwhile, the pervasive gospel of progress through mechanical invention caused venerable weapons such as "Brown Bess" and the sailing ship-of-the-line to be perceived as more and more anachronistic. So, within and without the military services, it began to occur to inventive souls that things could be made better.

As in the past, the motives for improving armaments were less warlike than technical and economic. Yet now there was a significant shift in emphasis. Whereas the majority of prior weapons developments, including those of the gun, had been intended originally for hunting other species, not men, from this point arms innovations were much more frankly aimed at military use, or at least possession.[1] But even so, the major intent was not mayhem but a desire to capitalize on markets created by enlarged force structures and the need to replace obsolescent weaponry. On the other hand, until World War I, it was generally argued that weapons of increased efficiency made war less, rather than more, likely, due to their deterrent effect. Meanwhile, it was both true and significant that weapons developed during this period in the West tended to be used first externally against non-Caucasians living in strange and exotic circumstances. As always, new armaments were most easily employed if their victims could be conceptualized, however implausibly, as belonging to another species.

Nevertheless, the impact of the mechanization of arms was profoundly disruptive at home, not only to the bureaucratic patterns of Western armies and navies but to the most fundamental conceptions of what constituted the proper conduct of war, both on land and at sea.

Yet the military profession was a calling rich in cultural heritage and alternative behavior patterns. And as Western soldiers and sailors struggled to find the basis for a new military ethos, they would draw instinctively and repeatedly upon the past, resurrecting a number of ancient martial archetypes and applying them to weapons that were unprecedented, at least in a material sense. Some of these combinations were outlandish and failed miserably. Yet others worked, and in the end the military profession succeeded in forging a new context for war which accommodated the reality of industrialized weapons technology fairly well. Yet what worked for the military profession was far less successful politically and in terms of society as a whole. Then again, the era of the gun and chemical energy–based armaments was drawing to a close.

Change is by definition relative. The transformation of arms which took place between 1840 and 1945 is frequently referred to as revolutionary. In a material, tangible sense, this is true enough, but it is also misleading. Most of the weapons which came to dominate warfare in the first half of the twentieth century had been conceptualized at the very dawn of the era. This is important to realize since there is a decided tendency to view nuclear weapons as the logical extension of this spiral of arms developments. Although the active state of military research and development certainly helped bring the bomb to fruition, nuclear weapons themselves constitute a fundamental break with the past, and they have transformed politics accordingly. On the other hand, the arms innovations which will be examined in the next several chapters are contiguous with developments which began much earlier. A revolution, perhaps, but one which transpired within the long shadow cast by Leonardo da Vinci.

II

Although the transformation of weaponry would eventually become dependent on an entire complex of inventions, many of which were of general rather than specific military utility, the first innovations to have major impact upon warfare were aimed directly at improving military firearms. Moreover, it was these changes—the ability to shoot faster, more accurately, and with increasingly devastating effects—which would alter the entire cast of warfare.

The process would begin almost randomly with a few key, but basically uncoordinated, improvements. However, as momentum gathered, gun-based innovations began to stem from more rational analysis and to conform to general paths of development. Englishmen frequently led the way, but from the beginning it was an international phenomenon, with military inventors across Europe and North America capitalizing on each other's work.

Since its appearance, the musket, both matchlock and flintlock fired, had been severely handicapped by inclement weather, being generally incapable of detonation in either heavy wind or rain. However, around the turn of the nineteenth century, fulminate of mercury, a practical explosive capable of detonation upon impact, was discovered. Within a few years the Reverend Alexander Forsyth, a sports-loving Scottish clergyman, successfully applied the principal to a hammer-fired hunting rifle. This, in turn, led directly to the development of a simple, effective percussion cap which could be fitted to any flintlock and became available for military use around 1820. Conversion proceeded slowly, though, the British Ordnance Department being typical in resisting the trend until 1839. But two years later an event took place in the Orient which brought the advantages of firing caps sharply into focus. Two companies of British marines armed with percussion-fired muskets succeeded in rescuing a small body of Indian sepoys beset by a thousand Chinese and a rainstorm which rendered their flintlocks useless. The resulting piles of wet, dead Chinese demonstrated as well as anything could that fire fighting was no longer a fair-weather pursuit.[2]

Meanwhile, other significant changes were taking place within the firing chambers of the traditional military musket. Of prime importance was the evolution of the cylindroconoidal bullet. Although a number of alternatives had been tried over the centuries, the necessity of maintaining a tight bore seal continued to make the military rifle vastly harder to load than its quick-firing but wildly inaccurate smoothbore cousin.

This began to change around 1832, when a Captain Norton of the British Thirty-Fourth Regiment became interested in the blowgun darts he saw during his tour in southern India. Crafted with a base of lotus pith which expanded when shot to seal the inner surface of the tube, these darts planted the seed of an idea in Norton's mind. The principle, he reasoned, might be extended to a rifle bullet, which could be designed with a hollow base shaped to deform upon firing to create a tight seal with the gun barrel, while still allowing it to be dropped easily through the bore and loaded as rapidly as a musket ball. The concept was enthusiastically taken up by Captain Claude-Etienne Minié, the Frenchman who gave his name to the perfected projectile when it appeared in 1849. By 1851, Minié ball–firing rifles were issued to British troops for use overseas, and one year later were first employed against Bantu tribesmen. They proved exceedingly accurate, and British soldiers were amazed to discover that Bantu could be picked off at up to thirteen hundred years, or at least four times the extreme range of smoothbore muskets.[3]

In Prussia the problem of rifle loading was being attacked, quite literally, from another direction. Almost from the beginning of the gun's evolution, it had been recognized that the problems inherent in forcing a projectile down the bore could be circumvented if a safe, foolproof means were found to load it at the breech.

Now improvements in metallurgy and fabrication were making this a much more viable proposition. Consequently, in 1840 Prussia's King Frederick William was able to make the bold decision to begin secretly equipping his army with the newly invented Dreyse breech-loading rifle, better known as the needle gun after its elongated firing pin. Due to a chronically leaky breach seal, the needle gun's range was not much more than half that of the Minié rifle, but it could fire seven shots per minute to the Minié's two. Still more important tactically, as J. F. C. Fuller points out, the needle gun could be loaded in a prone position, while the muzzle-fed Minié rifle required its operator to stand up to load, thereby creating a much larger target to shoot at.[4]

So advantageous were the characteristics of the needle gun that the Prussian king and his advisors made an initial order of sixty thousand rifles and did everything in their power to hasten the reequipment. Yet seven years later, in 1847, the inventor Johann Nickolas von Dreyse, had only managed to expedite production to the level of ten thousand rifles per year. Consequently, in 1866, when the needle gun had its first real test in battle, it had already required twenty-six years to reequip the three hundred thousand man Prussian army with the quick-firing rifles.[5] Clearly, if qualitative improvements were to be fully useful with available force structures, something had to be done to speed production.

This, too, was coming. Although a large-scale enterprise since the early sixteenth century, when the Liègeois began specializing in small-arms production, gunsmithing had remained a craft-bound cottage industry. Under such circumstances, numerous specialists worked as subcontractors for entrepreneurs, who in turn agreed to deliver a specified number of finished guns (each one essentially hand made and therefore not identical) to the central authorities. However, in America, as William McNeill notes, due to a persistent shortage of skilled gunsmiths, a new, more capital-intensive system evolved between 1820 and 1850, both at the U.S. arsenal at Springfield and among private producers of the Connecticut valley. Based on a series of automatic and semiautomatic milling machines working on the pantographic principle, first used during Hellenistic times to replicate statuary, the system reproduced gun parts so exactly that they became interchangeable. This fact was graphically illustrated in England during the Great Exhibition of 1851 when Yankee entrepreneur Samuel Colt disassembled a number of his revolvers, mixed up the parts, and then put them back together in working order with pieces chosen at random.[6]

This demonstration was of particular interest since, not only were local British craftsmen in the midst of a work slowdown brought on by the Minié rifle's closer parts tolerances, but the Crimean War would soon create a tremendous demand for the precisely made rifles. While the necessary machinery could not be imported from America and fully installed before 1859 (three years after the war had ended), from this point the English small-arms industry was increasingly committed to mechanization and automation. Soon domestically designed machines were turning out 250,000 Minié bullets and 200,000 finished cartridges per day at the Royal Arsenal.[7] Nor was this an isolated phenomenon. Charles H. Fitch, in a report to the U.S. Congress, would boast that, by 1870, Russia, Spain, Turkey,

Sweden, Denmark, and Egypt had all purchased American milling machines to make guns.

In the past, small arms had been plentiful largely because they could be acquired cumulatively, collected from a limited stream of roughly standardized models over a long period. Now firearms might be changed dramatically and supplied in huge quantities of exact copies in a matter of a few years. The military implications were profoundly destabilizing. Practically overnight an order-of-magnitude shift in the balance of individual firepower might be accomplished, potentially leaving an equivalent number of adversaries virtually helpless.

To compound matters, in roughly the same time frame, changes of nearly equal significance would begin to take place in artillery. And in this case the effects would be felt not only on land but at sea as well. Again it was the Crimean War which would provide the stimulus.

According to J. D. Scott, William Armstrong, previously a producer of hydraulic equipment, was sitting in his London club reading an account of the Battle of Inkerman, during which British troops saved themselves by finally succeeding in wrestling their ponderous smoothbore artillery into firing position, when he was heard to exclaim that it was "time military engineering was brought up to the level of current engineering practice."[8] With that he promptly drew up plans for a revolutionary breech-loading piece which, rather than being cast of homogeneous metal, was built up from a series of metal strips (later wire) wound around a central core and sheathed with an outer hoop heated to fit around it and then allowed to cool so as to exert tremendous pressure inward. Not only was the prototype a success, but, as McNeill points out, its strength-to-weight ratio was so superior to that achieved by traditional methods that it pointed the way to guns vastly larger than those which could be cast as a single piece and expected to stay together when fired.[9]

Three years earlier an event had taken place which would literally blow three hundred years of military naval architecture out of the water. As noted earlier, explosive projectiles with improved fusing had been available since the late eighteenth century. Because they had been confined to high-trajectory weapons like mortars, they were largely ignored, particularly at sea, where a ship's rocking motion made anything other than flat-shooting guns virtually impossible to aim. In 1824, however, Henri Paixhans developed a horizontal-firing shell gun with which he successfully broke up an old naval hulk in a test. More than a decade would pass before the French and the British navies got around to officially adopting Paixhans's guns, but it was already an open secret that every wooden warship afloat was now a great deal more vulnerable.

Just how vulnerable was demonstrated on 30 November 1853, when a flotilla of ten Turkish ships sent to fire on the Russian coast was encountered in the Bay of Sinope by a squadron of czarist men-of-war mounting Paixhans's guns. In a hail of splinters and flame, the Russians sank all but one of the Turkish vessels, killing four thousand men.[10] But the real victim was the oak warship and the European navies for which it had been a mainstay for so long.

The bursting effect of the shell, as Henri Paixhans realized thirty years before, suggested its own antidote—armor plate. Since the explosive projectiles could not penetrate much below the waterline, relative invulnerability to shell fire seemed at first attainable through sheathing only those surfaces exposed to the air with a relatively thin coat of armor.

But it was now possible for naval guns and the shells they fired to be made much larger, a contingency which logically demanded thicker armor. But wrought iron, or other suitable material, was extremely heavy—so heavy, in fact, that even limited use of armor plating imposed a weight penalty so severe that it called the whole proposition of wind-powered propulsion immediately into question. For it was clear from the beginning that sails would be incapable of generating the motive force to drive such weighty vessels through the water.

Once again technology provided an alternative in the form of a parallel revolution, already well underway, in steam engineering. Since 1807, when Robert Fulton had demonstrated the feasibility of applying the reciprocating steam engine to drive a vessel up the Hudson River, astonishingly rapid strides had been made, and more would soon come. For example, just thirty years were required before a steamship, the paddle-wheeler *Sirius,* managed to cross the Atlantic with an engine rated at six hundred horsepower. Barely twenty years later, steam engines with a combined total of 11,500 horsepower would propel the 27,000-ton, 690-foot *Great Eastern* at nearly fifteen knots.[11]

Yet these ships were paddle wheelers whose vulnerability and location along the sides of the hull, well above the waterline, left little room for armament and argued strongly against military application. However, the screw propeller, based on Bernoulli's principles and first applied by David Bushnell in his ill-fated *Turtle,* provided an elegant alternative. By 1843, Swedish inventor John Ericsson, under the patronge of an energetic American, Captain Robert F. Stockton, had built the first prop-driven warship in the world.[12] The ship's screw propeller, besides being considerably more efficient than the paddle, allowed most of the steam equipment to operate out of harm's way below the waterline, clearing an increased portion of the deck for armament. In what amounted to a puff of smoke, the warship had become a self-propelled entity, liberated from the vagaries of the wind and free to grow in virtually any direction dictated by guns and armor.

Although there would be transitional vessels like the French *Gloire* (1858) and its British counterpart, *Warrior,* almost from the beginning it was clear that the internal logic of these trends would lead to ships with fewer, much bigger guns, armor plate in profusion, even more powerful engines, and iron-only construction strong enough to bear the weight of all this technical progress—in short, vessels whose general configuration and appearance bore little resemblance to the great wooden ships-of-the-line which had for so long held front and center upon the stage of European naval history. In their place would emerge, very early in the design cycle, a sort of primitive, generalized steam battleship which, like man's primary ancestor *Australopithecus afarensis,* had all the elements necessary for final development and awaited only a better interrelationship of its parts.

These few developments—long-range, rapid-fire small arms; large, explosive-shelled artillery; and the steam battleship—were at the heart of the first wave of weapons which would sweep down upon warfare and change it so dramatically in the second half of the nineteenth century. Yet on the eve of the American Civil War, their significance was apparent to literally no one—least of all the inventors.

The founders of the modern military-industrial complex were not a great deal different in their motives than the latter-day board chairman of Lockeed or General Dynamics, nor did they necessarily part company with the military inventors who preceded them. The differences were in the power of the technologies available for application and in the continuity implied by the institutionalization of research and development. Often enough the men who fostered the first changes in the tools of war came from a military background, frequently serving on active duty when they began their careers as inventors. Yet without exception they were neither great military leaders nor aristocrats at the pinnacle of the rank hierarchy. Rather, they tended to be of middle- and upper-middle-class origins, marginal officers who often left the service with their innovations, hoping to make money producing them. Quite clearly, it was less patriotism and an ambition to revolutionize their particular service's fighting ability than it was the desire to make a quick dollar—or pound, or mark, or franc—which drove these men.

It was that and also the sheer intoxication with power which pervaded not only military technology but the whole complex of inventions brought to fruition during the nineteenth century. From our own jaded perspective it is easy to see only irony in the sense of liberation and potency which accompanied the introduction of steam-based technologies, freeing man virtually overnight from ancient limitations, multiplying his strength a thousandfold. Suddenly capable of casting, beating, and bending metal into unheard of shapes and in gargantuan quantities, and then driving them along case-hardened rails or through the bounding sea at impossible speeds, industrialized man and, in particular, the inventors were given every reason to celebrate their prepotence. And what better talisman of force could there be than the implements of death? So these men, or at least a representative sample, saw to their mechanization.

Given their outlook, a Shrapnel, Minié, Dreyse, Paixhans, Colt, or Armstrong generally had little conception of what their inventions might mean for the actual conduct of war. Nor did they seem to care a great deal. They and their apologists frequently voiced a belief that modern weaponry would make combat so terrible as to render it unbearable and therefore unlikely. Yet this was clearly a superficial judgment, the kind of glib platitude easily spun off a mind not particularly concerned with the darker side of life. By and large these were not guilt-ridden men, nor were they particularly bloodthirsty. They were simply militarized analogues of the proverbial entrepreneur, believers in mechanical invention and infused with the optimism it engendered. They were in the process of creating something terrible and awe-inspiring. But they hardly suspected it.

Nor were they alone. Professional military and naval officers faced the first flood of new weaponry with something approaching somnolence.

Initially, the bristling protests and reactionary maneuvering symptomatic of later military responses to arms innovations appear to have been muted and relatively rare. Instead, passive acceptance was the order of the day. For like the civilian world, the ranks of the warlike had been largely removed by time from firsthand knowledge of their trade. The long era of peace and the day-to-day rituals of small, professionalized force structures apparently dulled the memory of what mass warfare could be like and what improved weaponry might mean in such a context. And since the eighteenth-century version of arms control was based on unspoken assumptions, there was little to alert their collective imaginations to the danger.

So it was that change came to Western arsenals, at first in a halfhearted trickle and then, as the pace picked up among European and American services, in a torrent. By 1860 percussion caps and Minié ball rifles had become virtually universal, with true repeaters not far behind; rifled cannon and early breechloaders were making steady inroads in artillery parks; and steam-powered, armor-clad warships were the only major units being added to Western flotillas.

Amid the deluge, up to their necks in change, officers seem to have said and thought very little about it. Disarmed by the obvious technical superiority of what was being made available, and momentarily without coherent counterarguments, the military simply let it happen.

And when it came time to actually fight, Western officers initially faced the deadly hail of Minié and other bullets with tactical schemes basically unchanged from the previous era. Finding their ranks shot to pieces, they would then look to the heroic past for answers. At sea, where the transformation was rather more obvious, the Homeric urge to close was dredged up even faster in the form of the ram. Yet, in essence, both response patterns were similar. That they proved incorrect was less important than their capacity to accommodate the new weapons in some meaningful military context. For the near certainty of death, it seems, was preferable to tactical anomie to officers. Meanwhile, their men did what they could to stay alive.

And what of politics and its inevitable relationship to warfare? Here, in the last analysis, was the most damage done, the distortions the most profound. For in their prodigious capacity to kill, weapons gradually took control of events, capriciously bending what were intended to be limited conflicts into acts of slaughter so excessive that, in the end, war became the natural environment of only the most bestial of transnational tyrants. It would seem that this was the destiny of an era begun with Charles VIII's invasion and postponed only by the eighteenth century's resort to arms control. Now it would come to fruition, not in the limited intentions of Lincoln, Bismarck, and Lloyd George but on the apocalyptic battlefields of Gettysburg, Sedan, and the Somme. And, like the inventors and the soldiers, the politicans had only the barest idea of what was happening. Instead, they temporized and pontificated and looked everywhere for the cause of their troubles except at the arms with which they sent their men to fight.

III

It could be said without exaggerating overmuch that the Civil War remains the central event in American history, a watershed which fixed the political and constitutional future of our nation, marked its transition to an industrial state, and charted the course of subsequent race relations within our borders. And, as such, it has drawn students of American history like a magnet. But precisely because of its multifarious significance, its importance as a purely military experience has been frequently underestimated. Even when the martial side of the war has been addressed, it has been largely in terms of the thoughts and actions of its leaders or in sterile tactical studies.

Yet, in the end, the American Civil War stands out as the first truly modern conflict, and like subsequent wars of this nature, its course was to be primarily determined by factors of production and, more specifically, weapons technology. Central among these was the influence exerted by small arms, as Grady McWhiney and Perry D. Jamieson have shown in their recent book, *Attack and Die*.[13]

Ironically, it was Jefferson Davis, then U.S. secretary of war and future president of the Confederacy, who announced in his 1854 annual report the preliminary results of tests on the Minié ball rifle showing "that the new weapon, while it can be loaded as readily as the ordinary musket, is at least equally effective at three times the distance."[14] Though momentarily urging caution, by the next year Davis was indicating that the national armories had ceased all musket production and would commence manufacturing the new military rifles by the end of the year. Soon after hostilities began, the Model 1861 Springfield rifle, capable of killing fire at a thousand yards, would become the standard issue for Union infantry, while Confederate troops were being equipped with small arms equally as good.

The result was mass slaughter. For the tactical conceptions and practices of both Union and Confederate commanders changed far more slowly than was warranted by the weapons in the hands of their troops. Meanwhile, the careers of numerous Northern and Southern military leaders, including Grant, Lee, McClellan, Beauregard, Hancock, Longstreet, Hooker, A. S. Johnston, Thomas, Jefferson Davis, Meade, and Bragg were shaped by the Mexican War, a conflict in which smoothbore muskets far outnumbered rifles in all decisive actions.[15] Here, closed-rank linear formations and very aggressive Napoleonic bayonet charges bore spectacular results and relatively few casualities in a series of stunning American victories. It was a lesson the participants would not soon forget. Therefore, although there were some accommodations to the rifle in William J. Hardee's update of Winfield Scott's basic tactical manual, nearly all commanders on both sides, particularly the Southerners, entered the Civil War assuming that what had worked against the Mexicans would work against each other.

Instead, the opposing forces found themselves locked in a bloodbath, with the aggressive Southerners, urged on by the ever-combative Jefferson Davis, suffering particularly intensely. In eight of the first twelve big battles, Confederates assumed the tactical offensive, and lost ninety-seven thousand men doing so. Altogether, the South suffered 175,000 battle casualities in the first twenty-seven months of fighting, a figure somewhat higher than the entire Confederate military establishment in 1861.[16]

"It was not war—it was murder," concluded General Daniel H. Hill after his division lost two thousand of its sixty-five hundred men attacking Union positions at Malvern Hill.[17] Or, rather, it was mass suicide. For, as McWhiney and Jamieson conclude, the South, in the process of winning a series of Pyrrhic tactical victories, bled itself white during the first three years of war.[18]

There was little recognition of what was happening. Instead, Robert E. Lee bemoaned losing the tactical initiative, and Jefferson Davis persisted in sacking generals such as Joseph E. Johnston who saw virtue in the defensive and calculated retreat.

Nor was the level of understanding necessarily any higher on the side of the blue. In most cases Northern military leaders expressed regret at assuming the defensive, and cautious generals like George McClellan often found themselves unemployed. Instead, Ulysses S. Grant became the Union commander par excellence. "He fights," Abraham Lincoln was heard to say, summing up his favorite general's virtues.[19]

And fight he did—accumulating sixty-four thousand casualties during the three months of his sledgehammer Wilderness campaign and taking as the major sign of victory, in late May 1864, the fact that a battle with Lee's troops "outside of entrenchments cannot be had."[20] Yet the Confederates would remain unbeaten inside their trenches for almost a year more. And, in fact, a better indication of the true tactical situation was the spectacle of Union troops pinning their names to their uniforms shortly before the notorious frontal assault on Confederate positions at Cold Harbor on 3 June so that their corpses might be better identified after the battle.[21]

Unlike their officers, foot soldiers drew an altogether more practical, if less heroic, conclusion as to the tactical significance of new weaponry, and sought cover and defensible positions whenever possible. Thus, by mid-1863 both sides were becoming addicted to trenches, whenever possible "digging at the ground like terriers," as Stephen Crane's fictional hero of The Red Badge of Courage describes the veterans on his flank shortly before his first action.[22] Archetypical in this regard was William Tecumseh Sherman's Army of Tennessee, which Bruce Catton describes as not having drilled for two years but refusing to let wagons carry their spades so as to have them handy for emergency digging.[23] Writing his wife from Spotsylvania Court House, Colonel Theodore Lyman made much the same point about the Confederates: "It is a rule that when the Rebels halt, the first day gives them a good rifle pit; the second a regular infantry parapet with artillery in position. . . . You would be amazed to see how this country is intersected with field works."[24]

As far as they went, field fortifications were an entirely correct solution to the revolution in small arms, the long-range rifle having roughly tripled the advantage of defense over offense by putting attacking troops under deadly fire almost from the moment they became visible. Yet trenches also prefaced a very static and inconclusive sort of war, as the siege of Richmond-Petersburg indicated. Thus, at some point it became necessary for troops to physically overcome opposing trenches. Logically, this required an advance made all the more costly by the prepared nature of the objective. Troops were encouraged to move faster and in looser formations, but there were clearly limits to these measures, and very few fixed positions were taken by frontal assault during the Civil War. With considerable ingenuity Federal forces sought a substitute in a huge explosive mine dug under Confederate positions at Petersburg. But this, like its successor at the Messines

Ridge during the 1917 Flanders offensive, proved spectacular but indecisive.[25] (It did, however, represent a renewed willingness to employ a true weapon of mass destruction, a phenomenon pioneered during the Dutch rebellion with the "Hell-burner of Antwerp.")

Long-range small arms continued to present two basic alternatives to the traditional close-order firing line: the first, a passive analogue of the previous formation—linear trenches made continuously longer by efforts to flank; and the second, a Homeric throwback—closing with opposing forces as rapidly as possible. The first became the proverbial choice of the common foot soldier, the second, the preferred solution of the military profession. Neither was satisfactory. And although major improvements in artillery would soon add another variable, it was on the horns of this dilemma that millions of fighting men would perish over the next sixty years.

The second major outcome to emerge from the availability of long-range small arms during the Civil War was the sheer magnitude of their dominance. This can be illustrated by statistics cited by Gilbert Beebe and Michael DeBakey indicating that of a representative sample of 144,000 Civil War casualties, 108,000 were caused by conoidal rifle bullets and only around 13,000 by cannon-fired ball and shell—a major shift when it is considered that artillery had traditionally inflicted around one-half of battle injuries.[26] Such figures leave little doubt that in the space of a very few years the long-standing and balanced relationship between infantry, artillery, and cavalry had undergone major realignment.

In the most immediate sense this had significant tactical implications for the other traditional arms. Truly effective rifled artillery and explosive shells being still a few years off in the future, Civil War smoothbore cannon had consistent trouble outranging rifle-equipped infantry. Consequently, their crews frequently found themselves under heavy and accurate small-arms fire as they attempted to work their pieces. Although cannon remained relatively potent on the defensive against charging troops, they lost virtually all of their importance as implements of the offense. But this shift, at least, was temporary.

Cavalry, on the other hand, was deeply and permanently undermined. The fate of the saber charge was epitomized by the deaths of one Major Keenan and his adjutant, who jointly led a column of the Eighth Pennsylvania Horse in a desperate advance against Stonewall Jackson's victorious infantry at Chancellorsville. Not only did the charge fail miserably, but after the battle the bodies of Keenan and his adjutant were found to have thirteen and nine bullet wounds, respectively.[27] Given the prospects of surviving such a charge, sabers were employed so rarely that John S. Mosby of the First Virginia Cavalry noted that "the only real use I ever heard of their being put to was to hold a piece of meat over a fire for frying."[28] Instead, mounted troops learned to rely on firearms and fight dismounted as dragoons, even against each other.

Superior mobility continued to endow Civil War cavalry with some use for strategic reconnaissance and as raiders, but their traditional fighting role on the battlefield virtually disappeared and would not return. Subsequent proponents would do all in their power (particularly in peacetime) to suppress this iconoclastic notion. But the fact remained that charging cavalry presented targets too large and vulnerable to ever stand a reasonable chance of closing to within saber range against even disorganized infantry.

A similar fate befell that other heroic throwback, the bayonet. Despite frequent expressions of confidence by commanders on both sides, the bayonet played a minuscule role in the killing during the Civil War. Not only were most bayonet charges turned aside by rifle fire, but even when they did succeed, the defending troops almost invariably ran away before these weapons could be employed. Hence, Prussian observer Heros von Borcke, after examining numerous corpses for signs of stabbing, would conclude, "Bayonet fights rarely if ever occur, and exist only in the imagination."[29]

As with the cavalry saber, advocates of the bayonet would gloss over such evidence, basing their future rationales increasingly on metaphor and the psychological impact of the so-called arme blanche and "cold steel." Yet such arguments did little justice to available evidence, especially since the small-arms revolution had not yet even reached a plateau. For the introduction of the Spencer and Henry repeating rifle as well as the nascent development of the Gatling machine gun left every reason to believe that improvements in range would inevitably be complemented by dramatic increases in rate of fire. Whatever their intentions or preconceptions, those in the future who dared to close with opposing infantry lines would be met by a tempest of flying lead.

In more general terms, though, the very rapid ascent of small arms between 1861 and 1865 also spoke volumes about the future of warfare as a whole. Technology was taking control. At any moment, the very bedrock of military thought might be overturned by some new gadget or device. Nowhere was this more apparent than in lower Chesapeake Bay during the first few days of March 1862.

Because of its economic specialization and reliance on importation for virtually all manufactured goods, the Confederacy was particularly vulnerable to economic warfare. And by late 1861 the South was beginning to be strangled by a garrote of Northern ships blockading all of its chief ports—the so-called anaconda policy. In a mood that must have bordered on desperation, Confederate Naval Secretary Stephen Mallory turned to the revolution in naval architecture for salvation. "One armored battleship," he wrote in 1861, "could traverse the entire coast of the United States, preventing all blockades and encounter with a fair prospect of success, their entire navy."[30] So it was that the Confederacy committed the labor of fifteen hundred men and a considerable portion of its tiny iron-working capacity to the conversion of the captured steam frigate *Merrimac* into the armored central-battery ship CSS *Virginia*.

Searching for an antidote to this theoretically "ultimate" weapon, a committee of U.S. naval officers, commissioned to formulate ironclad policy, settled on an unorthodox design submitted by John Ericsson calling for a small, ungainly, single-turreted craft, practically without freeboard and destined to gain fame as the USS *Monitor*. Rushed to completion, the *Monitor* began its journey from New York to Hampton Roads on 6 March—not a moment too soon.

For the South would draw first blood. On 8 March the ponderous *Virginia* left Norfolk and attacked what by previous standards was a formidable force of wooden vessels. Yet before nightfall cut short the carnage, the *Virginia* had destroyed two vessels, badly damaged a third, and scattered the rest. It was this depressing scene that greeted the *Monitor* as it arrived belatedly at nine that evening, setting the stage for the next day's climactic encounter.

On 9 March the morning fog lifted over Hampton Roads to reveal the *Virginia* intent on further destruction. To protect the damaged steam frigate *Minnesota,* the *Monitor* moved out to confront her Confederate adversary. After a few preliminary shots the two ships closed to point-blank range and discovered (presumably to their mutual horror) that neither could pierce the other's armor. For the next four hours the ships circled and with fierce resolution sought unsuccessfully to pound this revelation into oblivion. Significantly, both tried to end the stalemate by ramming, but this, too, failed and the day ended in complete tactical frustration.[31]

Yet this inconclusive confrontation provided a glimpse at the real nature of Western man's warlike partnership with machinery. Technology had laid its hands on the affairs of men, and its grip was like a vice. No amount of tactical skill, inspired leadership, or personal courage could keep those cannonballs from bouncing off the sides of ships. Technology was as fickle as it was callous—one day slaughtering hundreds, the next sparing all but a few. This melodrama upon the shallow waters of Hampton Roads was an archetype of future events. The first act had provided the taste of blood that would forever be the motive for improved weapons, while the second act had demonstrated the essential futility of the vision. The Southern plan had failed. Her invincible ironclad, like all ultimate weapons, simply brought forth a symmetrical response. The blockade would remain, and the Confederacy would strangle. On the other hand, the Northern *Monitor,* by simply existing, had won an important strategic victory oddly in contrast to her tactical ineptitude. Much the same thing would happen fifty-four years later at a more elaborate comedy of errors, Jutland.

The American Civil War cost a great many lives. Estimates range up to over six hundred thousand, making it still the most costly conflict in U.S. history. On the surface this may not seem surprising. Civil wars are among the most bitterly contested of struggles, and this one was waged for four long years, to the point of Southern capitulation. Besides, both sides were made up of Americans, so casualties were bound to be higher.

This is misleading, however. Unlike most civil wars, this was not an internal but a regional struggle. Neither side differed significantly in terms of race, religion, or basic political philosophy. Rather, the war was fought over some fairly abstract economic and moral points, not against but for the sake of a divergent racial group. Nor do we see the kinds of extreme predatory behavior characteristic of the Dutch rebellion or the Spanish revolt against Napoleon. Instead, both sides behaved fairly moderately, with continual fraternization taking place between engagements. Considerable property was destroyed in the South, but this is about as far as reprisals went. Certainly, there was no organized effort to kill civilians, nor were vanquished white soldiers slaughtered after combat ceased (there were some incidents of black prisoners being killed by Southerners). Casualties accumulated primarily during the heat of battle, mostly as a result of wounds inflicted by small arms. Hence, it is logical to conclude that it was less willful enmity than the weapons themselves that turned the Civil War into such a deadly undertaking.

The omnipotence of arms, the shaping of warfare through weaponry, beyond all political and psychological intent, was a new phenomenon, and one which went largely unrecognized by professional military men. Such an intimate participant as Ulysses S. Grant, the author of probably the Civil War's best memoir, went through two entire volumes with barely a mention of weapons or their impact. Jay Luvaas also notes that while a number of Europeans drew attention to new armaments, few took any real notice of their effect.[32]

However, it is and was possible to draw a somewhat different conclusion. The American Civil War was the first conflict since the time of Napoleon to be waged with mass armies composed of troops with a real stake in the fighting. But the forces confronted each other with weaponry radically more deadly. As we have seen with the Greek city-states and eighteenth-century Europe, excessive lethality had been traditionally dealt with belatedly through sharply limiting the number and motivation of combatants, the ritualization of tactics, and by freezing weapons development. None of these palliatives were available to the participants in the Civil War. Their only option was to bear up in the face of slaughter. In the near term this meant compulsive digging of trenches to hide in. Yet in the longer run there were signs of deep resentment. These were free men who had for the most part volunteered to fight. Yet when conscription was begun in the North, serious rioting occurred. More to the point, once the war was over, Americans turned their collective backs on things military. In part this was the natural reaction of a people with no geopolitical need for a large standing army or navy. But the immediate postbellum period was a time of great sadness, full of regrets. It would seem that free men had not liked being cannon, or more properly rifle, fodder. While they may not have fully grapsed the implications of continuously improving weaponry, the immediate consequences were clear. For a democratic society the experience of modern warfare had been largely a negative one, and when the opportunity arose, it was rejected.

IV

So it was that the Western world's attention shifted to an entirely more pleasant series of wars and their chief beneficiary, the new military colossus of Europe.

Prussia, that proverbial army masquerading as a state, had risen out of its own ashes. Smashed at Jena-Auerstedt by Napoleon, it would reemerge not chastened but remilitarized, having learned nothing more about warfare than God's reputed preference for bigger (and better) legions. Gone were the Potsdam giants and the Hohenzollern's automata professionals, replaced by a *volks* army and a centralized military brain, initially crafted by Scharnhorst and his fellow reformers and brought to fruition by the labors of Helmuth von Moltke. It was this army that would win Prussia greatness and unite Germany through a string of almost effortless military victories. But in the process it would reinforce a dangerous leitmotif of bellicosity that would eventually bring ruin and devastation.

While it was clearly a trans-European phenomenon, postindustrial militarism was epitomized in the policies and development of Prussia. It was here that peculiarities of geography, economics, and politics combined to form such an apparently coherent and self-reinforcing whole. Meanwhile, the fatal internal contradictions of the system remained buried, hidden for decades by a combination of good luck, leadership, and self-satisfaction.

Geography was omnipresent. Prussia remained a series of disparate holdings stretching from the Rhine to the Vistula and subject to attack by one or more of three great powers: France, Russia, and Austria. As before, the army remained the sole national institution capable of protecting the state and binding it together. Yet more than with other polities, the precarious military situation required carefully defined plans of action and a clear sense of priorities. Thus, even before 1820, Prussia led the way in developing a designated planning and control element, known henceforth as the *Grosser Generalstab,* or Great General Staff. Four decades later it would be transformed by the elder Moltke into a self-conscious military-intellectual elite meticulously selected and symbolically set apart from the rest of the army by their distinctive red trouser stripes.[33]

Its success, however, was less a matter of personnel than technology. For the Great General Staff, charged with developing a series of hypothetical but comprehensive war plans, was preoccupied with communications and troop movement; only through these media could the intricacies of mobilization and concentration be accomplished and the initiative retained over Prussia's numerous potential enemies. And by the decade of the 1860s two new inventions, the telegraph and the railroad, were beginning to work miracles on the possibilities for command and control.

For the first time a centralized headquarters might maintain theoretically instantaneous communications with an advancing army simply by spinning out a strand of copper wire in the wake of its advance. In practice there were frequent breakdowns and delays, but, to an undreamed of degree, Moltke and his staff might now monitor the deployment of its forces on a real-time basis.[34]

Meanwhile, their numbers and speed of movement were being hugely amplified by the second of the Great General Staff's key tools, the railroad. As we have noted, throughout the eighteenth century the size and mobility of European armies had been strictly limited by the necessity of creating massive logistical establishments along their lines of march. Napoleon had sought to remove these shackles by encouraging his troops to supplement their regular sources of supply with organized pillage and, in doing so, made armies in the multiple hundreds of thousands possible. This recourse, however, not only resulted in serious civilian deprivation and economic injury but, as Michael Howard notes, the disaster which overtook the six hundred thousand man Grand Army in Russia also revealed the military dangers of such ruthless improvisation.[35]

The introduction of railroads obliterated all of these difficulties, for a single train had the carrying capacity of thousands of horse-drawn carts and could traverse ten times the distance with equal ease. Now supplies could be drawn in vast quantities from many hundreds of miles away, while huge numbers of men could be transported similar distances with unprecedented speed. And more subtle, perhaps, but of no less significance, these troops were to be spared the hardening rigors of the march, enabling virtual civilians to take their place in the front lines.[36] Suddenly, every man of military age became a potential soldier. Armies in the millions were possible. And while Prussia's gravitation toward universal conscription was halting and subject to deep internal political divisions, after 1857 the Army Reform Movement, by relentlessly enlarging the available manpower pool, made it all but inevitable. And as Prussia went, so went the rest of Europe.

Of course, dealing with such numbers introduced enormous complexity into the planning process. This was where the Prussian Great General Staff truly shone. Good use of railroads had already been made during the American Civil War and the Franco-Austrian war of 1859, but it had been largely a piecemeal, ad hoc process. The Prussian Great General Staff, on the other hand, set about in a very calculated fashion to make this new tool the centerpiece of its strategic doctrine.[37] A railway planning section was established, and construction, particularly in vital directions, was encouraged. "Every new development of railways," wrote Moltke, "is a military advantage."[38] For it was becoming increasingly apparent that the new means of transport could transform Prussia's central position into a geographic asset, allowing her to concentrate troops on any border to repel an assault. All that was required was planning and maintaining the initiative.

Numerous mistakes were made, particularly in the wars against the Danes and Austrians, but gradually Prussian strategy took on the level of detail and inevitability of Swiss railroad timetables. War in this context became primarily a matter of boxcars, locomotives, and precisely scheduled troop movements, while political contingencies were reduced to the level of complicating factors. In the minds of the Prussian Great General Staff there could be no greater sin than political vacillation and failure to initiate the plan. Beyond this there was only defeat.

In most respects the last element of Prussian military success, the application of progressive industrial technology to the arming of her troops, was the least likely of all. But again the key was geography.

Traditionally, Prussia had been an agricultural state, with major holdings in what is now Poland. After Jena-Auerstedt, however, she had been shorn of much of the eastern territory, and at the peace conference following Napoleon's defeat, ceded most of the former Rhineland states in the West as compensation. At the time, the Prussians would have preferred the return of all of their portion of Poland.[39] Yet time proved them utterly wrong. They had traded some relatively worthless agricultural lands for what would soon become the richest single industrial area in the world and, in doing so, tied themselves inadvertently to the technical and economic future. For the wealth of these territories provided not only a stimulus for their defense but the means as well, in the form of factories to build railroads and eventually the best and most modern weapons in the world.

In large part this was the story of Alfred Krupp, the redoubtable Cannon King. He was fourteen when his father, Friedrich, died in despair, leaving young Alfred and his mother, Therese, with seven sullen workers, the crumbling remnants of a cast-steel factory, and a water-powered hammer positioned on a stream that was generally dry.[40] Out of this meager legacy Alfred would set about creating the biggest industrial empire in Europe and filling it, in the process, with his magnificent instruments of death. Tall and whippet-thin all his life, he was a mass of energy and neuroses—at once an insomniac, a hypochondriac, and a workaholic dynamo of business schemes. Although he did not discover weapons until almost twenty years of his frantic career had passed, he exhibited from the beginning the central contradictions of the industry. For Alfred was always patriotically insistent that the Prussian government should nurture its infant Krupp *Gusstahlfabrik*. Yet when given the chance, as both William Manchester and Peter Batty agree, Krupp would sell anything to anyone with money.[41]

In the early days this was a matter of necessity. Prussian bureaucrats and army officers remained notably unimpressed with Krupp's wares. Typical was the reaction of the Artillery Test Commission when, in 1847, after three years of experimentation, Krupp succeeded in delivering a 6.5-centimeter crucible steel cannon to the Spandau arsenal for evaluation. The authorities left the gun out in the weather to rust for nearly two years without even bothering to fire it, and when Alfred finally brought pressure on them to do so, they blandly informed him that although his steel gun was virtually indestructible, only bronze pieces were adequate for the purposes of field artillery.[42]

Consequently, where Alfred the chauvinist failed, Krupp the showman took up the slack—exhibiting his polished cannon at a string of international exhibitions, courting royalty and officialdom whenever and wherever he could, and peddling his guns on an endless series of business trips back and forth across Europe. In his relentless salesmanship Krupp perfected and epitomized the role of the modern military-industrialist. Nor did this change early in the 1860s when the accession of his patrons, the militaristic Wilhelm I and his Iron Chancellor, Count Otto von Bismarck, assured Krupp a steady domestic market for his new steel cannon. The arms trade and the technological progress which fueled it remained, and would remain, very much an international phenomenon. Although conflicting loyalties, personified by military capitalists such as Wallenstein, had been partially resolved through the tight control of armies by governmental entities, this would never be entirely the case with weapons.

Overtly, however, armaments competition would be perceived as a function of the state system. At this level the course charted by Wilhelm I and Bismarck, and its relationship to the burgeoning *Krupp-werke* had a major effect on the political destiny of Europe. For it became a matter of conscious policy to use the country's newfound industrial might to diligently improve the weapons issued to the Prussian army,[43] itself slated to embark on a series of expansionistic wars. In part the process had begun earlier with the decision to proliferate the needle gun. But the industrial base required for the transition from bronze to steel artillery was much more massive and the investment proportionately larger. Prussia was not alone; other European states were involved with similar programs of rearmament. Yet nowhere else was the process so clearly thought out or so thoroughly implemented.[44]

In retrospect, the Prussian military system—the Great General Staff, its deterministic war and mobilization plans, universal conscription, the industrial nexus's relationship to the development of the strategic rail net, and the massive expansion of the armaments industry—all fit together so tightly and were so self-reinforcing that they imbued the Prussian worldview with a highly mechanistic potential. When all else was stripped away, the state existed to wage war—blindly, inevitably. That this did not become apparent sooner was largely a historical accident.

It seems clear that Prussia and Germany reached a major crossroads with the revolution of 1848. Had the liberals prevailed, a different and much less militaristic future could have been expected. But, instead, the extreme conservatives were left to define the state's political character. This had two effects: it exaggerated the societal authoritarianism which was the behavioral essence of the lockstep military machine, and it produced a genius whose virtuosity was sufficient to disguise the deterministic core of Prussian politics.

Otto von Bismarck was a man who knew what he wanted. His maneuvering was endless, his tactical flexibility without limit. Yet he never lost track of his priorities. At home this meant conservative domination even if it required stealing his opponent's own program. In the international sphere he was equally steadfast. "When I come to power," he told Benjamin Disraeli in 1862, "my first care will be . . . to reorganize the army. . . . [Then] I shall seize the best pretext to declare war on Austria, dissolve the German diet, subdue the minor states, and give national unity to Germany under Prussia's leadership."[45]

Reality proved slightly more complicated. Yet to a remarkable degree Bismarck was able to forge his dream into the stuff of modern German history. Opportunistic and violent personally, he grasped Prussia's superb army and its new weaponry like the haft of a fine sword. "The great questions of the day will be decided, not by speeches and majority votes," he harangued a group of parliamentarians shortly after he took power, "but by blood and iron."[46] Within a decade he would deftly maneuver his intended international victims out of reach of potential allies and wage three successive conflicts (the Danish War of 1864, the Austro-Prussian War of 1866, and the Franco-Prussian War of 1870), at the end of which his program would be fulfilled and Germany unified as a state of over forty million astride the center of Europe.

Yet for all his success with violence, war remained only a tool for Bismarck. In each of his three martial adventures, he began searching for peace at the very moment his political objectives came within reach. "I have the ungrateful task of pouring water in the foaming wine," he wrote his wife in 1866. "If we are not immoderate in our demands, and do not imagine we have conquered the world, we shall acquire a peace which will be worth the trouble."[47] This remained his attitude throughout. And having gotten what he wanted, he spent the next twenty years quietly consolidating his gains.

But Bismarck would not be remembered for his pacific endeavors. His own and Germany's reputation would be based on calculated aggression. And war itself, basking in the reflected glow of Teutonic achievement, took on a new aura of glamor for the rest of Europe.

As both William McNeill and Eric Leed have indicated, these short, relatively bloodless Prussian wars, as opposed to the long, terrible American Civil War, provided an extremely attractive model to European societies caught up in the throes of industrialism. Spurred on by social Darwinian concepts of "struggle" and "survival of the fittest," citizens at all levels came to view military life and its culmination, armed conflict, as an equipoise to the tedium and uncertainty that was coming to characterize daily existence in the urbanized, factory-ridden states of late-nineteenth-century northern Europe. On one hand, military rank and the chain of command preserved the older world of ascribed status and unquestioned obedience which were fast disappearing from the modern social setting and casting men into a perpetual search for identity.[48]

Perhaps equally important as this escape from freedom was, paradoxically, the potential for adventure which Prussian-like conflicts seemed to promise the average man. Combat came to be perceived as a short interlude in which young males might purge from their lives civilization's supposedly corrupting influence and test themselves against the traditional, intraspecific aggression-based code of the warrior. This "war as summer camp" mentality would persist throughout the last quarter of the nineteenth century, culminating in the ecstasy with which Europe marched off to fight in 1914. Of course, the bizarre reality of trench warfare brought a quick end to most of these sweet dreams of heroics. Yet as long as it lasted, this highly romanticized vision of combat provided a social climate in which general military expansion and the intensification of weapons development and acquisition were not just acceptable but popular.

Given the natural propensity for seeing what is desired, this was perhaps inevitable. Yet had contemporaries cared to bathe Prussian military success in the harsh, flat light of skepticism, they might have caught a glimpse of an entirely different, more disturbing picture.

As always, there were the traditional shortcomings—inexperience, confusion, and reliance upon chance—which had bedeviled the planning and execution of armed conflict since its inception. During the ten-week Danish War, the Prussian command ignored Moltke's brilliant war plan and bungled matters so badly that the allied Austrians were forced to take up the slack. Meanwhile, Prussian troops, not having fought foreigners since 1815, proved initially gun-shy, and it was not until Moltke was able to direct the assault at Düppel that they began to show a real taste for battle.[49] By the same token, the Great General Staff's intricate logistical tables misfired badly during the seven-week Austrian campaign, while the single great action of the war, Königgrätz, was won by the fortuitous arrival of Crown Prince Frederick with Prussian reinforcements. Even then, the war's termination was as much a product of the Austrian's continued adherence to the tradition of capitulation after a serious defeat as it was due to Prussian force of arms.[50]

The Great General Staff's planning worked better in the War of 1870, and within eighteen days the railway system delivered an army of almost five hundred thousand to the French border. Almost immediately, Prussian troops inflicted two shocking defeats on the French at Sedan and Metz. This done, however, Bismarck and Moltke were faced with the problem of forcing the still-bellicose French to surrender, a solution for which, as Michael Howard points out in his very thorough study of the war, they became increasingly desperate to find as Gallic resistance degenerated into the guerrilla campaign of the *Francs-Tireurs*.[51]

That they found a way out within four months only served to obscure the manner in which the revolution in logistics and conscription-based armies might prolong, rather than shorten, warfare. Although draftees were inducted on the understanding that their term of duty would be relatively short, bountiful advances in domestic economic productivity made much longer service feasible, as demonstrated by the American Civil War, had anyone cared to look. And as long as governments continued to engage the national sentiments of their populations to fulfill manpower requirements and the political ends of the state, the likelihood of this happening remained undiminished.

Meanwhile, purely military technologies were exerting themselves as never before. And here, too, the events of Prussia's serial wars, particularly the last, spread a puffy cloud of optimism over what were really some very ominous developments. To be sure, there was a growing awareness of the importance of new weaponry and the resulting potential for battlefield asymmetries. Yet attempts to analyze implications and directions remained superficial and self-serving. Thus, the needle gun's success against the Danes, and particularly the Austrians, was clearly recognized by the French, who began almost immediately equipping their own troops with an even better breechloader, the chassepot. That over a million of these rifles could be produced between 1866 and 1870 was a remarkable industrial achievement,[52] but it also served notice how rapidly even significant imbalances in armament could be redressed.

In a replay of the Civil War experience, the ability of both national combatants in the Franco-Prussian War to acquire new weapons clearly exceeded their capacity to use them reasonably, let alone to maximum advantage. Therefore, after initially appearing to have recognized that fast-firing small arms bestowed a tremendous advantage on the defense, German, and particularly French, infantry leaders in the heat of battle and as a long-term proposition simply could not accept the permanent subordination of the offensive. Instead, they retreated into a mythology which held that courage alone could overcome a multitude of bullets. Much the same thing could be said of the cavalry, which like their Civil War counterparts were shot to pieces by small-arms fire during the War of 1870, yet lived on afterward in a military state of grace which amounted to blind idolatry. Even the humble bayonet, by now a tactical relic, retained its advocates.

Yet all of this self-hypnosis was made even more remarkable by the emergence of Alfred Krupp's breech-loading crucible steel artillery, which provided the Prussians in 1870 with a major tactical advantage over the bronze muzzle-loaders of the French. Here, again, the central reaction of Moltke and the high command, upon realizing the magnitude of their edge, was reasonable enough: they withheld their infantry, whose needle guns were outranged by enemy chassepots, and blew the French apart with concentrated artillery fire. This was how Sedan was won.[53]

Yet during the forty-four years which separated this battle from the initial campaigns of World War I, penetrating thought about the implications of such artillery, particularly if both sides were so equipped, was singularly lacking within the military ranks. Rather, the major military-intellectual figure to emerge from the Franco-Prussian War, albeit posthumously, was Colonel Ardant du Picq (killed, appropriately enough, by a Prussian artillery shell near Metz), whose *Battle Studies* were filled with elevating aphorisms: ''Battles now more than ever, are battles of men. . . . Attack is always, even on the defensive, an evidence of resolution and gives moral ascendancy. . . . The improvement of firearms continues to diminish losses. . . . Rifled cannon and accurate rifles do not change cavalry tactics at all."[54]

While du Picq was neither blind nor an utter reactionary, a much more accurate indication of what was really happening on the battlefield was evidence showing that, during the Franco-Prussian War, it was artillery which had become the dominant weapon, when just a few years prior, in the American Civil War, it had been improved small arms.[55] In truth, Western man's warlike traditions were being batted back and forth by a group of hungry mechanical predators.

It was no longer primarily courage or leadership or training that killed men and won battles; more and more it was the latest weapons. Yet it was equally true, and supremely ironic, that the pursuit of better armament would almost always prove futile. For as weapons development accelerated, the iron laws of armament symmetry easily kept pace. The Prussians were exceedingly fortunate to declare war, first on Austria, then on France, at the moment when two unusually successful weapons, their needle gun and then their steel artillery, were unmatched. Yet this would prove exceptional. Almost immediately, the rest of Europe would go to great lengths to duplicate arms which proved so formidable in battle. Meanwhile, the timing of war remained largely erratic and incapable of being synchronized with weapons innovations, whose actual worth was a matter of uncertainty until proven in combat.

Theoretically, however, there was one way around this logical treadmill, the creation of an armament of obvious potency, but carefully veiled in obscurity— the proverbial secret weapon. And the Franco-Prussian War provided a perfect example in the ill-fated mitrailleuse. Basically a multibarreled, hand-cranked machine gun similar in conception to the American Gatling gun, the mitrailleuse was first tested in 1860 and went into production in 1866. Yet, so heavy was the curtain of secrecy surrounding the new weapon that training and critical discussion as to how it might be used were virtually impossible.[56] Instead, the mitrailleuse remained a military panacea, Napoleon III's ace in the hole, untried but surely capable of great things once sprung on the unsuspecting enemy.

As a result, when war was declared and the two hundred or so available guns were released to French units, hardly anyone knew how to work them. Michael Howard reports that in one division before the Battle of Froeschwiller, only a single noncommissioned officer could be found knowledgeable enough to operate the gun.[57] Even worse was a tactical doctrine which called for mitrailleuses to be placed in batteries out in the open and fired at maximum range as artillery. Not surprisingly, German cannon simply blew them apart with high explosives, and the rapid-firing gun's part in the fighting proved negligible. In fact, the mitrailleuse was a potentially devastating piece of military hardware, and a great deal more would be heard from machine guns.

Yet for the moment their role would be largely allegorical. For the very act of keeping a secret weapon secret tended to relegate it to tactical obscurity. Frequently, it was only by disseminating a superior weapon that its potential could be fulfilled. But this, in turn, almost inevitably led to its symmetrical adoption by others. So it was that arms racing, rather than granting a significant military advantage, often simply raised the level of violence. Of course, the paradoxical nature of these mechanisms was hardly apparent at the time, and to this day, particularly among totalitarian regimes, weapons development programs are treated with obsessive secrecy. Yet it is not only advances in communications and observation which continually erode military secrets; they are by their nature self-defeating.

Time would show Prussia's string of victories to be largely a mirage. Yet the illusion was undeniably an attractive one—short, purposeful wars waged in a civilized fashion with weapons which embodied the best of modern technology. Who could really blame those who jumped to the conclusion that these elements were naturally reinforcing rather than profoundly contradictory? Given the available evidence, industrialized militarism seemed a viable national option, at once economically and politically sound, while replete with an invigorating bravura which seemed just the tonic for the enervation of urban industrial life.

For its part, the uniformed military had every reason to be satisfied with the professional implications of Prussian success. It had apparently salvaged their worldview. As noted earlier, the first wave of modern weapons development caught the ranks of military men with their guard down, and they underwent rearmament in something approaching a state of shock. The American Civil War had not helped matters. The reassertion of the Homeric urge to close in the face of vastly improved small arms had proved nearly suicidal, and trench warfare remained the only apparent alternative. But after Appomattox Americans had turned to peaceful pursuits. And in far-off Europe military men found it easy to ignore the Civil War's bitter lessons, concentrating instead on a highly selective interpretation of the Prussian experience.[58]

What emerged was the resurrection of the traditional, intraspecific, aggression-laden code of combat, slightly modified to accommodate new weaponry. Symptomatic of this syncretism was the repeated assertion that the basic relationship between infantry, cavalry, and artillery had not changed, and that new armaments, whether rapid-firing, rifled small arms or steel, breech-loading artillery, would favor the offense, not the defense.

It was, as Jean Renoir called it, a "grand illusion." When given the opportunity, firepower would overwhelm courage and slaughter attackers with predatory efficiency that would make a mockery of the warrior ethic. Rather than a stage for posturing and heroics, the battlefield would become a no-man's-land where the enemy was invisible and the killing accomplished at extreme ranges in a spirit of methodical indifference. In short, the warrior would find himself at the mercy of his tools.

Yet until the fighting began in earnest, it remained possible for the professional military to maintain the fiction of control. So they would plan for wars that could never be fought, carefully screening and applying new weaponry, excluding the most brutal instruments. In the end the Great War would rip away the honorific shrouds hiding the true nature and dimensions of the death machine. But if the effort at concealment was a sham, it was a noble one. Who would not prefer war in the grand style to the horror of the western front?

Meanwhile, the Continental body politic remained nearly as out of touch with reality. As Stephan Van Evera has persuasively argued, pre-1914 Europe was in the grip of a series of delusions which caused each power to teach its people a mythical history which falsely magnified national differences; allowed war to be seen as fundamentally beneficial and bountiful in its rewards; overestimated the hostility of neighbors and the efficacy of threat behavior; and, finally, maintained an undeserved faith in the need to strike first once hostilities began.[59]

And nowhere was the grip of fantasy stronger than in the new Germany. Smaller than Russia, France, and even Spain, it had grandly labeled itself an empire and its ruler, the kaiser (Caesar). While Germany was modern in its industry, its scientific and educational establishment, and its efficient bureaucracy, the national imagination was nevertheless immersed in a primitive and largely fictitious past. In a people rich in dissent since Luther, authoritarianism and mindless obedience came to be associated with strength and political success. And most important, a nation steeped in the peaceful pursuits of hard work, acquisition, and materialism had come to love war like no other.

The new German Empire was an explosive mass of contradictions, a veritable time bomb. For, lacking a strong guiding hand, there would remain only the Great General Staff and its war plans, ever ready to mobilize over a million men, pack them into railway cars, and send them racing toward the borders.

So long as state policy was in the iron grasp of Otto von Bismarck, all of this remained implicit, and Germany retained its equilibrium through a subtle mix of diplomacy and alliance. But in March 1888 ancient Wilhem I finally died, only to be succeeded by the liberal but mortally ill Frederick III, whose rule would last ninety-nine days.

His successor, Wilhelm II, was just twenty-nine when he took the title of kaiser. Intelligent yet bombastic, cultivated but overaggressive, he was as erratic as his newly formed dominion, and in many ways the two deserved each other. Within two years Bismarck would submit his resignation. Soon Russia would begin the long tilt toward France. And even worse, the young kaiser decided to build a navy, thereby earning the unending rath of Great Britain.

The course had been set, and Germany's ruin, though still distant and unseen, lay awaiting her like an iceberg half-submerged in a dark, night sea.

Chapter 12

ON THE HIGH SEAS
AND OUT OF SIGHT

I

It was axiomatic. Britannia ruled the waves—not just in a physical sense, though her fleet remained clearly the strongest until 1921, but psychologically as the touchstone of all naval thought and action. For if the sea separates mariners from home and country, it unites them with each other, driving them together to fraternize like no other military arm, sharing common customs and following the example of those perceived as leaders. So it was that German officers such as Reinhard Scheer, destined to command the High Seas Fleet at Jutland, came to view "English ships as models, the external appearance of which, alone produced the impression of perfection."[1] Similarly, when the budding Japanese navy built its service academy at Etajuma, it was designed to be a replica of the British academy Dartmouth, and was ceremoniously furnished with a lock of Nelson's hair.[2]

Yet no service was more enthralled by its British counterpart than the American navy. This had not always been so. But after the Civil War the two English-speaking powers began a gradually accelerating process of reconciliation which was paced and foreshadowed by steadily more intimate relations between British and U.S. naval officers. For their part, the English increasingly perceived the Americans as potential junior partners in the naval Pax Britannica, thereby freeing significant portions of the Royal Navy to deal with the kaiser's rapidly expanding armada in home waters. The Americans, in turn, viewed the British service as simply the paragon of all things naval. Indeed, it was an American who would explain the Royal Navy to the world.

To understand the role and motives of Alfred Thayer Mahan, it is necessary to be aware of the U.S. Navy's plight during the twenty years following the Civil War. No member of the world naval community better exemplified the problems attached to the mechanization of the very traditional realm of the naval officer and the difficulties of generating suitable responses.

Not only did the American citizenry turned their backs on the navy after 1865, but its line officers used the service's decline to rid themselves of steam power, newfangled weaponry, and naval engineers—all introduced during the emergency of the war years. The result was not only a tenfold contraction in ships and guns in less than a decade but a wholesale and deliberate policy of technical retrogression.[3] Clearly, at the heart of this trend was a strong desire to return to the days of sail, a skill which constituted a major element of the naval officer's body of knowledge and expertise. Since not only steam propulsion but high-powered guns and armor were responsible for the demise of the wooden sailing ship, all were suspect. Thus, a combination of poverty and institutional neglect insured that for more than twenty years, as William Hovgaard notes, no seagoing armored vessels were built in the United States.[4] Meanwhile, the more intense naval environment across the Atlantic forced European admiralties to forge ahead with the rapid evolution of the warship, creating a gap epitomized by the reply of Oscar Wilde's Canterville Ghost to the complaint of a young American that her country had no ruins or curiosities: "No ruins! No curiosities! You have your navy and your manners!"[5]

At this juncture, amid the chaos, the privation, and the gloom, there appeared in the ranks of beleaguered and discouraged American officers a prophet. As is typical of such beings, his guise was not what might have been expected. Alfred Thayer Mahan was no war hero or service politician; he was, instead, a naval historian, the least likely of messiahs.

Though clearly more scholarly and thoughtful than his contemporaries, Mahan's early career was not unordinary. Like his brother officers he was not happy about the technological turn war had taken, and worried openly about the growing influence of naval engineers. But he was also mortified by the postwar service's decline and remembered with particular bitterness the condescension of a visiting French admiral who referred to the guns of the future naval prophet's ship as *l'ancien système*. Mahan's response was an urgent desire to "raise the profession in the eyes of its members."[6]

His chance came in 1884 when his former commander, Rear Admiral Luce, invited Mahan to prepare a series of lectures to be delivered at the newly established Naval War College in Newport, Rhode Island. The recruitment of Mahan and the existence of the war college were products of both Luce's persistence and the growing realization among officers that if the navy was ever to be aroused from the doldrums, some form of intellectual framework had to be created upon which to base modern naval policy. This was to be the prophet's great contribution.

Characteristically, Mahan met the dynamic thrust of mechanization with a strategic retreat into the past, working for two years on his lectures, which would appear in print in 1890 as the *The Influence of Sea Power upon History: 1660–1783,* one of the most influential American books ever published. "It is doubly necessary thus to study critically the history of naval warfare in the days of sailing ships,'' he wrote in the introduction, ''because while these will be found to afford lessons of present application and value, steam navies have as yet made no history.''[7]

What Mahan found was profoundly reassuring. Nothing really had changed. The galaxy of improvements which seemed to be turning the naval world upside down were doing so only superficially, leaving unchanged the central premises of traditional naval strategy. These, as every naval officer knew, had been laid down and confirmed by the invincible Royal Navy in the endless wars of trade of the seventeenth and eighteenth centuries. History had shown time and again the importance of fleet concentration and the validity of blockade. Only fights between massed battleships, and never raids on commerce, had proved decisive at sea. Consequently, it was unthinkable to Mahan that sea power could ever be based on anything other than the possession of a fleet of numerous, largely homogeneous battleships—modern equivalents of the great sailing ships-of-the-line.

Unfortunately for Mahan and his followers, his analysis was based on historical analogy, not technical reality. He had confused the stability of the past with the immutability of naval warfare itself. In fact, much of what was happening really was unprecedented. Yet Mahan's approach was understandable; he was only doing what military men inevitably did when faced with significant technical change. He instinctively sought to accommodate it within a usable and traditional framework.

Whatever its technical merits, Mahan's capital ship theory had very definite implications for national and international policy. For Mahan, a fleet was not simply a defensive instrument but the key component of a self-reinforcing system of national aggrandizement, which also included rapidly expanding international markets, a resurgent merchant marine, an isthmian canal, and a network of overseas bases to serve as commercial outlets and coaling stations. Here, too, the model from which the prophet wrought his strategic vision was the queen of the naval world, the imperial power par excellence, Great Britain. It was her trade, her merchant marine, her Suez Canal, her net of bases, and above all, her mammoth fleet which inspired Mahan and his readers. Yet Mahan's work was not simply a reiteration of the obvious. He articulated what had been heretofore only implicit. And in doing so he would drag not just his own navy but the entire naval world and its battleships out of the morass of technology induced confusion and hitch their respective futures to the rising star of imperialism.

Mahan's efforts did not go unrewarded. He was no prophet without honor. Instead, naval officers and like-minded politicians in all the major maritime powers, save France, took Mahan into their hearts and raised his thoughts to the level of dogma.

In the United States, not only were several generations of naval thinkers brought up on Mahan, but the sacred text was read and used by Theodore Roosevelt, Henry Cabot Lodge, and two key secretaries of the navy, Benjamin F. Tracy and Hilary A. Herbert, as a prime justification for the battleship-based navy which would spring to life in the United States during the 1890s.[8]

Meanwhile, on the other side of the Pacific Ocean, Mahan became required reading for the officers of the Imperial Japanese Navy, and more of his books were translated into that language than those of any other foreign author. Kaiser Wilhelm II, for his part, "devoured" *The Influence of Seapower,* "trying to learn it by heart."[9] He was so impressed that he ordered it to become standard equipment aboard all of his ships.

But nowhere was Mahan better received than in Great Britain, where he became, in the words of naval historian Arthur Marder, "practically the naval Mohammed of England."[10] It could hardly have been otherwise. Yet the praise he would receive from the most influential body of officers in the world was in itself a significant factor in Mahan's acceptability to the rest of the naval profession. And the glorification of Mahan could only lead to further deference being paid to the Royal Navy. So it went. In reaction to change, tradition fed upon itself and flourished. With Mahan in their heads and the overpowering example of Britain's armada close to their hearts, the major naval contestants would sail in unison toward the twentieth century, building battleships.

Yet the primary means by which the tactical and strategic capabilities of the new generation of warships were deduced is worthy of some consideration. The problem lay in the fact that for virtually all of the first four decades of their lives, steam-powered warships experienced no massed combat worth mentioning. Consequently, for the first time in the history of a major weapons system, military planners had to resort primarily to simulation to provide answers to their tactical and strategic questions.

Although details and procedures varied among maritime powers, the U.S. Navy was archetypical in conjuring up the naval future through the repeated playing of a series of naval board games, invented by a retired lieutenant named William McCartney Little and introduced into the war college curriculum by Mahan in 1892.[11]

The games were three in number and embraced all aspects of surface warfare. A "strategic" game was played on actual charts and was devised in order to test the practicability of war plans. When two hostile fleets came within combat range, a second, or "tactical," game commenced, intended to measure the fighting potential of opposing battle lines, suggestively represented by model sailing ships. Finally, the "duel" simulated head-to-head confrontations between capital ships, ostensibly providing a player with experience in handling an individual warship as well as testing the effect of various ship characteristics and gun-armor combinations.[12]

While the details varied from navy to navy, taken as a whole this sort of gaming was accepted as a reliable analytic tool and substitute for combat, in large part because it consistently produced results which struck naval planners as intuitively correct.

First and foremost, the games demonstrated the necessity for fleet concentration. For example, with the aid of statistical probabilities, Captain Bradley Fiske was able to demonstrate that if two forces of similar battleships, numbering 8 and 10, respectively, met in combat, the smaller would be reduced to 0 before the larger lost even half of its ships. On the other hand, if a force of 10 was fortunate enough to engage two bodies of 5 each, the outcome would leave the unified party with 5.69 ships, while the bisected adversary would be left with none.[13]

Numbers were not the only measure of concentration. The games, particularly the "duel," tended to show that larger guns held an inordinate advantage. All things considered, the safest means of reconciling the contradictory ends of numerical and individual concentration was the possession of the largest possible number of the biggest ships available.

Also, while scouting the no-man's-water between opposing battle lines might call for successively larger destroyers, light cruisers, and armored cruisers, gaming and statistical comparisons indicated that it was clearly battleships that were, in the words of Rear Admiral Stephen B. Luce, "necessary to oppose battleships."[14]

In such confrontations the tactical game served also to emphasize the need for unity of command and its natural correlate, line-ahead tactics, in that these maximized the chances that all turret guns might be brought to bear on an enemy. Moreover, a scoring bias that rated hits as being eight times more likely at one thousand yards than at four thousand made it obvious that decisive results could be best obtained at short ranges. "With two well-handled fleets," wrote Lieutenant Commander Richard Wainwright in 1895, "the combat may be expected to be carried on with the ships in column and steering in nearly parallel directions, the interval gradually closing, until one or the other, threatening to charge, . . . the fleets come together."[15] The goal was either to ram on one side or to flank on the other, thereby crossing the opponent's T and effectively blanking a large portion of his turret guns, while exposing him to a maximum concentration of fire prior to his closing. In either case speed was of the essence, both corporately and in individual ships.

All told it was a convincing picture of the future painted on the game boards of the U.S. Naval War College and other thoughtful establishments around the naval world. Just as Mahan had said, technology was not proving to be as revolutionary a force as once feared. On the contrary, to naval planners it seemed to have reinforced several of the traditional features of war at sea. The hierarchy of ship types, for example, seemed even more firmly founded in that larger ships, instead of being armed with guns common to all classes, now mounted progressively bigger and more powerful ordnance and were sheathed in armor to boot. Therefore, the common emphasis on battleships and the relative neglect of lesser types seemed entirely logical. Moreover, the regularity of steam propulsion and the rapid advance of communications made centralized command and follow-the-leader tactics even more advisable than in the days of sail.

As plausible as this appeared at first glance, simulation through naval gaming contained several hidden preconceptions decidedly out of phase with naval reality. Game boards were flat and hard and therefore capable of representing combat in only two dimensions. This was no problem so long as naval combat continued to take place only on the surface. But at this very time, ingenuity was making it possible to plunge beneath the waves and dream of flying above them. Toy submarines and model airplanes might be represented on game boards, but their peculiar spatial advantages would not be apparent.

Similarly, the two-dimensional nature of the game board tended to reinforce the primacy of the gun and, to a lesser extent, the ram as instruments of naval destruction. While the careful gradation in the size of naval rifles was becoming a major prop to the hierarchy of ships, it was intuitively obvious that only a large vessel could ram with sufficient momentum to do mortal damage to another capital ship. The effect of such weapons could be adequately represented in two planes, but the potential of their submarine alternatives, the torpedo and the mine, could not be and was therefore consistently underrated in such an analysis. Significantly, the latter two, by circumventing the tight relationship between guns and armor, were much less deferential in their destructiveness. They could sink the largest ship or the smallest, it did not matter.

This is suggestive. Ultimately, the shortcomings of naval simulation were more than just a function of the games themselves, they were matters of choice. Mahan's defense of the battleship-based naval orthodoxy and its technical elaboration through naval gaming made sense in a way that was basic to the manner in which military men had always valued weapons. From this perspective the modern battleship was close to ideal, probably closer than any other weapons system in recent history. And, as such, naval officers around the globe would cling to it with a faith and determination that even a virtually unbroken string of combat failures could not quench. So it is that we presently find the U.S. Navy refurbishing, at great cost, several forty-year-old Iowa-class dreadnoughts, while at the same time the Soviet navy has actually constructed three new battle cruisers, a class abandoned shortly after World War I. The members of the naval world have never forgotten their battleships, and it would seem that they have been biding their time to get them back.

This remarkable loyalty becomes more understandable if the morphology of the great ships is examined in detail. Almost from their initial conception, steam battleships were designed and built to be at once paragons of size and belligerence, and exemplars of the traditional weapons virtues. Therefore, it was particularly appropriate that the primary naval weapon during the two thousand year reign of the oar-powered warship, the ram, was rehabilitated and grafted on the prow of nearly every capital ship up to the construction of the HMS *Dreadnought* in 1906. Meanwhile, it was conveniently overlooked that in combat the ram proved less than formidable—its total success amounting to one ship dispatched at the Battle of Lissa in 1866 and another during the War of the Pacific—while in peacetime its presence turned several collisions into disasters, culminating in the sinking of the battleships *Grosser Kurfurst* in 1878 and *Victoria* in 1893, both with heavy loss of life.[16] The resurrection of the ram symbolized not only the persistence of Homeric fighting values and the urge to close but also a deeply conservative approach to potentially revolutionary technologies. For the most part, mechanical innovations were tolerable only to the degree that they could be accommodated and measured according to familiar and appropriate military standards.

In this respect the new naval rifles proved not only much more useful than the ram but almost equally satisfying to the soul of the naval warrior. British observer H. M. Le Fleming was suitably impressed that battleships, "when firing, were momentarily blotted out by globes of orange flame followed by the tremendous concussion of the guns whose blast caused ripples and a flurry of spray on the water."[17] In such circumstances, to doubt the absolute relationship between a powerful bark and an equally potent bite was more than could be expected from the orderly ranks of naval officers.

So, too, the sheathing of battleships in progressively harder and more cunningly designed defensive plating not only served to protect them against hostile shells, but played to the traditional expectation that major combatants should be suited in armor.

Similarly, the emphasis on pure speed did have clear tactical advantages, but the engineering sacrifices made in its pursuit indicate that the traditional preference for fast heroes also entered subtly into the design equation.

Of course, bigger guns, heavier armor, and more powerful propulsion translated into irresistible arguments for why battleships must grow. And grow they did, roughly tripling their displacement in the fifty years between 1890 and 1940. Yet the chronic swelling of the battleship only served to increase its perceived formidability. For size had always been a military virtue, and in this idiom the naval officer's every instinct told him that the perfect warship was a perfectly enormous warship.

Such a conclusion could not but reinforce the self-evidence of the hierarchy of ships. "A big prize-fighter, trained to the ultimate," wrote Commander Homer C. Poundstone, a key figure in the evolution of the dreadnought type, "is invulnerable to smaller-sized fighters of the same identical quality. . . . So with the supreme type of battleship in their encounters with smaller units."[18]

In naval eyes the battleship was an aristocrat among naval combatants, threatening impudent members of the underclasses with instant mayhem and meant really to fight only equals. Significantly, such combat was characteristically conceptualized in individual terms—single battleship against battleship. In part this was because line-ahead formations lent themselves to such pairing off so long as the lines remained parallel. Yet the stereotypical nature of this vision of combat, along with the almost compulsive comparison of individual ship displacement, gun sizes, and armor thickness, leads to the conclusion that an underlying motif of intraspecific aggression was subtly guiding the course of naval architecture.

As such, steel, steam, and naval rifles became the tools to transform the wooden ships-of-the-line into something even better, fire-belching leviathans, veritable floating Achilleuses, or more accurately, aesthetic embodiments of the entire heroic tradition. Visually, the great ships were paradoxes of power and beauty. Great floating fortresses, guns bristling from slab-sided turrets, crowned with massive steel superstructures, they literally oozed defiance. When viewed from either end, they were squat and immovable as castles. Yet they appeared almost delicate and graceful when seen lengthwise.

These were weapons as men dreamed they should be. And, as such, they themselves became totems of armament, archetypes to be measured against future death machinery to help define its form, if not its function. As much as anything,

Figure 11. The British dreadnought *Neptune* at Portsmouth in 1911. National Maritime Museum, Greenwich, England.

this is why, even today, navies bring them out of mothballs and refuse to let them die.

<h2 style="text-align:center">II</h2>

Unfortunately, heresy lurked beneath the waves. The reassertion of orthodoxy in naval architecture was based on a profound misperception of water, upon which all else rested. Unlike land-based cathedrals, it was the steam battleship's misfortune to exist in a medium even less substantial than the body of belief which brought it into existence.

However, the ocean's eternal willingness to swallow leaky ships was strangely contradicted by its remarkable noncompressibility when subjected to sudden stress. This quirk of physics was the fatal flaw in the logical structure which supported large surface vessels. Because of the immense inertial resistance exerted by water, the entire force of a submerged explosion next to a ship's hull must be directed inward, along the line of least resistance. Seen in this way, a battleship was not the impregnable floating fortress perceived by Mahan's followers but little more than a bubble clad in a thin layer of steel. This had remained basically irrelevant during the long era of sail, and with the coming of steam, little had apparently changed.

As we have seen, there had been isolated experiments with submarine attack— David Bushnell's *Turtle,* Robert Fulton's stationary torpedoes. In 1843 Samuel Colt developed a mine with an electrical triggering device which succeeded in sinking a vessel five miles out at sea. The Civil War brought fairly widespread use of such mines, particularly by the blockaded Confederates, to protect estuaries and harbors. Consequently, a total of twenty-eight vessels had been sunk by such devices. Yet all of this amounted to no more than a few ripples when compared with the torrent of innovations simultaneously engulfing surface ships. Mines might make close blockading dangerous, but they were strictly coastal weapons and almost worthless on the high seas. Besides, they were a passive armament—warheads without delivery systems—requiring the unwitting cooperation of the enemy by venturing into the danger zone.

This would soon change. The year 1864 marked the conception of what Richard Hough calls "the most destructive weapon at sea until the arrival of nuclear power."[19] At this point an obscure Austrian naval captain named Lupius drew up plans for a small, self-propelled torpedo powered by either clockworks or steam carrying a charge of gunpowder detonated by a pistol in the nose. Almost immediately, Robert Whitehead, an English manager of a nearby engineering firm in Fiume, became intensely interested in the project and took over development. Two years later he completed construction of his first torpedo, a rather feeble device which could barely make six knots over its short range and was extremely erratic in its vertical motion. By 1868 Whitehead had corrected this difficulty by incorporating a hydrostatic depth regulator, enabling the torpedo to run true at a predetermined distance from the surface.[20] In 1885 accuracy was further improved with the addition of a gyroscopic rudder control, an American invention. As the mechanical details of the Whitehead torpedo were worked out, its performance steadily improved, and by 1900 the torpedo's speed had been increased to twenty-nine knots and its range stood at about eight hundred yards.[21]

Yet it was also clear that the torpedo's development was nowhere near its technological limits. As for its destructiveness, it is worth noting that while a contemporaneous armor-piercing shell carried a charge amounting to no more than 5 percent of its weight, 20 percent or more of a torpedo consisted of explosives. So, statistically, this was already a weapon to be reckoned with. But in actual combat the torpedo would require another vehicle to transport it to within range of the target. There were two possibilities.

The first was to mount the lethal mechanical fish on a small, fast auxiliary surface craft. The appearance of the torpedo boat in the early 1850s created such an uproar in the naval world that at its height, as Theodore Ropp recounts in his excellent piece "Continental Doctrines of Sea Power," the navies of Germany, Austria, and Russia momentarily abandoned their battleship programs.[22] But nowhere was the impact greater than in the French navy, where, after the frustration and humiliation of Trafalgar, the idea of circumventing the battleship concept must have been particularly fascinating. Admiral Theophile Aube and his fellow theorists of the *Jeune Ecole* hailed the torpedo boat as the warship of the future. They reasoned that industrial Britain's increased dependence on foreign trade, combined with the introduction of the torpedo, had tipped the scales in favor of commerce raiding as the prime means of naval warfare, thus rendering the huge English battle fleet superfluous.

Aube's logic was penetrating but, in the long reign of peace in the nineteenth century, hard to prove. Meanwhile, the defenders of naval orthodoxy, like aroused antibodies, moved to engulf the unwanted invader. The publication of *The Influence of Sea Power* buttressed the venerable hierarchy of ships, while the development of quick-firing secondary armament, underwater structural subdivision, and bulky torpedo nets provided at least an aura of protection to battleship dwellers. (Actually, the nets proved virtually worthless as defenses against torpedo attack, but the rigging and unrigging of net defenses did provide an invaluable substitute for the furling and unfurling of sails, a traditional exercise by which the relative efficiency of crews was judged.)

In order to deal with the pesky craft in a more active manner, the British navy began developing boats specifically designed to hunt and destroy them. After experimenting unsuccessfully with a gun-based torpedo-boat killer, the Royal Navy concluded in 1893 that a vessel capable of performing this mission must be a torpedo boat itself, only larger, faster, and better armed. The useful type that resulted came to be known as a "destroyer" and was universally adopted as the prime means of screening a battle fleet from harassment.[23] The torpedo boat, on the other hand, quickly fell into disfavor.[24] Thus, by a neat sleight of hand, the naval establishment domesticated a potentially very dangerous enemy.

Yet the second carrier of the torpedo, the submarine, was not so easily co-opted and turned to defensive purposes. Therefore, it was alternately ignored and despised.

Theoretically, however, the union of the submarine and the torpedo held vast potential, not only because submersibility would render such a vessel invisible and virtually invulnerable, but also because, unlike the gun, the torpedo could be fired underwater.

Yet, practically speaking, a successful submarine would have to await the development of a suitable propulsion system and the end of the fallacious notion that a submarine must descend and rise on an even keel. Yet these conundrums would soon fall prey to young Irish nationalist immigrant to America, John P. Holland. Dreaming of a weapon capable of humbling the British battle fleet and financed with sixty thousand dollars of Sinn Fein money, Holland, in 1881, built the *Fenian Ram,* the first boat designed to dive by planing and also capable of firing a torpedo while submerged. Yet the high oxygen consumption of its Brayton petroleum engine severely circumscribed its underwater range.[25]

With little outside support, Holland struggled with the problem for fifteen years until he finally succeeded in building the *Holland VI,* a craft which incorporated the revolutionary idea of combining battery-powered electric motors for submerged operation with the newly developed internal combustion engine for surface running. The boat was an immediate success, traveling twice the distance submerged which the U.S. Navy required for acceptance. Yet still the service hesitated. "What will the Navy require next," Holland's biographer Richard Knowles Morris quotes his long-suffering subject, "that my boat should climb a tree?"[26]

Quite probably most naval officers, if they had heard of Holland and his boat at all, simply wished they would disappear. The submarine's sole redeeming feature from a U.S. perspective was its potential as a coast defense weapon. Thus, George Dewey, the hero of Manila Bay and later a major figure in the development of the fleet, testified before Congress in 1900 that "with two of those in Galveston, all the navies in the world could not blockade that place."[27]

Yet far from being tied to coastal waters, the submarine had seakeeping abilities which would soon amaze even its most ardent supporters. Inherently able to dive below bad weather, the submarine's range and endurance grew at an astonishing pace. Prodded by a series of rapid-fire improvements, the process culminated in 1912 with the installation of the newly developed diesel, an engine requiring no ignition apparatus and burning safe fuel oil at such an economical rate that the scope of underwater craft immediately became truly transoceanic.[28]

Meanwhile, out on the high seas the torpedo's possible influence was beginning to be felt. Whereas a gun was most accurate when fired at an approaching target, the reverse was true of the torpedo, which was most likely to hit an opponent broadside. The implications were particularly ominous for parallel line-ahead tactics, where two hundred yard long ships were commonly spaced at five hundred yard intervals. "Some torpedoes run erratic courses," explains Bernard Brodie in *A Layman's Guide to Naval Strategy,* "but so long as they run at the proper depth they would have to be extremely erratic to miss a battle line." The only clear solution lay in separating the battle fleets beyond the reach of torpedoes. The problem, as a panel at the U.S. Naval War College recognized in 1909, was that "the torpedo would prevent a battle fleet from closing within effective gun range."[29]

Oddly enough, however, when war came, the threat which the submarine presented to military targets would prove secondary to the challenge it posed as a commerce raider. Even Admiral Aube never made the connection between *guerre de course* and the submarine. Yet it was there and, when recognized, the submersible warship would become the deadliest menace to ocean-borne trade ever devised.

But the fear and dislike which the submarine inspired in the international naval fraternity cannot be attributed solely to its destructive potential. Without doubt, early submarines were miserable and dangerous craft on which to serve. In contrast to the commodious battleship, the inside of a submarine was a claustrophobic, foul-smelling environment, where the starch of naval custom quickly wilted and battery-acid fumes, continual temperature changes, and the high noise level often undermined the health of the most robust submariners. To compound matters, every time a submarine dove underwater there was the distinct possibility that it would not come up again, but would instead drag its crew to the bottom to drown, suffocate, or simply be crushed by water pressure. Yet it was the submariners themselves who suffered these indignities, and they were for the most part volunteers.

Members of the surface navy resented these craft as much for what they implied as for what they were. For the submarine and its torpedoes flouted almost every value that had come to be associated with the proper and traditional conduct of naval warfare. Not only had they added another dimension to the hitherto flat world of the naval officer, but their very mode of operation was the essence of unpredictability. Unlike the carefully regulated and articulated surface fleet, the submarine by nature traveled alone or in small groups, largely free of control by higher authority. It was the nautical counterpart of the guerrilla fighter—invisible, ubiquitous, capricious, and terrifying. To make matters worse, both submarine and torpedo operated in fundamental oblivion to the hierarchy of ships. Since submarines sought invulnerability through stealth rather than size, they tended to be small, replaceable craft. And because the torpedo was self-propelled and therefore required no complicated launching devices, even the most diminutive of warships now could carry a weapon capable of sinking the largest. To the conventionally oriented officer, such a situation must have seemed not only potentially disastrous but tantamount to tactical insubordination.

Even the quiet discharge of the submarine's lethal torpedoes must have seemed queer to ears accustomed to the reassuring thunder of great guns. Yet the submarine was simply not a weapon based on confrontation, and herein lay a major reason for its unpopularity. The whole manner of its attack implied skulking, treachery, and deception—qualities warriors traditionally had disdained. British Admiral A. K. Wilson spoke for the entire naval establishment when he described the submarine as "underhanded, unfair, and damned un-English."[30]

This being the feeling at the hub of the naval world, it was not until 1904 that a small British submarine development program was begun, ironically, through a funding subterfuge engineered by First Sea Lord Sir John Fisher, the iconoclastic chief sponsor of the HMS *Dreadnought*. Yet familiarity with the submarine in the Royal Navy bred only contempt, as exemplified by the reaction of a flagship, thrice torpedoed during maneuvers and politely requested by its submarine antagonist to remove itself from the fleet problem. "You be damned!" was the signal flashed back.[31]

While not so vehement, the Royal Navy's three major rivals would pursue basically similar policies in regard to submarines. In the Orient the Imperial Japanese Navy built submersible prototypes but concentrated on surface ships. Across the North Sea the German navy's underwater weapons program was a remarkable success technically, producing the first true oceangoing submarine, the U-19, one of the deadliest weapons yet conceived. Yet the emphasis remained squarely on the surface fleet, which consumed 1.5 billion dollars during the twenty years prior to World War I and so dominated the building ways that only twenty-five seagoing submarines would be ready for service in August 1914. Meanwhile, in the United States efforts aimed at perfecting the submersible warship proceeded haphazardly at best. While Congress proved sympathetic, the navy demonstrated little enthusiasm for building up an underwater flotilla. Consequently, after three years of watching the submarine dominate combat at sea, American entered World War I without a single submarine fit to fight.

So the submarine languished, exiled to the nether reaches of the naval consciousness. Yet it was more than innate dislike which blinded conventional thinkers to its possibilities. Navies everywhere had been dazzled by a weapon so apparently formidable that virtually all classes were to some degree neglected so as to accommodate its gargantuan appetite for men and money and metal. Enter the dreadnought.

III

As noted earlier, the most immediate influence of torpedoes was a grudging recognition by naval theorists that, to be sure of avoiding them, opposing battle lines would have to engage each other at ranges progressively in excess of those of the mechanical fish. This not only flew in the face of the Homeric urge to close but was highly impractical. For although the size and reach of naval rifles had increased dramatically, attainable accuracies certainly had not.

This began to become apparent around the turn of the twentieth century, particularly within a group of vigorous British and American naval officers including John Arbuthnot Fisher, Percy Scott, and John Jellicoe among the former, and William Sowden Sims, Bradley Fiske, William Fullam, and Homer Poundstone among the latter. This Anglo-American clique was interesting not only for its accomplishments, which were numerous and would be a prime factor in determining the course of military naval architecture for the next fifty years, but also for its outlook.

All were line officers and very much a part of the naval mainstream, but they were also innovators and intimately involved with weapons acquisition. For the first time military services were beginning to generate not just an internal constituency for new arms but a component actively dedicated to their development. But, unlike their civilian equivalents, this group would consistently retain a very clear sense of military tradition and propriety, and would formulate their creations accordingly.

This was certainly the case with gunnery reform. Between 1898 and 1900, while stationed with the Royal Navy's Asiatic Squadron aboard the HMS *Scylla* and HMS *Terrible,* Captain Sir Percy Scott developed a series of techniques to maximize accuracy at long ranges and soon was achieving some very respectable figures at nearly two thousand yards, while traveling upward of twelve knots.[32] Although Scott's methods were somewhat contrived—consisting of ships firing singly in smooth water at targets unobscured by smoke—they constituted a major improvement and were accordingly treated as carefully guarded secrets, of which the French and Germans were told nothing.

But the American navy was different. Almost unconsciously, a decision had been made to treat it as a little brother whose growth and increasing competence was seen not as a threat but as a matter of family pride. Therefore, when an enterprising young U.S. intelligence officer, William Sowden Sims, visited Scott in Hong Kong during 1901, he was shown everything.[33] No sooner had Sims learned the rudiments of the system than he was proselytizing it within the American navy. By autumn of the following year, at the intercession of Theodore Roosevelt, he was made inspector of target practice and given basically a free hand to institute "scientific" marksmanship. Working hand and glove, Scott and Sims soon had their respective fleets locked in a friendly competition to increase the accuracy of their shooting and improve the precision and magnifying power of their sights. (Sims and Scott regularly exchanged the most intimate data, and at one point conspired to inflate each other's shooting scores to spur on their home authorities.)[34]

But even if they had ceased comparing notes and remained isolated on either side of the Atlantic, logic and ordnance technology would have led them in exactly the same direction. For as naval antagonists drew farther and farther apart, the problem of the gunner, like that of the basketball player beyond the foul line, became increasingly less one of aiming than of shooting the proper distance.

The best means of establishing an unknown range was to create an imaginary triangle and find its tangent. But beyond six thousand yards the angle created became too acute to be measured accurately unless one of the legs of the triangle was lengthened by mounting a spotter high above the ship where he might calculate the range and check himself by observing the shell splashes around the target. Yet producing a recognizable splash pattern required that the shells be fired at the same time and that they be as nearly identical as possible. It was also true that the heaviest shells, due to their steady flight characteristics, were consistently the most accurate at extreme ranges.

The conclusion was all but unavoidable. The best resolution to the manifold problems of long-range naval fire fighting lay in the construction of a battleship with a single-caliber main battery composed of the largest naval rifles available. So it was that the all-big-gun concept captured the imagination of the naval world.

By early 1902, Sims's friend Homer G. Poundstone ("Lbspierre"), invalided by severe rheumatoid arthritis and liberally dosed with morphine, was working on plans for an all-big-gun battleship, the *Possible,* which quickly found its way into the hands of a sympathetic President Theodore Roosevelt.[35]

The next year Vitorio Cuniberti, a romantic Italian naval engineer, published an article in the semiofficial English naval annual, *Jane's Fighting Ships,* projecting a vessel armed with a dozen twelve-inch rifles and a "very high speed— superior to that of any existing battleship." Cuniberti argued that his *Invincible* not only carried enough armament to reduce anything else at sea to a smoldering hulk but also possessed the speed to escape any trap or combination of opponents.[36] Once again the mirage of an ultimate weapon appeared on the horizon, this time to dazzle the naval world.

Lord Admiral John Arbuthnot Fisher reacted as if hypnotized. Only dimly remembered today, Fisher was one of the most colorful and influential British naval leaders of all time. Robbed by the long peace of a chance to immortalize himself in battle, Fisher's significance rests largely on his influence over British naval construction and his amazing personality. At once a brilliant visionary, charismatic and charming, he was also dogmatic, chauvinistic, and utterly pugnacious. ("If a man throws a glass of wine in your face, do not throw a glass of wine in his. Throw the decanter stopper!")[37]

In these last qualities Fisher epitomized the anger and suspicion with which the English nation and the Royal Navy viewed the kaiser's growing fleet. An avid supporter of Scott ("I don't care if he drinks, gambles, and womanizes; he hits targets!"),[38] Fisher was fully aware of the advances in naval gunnery. When he was appointed first sea lord in 1904, he was, according to his biographer, Arthur Marder, determined to act on them by building an all-big-gun battleship.[39] Such a ship, he knew, would make every capital vessel in the German navy hopelessly obsolete. That it would do the same to the British and American fleets was of secondary importance. Fisher and his counterparts in the United States were not thinking in terms of single units; they were already bent on rebuilding their entire battle lines. And news of the great Japanese victory at Tsushima on 27 May 1905 only served to reinforce this commitment—this despite the fact that fully half of the vessels sunk during the Russo-Japanese War had fallen prey to mines.[40]

The ship, the HMS *Dreadnought,* was undertaken in absolute secrecy and rushed to completion in eighteen months. In December 1906, Sims visited England and was brought in civilian clothes to the Portsmouth navy yard by Scott and John Jellicoe and given a thorough tour of the revolutionary battleship. Displacing nearly twenty-one thousand tons and mounting ten twelve-inch guns, the *Dreadnought* was the first capital ship in the world powered by steam turbines, giving it the remarkable speed of twenty-one knots.[41] Sims left convinced that the reciprocating engines of the two American all-big-gun ships already under construction, *Michigan* and *South Carolina,* were insufficient, and that henceforth American battleships would require turbine engines to make them true dreadnoughts.

Yet even Sims underestimated Fisher's passion for speed. For work was already under way on three British supercruisers, *Invincible, Inflexible,* and *Indomitable,* each armed with all big guns but largely shorn of armor—the weight saving going into turbines of nearly twice the horsepower of the *Dreadnought,* giving these ships sustained speeds of up to twenty-eight knots.[42] The supercruisers represented the triumph of naval theory over experience, the game board over reality. In Fisher's overheated imagination they could run down anything at sea, outgun it, and then break off the action whenever desirable; nothing could stop them.

This was not the first time British naval construction had fallen prey to this fantasy. Three hundred twenty-five years before, at the dawn of English naval supremacy, John Hawkins had become wed to the identical proposition, only to find that it didn't work in battle against the Spanish Armada. Now, in the twilight of British dominance, fate would soon have an even less pleasant surprise in store for the Royal Navy.

But, in the meantime, British maritime prestige and the subtle mechanisms of weapons symmetry conspired to set the world building equivalent dreadnoughts at an astonishing rate. Not since the macrogalley building orgy of the Hellenistic monarchies had the world seen a naval arms race of such intensity and with such a wholehearted commitment to large ships.

Germany's reaction was instructive. No other naval power had been more inconvenienced by the appearance of the HMS *Dreadnought*. Not only was the kaiser's entire battle fleet instantly outdated, but the country's most important strategic waterway, the Kiel Canal—a sixty-one-mile shortcut between the Baltic and North seas—was rendered almost equally obsolete for lack of locks capable of handling ships larger than thirteen thousand tons.[43] Thus, construction of Teutonic dreadnoughts would almost automatically necessitate canal alterations costing 12.5 million pounds sterling. If there was ever a time to cast aside aspirations of naval power as not worth the price, or to follow the alternate track of the submarine and the torpedo, it was at this point.

Yet, instead, the ante was laid down with hardly a grimace. For by this time the kaiser had come to look upon his fleet as a solution to his personal frustrations and those of his adolescent nation. "All the years of my reign," he told the king of Italy, "my colleagues, the Monarchs of Europe, have paid no attention to what I have to say. Soon, with my great Navy to endorse my words, they will be more respectful."[44] It was a revealing statement. To the kaiser, his herd of battleships implied not only power but acceptance. Most of all, Baron Friedrich von Holstein would write, the "Kaiser want [ed] a fleet like that of England."[45] Seen in this context, the *Dreadnought* constituted both a calculated affront and a supreme challenge which he was unlikely to ignore.

Even if the kaiser had displayed no interest in naval weaponry, the results probably would not have differed markedly. For German naval officers were no less wed to the example of the Royal Navy and the battleship than was their monarch. Moreover, the logic which had been devised to justify the birth of the High Seas Fleet demanded that Germany follow Britain's lead in constructing dreadnoughts. *Risk fleet* was the term invented by the construction program's bureaucratic architect, Admiral Tirpitz, to describe this oblique attempt to paralyze the Royal Navy by building only enough battleships to prevent the English navy from challenging its German rival without fatally weakening itself in the face of the remaining naval powers. As a prescription for naval power, notes Jonathan Steinberg, risk fleet proved a sterile hybrid of orthodox naval theory and political wishful thinking.[46] Not only did it ignore the fact that the remaining naval powers—America, Japan, and France—were either allies of or well disposed toward England, but it condemned the High Seas Fleet to a perpetual second place, which, when the time came, would stifle virtually all combat initiative. Meanwhile, to retain credibility as a deterrent, the German battle fleet had to be kept in some meaningful relationship to that of the Royal Navy which translated into the construction of seventeen all-big-gun battleships and five dreadnought battle cruisers before August 1914—a fleet large enough to fuel a naval arms race but too small to fight.

Across the Atlantic, the Americans rapidly followed suit. Sims got his steam turbines in the first true member of the American dreadnought battle fleet, the USS *Delaware*, which mounted ten twelve-inch guns and weighed in at a hefty twenty thousand tons.[47] Others would soon follow. But not before loud voices were raised in protest, not just in Congress, which had always remained somewhat skeptical on the subject of battleships, but also from the naval prophet himself, Alfred Thayer Mahan, who complained: "We are at the beginning of a series to which there is no logical end, except the power of naval architects to increase size."[48]

President Theodore Roosevelt reacting cannily, first asking Sims to write a rebuttal and then concocting a gigantic publicity stunt. Gathering together all the outmoded American mixed-caliber battleships, he had them painted white, lined up like mechanical pachyderms, and sent out to sea on an around-the-world tour. Having shorn the Republic of its white elephant fleet, Roosevelt then explained to Congress the virtues of dreadnoughts, asking for four per year. Angrily, the legislative body cut his request in half. But in time Roosevelt and Sims would have their way. The American fleet would be rebuilt with dreadnoughts, with thirteen being authorized by 1914. Meanwhile, Mahan's original concept of a battle fleet as an integral component of a vast scheme of national aggrandizement was more and more overlooked. American dreadnoughts were built largely because other dreadnoughts existed.

Elsewhere it was much the same. The Japanese, fresh from their triumph at Tsushima, responded almost immediately to the *Dreadnought* with their own *Satsuma* and continued building all-big-gun ships as rapidly as their limited industrial base would allow. The French, though no longer much interested in sea power, would not long resist the trend, and by 1911 the first true Gallic dreadnought, the *Jean Bart,* was sliding down the ways. In 1910 the Italians added the nineteen thousand ton *Dante Alighieri* and kept on building. The Russians, after losing virtually their entire fleet in 1905, were naturally susceptible to dreadnought fever, laying down the Pervozvannyi class as early as 1906 and then the Gangut class in 1911. Even Austro-Hungary, with precious little seacoast to defend, built the twenty thousand ton *Viribus Unitis*. Those that could not build dreadnoughts of their own, like Turkey and Brazil, simply ordered them built by others.

Yet nowhere was the enthusiasm for dreadnoughts greater than in their birthplace, the naval-industrial womb, Great Britain. With Lord Fisher at the helm, the Royal Navy steered a course of naval expansion which left the rest of the naval world wallowing in its wake. With the single-mindedness of all great naval builders from Hawkins to Gorshkov, Fisher generated momentum which even his most reasoned critics were powerless to slow. The dreadnought-building frenzy would climax in 1909 with Parliament's authorization of eight of the mammoth warships. Winston Churchill, astonished at the progenitive power of military technology, would comment: "The Admiralty had demanded six ships; the economists offered four; and we finally compromised on eight."[49] Not every year proved as fruitful, but by the fateful summer of 1914, the Royal Navy had accumulated twenty-one all-big-gun battleships and nine battle cruisers—a grand total of thirty dreadnoughts, or a bit under three-quarters of a million tons of capital ships.

Instead of freedom to wander the world's oceans unmolested, this vast expenditure of metal and effort brought only uneasiness and the necessity to keep the lion's share of the appropriately named Grand Fleet concentrated in home waters to thwart the equally immobile but thoroughly mislabeled High Seas Fleet.

In fact, geopolitical considerations were increasingly cast aside in favor of statistics. The great battleship-building race was driven by little other than its own internal logic. Gun size, broadside weight, turret armor thickness, and speed differentials of a few knots were the only meaningful variables in the closed system of dreadnought logic—these and pure numbers. There were, of course, war plans, but when the time came to implement them, they proved little more than window dressing. In its essence, the dreadnought rivalry was a classic example of intraspecific competition sublimated into weaponry. Not only were the products large, loud, armor plated, and festooned with phallic naval rifles, but the actual competition was utterly symmetrical. Of over fifty dreadnoughts built worldwide prior to World War I, none differed in any major respect from any other. Indeed, the British, American, and German navies might have traded ships and not felt very much out of place.

Meanwhile, something very fundamental had happened to the armored warship. By underwriting the step-by-step evolution of the surface artillery ship, the mainstream of the naval world led itself out on a technological limb. The character of the battleship had been decisively altered. The capital ship was no longer a brawler built to slug it out at point-blank range but a weapon of precision whose entire destructive potential depended on the pinpoint accuracy of relatively few guns firing at ranges exceeding eight miles.

Behaviorally, the transition was eased by the well-established patterns foreshadowed by the duke of Parma's ill-fated luncheon. Rather than swinging a saber in yardarm-to-yardarm confrontations, an admiral might feel suitably heroic standing on the bridge of a dreadnought, eyes fixed to the horizon, oblivious of the giant shell splashes which threatened to engulf his ship.

Operationally, however, such spectacular misses would prove far too frequent. In fact, the variables impinging on the precision of naval gunnery would overwhelm the devices available to control them. When war came, ballistic peculiarities, smoke, and uneven lighting conditions would confound the dreadnoughts' ability to fight decisively while subsurface weaponry would steadily erode their ability to seek each other out. Until such a time, though, the great ships were magnificent in the shipyards and building ways.

Yet if, as noted, geopolitical considerations had progressively less to do with the proliferation of dreadnoughts, the reverse was hardly the case. The naval arms race clearly served to exaggerate tensions endemic in the pre-1914 European state system. It is ironic that, not only can a persuasive case be made that these tensions were based on a series of misperceptions of the politico-military environment, but also that the various dreadnought fleets were really rather harmless as weapons go. Nonetheless, the bad feelings they provoked were very real.

Interestingly enough, it was the dreadnought's very failings as an instrument of destruction which provide the major point of comparison with our own nuclear deterrent. In essence, each was or is very much better not used than used. In the latter case this is more or less overtly understood; in the former it was merely an accident of technology and in no way accepted by the potential users. Yet the central point stands.

In this sense the dreadnought represented a groping prototype of deterrence, a weapon of last resort whose presumed formidability underlay all political relationships. Unlike the pre-1914 land armies to whom every advantage seemed to lie with preemption, there was no perceived need to rush into battle with dreadnoughts. In this sense they were stabilizing. Also, had there been an agreement to stabilize numerical relationships, the possession of a battle fleet might have bought a sort of naval legitimacy short of war. But, of course, there was no such agreement, and this is why risk fleet could not work and why the proliferation of battleships continued to exacerbate tensions. Today the dynamics remain much the same, though we understand them somewhat better. At least that is the presumption.

Chapter 13

PRELUDE

I

If the dreadnought stood for intraspecific valuation and the stablilizing potential of pure threat, there existed in pre-1914 armories a series of weapons much more predatory in their implications and a great deal more usable. The submarine was one. The machine gun and the dumdum bullet were others. So long as peace persisted, the overwhelming tendency was to suppress them. Yet development continued, and when deemed appropriate, there was experimentation with use. The manner in which this took place illustrates the enduring aspects of weapons development. For it was very much a part of the white man's burden.

Just as the first great spasm of European colonization coincided with the introduction of firearms, the second climactic period of Western imperialism fell neatly in sync with the multifarious improvements in arms which took place during the latter half of the nineteenth century. Even more than in the first instance, it was precisely these weapons and their ruthless application which allowed small and frequently semiofficial bands of Europeans to conquer virtually all of Africa and large chunks of Asia with almost ridiculous ease. Never had the martial superiority of the West been more apparent. Yet the magnitude of the triumph could not mask the contradictions upon which it was based, and in the end Europe would be shaken to its foundations by the backlash from these easy victories.

Rather than face up to the paradox of weapons which killed too easily, Westerners found it expedient to use such devices far afield against those who looked and acted differently, all the while reassuring themselves that these armaments would never be employed against Europeans. That this course of action proved a sham in no way contradicts the fact that it was supported by precedents extending back to the origins of humanity. Man had almost always initially applied new weaponry toward predatory ends. In Europe the theme of arms control at home, and their ruthless application abroad, against those deemed alien, can be traced to the Church Edict of A.D. 1139, outlawing the use of the crossbow among Christians but not against Muslims. It could be said that the victors of El Teb, Omdurman, and Shangani were merely walking in those holy footsteps.

The first use of shrapnel in Surinam, the introduction of the percussion-fired musket against the Chinese, the Minié ball against the Bantu, and the bombardment of many a native enclave by steam-powered warships all illustrate the point; but it was the employment of the dumdum bullet and the machine gun which brought it mostly sharply into focus.

Given the success of the exploding shell, the development of a fragmenting small-arms projectile was a logical, if not entirely welcome, step. In 1863 the Imperial Russian Army was first to introduce a bullet capable of bursting on contact with hard surfaces, ostensibly for use in blowing up artillery wagons. Three years later, however, a modified version became available which was designed to explode upon colliding with substances as soft as flesh.[1] Recognizing the danger that such a bullet might be employed against Russian troops, the Imperial War Ministry advised Czar Alexander II to take the unusual step of calling an international military commission to outlaw such bullets. The resulting convention at Saint Petersburg in 1868 not only marked the origins of the characteristically self-interested Russian resort to arms control but also succeeded in banning exploding projectiles under four hundred grams in weight, at least among signatories.[2] This was significant since of the nineteen state parties, sixteen were Europeans, including the United Kingdom.

Here matters stood until approximately 1895, when British colonial authorities discovered, or thought they discovered, that the standard-issue .303-caliber Mark II high-velocity bullet shot by the new Lee-Metford rifle was doing remarkably little damage when it hit native insurgents in the Chitral. Alarmed by stories of individual enemies surviving as many as six wounds, Major General Gerald de Courcy Morton, the adjutant general in India, set his ordnance experts at the ammunition factory at Dum Dum working to develop a bullet which expanded on impact like those used in big game hunting. The resulting dumdum, and later the Mark IV variant, almost invariably produced large, jagged wounds, ideal for stopping native combatants in their tracks; but also raising questions about their legality under the Saint Petersburg Declaration.

The British defense of their actions could hardly have been more revealing. As Surgeon Major General J. B. Hamilton and Sir John Ardagh explained at the International Peace Conference at The Hague in 1899, the enemies encountered in the colonies were not to be equated with signatories of the Saint Petersburg Declaration, nor should they be treated as such. "Civilized man is much more susceptible to injury than savages. . . . The savage, like the tiger, is not so impressionable, and will go on fighting even when desperately wounded."[3] Under the circumstances, the dumdum bullet was deemed entirely appropriate, and, as Edward M. Spiers explains in his excellent article on the subject, the racist assumptions underlying their use were never questioned.[4]

When war came that same year in South Africa, however, the fact that the

Boers, though frequently depicted as primitive farmers, were still white farmers insured that British field forces would fight with fully jacketed ammunition.

This pattern held when general war came to Europe in 1914. The dumdum-type projectile remained something of an exotic and would not see much combat until the so-called tumbling bullets of the American AR-16 and the Soviet AK-74 were used, respectively, against the Vietnamese in the 1960s and the Afghans in the 1980s—enemies, once again, easily perceived as vastly different from the "civilized" troops fighting them.

Yet there was an alternative to the dumdum which capitalized on a much more acceptable and traditional line of development—rapid firing. Since the failure of the mitrailleuse, the subsequent development of the machine gun, notes John Ellis in his *Social History of the Machine Gun,* was carried on almost entirely by private entrepreneurs, the four most significant—Gatling, Maxim, Browning, and Lewis—all being Americans.[5] Although they were able to demonstrate repeatedly the relatively low cost and startling capabilities of their weapons, all four met with consistent frustration when dealing with military authorities. While the Germans and the Russians proved slightly more receptive, in general the armies of Europe took to the machine gun with great reluctance. "For," as Ellis explains, "military reactions to the machine gun were not a rational response to either technical or financial considerations. They were rooted in the traditions of an anachronistic officer corps whose conceptions of combat still centered around the notions of hand-to-hand combat and individual heroism."[6] A weapon which sprayed bullets like a garden hose sprayed water not only contradicted these values, it promised to make a mockery of them.

Nevertheless, the machine gun's cool reception at home was very much contrasted by the eagerness with which European, particularly British, colonial forces took up automatic weapons. Seen from an imperialist standpoint, the machine gun was nearly the perfect laborsaving device, enabling tiny forces of whites to mow down multitudes of brave but thoroughly outgunned native warriors. Archetypical was the 1898 Battle of Omdurman in the Sudan, where the disciples of the Mahdi, the fabled dervishes, repeatedly hurled themselves against British lines, only to be repulsed each time by six Maxim guns firing six hundred shots per minute. "It was not a battle, but an execution," reported G. W. Steevens. "The bodies were not in heaps . . . but . . . spread evenly over acres and acres. Some lay very composedly with their slippers placed under their heads for a last pillow; some knelt, cut short in the middle of a last prayer. Others were torn apart."[7]

An even more lurid example was provided by a battle which took place in Tanzania during the early 1890s between representatives of the German East Africa Company and Hehe tribesmen. At the height of the action a German officer-surgeon and his assistant dragged two machine guns and plenty of ammunition into a mud hut with a clear field of fire, and from there killed around a thousand native combatants.[8] Two men, two guns, a thousand dead—if ever there was a device capable of giving vent to man's predatory instincts, it was the machine gun. And in such circumstances these feelings cannot have been far below the surface.

Figure 12. Hiram Maxim firing a Maxim gun. Reproduced by permission of the Bettmann Archive.

Consider the case, cited by Ellis, of one British machine gunner on a punitive expedition to Tibet in 1904 who, in the middle of a battle, got so sick of the slaughter that he ceased firing, only to be reminded by his commander that he should not regard his victims as anything other than so much game.[9] While obviously a rationalization, this and other similar statements constitute an admission, however dim and backhanded, that such weapons were inappropriate for use against actual human beings. Only by expelling these native victims from the ranks of *Homo sapiens,* a process made easier by their divergent physical characteristics, could such acts of slaughter be easily countenanced.

But it was, of course, a sham which in the end fooled no one. Machine guns were not hunting instruments. They were designed to kill men—black or white or yellow, depending on who possessed them. So ultimately, Europeans fell back on pure self-interest, epitomized in the words of Hilaire Belloc's Captain Blood: "Whatever happens, we have got: the Maxim gun, and they have not."[10] For the moment, at least.

Just as the South American Indians had lapsed into passivity in the face of the conquistadors' arquebuses during the first wave of European imperialism; so too did the nineteenth-century natives of Asia and Africa resign themselves to the European's machine guns and dumdum bullets during the second. "And the white man came again," moaned one Rhodesian tribesman after an encounter in 1893, "with his guns that spat bullets as the heavens sometimes spit hail, and who were the naked Matabele to stand up against these guns?"[11] Had his new overlords cared to listen, they would have heard not the plaintive cry of quarry but the voice of a man articulating the dilemma of all men faced with weapons which killed too easily. "War now be no war," commented one Nigerian. "I savvy Maxim gun kill Fulani five hundred yards, eight hundred yards far away. . . . It be no black-man . . . fight, it be white man one-side war." [12]

And so, whether black, brown, or yellow, they had to submit—open their ports to the white man's smoke-belching ships, accept his one-sided trade, his strange laws and arrogant officials, even his religion. Yet underneath this passive demeanor was a sullen rage and a growing awareness that, as Mao put it, "power grows out of the barrel of a gun."

Reactions to this revelation took several forms. At first it would periodically result in acts of rage and incoherent violence, the most memorable being the great sepoy mutiny. This epidemic of mass hysteria and bloodlust which swept across India in 1857 was undoubtedly fueled by the pent-up frustrations of 150,000,000 natives ruled by a tiny European minority. Yet, as Christopher Hibbert points out, the rebellion began among the relatively privileged native colonial infantry, or sepoys. More to the point, it was the rumored introduction of a cartridge greased with tallow, for the new Enfield rifle, which drove the sepoys to mutiny. [13] Since loading procedures required the marksman to bite off the end of the cartridge, and tallow was known to contain beef or pork fat, the sepoys, both Hindu and Muslim, not unreasonably feared defilement. Yet the tallow-coated cartridges were never actually issued, and the British authorities even offered to allow the men to grease their own ammunition with a vegetable-based substance of their choosing. Even this did not allay sepoy suspicions, and soon rumors were circulating that the rifles themselves had been packed in cow's fat. [14]

The result was a rebellion which probably cost the lives of several hundred thousand people, mostly Indians. Hibbert is right in labeling it "not so much a national revolt [as] a last passionate protest against the relentless penetration of the West." [15] Nevertheless, it seems more than coincidental that the primary object of Indian hatred was the ammunition for the white man's new rifles. It would appear that beneath his fear of defilement was an unconscious belief that these weapons were polluting his way of life and were at the root of his subjugation.

This brand of unfocused violence would persist to the Boxer Rebellion and beyond, but it was no solution to imperialism. A few of the white devils might die, but always more would come, and their retribution was terrible.

II

There was an alternate route to power, however, one taken by a strange island nation whose geographical relationship to the Asian landmass was similar to that of the British Isles to Europe. But unlike the English, who had exploded outward during the seventeenth century, the Japanese had turned inward and, since approximately 1640, had successfully closed their island to the rest of the world.

Although foreign attempts at penetration and reciprocal Japanese awareness of outsiders had increased, the arrival of Commodore Matthew Perry's powerful squadron of American warships in 1853 was nonetheless a profound shock to both the Tokugawa shogunate and its subjects, notes Pat Barr.[16] For over two hundred years Japanese society, culture, and technology had remained crystallized. Suddenly, Perry confronted the Japanese with devices such as the telegraph, the steam locomotive, and, most disturbing of all, massively superior armaments which he used to browbeat the Tokugawa shogunate into signing a commercial treaty, soon followed by similar arrangements with other imperial states.

Like other traditional societies thrust into the same predicament, the Japanese were humiliated and fearful of further encroachment. Yet their reaction was quite different. Rather than accept their fate passively, the Japanese almost instinctively set about to redress the military imbalance.

Up to this point Japanese military power had been concentrated exclusively in the hands of a hereditary caste of samurai, and it might be expected that this class would have provided the primary impetus for a military renascence. In the main, this did not prove true.

In Choshu, as a result of an internal struggle, a group of radical young samurai had become the dominant force internally and, at the behest of the eldest local lord, began reorganizing his army under the brilliant leadership of Takasugi Shinsaku. A close student of Western military science, Takasugi was also a violent partisan of the *sonno joi* (revere the emperor, expel the barbarian) movement. With the European example as a reference point, he began recruiting a force without regard to social background and equipping them with the latest Western Minié ball–firing rifles. Still wed to traditional military practice, the Tokugawa samurai sent to put down this well-armed, peasant-based force relied on the bow, the sword, and the tactics of old Japan, and was defeated accordingly.[17]

Out of the resulting political ferment there arose, in 1868, the so-called Meiji restoration, a coup d'état which replaced the Tokugawa regime with a group of younger samurai intent on eliminating most feudal privileges, including their own, and substituting a thoroughly revamped and modernized political and economic structure. Central to this program was a conscript-based army and a state-supported weapons industry. Between 1873 and 1877, the samurai revolted four times. After the last and largest of these uprisings, the Satsuma Rebellion, the power of the samurai was forever broken, and, as E. H. Norman notes, the Meiji resolutely set about expanding still further its weapons programs, increasing land arms expenditures 60 percent and naval estimates 200 percent over the next decade.[18] By 1903, according to Clive Trebilcock, a higher portion of Japanese national income (10.3 percent) was being spent on arms, than that of any state in Europe.[19] And although the evolution of arms production provided a basic model for the growth of Japanese heavy industry in general, there was one major difference. While other state-incubated industries were gradually turned back into private hands, the Japanese military-industrial base continued to be held tightly in the grip of the state, and would remain so until World War II.[20]

At the same time the weapons nexus was taking shape, conscription was becoming the basis for the manpower needs of the army. The intellectual child of another student of Western military practice, Omura Masujiro (assassinated by reactionary samurai before his plans could come to fruition), conscription was first written into the law in 1873. It was not until after 1877 and the failure of the

Satsuma Rebellion, however, that it was practiced on a massive scale. It was then, argues E. H. Norman, that the transition from an army intended for purely home defense to a force aimed at use abroad took place.[21] Japan would not only build an army based on European arms and personnel practices, she would become an imperial power herself and, in doing so, render a clash with one or another Western state practically inevitable.

This did not occur until 1904, and the opponent was to be the least developed of the great European powers, Russia. However, Japan's stunning victories, particularly the virtual annihilation of Admiral Rozhdestvenski's fleet in the Tsushima Strait, marked a fundamental change in world history. Since the fifteenth century, when the Turks adopted the gun, no other non-Western society had shown a real affinity for state-of-the-art weaponry. Now the Japanese served notice that the Western weapons tradition, the key element in four centuries of military dominance, was no longer the exclusive preserve of the West. It is true that the Japanese still imported some arms and copied the designs of others. Yet this was hardly an unknown phenomenon in the West and had, in fact, always been a major mechanism for the proliferation of new developments. What mattered was that the Japanese had learned to acquire advanced weapons technology and had used it successfully to defeat a major Western state. Even more important, they would show that the process was open to exploitation by others.

Coming at what appeared to be the peak of Western martial ascendancy, Japan's victory over Russia might be expected to have been a shocking revelation. But it wasn't. The Japanese were perceived basically as an aberration—a plucky race, good at copying things, but with little potential for creativity. As for the larger implications, there was little concern that others would or could follow in their footsteps.

This was symptomatic. Almost unanimously, professional opinion in the developed West saw what it wanted in the Russo-Japanese War. At sea, if mines sank as many ships as all other naval weapons combined, the fact was conveniently overlooked. If, on the other hand, naval gunfire proved ineffective except at very close ranges, this was used as an argument for bigger guns.

On land it was much the same. The war, as Theodore Ropp reports, was observed by some of the world's ablest soldiers, including John J. Pershing, Ian Hamilton, and Max Hoffmann.[22] Yet their dispatches were selectively interpreted in a manner which screened out the enormous power of field entrenchments, the deadliness of machine guns and quick firing artillery, and the futility and inevitably huge casualties accompanying frontal assault. And so this prelude to Armageddon passed if not unnoticed, then at least thoroughly misunderstood by the military establishments which, in less than a decade, would have to suffer the consequences.

III

In contrast to the general state of oblivion which had settled over the ranks of the military and most civilian elements in the industrialized world, there were perceptible signs of unease as 1914 approached. I. F. Clarke notes, for example, the increasing numbers and popularity of published war fantasies after 1880.[23] Also of significance was the steady growth of organized peace movements and, in particular, efforts to further codify warfare and limit arms. While the official response to this public ground swell was decidedly restrained, it did result in two major disarmament conferences at The Hague in 1899 and 1907.

All but forgotten today, these conferences did little more than register the international apprehensions of a hypocritical age which characteristically preached one thing and did another. Nonetheless, they do illustrate the subtle but growing fear of modern war and weapons, along with providing a suggestive prelude to the subsequent evolution of modern arms control.

As with the Saint Petersburg Declaration, the impetus for both conferences came from Imperial Russia, and despite characteristic appeals to humanitarian sentiments, the element of self-interest was obvious. In 1898, seeking to avoid the expense of replacing a range of obsolete artillery with new crucible steel, quick-firing pieces, the Imperial finance minister, Witte, convinced the czar to issue a "rescript" on armaments, calling for an international conference to "occupy itself with this grave problem."[24]

By and large, the twenty-six nations which met at The Hague in 1899 followed a Russian-formulated agenda calling for, among other things, a prohibition of "any new kinds of firearms [and explosive] whatsoever," as well as a ban on bombardment from balloons, the outlawing of submarines, and a general five-year freeze on military budgets and the size of armies.[25]

Having lost tremendous quantities of equipment in the Russo-Japanese War, the czar's agenda for the 1907 conference shifted from arms, which he now had every reason to want to replace, to the conduct of war, stressing the arbitration of international disputes, provisions "concerning the opening of hostilities" (the Japanese had begun the campaign against Russia with a surprise attack), and the laws and customs of maritime warfare.[26]

Looking at the record, it is immediately apparent that there was a strong bias against unconventional arms. Not only was the czar's suggested ban on balloon bombardment affirmed in both 1899 and 1907, but the conferees in 1899 agreed "to abstain from the use of projectiles the sole object of which is the diffusion of asphyxiating or deleterious gases."[27] It is notable that neither means had as yet been used in combat; in the latter case it was explicitly recognized that "it is logical to prohibit new means above all when they have a barbarous character and partake of treachery . . ."[28] Similarly, the 1899 conference reaffirmed, over British objections (see p. 232), the earlier Saint Petersburg injunction against exploding bullets, while the 1907 conference placed the use of seaborne mines under strict regulation.[29] However, it is interesting that the proposition to ban torpedo-firing submarines was postponed, as was an effort to eliminate small-arms firing over twenty-five rounds per minute. Russian proposals to prohibit exploding shells and quick-firing artillery were decisively rejected, as were the suggested freezes on military budgets and the size of force structures.

Other than these attempts to regulate arms and armies, the conferences' major acts were aimed at further codification of the rules of land and naval warfare, particularly with respect to neutral rights. But with absolutely no provisions for monitoring or enforcing compliance, this edifice of legalism quickly would be reduced to a shambles by the desperation of the combat in World War I.

Even if the provisions had been better written, the seriousness of the conferees might well have been questioned. There was an element of lip service, an air of unreality which hung about the deliberations at The Hague. This was typified by the conduct of Russia, which called the first peace conference, fought a desperate war with Japan, and then called the second peace conference—all in less than a decade.

This, too, was symptomatic. In the strange, anesthetized atmosphere of pre–World War I politics, attempts to come to grips with reality were most conveniently relegated to paper exercises, while the pressures of nationalism and technology silently built to an inevitable crescendo.

This was nowhere more evident than in the remarkable outpouring of combat fantasies which found their way into print as the Great War approached. Much of this literature was puerile and obviously motivated by naked chauvinism. Yet in the case of a few, the authors demonstrated real insight into the nature of the impending catastrophe and even the still more profound changes that would follow in its wake.

One of these was a rags-to-riches Polish banker, I. S. Bloch. Though Bloch was to die in 1902, his massive and impeccably researched six-volume work, *The Future of War,* would predict with uncanny accuracy the unfolding of the most bizarre two decades in Western military history. Bloch's thesis was simple: war had no future, and mechanical invention was making it impossible to fight, except at suicidal cost.

> At one time war appealed to the imagination of man, and the poets and painters found no theme so tempting as depicting the heroism of the individual warrior. . . . All that has long gone by the boards. War has become more and more a matter of mechanical arrangement. Modern battles will be decided, so far as they can be decided at all, by men lying in improvised ditches they have scooped out to protect themselves from the fire of distant and invisible enemy. . . . War, instead of being a hand-to-hand contest . . . will become a kind of stalemate, in which neither army [will be] able to get at the other.[30]

Moreover, Bloch made clear, the consequences of such prolonged conflicts would not be measured simply in casualties and material loss but also in terms of the potential disruption of the social order. Modern war, Bloch warned, had the capacity to rip apart the social fabric.[31]

Bloch's understanding of the naval future, while less comprehensive, was nearly as cogent. He grasped the significance of the torpedo, especially in combination with the submarine, and saw how both, when applied ruthlessly to seaborne commerce, might render great battle fleets irrelevant.[32]

Yet it remained for A. Conan Doyle, the opium-smoking creator of Sherlock Holmes, to fully elaborate this conception in a remarkable war fantasy entitled *Danger,* which he wrote eighteen months prior to World War I.

The story opens by describing an uneven dispute between England and Nordland, a small, imaginary European nation. Lacking an adequate surface navy, the latter's king is about to submit when he is reminded of his flotilla of eight submarines by an enterprising officer, John Sirius. "Ah, you would attack the English battleships with submarines?" asks the worried monarch. "Sire, I would never go near an English battleship."[33] Instead, he proposes to wage a merciless campaign against merchant shipping, thus striking at the Island Kingdom's vital dependence upon seaborne foodstuffs. As soon as the plan is put into operation, numerous transports are sunk without warning. "What do I care for the three mile limit or international law?" growls Sirius at one point.[34] England is quickly pushed to the edge of starvation and forced to accept a humiliating peace.

The story was widely read but received only scant attention in military circles, particularly within the Royal Navy. "I do not myself think any civilized nation will torpedo unarmed and defenseless merchant ships," maintained Admiral Penrose Fitzgerald, speaking for most of his brother officers.[35] He was wrong, of course, but this observation was not a ridiculous one. *Danger* served to expose the fragility of industrial society and the ease with which modern weapons might strike at its heart. Like Bloch's terrestrial insights, Doyle's naval cogitations led directly to the conclusion that modern war, by its very nature, would transgress nearly all the institutions which remained to contain it.

Still more striking than the works of Bloch and Doyle was a tale called *The World Set Free*, published early in 1914 by H. G. Wells. As literature it falls short of the standards set by *The Time Machine* and *War of the Worlds*, but it marks, in the words of I. F. Clarke, "one of those rare occasions when fiction becomes truly prophetic."[36] For the subject is radioactivity.

The story begins with a professor holding a phial of uranium oxide before his audience and foretelling "a source of power so potent that a man might carry in his hand the energy to light a city for a year."[37] Yet peaceful uses do not prove the ultimate objective when men finally harness atomic energy in 1953. Instead, six years later, the world erupts. "By the spring of 1959, from nearly two hundred centres, and every week added to their number, roared the unquenchable crimson conflagrations of the atomic bombs. . . . Most of the capital cities of the world were burning; millions of people had already perished, and over great areas government was at an end."[38]

In a single white-hot image this writer of fiction captured what the work of Rutherford, Einstein, and Planck made inevitable. While others were envisioning the end of the previous era, Wells looked beyond to the beginning of the next. That his conception was apocalyptic should come as no surprise; an awareness of the potential for apocalypse is the basis for the only sanity we now know. The critical point is that Wells caught a glimpse of that which would transform everything. As the day of transition approached, others would come to share parts of his vision, and like the killing zones Edward III set up for his longbowmen at Crécy-en-Ponthieu, bits and pieces of the new order would begin to accumulate prior to the decisive emergence of its key element.

Meanwhile, thirty years of the chemical energy–based era remained, and Western man would be called upon to render up to the gun a terrible and long-overdue price. For the arsenal of da Vinci would be completed at last, and not since the Thirty Years' War would there be such a harvest of blood.

THE GREAT WAR

I

Until 1939 the term *World War I* was unknown. This might appear intuitively obvious since without a second world war, it would hardly seem necessary to designate a first. Yet there is more to it. Prior to this time the conflict which took place between 1914 and 1918 was known simply as the Great War. It was a stark, monumental, and entirely appropriate appellation. As with other watershed events— the Black Death, the Reformation, the Great Depression—there was no perceived need for further description. There had never been a war remotely like it, and it was assumed that it would remain forever unique and recognizable. Of course, contemporaries failed to foresee the scale and pervasiveness of its sequel. Yet today their original judgment once again seems correct. The war touched off at Sarajevo remains unparalleled, if not in its gross statistics, then at least in its significance to our present situation.

It has been noted repeatedly, most recently by Bernadotte Schmitt and Harold Vedeler,[1] that it was in the crucible of the Great War that our own political world was initially forged. As institutions of real authority, monarchy and fealty-based empire (though not necessarily transnational tyranny) received deathblows, and out of the superheated remnants of empire there emerged a body of new states which remade the map of Europe in essentially its present form. Meanwhile, democracy and socialism made huge strides, and with them occurred a radical shift in economics, the status of social classes, and the relative place of women. On the larger geopolitical plane, the Great War also marked the real end of the colonial era and, in the revolt of the Arabs, the origins of the Third World. But most important, the whirlwinds of the fire storm pushed power out and away from Europe and deposited it at the edges of Western civilization, in America and Russia.

Yet there is clearly more. The Great War had a profoundly lasting and dele-terious effect on Western man's view of himself and his civilization which cannot be explained solely in political terms. Rather, it will be argued here that at the root of this crisis of morale was a sudden awareness, engendered primarily by the stalemate on the western front, that military power, when applied, had grown uncontrollable, and that this was directly attributable to weapons technology. This judgment has not changed essentially to this day. Yet the abruptness of this oc-currence, the wholesale discrediting of a factor largely responsible for three hundred years of political transcendence in a mere four years of war, was such a shock, and raised such profound questions about the basic directions of Western civili-zation, that it created a crisis of the spirit unparalleled in modern times. To see exactly why this was true, it is important to examine the disaster in detail, not just its magnitude but its quality and impact on a number of different levels.

Around ten million men were killed in combat during the Great War. When compared with prior wars, this is undoubtedly a large number. On the other hand, during the six months between the fall of 1918 and the spring of 1919, somewhere between twenty and thirty million died worldwide as a result of the so-called Spanish flu.[2] This bout of influenza is, however, a historical footnote, while the Great War will never be forgotten.

The key, then, is not simply the quantity of death but its qualitative element. And what distinguishes this particular war, sets it apart from even the most hor-rible, is futility. Most of the victims died for nothing more than a few feet of rat-infested mud. The most carefully prepared war plans were reduced, sometimes in a matter of moments, to antic apologies for slaughter. Age-old military verities, both on land and at sea, were twisted by circumstance into shapes that would have been funny had the results not been so awful. And perhaps most ironic, despite the enormity of the price and the total preoccupation of the participants, the war was fought, and peace was made, with very limited ends in mind. In short, the Great War was a nearly seamless evocation of Murphy's Law: virtually everything that could have gone wrong, did go wrong.

And behind it all loomed the factor of military technology. Like no other conflict that had come before, the Great War's course was determined by the weapons with which it was fought. And of these, many of the most important had seen no previous large-scale use in combat. Thus, a meaningful understanding of their tactical characteristics and strategic implications was almost invariably de-layed. Yet the emergency of wartime made it necessary to act on present assump-tions, whether accurate or inaccurate. So the course of the war was reduced to a blundering process of experimentation, conditioned by the inherent conservatism of military men and the very traditional ethos which surrounded the profession. Meanwhile the western front became an automated corpse factory, while the war at sea took the form of a mechanized charade in which the chief protagonist lurked below, not upon, the stage.

Even worse, arms did not simply dominate, they did so in a manner which made a mockery of the warrior ethic. With few exceptions the key weapons in this great conflict were devices which held little appeal according to the traditional criteria by which armaments had always been judged. Skill, strength, swiftness, cunning, and aggressiveness were rendered nearly irrelevant. Combatants were gassed, torpedoed, bombarded by invisible artillery, or mowed down randomly by puny-looking machine guns; there was hardly a heroic death to be had. Despite the scale of the combat, it was visually unimpressive. For the extreme lethality of the weaponry drove participants underground, huddled in trenches; so it was rare that either side caught a glimpse of a recognizable adversary. Life in the trenches reduced soldiers from warriors to statistics, casualty figures, so that the western front's quintessential action, Verdun, was fought not to gain a superior position or to drive the enemy from the field but simply to kill.

At sea, or more accurately, in port, life was less dangerous but even more boring. Soldiers sat aboard their magnificent dreadnoughts, behind torpedo nets, awaiting the decisive battle royal just over the horizon but forever eluding them. Meanwhile, the real naval action took place on the loathsome submarine, once again, below the surface.

There was, however, one towering exception. In the midst of the grinding impersonal slaughter there arose a weapon of such chivalric proportions that it would provide a counterpoint to the entire struggle and in doing so illustrate the durability and regenerative powers of the warrior code in even the most adverse circumstances. Far above the squalor of the western front, jousting at the edge of a dream, new knights of the air gathered to duel one another, reinvesting an element of intraspecific combat which might reasonably have been presumed irrevocably lost. Thus, the development of the fighter aircraft demonstrated that advanced technology was not necessarily incompatible with traditional preconceptions of war and weapons.

Nonetheless, it was also clear that the momentum was in the opposite direction. The fighter aircraft was just one of many new weapons, and even among flying machines, a much more predatory and random killer, the strategic bomber also evolved during the Great War. So, as had happened just prior to the proliferation of the gun, the foundations of organized violence were beginning to shift. Only this time more than just a reinterpretation of courage would be required to restore the equilibrium. For now weapons were turning against the war itself.

II

It is a singular fact that all three major Continental powers, Germany, Russia, and France, entered the Great War intent upon going on the offensive immediately, which they did with disastrous results. Everybody attacked, and everybody suffered, the consequences of which set the conditions for four subsequent years of stalemate and misery. Thus, the Schlieffen Plan (calling for German forces to sweep around the French in a gigantic wheeling movement), and the resulting invasion of Belgium were critical in bringing Britain into the war, provoking the very naval blockade which the kaiser and his advisors dreaded and hoped to avoid. France's ill-advised Plan 17, calling for a thrust in the direction of Lorraine and the Ardennes, allowed the Germans to occupy large portions of northeastern France, thereby hindering the operation of the wartime economy and insuring that the remainder of the action in the West would be fought primarily on French soil. Finally, the annihilation of the sluggish Russian advance into East Prussia not only wasted troops which could have been used to far better effect against the Austrians, but set the tone for further disasters which would lead directly to the Revolution.

In an interesting recent book, *The Ideology of the Offensive,* Jack Snyder makes the case that this confluence of offensive schemes was basically coincidence. Rather than explaining the phenomenon primarily in terms of a "pan-European cult of the offensive, rooted in long-term transnational causes," Snyder locates within the military infrastructures of each of the respective powers separate and individual reasons why an attack was planned and immediately carried out.[3]

Snyder's analysis is informative and incisive, at its best highlighting the irrational aspects of each plan. Joffre ignored reliable intelligence reports that the Germans were planning to use reserve units to extend far north into Belgium, thoroughly outflanking the French attack. The Germans, on the other hand, should have realized they lacked the troops and logistical support to do all the Schlieffen Plan demanded. And the Russians had only to gather their troops and wait in order to reap at least some of the benefits that time and numbers should have granted them.

Yet nobody waited and nobody listened to reason; this Snyder blames on bad strategy and institutional loyalty-based decision making. Others, such as Steven Van Evera and Scott Sagan, emphasize a more complicated set of factors leading to a tight network of offensive alliances.[4] Yet the actual results seem more immutable than is implied by even these explanations. To illustrate we have only to reduce Snyder's arguments to a logical absurdity in which all three powers take his advice and go on the defensive as soon as war is declared. Nothing would happen—certainly a more humane solution, but hardly a satisfying or lasting one given the late-nineteenth-century military mind-set.

Snyder, in particular, would have been better served had he delved more deeply into military sociology or technology. To be fair, he does mention the Prussian campaign of 1870 as a universally attractive model of a short, successful offensive war.[5] But he makes no attempt to analyze why they were so or why, once rebuffed initially, the participants in the Great War continued attacking whenever victory seemed even remotely possible. Similarly, Snyder and most scholars of the period do give weapons technology credit for having totally overturned the relationship between offense and defense, yet they fail to ponder the implications. The level of arms technology available in 1914 had made war, as it was conceptualized by the participants, literally impossible to fight. Yet fight they must. And it was the clash between these two imperatives which defined the tragedy. In essence, everybody attacked because nobody had any real alternative.

While the initial French and Russian offensives were so profoundly faulted that few have questioned the inevitability of failure the Schlieffen Plan has often been perceived differently. A number of commentators, a recent one being George Quester,[6] have chosen to emphasize how close the plan came to working. To explain its failure, apologists traditionally have blamed the supreme German commander, the younger Moltke, for transferring two corps from his right wing back to East Prussia, thereby fatally weakening the German forces along the key avenue of advance.

In fact, the Schlieffen Plan stood little chance of success under any circumstances, a conclusion reinforced by the remarkable German good fortune during its initial stages. Rather than move into Belgium to meet the advance head-on, the French obligingly marched off toward Lorraine. Next, the Germans were exceedingly lucky to seize the key Liège railhead. Had it been demolished as planned, German logistics would have been devastated. Finally, as the attack matured, the French continued to miss its real nature until the very last minute. Still even after this string of blunders, the French were able to escape the fate Schlieffen and the Germans had planned for them. And it was technology which saved them.

On a strategic level the French took advantage of their excellent rail net and internal lines of communication to redeploy their forces by train to achieve a numerical superiority opposite the German right just as the Battle of the Marne commenced.[7] The Germans, on the other hand, had to take the long way around, reaching the Marne on foot—tired, dusty, and hungry, their logistics stretched to the breaking point. Moreover, their arrival was greeted by an unprecedented array of firepower. Tactically, the improved range and rate of fire of small arms was quickly evident, and the machine gun would very soon play a major role, but at the Marne one weapon in particular wreaked havoc.

The French possessed a remarkable piece of artillery, the 1897 model 75-mm field gun, or more simply the French 75. As Henri Isselin explains, the key to the weapon had nothing to do with the gun itself but with its hydraulic recoil mechanism which, upon detonation, allowed the barrel to slide back on its carriage and then return to its precise firing position without upsetting the aim. This meant that 75s could be fired accurately as fast as they could be loaded, or up to twelve shots a minute. For Germans caught in the open, it meant sudden death, as it had for over two thousand members of the Lepel brigade mowed down in a beet field near Nanteuil-le-Haudouin by a battery of 75s in a matter of five minutes.[8] Because of the low trajectory of its shells, the French 75 would not prove particularly effective against troops in trenches, but at the Marne, against exposed, maneuvering Germans, it was devastating.

Exhausted, their ranks depleted, close to despair, the Germans reeled backward, defeated it seemed. To the elated French the time had come to chase them back to the border. "Legs!" General Foch told the Moroccan Division. "We need only legs now! The enemy is running away."[9] But it was not to be. On 13 September the pursuing Anglo-French force reached the southern edge of the Aisne valley. That morning Raymond Recouly, an officer attached to the Moroccan Division headquarters, overheard the commanding general on the telephone: "Barbed wire? Let them go round it or cut it!" The next sound Recouly heard was that of a tremendous fusillade to the north, punctuated by the rattle of machine guns.[10]

The Germans had dug in and turned on their pursuers, and in the process revealed the next lethal surprise of the war. Up to this point, the machine gun's usefulness was compromised by the fluid nature of the combat, but now, carefully emplaced in field fortifications, it mowed down charging French and British with ridiculous ease. In this regard, John Keegan makes the obvious but critical point that the machine gun was above all a machine, similar in some respects to a precision lathe. As such it had to be set up, but once this was done, it operated virtually automatically, shooting down anything in its path with a reliability far exceeding that of a rifleman.[11] Totally unable to penetrate the German line, the Allies had no choice but to dig in themselves. In this sector the two lines of trenches would remain at almost exactly the same spot for the next four years.

Realizing he could not go through the Allies, the new German commander, Falkenhayn, sought to envelop their flank by moving reinforcements out from the northern end of his line along the Aisne. Grasping his object, the Allies, too, extended themselves northward, trying to cap the German defenses. There ensued a month of mutual outflanking during which the front was extended from Noyon, through Picardy, Artois, and Flanders and to the English Channel near Nieuport. This so-called race to the sea left two parallel lines of continuous fortifications stretching like giant snakes from the Swiss border to the North Sea.

Having run out of room to flank, Falkenhayn next sought to break through at Ypres, a month-long encounter whose desperation and futility would set the tone for the rest of the war. Like the Dutch against the Spaniards nearly three-and-a-half centuries prior, the Belgians turned the sea loose against their adversaries, opening the sluices at Nieuport, forcing the Germans to break off. During the next phase, around Messines Ridge farther south, Falkenhayn threw the ardent but half-trained German youths of the Fourth Army against the English. The British line broke for a time, but in the end the attackers were slaughtered, in a massacre remembered in Germany as *der Kindermord von Ypern.* The final stages of the battle saw the Germans trying just to capture the city of Ypres itself, mostly as a face-saving measure. Even in this they failed. Both sides were exhausted, and the stalemate was complete. From October 1914 until March 1918, notes J. F. C. Fuller, no attack or series of attacks in the West was able to move the front line even ten miles in either direction.[12] Meanwhile, according to Dupuy, during the first three months of war, the French and the British had suffered around 940,000 casualties and the Germans, 677,000.[13] It would get worse.

III

The war at sea got off to an even more bizarre, if far less sanguinary, start. Both sides expected almost immediate combat and tangible proof of the mighty dreadnought's power. What ensued was a veritable satire of conventional naval wisdom.

Supplementing a tradition of victory stretching almost beyond recollection, the Royal Navy enjoyed a comfortable, if not extravagant, lead over its adversary in dreadnoughts, matching twenty-one all-big-gun battleships and nine battle cruisers against the Germans' thirteen and six, respectively. Yet in the eyes of the British Admiralty this was not enough, especially when two Turkish dreadnoughts, *Osiman* and *Rashadish,* were nearing completion at Armstrong's shipyard on the River Tyne. In short order, the two ships—payed for out of the contributions of the sultan's impoverished but patriotic peasants—were requisitioned.[14] The Turks were mortified. Yet retribution would not be long in coming.

For simultaneously in the Mediterranean in an apparently unrelated drama, the Royal Navy was stalking the German battle cruiser *Goeben* and her consort, the light cruiser *Breslau,* with two powerful forces: one made up of three battle cruisers under Admiral Sir Berkeley Milne ("Arky-Barky" to the service) and the other consisting of four armored cruisers—*Warrior, Defense, Black Prince,* and *Duke of Edinborough*—under Admiral Ernest Troubridge. Presuming that the *Goeben* and the *Breslau* must inevitably try to break out through Gibraltar in order to reinforce the High Seas Fleet, Milne positioned his battle cruisers to "prevent the German ships going westward."[15]

The German commander, Admiral Souchon, had no such idea. He had received a curt and startling message from Grand Admiral Tirpitz: "Alliance concluded with Turkey. *Goeben* and *Breslau* proceed immediately to Constantinople."[16] Yet his way remained barred by the four English armored cruisers. All were fourteen-thousand-ton ships mounting a total of twenty-two 9.2-inch guns, against which the Germans could answer only with the *Goeben's* ten 11-inch guns.

But as the two forces converged, Fawcet Wray, Troubridge's flag captain and ordnance expert, was providing his admiral with a gunnery specialist's version of naval reality. Using superior speed and gun range, the *Goeben* had merely to steam around the English force, picking off ships one at a time. For if the logic that produced the all-big-gun battleship was taken literally, the *Goeben* did constitute a superior force. Of course, it didn't, but Troubridge abandoned the chase. "Admiral," said Wray, "that is the bravest thing you have ever done in your life."[17] It wasn't, and Troubridge would be court-martialed.

So Souchon escaped, and three days later the *Goeben* and the *Breslau* arrived unharmed in the Dardanelles. Upon going ashore the German admiral was informed that his ships had been sold to the Turkish government—"replacements," as Tirpitz put it, "for the two the British stole."[18] The Turks, in gratitude, would declare war on England. So, in toto, Britain gained two dreadnoughts but acquired a nation full of enemies. A poor trade, indeed.

Yet interpreted differently, the *Goeben* affair was highly symptomatic of the participants. As befit the venerable juggernaut of the naval world, the Royal Navy's ponderous attempts to crush the fleeing German battle cruiser were strictly in accordance with the rules, while the Germans had shown considerable ingenuity.

It was characteristic. The young German service can best be described as liberal, bourgeois, and technical in orientation. As the single truly national institution created under the German Empire, the navy was immensely popular with the middle class. And the composition of the officer corps reflected this power base, with almost none of the High Seas Fleet's flag officers being nobles.[19]

Just as the spirit of the middle class pervaded the command structure, it found tangible manifestation in German dreadnoughts. They were durable, solid products of a society which placed special emphasis on quality—floating metaphors of Teutonic craftsmanship. Meanwhile, U-boats in 1914 were years ahead of their time, lethal instruments whose reliability was truly remarkable when compared with the sputtering craft which passed for submarines in other navies. Yet material excellence alone would not suffice.

Blessed with the active, inventive virtues of the middle class, the officers of the Imperial German Navy were plagued by the most bourgeois of afflictions, an inferiority complex on an institutional scale. They never really believed they could beat the English. This pessimism would cost them the war at sea. For German insecurity was the ultimate insurance that they would persist in fighting according to rules dictated by their foes.

In spite of its many advantages, the Royal Navy was an institution flawed at many points. Time and combat would beat through the impressive facade to reveal a system so tied to a particular set of assumptions as to be practically incapable of adjusting itself to reality. Not having fought for a hundred years, it had rusted from within. And this petrifaction of thought and action found its material representation in the Royal Navy's utter and complete reliance on the gun. If the Germans treated mines and torpedoes as devices with real possibilities, then this was evidence of their foolishness and inexperience in the eyes of the British. Big guns and big ships won wars.

And British battleships were the standard by which all other warships were measured. If they were revealed as carelessly built, lacking adequate sights and armor-piercing shells, and prone to sudden destruction, they never lost their mystique. Whatever happened, the Royal Navy was conditioned to maintain its confidence in English men and material. Such aplomb in the face of the void, as much as anything, undid the fierce but neurotic Hun.

A short, decisive contest in the North Sea was initially expected. Yet this did not prove the case. All too aware that his capital ships were outnumbered, Kaiser Wilhelm was not anxious to provoke a climactic and potentially disastrous encounter. Instead, he hoped the aggressive British, attempting a close blockage of the shallow, restricted Heligoland Bight, would be decimated by mines and torpedo boats. Then, when the sides were equal, the Germans might risk battle.[20]

Although contemptuous of underwater weaponry, the British had no intention of committing suicide. Minefields had simply made the traditional close blockade too dangerous. Consequently, by 1911 the Royal Navy had evolved a new policy of "distant blockade." The Germans would be confined to the North Sea by the British fleet poised at some northern anchorage, ready to spring upon receiving word that the High Seas Fleet had sailed.[21] Yet it was conveniently overlooked that the Germans might prove difficult to locate in the 120,000 square miles of the North Sea. In fact, distant blockade was to naval strategy what the "emperor's new clothes" were to menswear—both required faith on the part of all participants.

The upshot was that very little happened in the first few months of war. The Royal Navy fumed with frustration. Yet in truth it was hardly less cautious than its timid opponent.

This spirit was personified by the handpicked commander in chief of the Grand Fleet, John Rushworth Jellicoe. He was, in the words of Winston Churchill, "the one man who could have lost the war in an afternoon." And, fully aware of this fact, Jellicoe was determined "not to leave anything to chance in a fleet action."[22] An ordnance specialist who had made an important contribution to the design of the original *Dreadnought,* he would have great trouble seeing beyond the measured, long-range gunnery duel. When battle came at last, he would act correctly but strictly according to the rules, and opportunity would slip away.

Excessive caution was never a problem with Jellicoe's second in command, Sir David Beatty, the leader of the battle cruisers. Having risen through the ranks on raw courage, no one could have been better suited to these swift, flamboyant craft and more capable of bringing the elusive Hun to bay. Yet by the middle of September 1914, he was beginning to worry that "the rascals will never come out but will only send out minelayers and submarines."[23]

Practically unnoticed, the untried submarine slipped into the waters between England and Germany to dispute the crown of sea power with the ponderous battleship. For almost a month nothing much happened. Then a disaster struck. On 22 September, shortly before dawn, three twelve thousand ton British armored cruisers, *Cressy, Hogue,* and *Aboukir,* were sighted completing a leisurely sweep, by Otto Weddigen, the captain of the German submarine U-9. Within an hour he had sunk them all. Almost fourteen hundred men drowned. In terms of casualties, it was the greatest disaster the Royal Navy had suffered in almost three hundred years. But it was more than that, much more.

Somewhere deep in the imagination of the naval establishment, a laughing voodoo priest had just entered the pristine chapel of nautical orthodoxy. And as he polluted icon after icon, it would gradually become clear that this witch doctor who cast no shadow and waved a contract signed in human blood was man's new partner in warfare—technology, come to collect his due. In some weird approximation of revenge, the HMS Dreadnought would ram and sink Weddigen's submarine in March of 1915.[24] But it was only bravado. There were no real counters for the submarine.

All the Royal Navy had to offer were ridiculous panaceas. Picket boats armed with blacksmith's hammers were sent out to smash periscopes. When these didn't work, the little craft were armed with large steel nets to catch submarines like haddock.[25] Sea gulls would be taught to perch on periscopes to make them more visible.[26] The Royal Navy even attempted to train sea lions from the London stage to search out unwanted submerged intruders. (Bernard Brodie maintains that "the sea lions shrewdly appraised U-boats as inedible, or at any rate unsavory, and declined to waste effort upon them.")[27] It was not until July 1915, with the formation of the Board on Invention and Research, that the English navy made a wholehearted effort to generate effective countermeasures. But progress was slow, and it was June of 1917 before hydrophones, the first workable acoustical detection system, and depth charges became available in sufficient quantities to allow surface craft to seriously menace submarines.

Meanwhile, battleships became beasts of prey. By mid-September 1914, packs of U-boats were beginning to be sighted in the upper portions of the North Sea, lying in wait for the Grand Fleet.[28] At first it was thought that they were operating from a floating base that could be destroyed, but gradually it became clear that the endurance of the German submarines had been vastly underestimated.

When what appeared to be a periscope (now thought to have been a frolicking seal) was sighted within the main anchorage at Scapa Flow, the Grand Fleet beat a hasty retreat. After some wandering the fugitive dreadnoughts found a temporary home in Loch Swilly on the northern coast of Ireland, more than three hundred miles away. "Distant blockade" was becoming ever more distant. Yet even here there was no safety. On 27 October the new dreadnought *Audacious* struck a German mine and sank.

The incident seems to have unnerved Jellicoe, who on 30 October, wrote the Admiralty a letter with momentous implications for the future: "Experience with German methods makes it possible to consider the manner in which they are likely to be used tactically in a fleet action. . . . If the enemy turned away from us, I should assume the intention was to lead us over mines and submarines, and decline to be drawn."[29] This was exactly what would happen at Jutland.

Meanwhile, having found no safety in Ireland, the wandering dreadnoughts returned to Scapa, still far from secure from submarines. But their ordeal was nearly over. German submarines would soon desist from actively stalking the Grand Fleet. These wolves of the sea had found fatter, tamer flocks to plunder.

While A. Conan Doyle's *Danger* was quickly forgotten by the English, the book was called to the attention of Admiral Tirpitz and the Naval High Command, who kept it in the back of their minds through the first frustrating months of war. For the time being, submarines were used against Allied transports, but only after the crews had been warned and evacuated.

Then, on 7 November 1914, the chief of the Naval Staff, Admiral von Pohl, proposed that U-boats be allowed to sink transports without warning, arguing that "the gravity of the situation demands that we should free ourselves of all scruples."[30] The rather defensive nature of the request, however, may have been a factor in enabling German Chancellor Bethmann-Hollweg to resist the mounting pressure to use U-boats indiscriminately. Finally, in early February 1915, Bethmann-Hollweg capitulated, and the waters around Great Britain and Ireland were declared a war zone where all merchant vessels, including neutrals, might be sunk without prior notice.

Of course, the Germans had only twenty-two operational submarines at the time, and the blockade seemed at first to be something of a bluff. By the end of April, thirty-nine British ships, displacing 105,000 tons, had been sunk by U-boats, but this amounted to less than a quarter percent of all the United Kingdom's shipping, and could be dismissed as a nuisance.[31]

Then, on 7 May, something happened which could not be ignored. The giant thirty two thousand ton luxury liner *Lusitania*—whose continued presence on the New York to Liverpool run symbolized British control of the seas—was torpedoed off the coast of Ireland by the German submarine U-20. Heavily laden with munitions,[32] the ship blew up and sank in eighteen minutes, claiming 1,198 lives, including 128 Americans. Among the most vehement protests came from the United States, where President Woodrow Wilson seemed particularly outraged at the manner in which the *Lusitania* was sunk.

The British were quick to join the chorus of condemnation. Considering the Royal Navy's neglect of antisubmarine weaponry and its persistent opposition to merchant convoys for fear of depleting the Grand Fleet's destroyer screen, there was little else to do. Yet it was surprisingly effective. The broadside of English propaganda during the summer of 1915 solidified world opinion against unrestricted submarine warfare at a time when British merchant losses climbed to 135,000 tons per month. Finally, on 19 August the White Star liner *Arabic* was torpedoed by U-24, with the loss of forty lives, including two Americans. Wilson reacted immediately, threatening to break diplomatic relations with Germany unless such practices were stopped.

The German response was intriguing. Although it was apparent that America was not about to go to war, Germany conceded her every point. By the end of September the submarine campaign had been virtually abandoned, and with the exception of a two-month spate of sinkings in the spring of 1916, would not be begun again until Feburary 1917.

The Germans had deliberately relinquished a potentially decisive weapon at a critical point in the war. And they had been motivated to do so more by moral pressure than by fear of reprisal. This becomes even more suggestive when the relatively light casualties of the submarine campaign (less than thirteen thousand throughout the course of the war)[33] are compared with the prodigious man consumption of the western front. The submarine was not a wanton killer. Rather, it was the nature of the weapon that offended.

The German navy had broken a code that transcended casualty figures or even winning and losing, and what it felt must have been akin to guilt. Chief of the Naval Staff George von Muller referred to the submarine as a "desperate measure." And in 1916 Commander Bartenbach could write: "One has the feeling that instead of building every possible submarine regardless of the consequences we are trying to avoid having too many." Even hard-bitten Admiral Tirpitz was forced to admit that "our appearance of uneasy conscience encouraged the English case that the campaign was immoral."[34]

Meanwhile, the year-and-four-month suspension would give the British time to develop the antisubmarine weapons and defensive procedures that would eventually defeat the climactic, unrestricted campaign of 1917. So technology offered the crown of sea power to the officers of the Imperial German Navy. But something had frozen them on the terrifying brink of success. Perhaps it was their own insecurities, or possibly they noticed something even more portentous.

IV

Gridlock. "I don't know what is to be done—this isn't war!" fretted the bewildered Lord Kitchener, referring to the situation on the western front.[35] Two massive armies, strung out in a double line of trenches for hundreds of miles, each laying siege to the other and both locked in place by the other's weapons—not only was the situation without precedent in Western military history but, its permanence, in the face of every effort to break the stalemate, mocked the exertions of all those involved and transformed the entire corpus of tactical and strategic wisdom into a series of man-killing shibboleths. In retrospect, military thinkers might have been better prepared had they payed closer attention to the American

Civil War, particularly its later stages. But as Europeans they brought a more convenient, if ultimately far less realistic, model to the trenches—a fact which must have made the experience doubly shattering.

In spite of it all, military minds were not totally frozen by this new and bizarre reality, and even during the early stages of trench warfare there were attempts at innovation. In particular, Falkenhayn and the Germans were quick to capitalize on the advantages of the defensive. But in the end the omnipotence of the gridlock reduced even these efforts to little more than the thrashing of a trapped beast.

By the spring of 1915 the Germans had come to terms with the static nature of combat in the West and sought to turn it to their advantage by waging a war of attrition.[36] Appropriately, weapons were to play a major role in implementing this strategy. In addition to reinforcing their lines with more machine guns and a variety of heavy artillery, many of which had been stripped from fortresses, the High Command distributed a range of new arms and equipment optimized for combat in field fortifications. Among them were the trench mortar (a simple tube which lobbed antipersonnel bombs from one line to another), efficiently fused hand grenades, periscopes, and mining and demolition equipment.[37] With these devices German troops would inflict horrific casualties on the Allies who threw themselves against their lines.

Yet the Germans were simply making the best of a bad situation. They had not escaped from the trap along the western front, nor had they eschewed the hope of breaking through and reassuming the offensive. And this was demonstrated by the most notorious of their weapons innovations.

Late in the afternoon on 22 April 1915 members of the French Forty-fifth (Algerian) and Eighty-seventh (Territorial) divisions were amazed to see a vast, greenish yellow cloud spring out of the ground and begin rolling toward their positions along the Ypres salient. Within moments the cloud had enveloped them, and they found themselves choking and fighting for breath. Those who were not immediately overcome ran in panic, and a four-mile-wide gap was opened in the French lines. Although there had been some earlier Allied combat use of irritants (Stinkstoffe), this incident marked the beginning of modern chemical warfare.[38]

Following a carefully plotted scenario, special pioneer troops had released around 150 tons of compressed chlorine from thousands of storage cylinders buried in German trenches. The attack was the culmination of a process begun seven months earlier when General Falkenhayn, frustrated by shortages of high-explosive shells and their relative ineffectiveness in dislodging Allied troops from their trenches, gave personal instructions that a new type of munition be developed.

The chemists had an alternative. It was a tribute to the degree to which science had been enlisted in the German war effort that, as Ulrich Trumpener notes, five future Nobel laureates (Nernst, Haber, Franck, Hertz, and Hahn) would eventually be involved in the chemical warfare program.[39] When development of an actual chemical projectile was delayed, however, chemist Fritz Haber stepped forward with a neat interim solution, the release of bottled chlorine. Several senior commanders, including Crown Prince Rupprecht of Bavaria, expressed reservations, arguing that a gas attack would only provoke retaliation. Yet Haber reassured them that the Allied chemical industries could not possibly produce the requisite quantities of gas.[40] So the initial use was authorized.

While technically a success, the attack fell far short tactically. As Ian Hogg notes, the German staff had little faith in the new weapon and therefore made no provision to move reserves quickly into the gap to exploit it. Moreover, by the very next day, Allied medical services had identified the gas and provided improvised face pads of sufficient effectiveness to allow Canadian troops to hold their position when similarly attacked.[41]

The element of surprise had been lost in Ypres, and while chemical agents would inflict severe casualties in future campaigns, particularly against the Russians, never again would even this level of tactical success be achieved. Moreover, despite experiencing considerable difficulty, within a year the Allies would field workable chemical munitions of their own. Twice more during the Great War the Germans would raise the ante, improving the fill first with phosgene and then with the insidious blister agent, mustard. But each time, contrary to German expectations, the British and the French would respond in kind. Meanwhile, on the western front at least, protective devices would continue to be fielded fast enough to allow troops to bear, if not exactly emerge unscathed from, such attacks. In the end sixty-six million gas shells would be fired, inflicting 1.3 million casualties.[42] Yet strategically their effect would prove minimal. They would produce only suffering. Once again a secret weapon had fallen short.

Just as with the submarine, the initial use of gas brought immediate and widespread indignation throughout the West. The Germans sought to blunt the vilification by claiming Allied "provocation" for their first use of irritants and by taking refuge in legalism, arguing that they had not broken The Hague convention's prohibition against asphyxiating projectiles since they had used stationary canisters. Yet they were obviously on the defensive. While civilians like Haber occasionally took the position that chemical weapons were actually less cruel than high explosives, in general military men did not share this view. Colonel Gerhard Tappen, Falkenhayn's chief adviser on chemical warfare, was typical of his fellow officers in writing of its "unchivalrous nature" and calling it "initially repugnant" to everyone concerned.[43]

The use of gas continued, however. In large part this can be attributed to the fact that, unlike unrestricted submarine warfare, it was within the grasp of the Allies to retaliate in kind. Once weapons symmetry had been established, the campaign took on a life of its own. Yet it was equally clear that Allied troops were no more enthusiastic about chemical warfare than their German counterparts. To a degree this can be traced to the cruelty of the instrument and the residual nature of the injuries it inflicted. No one who was gassed ever forgot it, a fact attested to by the reaction of gas victim Corporal Adolph Hitler, whose memory of this experience was a major factor in German abstention from its use in World War II.

Yet the universally low prestige of chemical troops within major contemporary armies, along with the continued repugnance with which chemical weapons are viewed today, nearly seventy years after their last promiscuous employment in

Europe, argues strongly that something else is involved. Lacking instinctive inhibitions against the consumption of deleterious substances, we seem to have developed equivalent cultural mechanisms. The fear of being poisoned or, for that matter, suffocated, appears to be very strong and basic. Certainly, these are not commonly seen as heroic means of death or killing. Compounding this is the nature of the weapon itself, which, like the submarine, is virtually antithetical to the profile of arms favored in the West. Rather than being loud, visually impressive, and confrontational, chemical weapons are virtually invisible, silent, and capricious—so much so that a mere shift in the wind has been known to send them floating back upon their users. They are, in short, largely ineffective strategically, unreliable, and repulsive—a combination of factors which would insure that chemical armaments remained an object of revulsion and, more to the point, an object of arms control. It is significant that at the end of a war epitomized by senseless and impersonal killing, chemical weapons were singled out and their use made illegal in the 1925 Geneva Convention. It is even more interesting that during the Second World War, a conflict which saw the enthusiastic development and use of virtually every form of weaponry including nuclear, the combatants voluntarily abstained from using only gas. Even in an era of total warfare, apparently, there remained some limits.

There were not many though. The phenomenon of the western front was such a bizarre one in large part because so much energy was focused on generating so much futility. On the home fronts of the respective protagonists, as William McNeill notes, various bureaucratic structures which had previously acted independently, driven by market forces, "coalesced into what amounted to a single national firm for waging war."[44] Family life, rights of property, consumption patterns, and social and geographic mobility were reshaped in an unprecedented fashion by planning elites whose single aim was war production.

So organized, miracles were accomplished. The first order of business was the ammunition required for endemic extended barrages. France, shorn of much of her industry by German occupation, built a new production base and within two years had increased shell manufacture twentyfold over prewar levels. Germany, separated by blockade from many critical war materials, created entire new industries to produce substitutes, particularly nitrates, with such efficiency that the original products were hardly missed. Even Russia increased shell production 1,000 percent in one-and-a-half years.[45] Yet it was not just ammunition. By 1917 all the belligerents were manufacturing a wide range of weapons in the same staggering quantities, and entirely new arms were being rushed into production with a speed that would have been thought impossible just a few years prior.

And virtually all of this bounty was shipped to fronts dedicated to its consumption using the same assembly-line principles by which it was created. In economic terms it was a close approximation of a perpetual motion machine. In human terms, however, it was a nightmare. While the stated aim was always to break the stalemate, in fact armies were turned into little more than killing machines.

This condition reached a logical conclusion in 1916 with the two greatest battles of the war, Verdun and the Somme. In the first the German intention of "bleeding the enemy white" by focusing on a point the French would fight to hold regardless of the cost, produced a battle that literally defies description. "At Verdun," as Eric Leed notes in his brilliant book on combat and identity in World War I, "the combatant fought . . . in a landscape dismembered by explosives . . . [where] it was impossible to tell French from German; all were the color of soil. . . . In this unstructured space, time also lost its form and coherence."[46] Only death remained real. And in the end, after 302 days of the fiercest fighting, the Germans had suffered almost as many casualties as the French—nearly a half million apiece in an action the tortured poilus came to refer to simply as "the hell." The alternative was played out along the Somme, where conventional wisdom dictated that the British double and triple their artillery, attackers, and reserves to achieve a breakthrough through sheer chemical and human mass. However, as John Keegan has shown, the actual weight of explosives delivered by the 1.5-million-shell preparatory barrage fell far short of the amount necessary to obliterate the opposing German trenches.[47] The result, when the British "Tommies" went over the top, was the purest slaughter. "I heard the 'patter, patter' of machine guns," remembered a sergeant of the Third Tyneside Irish. "By the time I'd gone another ten yards there seemed to be only a few men left around me; by the time I had gone twenty yards, I seemed to be on my own. Then I was hit myself."[48] On the first day the British would suffer sixty thousand casualties and the Germans, six thousand. The Somme would continue for 140 days more, during which the initial disparity in losses would disappear. In the end each side would endure over six hundred thousand casualties for a prize of six or seven miles of strategically worthless ground along a thirty-mile front.

Plainly, the relationship between war and weapons was changing fundamentally. Not only had weapons come to dominate all other factors, but they were overrunning the categories and psychological mechanisms which had traditionally accommodated them. In political intent and general conduct, the Great War was essentially a moderate struggle. And it follows that the participant armies and their respective armaments were largely symmetrical. Yet beyond this, the equation broke down. It was a misperception of weapons and transportation technology which caused all sides to initially adopt an offensive strategy, and it was weaponry which enforced the defensive gridlock that actually occurred. Similarly, the slaughter that resulted was incidental to political or military designs, but had everything to do with weaponry. Intraspecific intent had resulted in predatory ends. War and weapons were profoundly at odds. Previously, excessive lethality had been enfolded in ritual and tactical moderation. But this had demanded major institutional and political adaptation, and now weapons technology was a great deal more robust and hard to control. So, a way out was sought through further recourse to new armaments. This was not an entirely hopeless avenue, yet ultimately it would only make the battlefield a more deadly place.

Meanwhile, life under such conditions stretched the concept of soldiering to its very limits. Even for those left unwounded, weapons were testing the capacity of human endurance, and mental survival demanded accommodation. At the extremes, combat-induced neurosis presented itself as a means of escaping an otherwise intolerable reality. Prior to the Great War, the most common psychic disturbance associated with military service was homesickness. Now, however, incessant shelling produced an unprecedented range of hysterical symptoms, known collectively as shell shock, an affliction destined to become an increasing problem as the war dragged on. This was no aberration. There was an extraordinary tendency, even among the vast majority of soldiers who retained their mental bearings, to fall under the sway of a variety of superstitions and myths, of which the angel of Mons, the "German corpse-rendering works," and the army of deserters living under no-man's-land were only the most famous.[49] At first the idea of such a fantasy-ridden mental landscape taking root in a war so representative of industrialism seems paradoxical. But, as Leed points out, closer analysis reveals these myths as characteristic features, "even necessary emanations of technological warfare."[50] However bizarre, they provided a means of explanation and adjustment to a phenomenon that was essentially alien and inhuman.

Among the other psychological mechanisms which made life bearable were identification with enemy soldiers and a proverbial hatred of staff officers, whose only function, it seemed, was to generate suicidal battle plans. Yet through most of the war there were very few overt acts of mutiny. The aim was to endure, not overturn, the system. Thus, when left to themselves, troops seldom initiated action but only retaliated. Indiscriminate sniping, for example, was frowned on during an enemy's mealtime. Similarly, certain portions of a line were ritually strafed each morning with a few rounds and then left alone.[51] Prisoners, once secured, were generally well treated, and spontaneous massacres, though they did occur, were rare. Also, while the nature of the trench system and the availability of firepower generally kept troops apart, there were a number of recorded instances of remarkable fraternization in which opposing troops literally met to embrace in no-man's-land. Here, again, the intent was not mutiny but a celebration of life and a revolt against the machine-enforced battle regimen. Of course, fraternization and forebearance had always existed in warfare. Yet the fact that it flourished in such a predatory environment seems to indicate that the troops realized that it was not simply the enemy who was responsible for their suffering.

V

At sea the nautical analogue of the stalemate persisted with equal constancy, locking both sides in strategic purgatory. After the inconclusive action off Dogger Bank, the High Seas Fleet had not shown itself in the North Sea for over a year, and by the spring of 1916 many members of the Royal Navy were on the edge of despair. Yet forces were at work that shortly would put both fleets on a collision course. For one thing, the new commander of the German fleet, Vice Admiral Reinhard Scheer, had been since the beginning of the war a leader among the younger officers who pressed for the battle fleet to take the offensive.[52] Even more important, by February 1916, pressure to resume unrestricted submarine warfare forced Bethmann-Hollweg and the government to unleash the High Seas Fleet as the lesser of two evils.

Scheer's scheme was just as Jellicoe had feared. He planned to use his second in command, Franz Hipper's battle cruisers to lure units of the Grand Fleet, hope-fully David Beatty's, over a line of U-boats and into the waiting arms of the rest of the High Seas Fleet.

But Scheer had no way of knowing that the British were planning an equiva-lent snare, or that they possessed a captured copy of the complete German naval codes and radio direction finders to let them know when their quarry left port and approximately where it would be. So it was that as the High Seas Fleet slipped out of its anchorage at Wilhelmshaven on 31 May, pressed into action by the knowledge that the U-boats could remain on station only one more day, the entire Grand Fleet was already at sea, waiting. The stage was finally set for the long-awaited battle royal. And as it happened, each would fall, in succession, for the other's trap.

First it was the Royal Navy's turn. In the process of investigating a suspicious merchant steamer, Beatty's six battle cruisers spotted Franz Hipper, who imme-diately turned his own five units as if to flee. Beatty took the bait like a hungry tarpon, and by 4:00 P.M. both squadrons had formed parallel lines and let fly at a range of over eight miles, all the while racing toward Scheer's battle line. Within a period of half an hour, Beatty's own *Lion* took a near-fatal hit in her Q turret, and both the *Indefatigable* and the champion gunnery ship of the Royal Navy, *Queen Mary*, were turned into fireballs by German shells, both sinking with a total loss of twenty-four hundred men. "There seems to be something wrong with our bloody ships today," David Beatty complained to his flag captain.[53]

There was indeed. Sixteen months earlier, at Dogger Bank, the fleeing *Seydlitz* had caught a 13.5-inch British shell in her aftermost turret, and insufficient anti-flash devices had almost allowed the resultant flames to reach her magazine and oblivion. The Germans had taken remedial action. But the Royal Navy had no such warning, and before Jutland was over still another of its battle cruisers, *Invincible*, would be shattered by this contagion of flame. Yet better antiflash protection would not have cured these ships. Products of John Fisher's febrile imagination, they were the purest of dreadnoughts, sacrificing everything for speed and big guns. Who, after all, had needed armor on prewar game boards where the victor either outranged or outran the vanquished? They had been billed as "Invin-cibles"; now in the heat of combat the English battle cruisers revealed themselves to be little more than intricately wrought bombs.

But if machinery had no respect for reputation, tradition still counted for something, and Beatty's squadron refused to panic. As they approached the main body of the High Seas Fleet, Beatty's scouts recognized the danger and signaled back. The battle cruisers reacted quickly, managing to reverse their course just before coming into range. By 5:00 P.M. the English would be clear and leading the combined German force straight into the jaws of Jellicoe just fifty miles to the northwest.[54] The hunter had become the hunted.

Meanwhile, John Jellicoe, absolute master of one of the clumsiest weapons in history, was a worried man. Before he could fight, the Grand Fleet's twenty-four dreadnoughts had to be deployed in a single file, an operation which took twenty minutes. If done too soon, the Germans could escape; if Jellicoe waited too long, leaving his ships bunched up, the results might be fatal. Exactly where were the

Germans? When the rumble of heavy artillery became audible, Jellicoe asked no one in particular, "I wish someone would tell me who is firing and what they are firing at."[55] Finally, at 6:14, he got the signal he needed. The Germans were approaching. The last British vessel joined the vast L-shaped line one minute before the Germans sailed into view, headed directly toward the center of the formation. The German T had been crossed, and the British were between the High Seas Fleet and its home base.[56] Had this been a game board, Scheer might have flipped over his pieces. But this was the North Sea, subject to all the imponderables of smoke and fear and confusion that dominate any landscape upon which men fight and die; here, in the heat of battle, the sterile logic which spawned the dreadnought would melt to nothing.

After only nine salvos had been fired, the Germans disappeared. At first Jellicoe thought that this was merely due to "a thickening of the mist" and did nothing.[57] But soon it became apparent that the Germans were really gone. The admiral was bewildered.

The answer lay with the Germans. Finding himself at an overwhelming disadvantage, Scheer had ordered a "battle turn to the right," a maneuver devised for desperate situations and unknown to the British. Rather than marching obediently around a common point to be pummeled, each German dreadnought turned along an individual axis, reversing the course of the line in less than four minutes.[58] The maneuver worked perfectly, and by 6:45 the High Seas Fleet had put an additional eight miles between itself and the dreaded English.

At this point, however, the balance between flight and fight appears to have shifted in Reinhard Scheer's endocrine system. Reconsidering his situation, he decided to risk "another determined advance. . . . It would surprise the enemy, upset his plans and, if the blows fell heavily, facilitate a night escape."[59] Hector had relied on similar reasoning.

By 7:12 it was clear that the High Seas Fleet had again run into the middle of the British line and, for the second time in a day, found its T crossed. "The van of our fleet was shut in by a semi-circle of the enemy. We were in a regular death trap," noted Commander von Hase on the *Derfflinger,* by now thoroughly battered.[60] Scheer promptly ordered another "battle turn," but the volume of English fire spread confusion in the German line, and the maneuver was botched. The High Seas Fleet was on the verge of falling apart. In a desperate attempt to divert the British barrage, Scheer ordered his battle cruisers to "close with the enemy and ram"—the so-called death ride of the battle cruisers.[61]

But just as the Jutland drama was about to culminate, fate, the eternal improviser, ushered a new player upon the stage. As a last resort, Scheer unleashed his destroyers, ordering all flotillas to attack the British line with torpedoes. Amid a deluge of secondary fire, the frail craft managed to launch thirty-one.

Poised on the brink of victory, John Jellicoe spied his nemesis. The attack he had dreaded for so long was materializing. He had warned the Admiralty in October 1914 that he would not allow the Grand Fleet to be subjected to a torpedo barrage, and now he would make good on his promise. Shortly after 7:20, hoping to outrun the deadly fish, Jellicoe ordered his entire line to turn away from the enemy.[62] By the time he returned, the High Seas Fleet was gone for good. After a harrowing night, Scheer would slip behind the Grand Fleet and make his way to safety. The two fleets would never again meet in battle.

Inevitably the question arose: Who won? Certainly, in terms of statistics, the Germans had the edge. They had sunk over 110,000 tons of British warships and killed 6,100 members of the Royal Navy, while losing 62,000 tons and 2,550 men themselves.[63] Yet it had been the Germans who had run away. In this fact the British could take heart; command of the sea had been maintained. But at a cost. "Never again would American or Japanese sailors be overawed by the powerful, even overwhelming force of British naval tradition," writes Jutland historian Holloway Frost.[64] In fact, the battle marked the end of a three-and-a-quarter-century reign. Britannia no longer ruled the waves.

Neither did the battleship. No amount of rationalization could erase the fact that twenty tiny boats firing torpedoes had chased the entire English fleet off the field at the critical moment. The dreadnought was simply not a decisive weapon. The combination of smoke and confusion had made accurate firing of the great guns, at the ranges torpedoes necessitated, impossible with available optics-based range finders. For the second time in Western military history, the basic naval unit and the mode of fighting it stood for had reached the point of obsolescence. Just as Lepanto had marked the end of the ram-based galley, Jutland signaled the demise of the ship-of-the-line. Battleships would continue to be built and would live on in the hearts of sailors almost everywhere, but a very important corner had been turned.

In his report to the kaiser on the battle, Reinhard Scheer conceded that "only the resumption of unrestricted submarine warfare—even at the risk of American enmity—[could bring] a victorious conclusion of the war within a measurable time."[65] The statement marked the official deemphasis of the battle fleet by the German navy. In late October 1916 John Jellicoe advised the first lord that the "ever-increasing menace of the submarine attack on trade is by far the most pressing question at the present time."[66] Shortly after, he would release a flotilla of the Grand Fleet's destroyers for antisubmarine work. The war at sea had entered its penultimate phase.

On 6 April 1917 the United States declared war on Germany. Two months prior, the kaiser had approved resumption of unrestricted submarine warfare, gambling that England could be brought to her knees before America could make a difference in the outcome. Now, on 9 April, the same William Sowden Sims who had so much to do with the invention of the dreadnought found himself arriving in England as the commander-designate of U.S. naval forces in Europe. He would have a most unpleasant two days: that morning his ship would strike a mine, and the next day John Jellicoe would inform him that British and neutral merchant losses to submarines were projected at nearly nine hundred thousand tons for just the month of April.[67] Worse yet, Jellicoe also made it clear that the Admiralty did not favor convoying transports with military vessels since any more attrition of the Grand Fleet's destroyer screen would threaten its ability to put to sea.

Sims remained outwardly calm, but he was appalled. If something was not done quickly to reduce these losses, there would not be enough tonnage left to import the food and armaments the British required to continue the war. They would have to surrender. Like Percy Scott, William Fullam, and a number of others who had been involved in the original gunnery revolution, Sims had watched the weird war at sea with a growing awareness that conventional naval weapons and warfare were proving irrelevant. Therefore, he advised Washington that the American battle fleet should be kept at home and stripped of its destroyers for convoy duty, while an immediate emphasis be put on the construction of destroyers and merchant bottoms—presumably even at the cost of the huge U.S. capital ship program.[68]

Almost immediately, British Prime Minister David Lloyd George seized upon Sims's recommendations as evidence for his own faith that the convoy system would work. By the end of April he had forced the Admiralty to acquiesce, which in turn put more pressure on the Americans to accept Sims's iconoclastic suggestions.

Woodrow Wilson and his secretary of the navy, Josephus Daniels, were ready for a change. Their chief naval advisors, the General Board, had proved hermetically sealed against reality; their official strategy, War Plan Black, called for a Caribbean Armageddon with the immobile German fleet, and their construction program focused on dreadnoughts. So in the end the administration would follow Sims's advice almost to the letter.[69]

The peremptory actions of Lloyd George and Wilson appear to have had the effect of loosening, if not removing, the conceptual straitjacket that had prevented effective action in the face of the submarine crisis. No one panacea was found, but a combination of new weapons, the convoy system, and fortuitous geographical factors proved sufficient, but just barely, to blunt the German naval offensive.

Submerged U-boats were no longer either invulnerable or undetectable. In January 1916 the British introduced the depth charge, basically an oil drum filled with 120 pounds of TNT set to explode at a predetermined depth. In August 1917 this was complemented by the perfection of a howitzerlike device capable of casting multiple depth charges up to forty yards in a tight pattern.[70] Also, by the spring of 1917, an underwater microphone, the hydrophone, had been improved to the point that it could pick up both the propeller beat and the general location of a craft far below. Of course, sinking a U-boat in this manner required exploding a depth charge within fourteen feet of the hull, a very good shot when there was seldom more than an approximate fix on the quarry. Yet the psychological impact should not be underestimated. A sustained depth charge attack was an absolutely terrifying experience, frequently inducing a number of the symptoms of shell shock.

Perhaps more important, these devices had a synergetic impact on the effectiveness of the convoy. Whereas lone merchant vessels frequently could be approached on the surface by submarines and sunk with gunfire, the convoy's fierce watchdogs, the depth charge–slinging destroyers, made submerged attack, later battery recharge and the use of precious torpedoes, all imperative. Under such circumstances U-boats were hard-pressed to claim more than one victim per convoy. And convoys, because they took up relatively little space, proved markedly more elusive. Rather than employing midocean scout submarines as radio relay stations to direct groups, or wolf packs, to specific convoys, the Germans reacted sluggishly, persisting in their singular tactics far beyond the point of diminishing returns.[71] Finally, the Germans were operating at a severe geographical disadvantage. Britain sat athwart the North Sea so as to reduce the most direct German access to the Atlantic to a thin band of water, the English Channel, a ready-made pressure point against the submarine. By effectively mining the Channel, the British were able to force U-boats to waste fuel rounding the tip of Scotland, and soon submariners were having trouble remaining on station long enough to dispose of even their limited supply of torpedoes. Compounding the problem, the American-developed antennae mine eventually enabled the Allies to lay a six hundred foot deep minefield across the 240 miles of open water between Scotland and Norway.[72] At war's end, U-boats were being effectively bottled up in their bases.

Statistically, the corner had been turned over a year before. By July 1917, monthly tonnage tolls ceased exceeding the Allied capacity to replace transports. Nevertheless, as Bernadotte Schmitt and Harold Vedeler concede, the U-boat was not so much defeated as mishandled.[73] The Germans had waited too long to use it promiscuously; they entered the final campaign with too few submarines; and they did not react quickly and effectively to Allied adjustments. So their last best chance of victory slipped away beneath the stormy waters of the North Atlantic.

VI

The Great War held no more ironic fate than that which befell the cavalry. It survived as a living relic of warfare, not discarded but kept behind the lines by traditionalists like Douglas Haig to exploit breakthroughs which never came. Useless and ignored, cavalrymen were also spared the futile deaths which claimed so many others. But to the realists among them, safety must have seemed transitory and their way of life and fighting irrevocably doomed. Remarkably, this did not come to pass.

In the fall of 1914, during the confused days of the "race to the sea," a troop of French cavalry would sweep down on a squadron of reconnaissance aircraft bivouacked in a field near the river Aisne.[74] Had they more insight into the immediate future, they might have hesitated. For these flimsy, ungainly flying machines were destined to provide an outlet for a style of fighting for which the cavalry had provided a repository since the invention of the stirrup. Far above the impersonal slaughter of the western front, the classic paradigms of intraspecific combat would bloom anew.

As with virtually all new weapons, the technical and tactical development of combat aircraft took place with blinding speed, spurred no doubt by the urgency of the Great War. Yet it is important to note at the outset that although the airplane lent itself to a number of military functions—reconnaissance, bombing, torpedo delivery—the major emphasis would be placed on plane-versus-plane combat.[75]

This sort of fighting grew out of the desultory encounters between observation aircraft, fought originally with a series of armaments ranging from bricks and steel darts to an assortment of small arms. However, the technological key which transformed the fighter type into an effective weapon was a mechanical synchronizer, developed nearly simultaneously by the French and Germans, which enabled a machine gun to be shot safely through the whirling blades of a propeller and the pilot, in turn, to aim at a prospective target by simply pointing the entire plane. Within weeks fighter pilots like Frenchman Roland Garros and the ambitious Germans Oswald Boelcke and Max Immelmann were stalking victims and locked in swirling battles, quickly labeled dogfights.

And in doing so these aerial pioneers invented a form of combat which apparently provided a reprieve from the grinding, impersonal death dealing into which war had degenerated. "They recall the legendary days of chivalry," British Prime Minister David Lloyd George would exult, "not merely by the daring of their exploits, but by the nobility of their spirits."[76] This was not merely hyperbole; there were definite parallels. Not coincidentally, cavalrymen flocked to the new squadrons, and literally hundreds of the most stalwart fighter pilots were knighted by their grateful homelands. More particularly, combat was individualized by both nature and design. Despite the rise of formation flying, nearly every important ace from Immelmann to Nunggesser, Navarre, and the brooding "Winged Sword of France," Georges Guynemer, to Britain's superaggressive Albert Ball, to the lethal American race driver turned pilot Eddie Rickenbacker expressed an absolute preference for fighting alone, and doing so in single-place, not dual-position, planes. Similarly, identification took on an obvious significance, with pilots decorating their planes with large initials and other colorful and highly visible escutcheons. The most brazen example was Baron von Richthofen's totally red aircraft, probably the most celebrated piece of combat equipment in the entire war. Equally in consonance with the characteristics of intraspecific combat was the frequently voiced contention that death dealing was a secondary consideration in aerial combat. Backing this up were incidents such as Georges Guynemer's deliberate cessation of a dogfight when German ace Ernst Udet's guns jammed. Eddie Rickenbacker claimed, "Though we were out to shoot down planes . . . I would have been delighted to learn that . . . any pilot I had shot down had escaped with his life."[77] Also, despite the very rapid advance of aerotechnology, opposing fighter planes remained nearly symmetrical in configuration. As Rickenbacker noted, "No matter what innovation one side might develop, the other was quick to find out about it, copy it, and incorporate it in a new design."[78]

It is also evident that the intraspecific nature of aerial combat was a welcome phenomenon, not simply among the pilots themselves but all along the western front. Despite periodically being strafed by fighter aircraft, infantrymen on both sides came to view their pilots as celebrities and heroes. Eric J. Leed opines that the myth of the flyer was "clearly a compensatory notion" to those fighting on the ground, symbolizing the freedom and ability to see and personify opponents which had been lost in land warfare.[79] But it was more than that. Just as armies had once stood aside to watch champions like Gilgamesh fight individually, the ancient institution of single combat had been resurrected. Thus diarists such as German artilleryman Herbert Sulzbach and English cook Stuart Dolden assiduously followed the progress of dogfights above them and the careers of their participants in dispatches and the press.[80] Among the most singular manifestations of this process were the elaborate funerals given downed fliers by their opposite numbers. Indeed, the last rites provided by the Australians for Manfred von Richthofen, the destroyer of eighty Allied aircraft, recalls in its essence the ceremonial truces of the ancient Greeks during which war dead were exchanged.

Despite all this, there were clearly contradictions in the intraspecific portrait of the fighter pilot. In fact, his combat environment was a good deal more predatory than was commonly acknowledged. For instance, the tactical characteristics of the single-seat fighter made it advisable to shoot an opponent from behind or, if possible, to dive upon him without warning. Although there were certainly instances of long and skillfully conducted duels between equally matched opponents, the majority of kills achieved by the major aces were at the expense of fledgling pilots, barely able to control their planes. Thus, the average life expectancy of a new airman on the western front was somewhere between three and six weeks. "I am really beginning to feel like a murderer," wrote Albert Ball, while the same Eddie Rickenbacker who denied any urge to kill his opponents was also capable of claiming: "I gave him a 10-second burst of machine gun fire. I saw the bullets hit the back of his seat. I felt no sympathy. He had made a stupid mistake."[81]

Rickenbacker and the others were not simply hypocrites. Rather, the elements of intraspecific aggression exhibited in air combat were seized upon, as Eric Leed suggests, in the spirit of desideration and systematically exaggerated to provide a counterpoint to the grim realities of ground warfare.[82] Similarly, it is reasonable to assume that the fighter aircraft itself was celebrated in large part because it provided a rare syncretism of warlike preconceptions and high technology. Swift to the extreme, loud, and visually impressive, here was a weapon capable of absorbing all manner of invention and still preserving its heroic essence. And as such it remains to this day an object of fierce loyalty and affection, not only among those who fly but also to large segments of the civilian population.

But if the fighter plane lives on as an icon of the compatibility between war and invention, it is a false and misleading one. True enough, technology can be manipulated by cultural presumptions within certain bounds, yet its dynamism is not easily contained and follows most naturally the laws of possibility, not men. Hence, military aircraft development moved readily in different, less salutary directions.

The evolution of strategic bombing during the Great War is a chapter which remains, perhaps not coincidentally, largely forgotten. While the postwar writings and activities of Giulio Douhet and William Mitchell are generally credited with having established the basis for strategic air power, it was in fact the Germans who gave birth to the concept and then waged the first systematic strategic air campaign in history. Although the initial and largely ineffectual segment of this assault, conducted by zeppelins, retains a certain notoriety due to its modus operandi, historian Raymond Fredette has had to dredge out of obscurity the much more important sequel, carried out by true heavy bombers.[83] The planes were of two types, both remarkable. The first and most common, the angular two-engine biplane, the Gotha G-IV, had a wingspan greater than that of any German plane used against Britain in World War II and a service ceiling of nineteen thousand feet. Yet the Gothas were dwarfed by their strategic companions, the aptly named Giants. These enormous four- and six-engine craft had a wingspan of almost 140 feet, carried a crew of up to nine and a maximum bomb load of nearly two tons, and could fly almost six hundred miles nonstop. Such aircraft once again bear witness to the extremely rapid evolution and early maturation of new weapons in general, as did the development of defenses against them. Fredette notes that the immediate British tactical response to the German bombers, the creation of a thoroughly integrated and coordinated air defense system, was, with the exception of radar, essentially the same one that would serve the English so well in 1940.[84] Yet it is also worth pointing out that on a strategic level the British responded in a symmetrical fashion, building their own heavy bombers (the Handley Page O/400 and V/1500) and using them in retaliatory raids.

Nevertheless, the fact that the natural tactical opponent of the bomber is not another bomber but a different weapon entirely—be it a fighter-interceptor, an antiaircraft gun, or later a surface-to-air missile—is in keeping with its predatory purpose. While the avowed aim of the initial German campaign was to draw British aircraft away from the western front for home defense, the central means, the nearly random bombing of civilian population centers, spoke of a larger and much more sinister design—wholesale warfare against noncombatants. "Single bombs from flying machines are wrong," argued the flinty Admiral Tirpitz. "[But] if one could set fire to London in thirty places, then what in a small way is odious would retire before something fine and powerful."[85] In fact, the Germans had such a means by late 1918, the magnesium-based Elekron incendiary bomb, and failed to use it only because they realized the war was already lost. Yet twenty-five years later, massive city-killing firebombing attacks were adopted with relatively little dissent. What followed constituted, in Liddell Hart's words, "the most uncivilized means of warfare that the world had known since the Mongol devastations."[86] It was one more strand in the cord which would strangle war as a viable instrument of policy and establish the paradoxical logic of deterrence as the central reference point in international affairs.

Less portentous and more immediately practical was the use of aircraft against purely military targets, particularly troop concentrations. Until nearly war's end, this had been largely unpremeditated, with planes strafing and bombing infantry in a basically haphazard fashion. Yet the essential problem of the western front—how to achieve a breakthrough—still remained, and by autumn 1918 an obscure American colonel, William Mitchell, was ready to apply military aircraft directly and systematically to achieving this goal. The essence of Mitchell's plans was the close coordination of tactical aviation and advancing ground units. "Our low flying system of attack in echelon, massing of bombardment on the field of battle and night pursuit operations, are new and efficient departures," he would tell his men.[87] Mitchell's most famous exercise of tactical aviation was the massive Anglo-American raid he staged in support of the Meuse-Argonne offensive, which encompassed around four hundred aircraft and resulted in seventy-nine tons of bombs being dropped on German munitions dumps and troop concentrations. Had the Armistice not intervened, Mitchell planned to leapfrog the western front by flying an infantry division, heavily armed with automatic weapons, behind enemy lines and dropping them into combat by parachute.[88] Mitchell had caught sight of the tactical future. Twenty years later, when Heinz Guderian unveiled blitzkrieg to a shocked world, intimate cooperation between infantry and tactical bombers, along with vertical envelopment using paratroopers, would constitute two key means of breaking up defensive formations.

VII

Yet something else was needed. Antipersonnel firepower was simply too lethal and available to allow infantry to maneuver outside of field fortifications with any degree of consistency. The problem which emerged at Shiloh, Gettysburg, and Cold Harbor, and christened the era of the bloodbath, remained to be solved.

Enter the tank. Not only was the idea of an armored fighting vehicle a logical one, but the concept had been nascent in the Western military tradition since the wheeled battering rams of the Assyrians and, much later, the armor-plated combat carts of the Bohemian Hussite Jan Žižka and drawings of equivalent mechanisms in Leonardo's notebooks. But like the birth of the airplane and the submarine, two other unrealized weapons conceived at the dawn of the era, the emergence of the tank had to await the availability of an appropriate power source. By 1914, however, this was no longer a problem. And, in fact, as hostilities commenced, both sides possessed wheeled armored cars powered by internal combustion engines, the British using theirs with considerable success until the trenches reached the North Sea, leaving these vehicles unable to either flank or traverse the continuous line of fortifications.[89]

It is surprising, but logical, that at this point the primary impetus for continued development of the armored vehicle should emanate not primarily from the army but from the Royal Navy, which after all pioneered such weapons at sea. A principal role was played by Winston Churchill, then first lord of the Admiralty. Inspired by Admiral Reginald Bacon's design for a caterpillar artillery transporter, along with the suggestions of Colonel E. D. Swinton, a British staff observer in Flanders, Churchill first referred the matter to Lord John Fisher, inventor of the dreadnought. He then formed a "landships" committee chaired by battleship designer Eustace Tennyson-d'Eyncourt to develop an armored vehicle capable of crossing trenches.[90] After several designs were considered and three prototypes constructed, the authorities settled on the so-called Mother type. This vehicle, with a characteristic lozenge-shaped hull and a track encircling the entire profile, was rushed into production in early 1916 and became the basis for all British heavy tanks that would fight in the Great War.

Typically, the requisite device technology was more easily acquired than a suitable doctrine of employment. In a clairvoyant memorandum written seven months before the first British combat commitment of armored vehicles, E. D. Swinton drew attention to the "moral" effect of armored vehicles and warned that they "should not be used in driblets" but be kept secret until sufficient numbers existed to launch "one great combined operation" coordinated with infantry.[91] Much later

Heinz Guderian would paraphrase these words when he directed his corps: "Don't dribble, pour!"

But in 1916 Swinton was largely ignored. While the actual developmental program was carefully concealed—the vehicles were labeled "tanks" so the Germans might think they were water-storage devices—the first available products were used immediately in small numbers on the Somme with almost no effect. Yet the British learned from this mistake. Accumulating tanks for over a year, they attacked the Hindenburg Line at Cambrai in late November 1917, with around four hundred of the new weapons. The result of the two-day battle was a six-mile salient driven into German territory, an advance unparalleled since 1914.[92] An equivalent gain was made by massed British armor on 8 August 1918, the so-called black day of the German army, and in July 1918 the French had achieved a similar success using almost five hundred independently developed Renault light tanks.

The Germans were slow to react. When they did, it was primarily with anti-tank weapons since severe raw material shortages made it nearly impossible to compete with the Allies in tank production.[93] By war's end, however, they had fielded very small numbers of the A7V "assault tank," and on 24 April 1918 one of these engaged a British Mark IV in the first tank-to-tank combat. But as the shooting stopped, the tank did not constitute a decisive weapon. As Schmitt and Vedeler point out, the Allies never succeeded in using tanks to disastrously disrupt the German rear.[94] It remained a frail, unreliable instrument with very limited endurance. Yet it had a future.

It was, in fact, a natural. Operationally, the tank addressed the major problem of ground combat, allowing combatants once again to fight out in the open. While the tank was initially developed as a counter to field fortifications, by war's end the laws of arms symmetry prompted a consensus that the tank was its own most appropriate adversary. Although clearly weapons of mass employment, combat among them naturally devolved into individual firefights. Aesthetically, the tank also fell well within the profile of the favored weapon, being by nature large, armor-plated, visually impressive, and loud. Not surprisingly, cavalrymen showed an immediate interest and would flock to armor units during the interwar years. Though not as romantic as the fighter aircraft, the tank did constitute a similar reconciliation between technology and the ethos of the warrior. Undeniably, the tank was effective and promised to become more so. Yet its tactical utility was complemented by its acceptibility, and this combination assured it a major and lasting place in the future order of battle. World War II has been called a conflict of airplanes and tanks. This did not come about accidentally.

There were other weapons that pointed even further into the future. In early 1918, American automotive innovator Charles Kettering unveiled a four hundred dollar, twelve-foot-long papier-mâché and cardboard drone with two Ford engines that could fly forty miles, following its Sperry guidance systems and deliver three hundred pounds of explosives—a prototypical cruise missile.[95] Even more portentous, in March 1918, Krupp's notorious *Pariskanone* began bombarding the French capital at a range of almost eighty miles, a harbinger of a day when cities would exist as perpetual hostages to ballistic projectiles aimed from halfway around the globe. Yet the promise of all of this, including the submarine, the tank, and the combat aircraft, would remain largely unrealized. The Great War, so hobbled by technology, would not ultimately be resolved by new weapons. Victory and defeat were a product of something much more mundane. Human endurance having been exceeded, whole armies simply began giving up.

It began on the eastern front. After two-and-a-half years of almost uninterrupted defeats, Russia was in terrible shape. The economy was near the breaking point, and the government had degenerated into a surreal state, with Czar Nicholas resembling a somnambulist and his court reputed to have fallen under the sway of the mysticism and sexual athleticism of Rasputin. All of this was not lost on the army, whose soldiers concluded that the war was a conspiracy of the officers and the propertied classes, and that their own interests lay elsewhere. They had at least one thing right. If ever a regime deserved to be overthrown, it was this one.

The inevitable commenced in March 1917, when a provisional government removed the czar but vowed to continue the war. Seeking to live up to this commitment, Kerensky's liberal-socialist cabinet approved a new offensive to begin on 1 July. It was a terrible mistake. Their remaining resolve undermined by German propaganda and widespread fraternization, Russian soldiers simply melted away at the first signs of a counterattack.[96] By the end of August virtually all Russian resistance had ceased. As November approached, the Russian high command concluded: "The army is simply a huge, weary, shabby, and ill-fed mob of angry men united in their common thirst for peace."[97] Into this vacuum stepped the Bolsheviks, committed to an immediate armistice, and the first manifestation of the Great War's true political legacy.

So long as the war lasted, the Germans avoided Napoleon's mistake of invading Russia, but at the subsequent peace talks their terms revealed a shortsighted greed. When the Bolsheviks walked out, the Teutonic High Command simply renewed operations. With no other recourse, the bitter Bolsheviks signed the Treaty of Brest Litovsk. The treaty would prove a two-edged sword for Germany. While its terms did not amount to complete conquest, they were harsh enough to afford the Allies ample opportunity to propagandize what a German victory might mean in the West. Meanwhile, peace with Russia opened the Fatherland to the corrosive Bolshevik propaganda so instrumental in destabilizing the home front.

As 1918 began, however, German prospects appeared bright. Free in the East, they now looked westward. Here Allied troops had grown dispirited. Although the Germans remained largely unaware of the situation, from April to September of the previous year the French army had been wracked by sporadic acts of mutiny affecting fully half of its divisions. Then, in late October, the Italian army met disaster at Caporetto. While only 40,000 men were killed or wounded, over 300,000 were taken prisoner and another 350,000 simply deserted. The totals would have been worse had not the Germans stopped the drive to gather strength for the contemplated spring offensive against the British and French.

Hindenburg and Ludendorff planned to end it all with a gigantic throw of the dice. Since early November, German troops had been arriving from the East at the rate of ten divisions a month. Of these, picked assault units were intensively trained in what was perceived by the high command as a tactical solution to the

stalemate: infiltration around strong points, short and very intensive artillery preparation, and advancement behind rolling barrages.[98] The aim was to hit enemy
lines fast and hard enough to create an irreparable breach, and then move to open
warfare. The juncture between the British and French armies at Arras–Saint-Quentin–
La Fère was chosen as the focal point.

On 21 March, enjoying a numerical superiority of twenty divisions, the Germans struck. Within days a twenty-kilometer gap was opened up between the
British and French, and to the south a forty-mile dent was created near Montdi-
dier. Yet, rallied by their new commander in chief, Marshal Foch, French troops
rushed into the breach and plugged it. On 9 April the Germans lunged forward
again, this time against the British alone. "Our backs to the wall," as Douglas
Haig reminded them, the stubborn British eventually broke the momentum of this
attack also, though with considerable loss of territory.[99] Twice more, in late May
and early June, the Germans renewed their assaults, though with progressively
less success. Particularly shocking to the battle-hardened but weary Germans was
the enthusiasm of American troops, whom they faced for the first time at Château-
Thierry and Belleau Wood. Moving forward even in the face of heavy machine
gun and artillery fire, these newcomers displayed the kind of audacity that had not
been seen on the western front since 1914. Worse yet, the number of Americans
in France had doubled between March and May, doubled again in May, and would
double once more by the end of August. In November 1918, the American Expeditionary Force would number some two million strong. The price of the belated
unrestricted submarine campaign was now being paid on the western front.

On 18 July Foch and the French went on the offensive accompanied by nine
double-strength American divisions. A series of attacks were directed against the
salients the Germans had formed. With worn out spirits and guns, the Germans
gave ground slowly. Then, on 8 August, confronted by over four hundred British
tanks, they broke and began surrendering in masses. Though the German army
remained essentially intact, mutiny spread and the retreat accelerated. On 26 September Ludendorff's officers discovered him on the floor foaming at the mouth;
the next day he would recommend an immediate armistice. It was arranged on 8
November, but the Allies insisted on a more dramatic date, even though it prolonged the killing. This was typical of the war. On the eleventh hour of the eleventh day of the eleventh month 1918, the shooting finally stopped.

But there would be no peace. It has come to be accepted as a truism that the
Versailles treaty was not a peace of reconciliation or one of vengeance but a
compromise—worse than either alternative. The role of armaments in the Great
War provides at least some perspective on this judgment.

From beginning to end, the Great War was fought as if it were a moderate
struggle. German war aims, embodied in the politico-economic concept of *Mitte-
leuropa* and the Treaty of Brest Litovsk, were evidently harsh but not millennial.
Nor, clearly, were those of the Allies. This did not change at Paris. In comparison
with what a Bonaparte might have demanded, even the conditions of the French
were exceedingly moderate. As Arno Mayer reminds us, the Congress of Vienna
was thought to be the most pertinent guide to action during the post-Armistice
deliberations.[100] Both Metternich and the Big Four were intent on ending a revo-

lutionary situation, reestablishing a lasting status quo, and insuring against future aggression on the part of a defeated but still formidable enemy. Therefore, politically, this perspective made sense, but for the nature of the Great War.

Bonaparte had undermined the foundations of the previous military era and set the stage for further dramatic change. Yet the course of the Napoleonic Wars did not present a situation that was perceived to be fundamentally new, either tactically or strategically. The Great War was unprecedented. It is supremely ironic that the weapons initially let loose on the western front and the North Sea could accomplish nothing useful. Yet this would soon change, and by the Armistice the necessary means to fight much more purposefully existed, albeit in a nascent state. Yet the primary condition was extant from the beginning. Tools were now available to kill beyond the wildest thanatotic fantasies. Under such conditions moderate war became a contradiction in terms. There were only two alternatives: no war, or war waged to its logical conclusion.

While the former held the true key to the future, Allied moderation condemned the combatants, first, to a dose of the latter. For the rapid reversal of Teutonic military fortunes, along with the continued integrity of their ground forces and the surrender of the High Seas Fleet, allowed many Germans to nurse the illusion that there had been no military defeat, that there remained unfinished business on the battlefield. Only by destroying Germany could the Allies have avoided the Great War's sequel.

Chapter 15

SEQUEL

I

Arnold Toynbee has drawn attention to the significance of the double war.[1] This phenomenon occurs when one great war is followed, within the span of a single lifetime, by a second, thereby intensifying the historical effect far more than twice what could be expected from a single such conflict. The Peloponnesian War was such a contest, as were the first two Punic Wars. Neither Greece nor Rome was ever the same, nor was northern Europe the same after the Thirty Years' War, which in most respects fits this category. It is our fate to live in the shadow of such a dual conflagration. Yet in a sense we view it from afar, for its cumulative impact was sufficient to push us into an entirely new era of history.

It has been estimated that nearly fifty-five million people died directly as a result of Word War II.[2] It was perhaps inevitable that the era of chemical-energy weapons would end in a crescendo of violence. Yet it is certainly true that the course of the second great war cannot begin to be understood except in light of the first. Regardless of its scale and destructiveness, World War II has limited independent meaning. Its roots are to be found tangled in the conflict which preceded it, not merely in terms of causation but also in the very manner in which it was conducted.

From the very early 1920s to at least 1935, postwar international politics proceeded on two separate planes. Most conspicuous was a sincere, though ultimately superficial, commitment to peace and disarmament. However, on another level—often hidden from public view—there existed another agenda entirely, one based on the military lessons of the Great War. Although both were contradictory, they were not mutually exclusive. Therefore, they could be pursued simultaneously at least until the later thirties, when Adolph Hitler tore away the shroud of political euphemisms and revealed that which had come to predominate.

Archetypical of this process was the Washington Naval Conference of 1921–22, the first and most successful of a string of post–World War I arms control gatherings. The conference has traditionally been viewed as something of an aberration, a utopian exercise which somehow established several useful guidelines for naval strength but also set a precedent for a style of public diplomacy which would eventually come to symbolize the feckless pacifism of the postwar era. In fact, it did both.

Due in part to the dramatic nature of Secretary of State Charles Evans Hughes's opening remarks to the conference in November 1921, a legend has persisted that his proposal to limit capital ships was more or less spontaneous and solely his own. This does not seem to have been the case. Rather, Hughes's statement appears to have been the product of a fairly intense bureaucratic struggle within the U.S. Government over the role and future of the battleship.

Despite the dreadnought's multiple humiliations in the Great War, peace did not bring a halt to their construction. Quite the contrary, Woodrow Wilson and his naval adviser, Admiral Benson, chose instead to revive and enlarge the massive U.S. battleship-building program of 1916, suspended after America's entry into the war, and brandish it over the Allies and later domestic enemies of the Treaty of Versailles, to enforce the president's conception of a just peace. Both the British and the Japanese eventually responded with programs of their own, so that two-and-a-half years after the greatest war in history, the world's naval powers were in the process of constructing thirty-six of among the conflict's least successful weapons. It was springtime for dreadnoughts, but winter for those who sought to avoid a major arms competition.

Yet the battleship was not without its enemies. Admiral Sims, along with Bradley Fiske, and William Fullam—all of whom had played a critical role in the invention of the dreadnought—had turned against the great ships. In particular, Sims, as president of the Naval War College, encouraged a series of war games which indicated that the aircraft carrier was destined to be the capital ship of the future.[3] It was an excellent choice. Unlike the lethal submarine, which contradicted virtually every premise of naval orthodoxy, the carrier, though still unproven in combat, was inherently a large surface ship which promised to bring the romance of flying to the fleet. Nevertheless, the conservatives on the General Board of the Navy protected the battleship-building program with the ferocity of a mother bear protecting her cubs. So at this point Sims, Fullam, and Fiske began playing a deeper, more conspiratorial game.

It is difficult to pin down who or what gave William Mitchell the idea of sinking the surrendered German battleship *Ostfriesland* with a squadron of his bombers, but it is clear that that he knew and corresponded with Sims.[4] At any rate, when the ship was sunk by Mitchell's planes in the summer of 1921, the new Republican administration's Secretary of State, Charles Evans Hughes, apparently alerted by Fullam, had developed more than a passing interest in the proceedings. (It is an interesting commentary on naval loyalties that when the Teutonic dreadnought slipped beneath the waves, former Secretary of War Benedict Crowell noted a number of American naval officers aboard the observer ship *Henderson* sobbing audibly.)

We may never know exactly what was said to Charles Evans Hughes. But it seems clear that by the time he made his startling proposition before the Washington Naval Conference, he had been thoroughly briefed on the latest naval developments and was aware that the ships he was prepared to forgo were not worth much in the first place.[5]

History obligingly took the line of least resistance. A fixed tonnage ratio for battleships of 5:5:3 was quickly established for the United States, Britain, and Japan, and they accordingly agreed to suspend their dreadnought-building programs. Also, the fate of a number of other naval weapons was determined at the conference in an equally pragmatic fashion. The aircraft carrier was the recipient of a particularly generous allotment—135,000 tons for the United States and Great Britain, and 81,000 tons for Japan. This was far more than any of these countries had vested in carriers at the time, but allowed the United States to convert two of its partially completed battle cruisers, *Lexington* and *Saratoga,* into flattops.[6] On the other hand, the extremely unpopular submarine was the subject of a serious attempt at prohibition. In the end, however, this came to nothing. The submarine, despite its unorthodox nature and bad reputation, had shown itself too valuable to give up, or even limit, for that matter.

Seen from this perspective, the Washington Naval Conference appears to have been a fairly realistic exercise. Obsolete weapons were curbed and some were scrapped. Favored weapons like the aircraft carrier were encouraged, and useful but unsavory items like the submarine were left alone. Yet all was done with great fanfare and a deliberate aura of disarmament. So the public was led to believe that millennial ends, if not yet achieved, were at least on the way.

Two subsequent postwar conferences on the reduction of naval armaments were held at London in 1930 and 1935, but they met with increasingly less success. At the first, conferees did manage to extend the moratorium on battleship construction and apply the tonnage ratios to cruisers, though at the cost of considerable bad feeling generated between the United States, Great Britain, and Japan. Once again, submarine construction was essentially left alone, and large aircraft carriers encouraged by the prohibition of any such ship under ten thousand tons.[7] At the second London conference the Japanese, after announcing they would abrogate the Washington Naval Treaty, proposed a "common upper limit" to replace tonnage ratios, and, when this was rejected, formally withdrew from the proceedings. This merely ratified the inevitable.[8] Negotiated naval limitation had served its military, if not its utopian, purpose and was of no further use.

Meanwhile, the naval lessons of the Great War were being quietly addressed within the services themselves, particularly the American and Japanese. In both cases the naval mainstream retained an intense loyalty to the battleship and gun-based fleet tactics. Nonetheless, technically progressive elements maintained sufficient initiative to explore and experiment with promising weapons.

A case in point was the imaginative band of American naval aviators who, under the inspired leadership of Rear Admiral William Moffett, managed to consistently improve the efficiency of air operations off carriers until they had forged a weapon nearly as formidable in practice as it appeared on the game boards. Moreover, despite the bad feelings engendered by William Mitchell's assertions that air power would drive fleets from the sea, this coterie of naval aviators was able to survive, if not exactly thrive, within the ranks of the navy. Therefore, they not only pioneered the lethal technique of dive-bombing, but were able have it tested in combat using Marine pilots against the Nicaraguan rebels of Augusto Sandino in the late 1920s.

Even more significant for the future was the naval aviators' participation in a series of fleet problems beginning in 1923. In spite of being tightly bound to the battle line to provide reconnaissance and air defense, the carriers quickly proved their worth. Yet their inhabitants longed for independent operations. Their chance came in 1929 when a sympathetic Sims protégé, William V. Pratt, became commander in chief of the battle fleet. In Fleet Problem IX, the first in which the *Lexington* and *Saratoga* participated together, over 260 carrier based aircraft were involved—the largest such exercise to date. More importantly, the *Saratoga* was cut loose from the fleet and allowed to operate independently, resulting in a devastating raid on the Panama Canal. In his critique Pratt announced: "Gentlemen, you have witnessed the most brilliantly conceived and most effectively executed naval operation in our history. I expect to fly my flag on the *Saratoga* on our return cruise north." [9] The carrier task force had been born.

Yet its primacy was far from assured. Until the fateful morning of 7 December 1941 the battleship remained, in the words of its countless naval defenders, the "backbone of the fleet." Meanwhile, the carrier's freedom of movement during maneuvers continued to be sporadic at best. But when the time came, U.S. naval aviation was sufficiently honed to allow the transition from dreadnoughts to carriers to transpire virtually overnight.

Conditions were not greatly different within the navy of Japan. Though increasingly independent, the Japanese navy remained a relatively junior member of the world naval establishment, and one nurtured since infancy on the writings of Alfred Mahan and the example of Britain and her battleships. Until just prior to Pearl Harbor, no key member of the naval leadership expected supremacy in the western Pacific to be settled ultimately by anything other than a clash of battleships. [10]

Nevertheless, the vast expanses of the Pacific and the correspondingly heavy requirements for reconnaissance made carrier-based aviation inherently attractive to the Japanese naval hierarchy. Consequently, the Japanese invested heavily in this arm during the interwar period. Like the Americans, the Japanese converted two capital ships, *Akagi* and *Kaga,* into carriers after the Washington conference and would enter World War II outnumbering the United States in this class by ten to eight.

Yet their real forte was planes and pilots. At the time of Pearl Harbor, Japanese carrier aviators were clearly the best in the world. Hardened by a Spartan and comprehensive training program, pilots by 1941 averaged over three hundred hours of flying time before joining the fleet, far more than their American equivalents. To complement their skill, the Japanese quietly developed a series of increasingly more capable carrier-based aircraft, optimized for a wide range of missions. Particularly impressive were the torpedo planes—the long-range Type 95 with a reach of almost thirteen hundred miles, and the tactical "Kate" type, which proved clearly superior to its American competitors. Yet most remarkable was the Zero fighter, in 1940 the most advanced fighter, carried-based or otherwise, in the world. Designed by Jiro Horikoshi and rushed into production at the insistence of Admiral Yamamoto, approximately thirty early models achieved 266 confirmed kills in China. Much to the amazement of its designer, however, it was virtually ignored in the West.[11] While only the Second World War would reveal the secrets of the Zero, and how lethal carrier aviation had become, it was clear to both sides much earlier that neither navy had been wasting its time in this area.

Not nearly as much could be said of the policies applied to that renagade of the high seas, the submarine. Had these stealthy craft been any less effective during the Great War, the international naval establishment would have gleefully cast them aside. This being impossible, domestication became the preferred option. Thus, the concept of the "fleet submarine" soon surfaced in both Japanese and American navies. In essence, the submarine, like the carrier, would be tied to the battle fleet as part of the screen and applied almost exclusively to military targets.[12] Because such duties required a high surface speed, the resulting units tended to be quite large and expensive, and corresponding few were built (e.g., only ten U.S. submarines were commissioned between 1924 and 1931).

As war loomed, however, reality took hold—at least among the Americans. By 1938, the U.S. fleet was taking antisubmarine warfare seriously, and the construction of smaller types, optimized for commerce raiding, was stepped up. By the time of Pearl Harbor, American submarines were the most technically advanced in the world.[13] Yet their torpedoes were among the worst.

The situation was nearly the opposite with the Japanese. As John Toland points out, they inherited the British aversion to unrestricted attacks on commerce, and paid virtually no attention to antisubmarine warfare[14] (a retired admiral could remember not even one prewar exercise of this nature). The major exception was the torpedo, which, according to Samuel Elliott Morison, constituted the prime technical achievement of the Japanese navy. Research between 1928 and 1933 led to the oxygen-fueled Type 93 model with a speed of nearly fifty knots, a range of 12.5 miles, and a very large warhead which, unlike its American equivalents, exploded reliably when it hit something.[15] Combined with the remarkable capacity of the Japanese for night fighting, these torpedoes would prove lethal indeed.

The parallel process of naval disarmament and the methodical exploration of new weapons concepts was no aberration. This pattern was faithfully reflected in the European context with regard to land-based weapons systems. While America and Japan emerged from the Great War nearly unscathed, Europe had been at its epicenter, virtually shorn of an entire generation of young men. War-weariness and the sincere desire for peace was pervasive in Germany, Italy, and Russia, as well as in England and France. The difference lay in governmental systems and their relationships to the respective military establishments. In the democracies, the pacifistic inclinations of their populations was faithfully reflected in official policy, while in the totalitarian states the military agenda counted for much more and could be pursued with equivalent rigor. Yet all engaged in the simultaneous quest for disarmament and better weapons.

It must have seemed to Europeans during the twenties and early thirties, particularly those whose only insight into policy was through the newspapers and governmental pronouncements, that the instruments of war were actually being cast aside. Throughout much of the period, the Continent was a ferment of pacifism, with Communists providing a biting critique of the links between capitalism and militarism, and "merchants of death" being denounced from every quarter. The fledgling League of Nations, whose charter called for "reductions of national armaments to the lowest point consistent with national safety,"[16] became a rallying point for disarmers, and its deliberations on the subject seemed to André Maurois more like religious services than parliamentary debates.

In retrospect, much of what resulted seems ludicrous. The 1928 Treaty of Paris, which outlawed war by fiat and nothing else, is frequently held up as the quintessence of "feel good" diplomacy and feckless utopianism. Similarly, the 1932 Geneva Conference on the Reduction and Limitation of Armaments, which had as its aim the abolition of "offensive weapons," foundered on its inability to merely define what constituted such an instrument.[17] Even the 1925 Geneva Protocol, which banned the use of poison gas in combat, was hedged by reservations, provided no means of enforcement, and left it perfectly legal to possess chemical weapons.

Nonetheless, these were not simply exercises in futility. Even the Treaty of Paris registered a developing awareness, soon to be ratified by the coming of nuclear weapons, that war was becoming ineffective as an instrument of policy. Although it failed, the Geneva disarmament conference provided the first rigorous, analytic dialogue on the basic nature of weaponry. Finally, and most unexpectedly, the Geneva Protocol proved to be lasting and useful. Much to everyone's surprise, chemical weapons would not be used in combat in World War II, a conflict notable for the promiscuous use of virtually every other instrument of destruction. Like the Washington Naval Conference, the Geneva Protocol addressed a weapon that was of marginal utility and registered a real consensus that it should not be employed. (Recent chemical weapons use by non-Westerners in the Iran-Iraq Gulf War, though relatively frequent, remains limited and largely without strategic impact. As in the past, however, it has caused significant casualties and much suffering. Even among the Iraqis, the major perpetrators, it is seen as a desperate measure which they have consistently tried to conceal).

Arms control during the interwar period was more than a sop to war-weary publics. It dealt with the question of weapons with unprecedented seriousness and achieved broad support among the populations of all state participants. However, it is still possible for countries to move in two opposite directions at once, and in this case, history was not on the side of the angels.

It is now apparent that the German army and its ancillary weapons producers had no intention of fully complying with the Versailles Treaty.[18] However, the specificity of its provisions, along with on-site inspection provided by the Inter-Allied Control Commission, insured that the German army and navy were reduced to one hundred thousand and fifteen thousand, respectively, and that the arms with which the Great War had been fought were for the most part surrendered or destroyed. Similarly, the Krupp Works' heavy-weapons production lines were dismantled under strict supervison, and by 1920 the industrial giant was in the process of diversification under the ambiguous slogan "We make everything."[19] As it turned out, they did.

For if the German army and arms industry had cast aside the immediate means to wage war, General von Seeckt and his revanchist colleagues in the contracted Reichswehr preserved the potential for rapid rearmament through a meticulously orchestrated program of covert noncompliance. Not only was a secret Krupp design bureau for tanks and other ground forces weapons set up in Berlin but artillery, antiaircraft guns, and light tanks were produced under license by Bofors in Sweden, U-boats were built in Holland, and virtually the entire aircraft factory of Tony Fokker was secretly spirited out of Germany.[20] The inherently international nature of the European military-industrial complex served the Reichswehr's covert strategy particularly well in the sphere of advanced weapons—tanks, poison gas, submarines, and miliatry aircraft—all forbidden to Germany under the treaty. Since, under the circumstances, domestic testing and manufacture (though not design) were too risky, the obvious solution was to perform these functions overseas.

In this regard no country was more helpful than the new proletarian polity which had sprung out of the ruins of Imperial Russia. By 1922 the once and future enemies, Germany and the Soviet Union, had joined forces to explore new ways of killing each other's soldiers. It was a partnership that would bring dividends numbering in the millions. As originally conceived, the relationship was to be essentially an exchange of German technical assistance in building a military-industrial base on Russian soil, for the space and privacy necessary to allow the Reichswehr to develop the theory and practice of forbidden weapons. Needless to say, the strictest secrecy was maintained from the beginning.

Although Krupp established an experimental factory to develop prototype "heavy tractors" (i.e., tanks), and Junkers manufactured some planes at Fili, military-industrial cooperation was, as John Erickson notes, plagued with serious difficulties practically from the beginning and led to almost nothing tangible.[21]

Nevertheless, in terms of developing new doctrine for advanced weapons and training with them, the partnership was most successful and intimate. "We show the German officers everything" were the words one senior Soviet officer used to describe the relationship.[22] By 1928 the joint tank school at Kazan, the chemical warfare school at Volsk, and the aviation center at Lipetsk were all operational and functioning with an efficiency which left future German War Minister Blomberg extremely impressed. Until Hitler ended the relationship in 1933, great progress was made in training Soviet and German officers in integrated battlefield concepts combining mobile artillery, mechanized infantry, and tanks—the essence of panzer warfare. "Will we not be so advanced in two years," a tipsy I. P. Uborevich would suggest to his German hosts during an inspection visit of the Rheinmetal and Zeiss Jena plants, "that we can set about a revision of the frontiers and slaughter the Poles? Indeed we must partition Poland again."[23]

More time would be required. But as the Germans left Russia, the conceptual framework, though not the tools of the coming land war, was set. For their part, the Soviets would aim for the long haul. At great sacrifice, they constructed an enormous military-industrial base during the first, second, and third Five-Year Plans which would bring forth, just when most needed, the flood of high-quality weapons necessary to prevail. The Germans, on the other hand, went for the quick fix.

While von Seeckt and the Reichswehr made the Wehrmacht and the Luftwaffe possible, it was Adolph Hitler who brought them into being. Whatever the German High Command might think, it was his army and his air force, and he created them to fight with. In terms of military strategy, Hitler was essentially a product of World War I. While he would have little feel for truly advanced weapons such as radar and the possibilities of nuclear energy, he had a remarkable grasp of what was needed to avoid the kind of stalemate that had ruined the Germans on the western front. "That's what I need! That's what I want to have!" Hitler exclaimed after seeing his first demonstration of Heinz Guderian's panzers in 1933.[24] From this point Germany's rearmament was assured. Yet it was a rearmament based on the here and now. Hitler knew from the beginning that if he did not win quickly, his prospective enemies would eventually outproduce him.[25]

By the midthirties Krupp's secret design bureaus had created a wide inventory of advanced land arms prototypes, including the remarkably versatile 88-mm high-velocity gun—outside of the Russian T-34 tank probably the war's most successful weapon. Yet until near the end, little else would follow. And by this time the Allies had caught up qualitatively and far surpassed Germany in terms of quantities. In fact, Germany's prewar land arms program was primarily based on the creation of the ten panzer divisions available in 1940 to form the steel tip of what remained a mass-conscript infantry force.[26] Even here the Franco-British defenders not only outnumbered the invading Germans in tanks, but the French "B" model was a better machine than anything the Wehrmacht possessed. The difference lay in the Germans knowing exactly what they wanted to do with their tanks.

The same pattern followed with the Luftwaffe. It was an air force essentially created out of four basic types: the twin-engined He-111-level bomber with a bomb load of only four thousand pounds; the Me-109 fighter with an excellent top speed of over 350 miles per hour but a short combat endurance; the Ju-52 transport plane; and the Ju-87 Stuka dive-bomber. By casting aside several superior prototypes and concentrating on these easy-to-construct models, Göring and the German aircraft industry were able to build up a combat-ready force of something under two thousand planes by 1940—though they claimed to have many more.[27] In fact, production was not particularly efficient, and when German aircraft were exceeded in performance by Allied models, the industry would have trouble creating and manufacturing better planes.

Yet German air doctrine was excellent. Probably as the result of experience in the Spanish civil war, the Luftwaffe learned to use the Ju-52 to transport bombs, fuel, and spare parts forward, leapfrogging from airfield to airfield, giving the air arm true strategic mobility.[28] Moreover, the Luftwaffe brilliantly exploited the possibilities of close air support, turning itself into a sort of strategic artillery for the ground forces, primarily through the use of dive-bombing. Exemplifying the rate of military cross-fertilization, World War I air ace Ernst Udet first observed the technique in America at the 1933 Cleveland Air Races, and had two Curtiss Hawks shipped to Germany for training. By the late 1930s the Luftwaffe had adopted the Ju-87 Stuka, a sinister-looking aircraft whose fixed undercarriage gave it the look of a swooping bird of prey, and whose siren (Udet called it the "trumpet of Jericho") further demoralized those below. Stukas, working in close coordination with German tanks, came to epitomize the blitzkrieg tactics that so shocked the world in 1939. Yet the plane was actually slow and vulnerable and, like the tactical concept, as much a psychological threat as a physical one. For the time it would be spectacularly successful. Yet eventually familiarity would breed if not contempt, then at least equanimity.

That England and France were unprepared for World War II is now axiomatic. And to a large extent the results of early campaigns speak for themselves. Yet it would be a mistake to assume that the pacific demeanor of their respective populations and governments totally paralyzed weapons-oriented research and development, or that neither party made a sincere effort to address the military lessons of the Great War while there was still time.

In the case of the British, efforts in this direction left them poised to wield what would prove to be their major contribution to the Allied war effort—air power.

The possibilities, both positive and negative, of strategic air warfare were widely publicized and discussed during the twenties and thirties. Books by William Mitchell and Giulio Douhet helped to create a climate of opinion which assumed the extreme vulnerability of population and industrial centers, and suggested that future wars would be won and lost entirely from the air.[29] Given the trends in military invention, these were not unreasonable assumptions. But they were conclusions drawn largely on the basis of theory. Britain, alone among the major combatants in the Great War, had experienced sustained bombing attack. Consequently, it was here that the most practical steps were taken to see to this new form of warfare.

Defensively, the British essentially recreated the integrated air defense system they had fashioned to counter the Gothas and Giants, with one very significant conceptual addition, radar. The idea of employing radio pulse and echo measurement to detect and locate planes and ships occurred to researchers in several countries around the same time, though the work seems to have been kept secret by all.[30] What differentiated the British program from its competitors was that the initial proposal was aimed at not just a device but an entire early-warning system. Thanks to the extraordinary foresight of Sir Henry Tizzard, by December 1935 five radar stations on the eastern coast of England constituted the world's first operational radar network. By the opening of the Battle of Britain, the system had been expanded to twenty-one long-range stations and an additional thirty low-level installations. The Germans, who had failed to develop an effective system of their own, paid these stations little heed in their targeting. It would prove a crucial error.

Yet defense was not enough. The depredations of the Gothas and Giants left the English convinced that they must have the capacity to reply symmetrically to bombing raids on their homeland. While other states found the doctrine of air power extreme, the British desire to avoid a repetition of the terrestrial bloodletting of the Great War and a long history of indirect warfare with their battle fleet made the concept of strategic bombing particularly attractive to English eyes. Unlike most other air arms, the Royal Air Force was separate and organizationally coequal with the army and the navy. Though small and bureaucratically frail, the service was free to develop its own aircraft for its own purposes. By 1940 the English air armada would include four twin-engined bombers with ranges of over one thousand miles (Blenheim, Whitley, Wellington, and Hampden).[31] Though most of the two-engine models were in short supply and disappointing in combat, a number of larger four-engined replacements were in the late stages of development, and by May 1942 the RAF would stage its first thousand-plane raid on downtown Cologne.

This was true terror bombing, the logical conclusion of the doctrinal path trod by the RAF during the interwar years. Once unleashed during the Battle of Britain, the RAF would pursue its campaign against German cities with a forthright ruthlessness unmatched by any other belligerent.

Finally, there was France. If strategic bombing proved disappointing in fact, it was still perceived as the wave of the future. On the other hand, France's distinctive contribution to the interwar arsenal, the Maginot Line, is remembered as the classic misreading of military trends. "A battleship built on land, a masterpiece in its own way. . . . And yet! It gives me but little feeling of security," wrote English General Alan Brooke.[32] He was right on the mark. "The shield of France," which had already cost seven billion francs by 1935, failed utterly to protect her. Yet in this failure were two components, military and political.

Seen purely as a weapon, the Maginot Line was not a bad idea. As we shall see, the element of mobility introduced by armored vehicles and tactical air support during World War II would be exaggerated by circumstances and the outlook of key leaders. When lines were properly constructed and defended, such as in Italy and along the Rhine in 1944, they proved exceedingly difficult to punch through, even for heavily armored forces. From a battlefield perspective, the most cogent criticism of the Maginot Line is that not enough of it was built.

For the armorers had left uncovered what Clausewitz called "the pit of the French stomach," the ancient invasion routes across the border with Belgium— the leks of European military history. Yet this was a political, not military, decision.

After October 1936, when Leopold III revoked the Franco-Belgian Treaty, France was free to extend the line to the sea without concern about leaving her erstwhile ally out in the cold. But Frenchmen proved unwilling to bear the cost and chose instead to live with their vulnerability. Yet on another level the Maginot Line, complete or incomplete, betrayed France's lack of political will. It was overtly protective at a time when her neighbors longed for conquest. In such an environment it invited attack and promised no retaliation. Meanwhile, the strategic future belonged to offensive symmetrical deterrence, not defensive counters.

Viewed as a whole, the development of the armaments destined to fight World War II revealed a singular inversion of intent on the part of the developers. Repeatedly, the very states which had been victimized by particular new weapons during the Great War fastened on these same devices and devoted considerable effort toward improving them, while the originators payed them much less attention. Thus, the Germans took up the concept of tank-based assault forces closely

supported by tactical aviation—respectively Anglo-French and American innovations—and advanced it, both doctrinally and in terms of materiel, far beyond the
state of the art among the western Allies. By the same token the English, and to
a lesser extent the Americans, grasped the strategic bombing mission and evolved
the techniques and planes to carry it out, while its Teutonic originators let it
languish. Similary, the Americans, who so loudly protested the submarine and its
unrestricted use in the Great War, led the world in improving these craft and used
them with utter ruthlessness to paralyze Japanese transport in the western Pacific.

This seems more than coincidental. Rather, it can be interpreted as a signal of
the motives of the prospective combatants. If the limited ends of the Great War
were confounded by predatory means, there would be no such discordance in
World War II. The instruments of battle would be perfectly adjusted to a conflict
which knew no moderation, a true fight to the finish.

If, as William James suggested, "history is a bloodbath," then it reached the
flood stage during the Second World War. Even taking into account such notable
episodes of slaughter as the Mongol conquests and the Thirty Years' War, it is
hard to point to a conflict more brutally fought than World War II, or to combatants more driven by the sheer urge to kill. While the Germans undoubtedly led
the way, the British with their prolonged campaign of terror bombing and the
Russians with their epic acts of retribution were nearly as enthusiastic. Nor was
the war in the Pacific any exception. As John W. Dower has recently reminded
us, the Americans and the Japanese waged a "war without mercy" which was
classically predatory in its overtones. In sum, there could be no more fitting culmination to the era of the gun.

II

The figure of Adolph Hitler towers above the sequel to the Great War. He was its
initiator, its architect. Without Hitler there would have been no Nazi Germany,
no *Sichelschnitt,* no Barbarossa, no Holocaust. But the man fit the times so well
that such speculation is rather pointless. If Hitler was not inevitable, he was hardly
inappropriate.[33]

Germany's führer was the apotheosis of the transnational tyrant. More than
any other individual in the history of Europe, he revealed the inner dynamic of
this recurrent governmental phenomenon, this virus of the body politic.

At the core was conquest. So baleful was the image he projected that initially
he managed to swallow entire nations through intimidation alone. Yet the intraspecific expedient of pure bluff had no lasting place in his plans. His true milieu
was war of the most predatory sort. Those who wonder what might have hap-
pended had Hitler not resorted to force in 1939 or not invaded Russia in 1941 are
dealing on the level of fantasy. The man was programmed for conquest.[34]

And the fate of Nazi Germany was just as predictable. The thousand-year
Third Reich was a contradiction in terms. By showing the inner workings of the
regime, Albert Speer unmasked its slapdash nature. It was a stage set, a facade
with a durability corresponding to its ephemeral future. The Wehrmacht was no

exception. What distinguished the Soviet and American armies, the true inheritors of military-industrialism, was a plenitude of weapons. This the Wehrmacht never had. Germany entered the war with arms production barely prioritized and fought the first year in Russia with a weapons output at only a fourth of what it had been in the fall of 1918. Three years later, in the spring of 1944, ammunition production was still below World War I levels.[35]

Martin van Creveld makes much of the Wehrmacht's "fighting power" in comparison with the of its enemies.[36] Yet these qualities—aggressivness of the troops, excellence of their training, and initiative shown by lower- and middle-level leadership—might just as well be attributed to the Roman army. And the comparison is not entirely irrelevant. For the ferocity of the Wehrmacht is beyond dispute. Whatever their weapons, German troops never lost their capacity to kill, and in doing so they acted as the true instrument of their leader.

For Hitler lived so that others might die. Death was the leitmotif of his regime—so much so that a major governmental function became the hunting and ritual slaughter of millions of noncombatants deemed subhuman, the Jews. (In this context it is interesting that the Jews were the only major group of World War II victims against whom gas was used.) This was no minor preoccupation. As Eberhard Jackel points out, the Final Solution was initiated on a large scale at the very moment, the summer of 1941, that Hitler's grand design in foreign affairs, the invasion of Russia, was undertaken. Indeed, there was a subsequent struggle over respective priorities.[37]

This was hardly out of character. Unlike Alexander or Napoleon, Hitler was not primarily a general. He was a gifted amateur in military matters, and what success he had in this area was the result of uncanny intuition and a penchant for the unorthodox. War was merely a means to an end—*Weltmacht oder Neidergang* (world power or ruin). If the latter proved true, Hitler told Raushning in 1932, "We may be destroyed, but if we are, we shall drag a world with us—a world in flames."[38] This was his true legacy.

Hitler had unfinished business with France. He had spent four years in the trenches of the western front, an experience he never forgot. The last thing he wanted was a repetition of this lethal stalemate.

The lightning campaigns in Poland and Norway should have warned the French and the English what was about to happen to them. Yet they allowed the so-called phony war to persist, caught in a trance of false security typified by the remark of a French sentry: "If we fire they will fire back."[39]

The Germans had other plans, specifically *Sichelschnitt* (the cut of the sickle), one of the most inspired and aggressive blueprints for victory in European military history. Conceived primarily by the canny Erich von Manstein and Hitler himself, it called for a Schlieffen-like feint on the extreme right to draw the Anglo-French defenders far forward into Belgium, followed by a panzer thrust through the lightly held French center facing the Ardennes, aimed at cutting off the extended Allied forces. It worked better than even its architects expected. The armored columns of Guderian, Rommel, and Reinhardt cut into the heart of France like the blades of Spanish short swords, isolating some sixty Allied divisions and precipitating the withdrawal of the British Expeditionary Force, minus all their heavy equipment, from Dunkirk in a desperate seaborne rescue mission. In six weeks, at a cost of less than thirty thousand dead, the Wehrmacht inflicted four hundred thousand casualties, captured nearly two million enemy soldiers, and conquered Holland, Belgium, and France. Only the badly shaken British remained standing against Hitler and the Germans.

The panzer–tactical air combination had been the key. Yet as revolutionary as this weapon appeared, it is interesting that it called forth some very archaic behavior. Protected by armor, commanders in particular became neoheroic. Guderian and Rommel took to stationing themselves right at the front lines, personally urging their men to attack at very close range. These hyperaggressive tactics were extremely successful. In fact, probably less than 10 percent of the total force structure did virtually all of the fighting for the Germans. This spoke volumes about both attackers and defenders. On one hand, the armored concepts of Guderian had been thoroughly vindicated. Motorized infantry, self-propelled artillery and tanks, teamed with leapfrogging air support, created self-contained tactical units which, once they broke through stationary defenses, were capable of independent movement of the most rapid sort. Yet the French had been ideal opponents. Already demoralized, they were particularly prone to the confrontational tactics of the Germans, proving themselves capable of neither staunch defense nor strategic retreat. However, the Germans would soon discover that against tougher, more adroit adversaries, the psychological component of blitzkrieg would not work nearly as well.

There is a famous photograph showing Göring and his staff staring across the English Channel at the cliffs of Dover. *"Was nun?"* (what now?), they must have asked themselves. It was a question that must have crossed the minds of many a German. Yet the man who would decide had no good answers.

Hitler had no great desire to pursue the war against the British. While it cannot be proved that he called a halt to his armored troops around Dunkirk to allow the English to escape, as a number have suggested, it is apparent that he was willing to grant them an easy truce as long as England accepted the Third Reich's domination of the Continent.[40] The British, of course, were adamantly determined to continue. Yet Hitler still had a choice.

Germany was decidedly ill equipped to wage war against England. It has been suggested by many, including Manstein, who would have commanded the initial landings, that if the Germans had only invaded Britain quickly during the summer of 1940, operation "Sea Lion" would have stood a good chance of success.[41] But this line of reasoning fails to take sufficient account of continuing British naval and air superiority in the Channel and the truly primitive nature of the armada slated to transport the German invasion force. Rather, it seems clear that an early invasion was not undertaken because it stood little chance of success. Besides, Hitler never had his heart in it

Yet his alternative was possible even worse. He would simultaneously seek to wage air war against the British and starve them by unleashing Admiral Doenitz's U-boats against their overseas commerce. Besides having neglected both U-boat and heavy bomber production,[42] and therefore lacking the requisite means for success, there were excellent political reasons why Hitler should have abstained from both. The United States had entered the Great War on the side of the Allies because of unrestricted submarine warfare, and, even considering American neutrality legislation, there was good reason to believe she would do so again. Also, despite the bombing of Rotterdam, which the Germans claimed was accidental, there were many who continued to hope such attacks on population centers could be curbed. Had the Luftwaffe abstained from bombing the British, it is quite possible that the Royal Air Force would have been reciprocally restrained from using its superior strategic attack force in an all-out assault against German cities. It seems unlikely that the British would have dropped out of the war, but their prime means of hurting Germany would have been blunted. Yet Hitler was Hitler. Calculated acts of moderation were alien to his nature. Therefore, he got the worst of everything.

The submarine campaign in the Atlantic was characteristically predatory in its conduct, calling forth an arms competition based, appropriately enough, on a very rapid-fire series of counter and counter-counter measures. For the first few months German submarine successes were modest. However, from March 1941 to December 1942, shipping losses averaged nearly 450,000 tons a month, a catastrophic figure.[43] U-boats now operated in flotillas, aptly named wolf packs, which were guided to convoys by reconnaissance aircraft, where they used their strength in numbers to wreak extended havoc, at times even shooting lifeboats and floating survivors.

The U-boats' enemies reacted with a host of new weapons. Most significant was sonar, a piezoelectric echo ranging device which, although countered by the Germans with gas bubbles to produce false returns, continued as the basic means of underwater detection. To locate surfaced submarines the British employed aircraft and ship-based radar, along with high-frequency radio direction finders. The Germans first responded with search receivers that warned submariners of such surveillance, and later with schnorkels allowing them to run submerged on their diesels to avoid search radars. As these various innovations held sway, tonnage figures surged back and forth. The Allies basically prevailed, but war's end brought no definitive answer to the U-boat.[44]

Yet a political decision was reached long before. While the Roosevelt administration was clearly pro-British, the German submarine campaign constituted the mechanism which inexorably drew America toward war. Each new hostile incident at sea further isolated the American isolationists and strengthened the president's hand to increase participation, until the U.S. Navy was escorting British vessels more than halfway across the Atlantic, under orders to shoot German submarines on sight. Yet Hitler did not back down. Instead, he used the occasion of Pearl Harbor to declare war on America, thereby bringing this onus upon himself and the world's largest industrial power down on Germany. It was a strategic blunder of the first magnitude.[45]

Yet the effect of the air blitz against the English was hardly better. After failing to knock out the British warning radars and grossly underestimating the strength of the RAF Fighter Command, the Luftwaffe allowed itself to be drawn away from attacks on vital air bases and aircraft plants to concentrate instead on terror bombing of civilian targets. It was a thoroughly feckless performance. After the cancellation of Sea Lion, the campaign served no real military purpose and only revealed the tactical weaknesses of German aircraft, particularly the bombers. Meanwhile, the chivalry of the Great War was forgotten by the defending British fighter pilots, who took pleasure in killing German airmen, even shooting them in their parachutes. "We hated those aeroplanes with their iron crosses and their crooked swastikas," remembered Wing Commander Douglas Bader, "flying them into our English sky and dropping bombs indiscriminately on our English towns."[46]

Yet true revenge would come from another source. During the blitz Winston Churchill visited a bombed-out neighborhood in poor South London where he was met not with panic or recriminations but with the angry cry "Give it 'em back." In February 1942 he found a man who would—Air Marshall Arthur T. "Bomber" Harris.

After a short series of costly and ineffective daytime raids, the RAF switched to bombing at night. Although losses were cut dramatically, so was accuracy. While the Americans insisted on the efficacy of daylight "precision" raids on German industry, the British developed another rationale, "dehousing." The concept was invented by Lord Cherwell, Churchill's science advisor, who, after analyzing the effects of the blitz, concluded that what most bothered victims was losing their homes—"people seem to mind it more than having their friends or even relatives killed." Extrapolating this to Germany, where twenty-two million people were concentrated in just fifty-eight cities, he estimated that a bombing campaign of eighteen months' duration could dehouse a third of the German population and thus "break the spirit of the people."[47]

It was the opening Harris needed. On 28 March 1942 the RAF burned the wooden city of Lübeck with incendiaries dehousing over fifteen thousand. Rostock followed at the end of April. A month later came the thousand-plane attack on Cologne. A year later, 722 RAF bombers lit the world's first fire storm in Hamburg. Many more Harris-inspired raids would follow, and by war's end much of urban Germany was in ashes. Millions were dehoused. Critics would argue that for much of this time German war production actually rose, yet this misses the point. By provoking the British, Hitler had subjected his people to what would be the future of war—or lack of it. Whatever the strategic value, it was a terrible price to pay.

Though it was not as great as turning east and provoking the two-front war German military planners dreaded. In the words of Marshal Montgomery: "One of the first rules of war is: don't march on Moscow."[48] Like Charles XII and Napoleon, Hitler did and was destroyed.

From the beginning, Hitler planned a fight to the finish—the Russians', not his own. Operation Barbarossa foresaw the occupation of the entire country west of a line stretching north from Astrakhan to Archangel—the fabled lebensraum of the Nazi dreamscape. This implied not only conquest but depopulation, and he warned his generals that they would not be fighting in a "knightly fashion." All captured commissars were to be shot, and the prosecution of German troops for crimes against Russian civilians was left optional. What was intended was a true race war against *Untermenschen,* "to be conducted with unprecedented, unmerciful, and unrelenting harshness."[49] Anxious to prevent a Russian withdrawal into the interior, as befell Napoleon, the famous Directive 21 stipulated: "The Bulk of the Russian Army . . . will be destroyed by daring operations led by deeply penetrating armored spearheads."

Total victory was to be achieved in just eight weeks, a figure symptomatic of the aura of unreality which suffused Barbarossa. Four-fifths of the invading German troops were not even provided with winter clothes.[50] Meanwhile, the Red Army was huge and heavily equipped. Facing the 136 invading German divisions was a force of something over 200 divisions. In tanks the Germans were outnumbered by more than 12,000 to 3,550, emphasizing the relatively small size of their panzer element. Worse yet, soon they would be confronted by very large numbers of an entirely new generation of Soviet armored vehicles, including the KV heavy tank and the incomparable T-34.

Nevertheless, as the Wehrmacht moved forward in late June 1941, divided into a northern, a southern, and a very strong central army group, it achieved virtually total surprise and seized the tactical and strategic initiative. Having had most of its command cadre slaughtered by Stalin and his secret police in 1937, the Red Army was ill led and deployed too close to the border in defensive lines full of gaps. The Soviet air force, numerically the strongest in the world, was dealt a catastrophic blow, losing over two thousand aircraft in two days.[51] Consequently, the panzer-led pincer movements accomplished almost exactly what they were instructed to do in Directive 21, enveloping huge masses of Russians.

Yet this was deceiving. The mobility of German armored units was exaggerated by a Great War–induced unwillingness to retreat, destined to bedevil not only Stalin and his strategic cronies but, later, ex-corporal Adolf Hitler. Even when surrounded, however, Soviet troops fought ferociously. "If you are wounded, pretend to be dead," recommended orders based on Soviet Provisional Field Service regulations. "Wait until the Germans come up; then select one and kill him! Kill him with gun, bayonet, or knife. Tear out his throat with your teeth."[52] Soldiers of the Wehrmacht faced no similar hazard in France.

Yet the Wehrmacht rolled on. By the middle of July, Smolensk was taken, two-thirds down the road to Moscow. At this juncture, however, the Germans redirected their efforts, driving into the economic heartland of the Ukraine. It was a strange decision. Hitler the transnational tyrant might have been expected to strike directly at the capital. Instead, he insisted that only the heavy manufacturing and coal of the Donets Basin would provide the basis for victory. His strategists Brauchitsch, Halder, Bock, and Guderian argued the opposite, pushing for a swift, decapitating strike on Moscow. Historians have generally sided with the generals, pointing out that this diversion plunged the Germans and their timetable for conquest into the midst of the Russian winter. Yet John Erickson stresses the gravity of this blow to the industrial vitals which, even in 1945, left the USSR shorn of approximately a third of its steel and petroleum capacity, and producing 10 percent less coal and electricity than in 1940.[53] Considering this, the Soviet military-industrial recovery becomes even more impressive.

The German push on the capital, which got under way in the first days of October, was finally blunted in early December, virtually in the shadow of the Kremlin. Reinforced by the implacable Georgy Zhukov, the new T-34, and tough and warmly dressed Siberian troops, the Russians counter attacked and threw the Wehrmacht back away from Moscow. Now it was Hitler insisting that his troops not fall back, and the Russian tanks threatening to encircle them. Both Alan Clark and John Strawson agree that in this instance Hitler's no-retreat order was correct, since the lack of natural strong points spelled the same sort of shattering withdrawal which destroyed Napoleon's Grand Army.[54] Yet as time passed, the Germans' führer would make a fetish of not giving ground, with appalling tactical and strategic results, only the worst of which was Stalingrad.

There would be many other battles, but the central crisis of the war passed before Moscow and in the process revealed a great deal about both the true nature of the conflict and the opponents fighting it. It is true the Russians suffered horribly. Not even counting battle deaths, they lost over two million men captured by 1 November. Three-quarters of their air force was destroyed.[55] Their tank park was in ruins. Yet their opponents, if less injured, were nevertheless badly bloodied. Not only had their equipment base been shattered by overuse, battle, and cold, but between 22 June and 1 February the Germans suffered over a million casualties. Blitzkrieg was a fond memory. At the beginning of 1942 the German army found itself once again in a brutal war of attrition.

This was to be a war without scruples, a predatory extravaganza. Mesmerized by the racist fantasies of their führer and taking his instructions literally, the Germans were the prime instigators. It is beyond dispute that their very cruelty was a major factor in uniting the Russians behind Stalin, particularly in the Ukraine. Of the Russian prisoners taken by the Wehrmacht, nearly 2,000,000 died in the camps and another 1,308,000 were listed under the sinister category of "exterminations."[56] Very large (but unverifiable) numbers were never allowed to surrender but were shot on the spot. When civilian casualties—those who starved or died of neglect—are added, the total number of Russian deaths is estimated in excess of 20,000,000. This was a new dimension in death dealing, and the Russian people reacted accordingly. They became a nation at arms. In their reliance on snipers, and in the partisan campaigns, they did not so much fight Germans as hunt them. At times they advanced under orders to take no prisoners. As is characteristic of such struggles, women became involved in the fighting, though on a larger scale than ever before, even flying combat missions, acting as snipers, and participating in human-wave assaults.[57] In short, the Russians fought with the desperation of those preyed upon.

German diarists and eyewitness reports on the eastern front repeatedly draw attention to two basic perceptions of the Russians: their courage and determination, and their apparently endless supply of excellent weapons. Of the two, the latter seems to have been the key to victory. The Poles had been brave and lost in a matter of days. The Germans themselves were redoubtable fighters, even under hopeless circumstances, yet ultimately they were buried under a mountain of arms.

Of the many Soviet accomplishments during this time of trial, none was more vital than the wholesale evacuation of its military-industrial complex. Certainly, it was the most complete and efficiently planned strategic component implemented during the first part of the war. Between June and November, the Russians completely disassembled over fifteen hundred industrial plants and thirteen hundred military enterprises, and transported them in hundreds of thousands of railway cars east to prepared sites along the Volga, in the Urals, and in western Siberia.[58] During much of the exodus, the Germans staged air raids by the thousands in an effort to break down the operation and interdict lines of transport.

Not only did this fail, but Soviet defense industries actually thrived during this period. The portion of gross national product devoted to the defense budget rose to 57 percent by the end of 1942. Meanwhile, for the twelve-month period beginning in June 1941, total Russian production of aircraft, tanks, artillery, and ammunition increased by 76 percent. Most critically, production of KV and T-34 tanks during the first half of 1942 tripled the numbers turned out in 1941.[59] By the end of the war, Russian industry would produce almost 110,000 tanks and self-propelled guns to the Germans' 23,000.

Ultimately, these statistics translated into a combat strategy based on drawing the Germans into vast, equipment-draining confrontations. Often fighting on the tactical defensive, the Soviets absorbed huge losses knowing that those they inflicted on the Wehrmacht could not be replaced with anything like the rapidity of which they themselves were capable. Kursk was the archetype of these clashes, but they were fought numerous times on a smaller scale as the Germans were gradually pushed back. In the end the Wehrmacht simply had very little to fight with.

If weapons won the the war for the Soviet Union, it was tanks, most particularly the T-34, which epitomized this superiority. Designed in August 1939 by the Medium Tank Design Group, the T-34 was the culmination of nearly a decade of extensive research on a wide range of components. The product was a masterpiece of integration, incorporating for the first time a powerful and fireresistant diesel engine, a high-velocity 76-mm gun (German Panzer III and IV tanks mounted 37-mm and 50-mm pieces), thick armor sloped to deflect shells, and advanced Christie suspension, combined with very wide tracks to provide exceptional mobility in snow and ice—all in a compact package weighing barely thirty tons. While there was some suspicion of better and heavier Russian tanks prior to Barbarossa,[60] the appearance of the first T-34s came as a real shock to the Germans. A single strange-looking, low-slung tank emerged out of the underbrush near the Dnieper for the first time in early July, and proceeded to cut a nine-mile swath of destruction through the Seventeenth Panzer Division, proving itself all but impervious to German shells. By early October, when the Fourth Panzer Division was very roughly handled by a covey of T-34s, it was perfectly apparent to the Germans that the Russians had a vastly superior tank.[61] In November a group of designers and engineers visited the front and were begged by officers on the scene to simply reverse engineer the T-34 and quickly mass-produce a German version. The vanity of the designers prevented this, and virtually nothing was done for all of 1942. Finally, the Germans settled on the huge Tiger, the complex Panther, and a variety of still-larger Porsche-designed models, none of which could be manufactured in sufficient quantities. Meanwhile, the T-34 would proliferate and eventually clatter down the broad avenues of Berlin.

The T-34 emerged from World War II as an icon of Soviet nationalism, truly

Figure 13. Soviet T-34 tank. Courtesy of the U.S. Army.

the "hero weapon of the Great Patriotic War," as Russian historians are prone to call it. Consequently, it has had an important effect on the subsequent weapons developments and deployments of the Soviet army, which to this day remains preeminently a tank-based force using lineal descendants of the original T-34. In an age dominated by nuclear missiles, the tank continues as the national weapon of the USSR, connoting exactly the political message the Party has traditionally stood for: "Threaten us, attempt to overturn the decision of World War II, and our tanks will roll." It is an outmoded message and a superfluous threat, but nonetheless an extant one.

The T-34 also says a good deal about World War II on a political and personal level. The struggle between Russia and Germany was a clash, perhaps the last one, of transnational tyrants. Of the two, however, Hitler was the purer type, Stalin a historical accident. The Russian dictator grew out of a system which made him possible and would also outlive him. Communism and what the USSR became evolved out of an interpretation of the industrial age. The economy was quite literally structured according to principles pioneered by Frederick Winslow Taylor and Henry Ford. It was about heavy industry, mass production, and steel, and the legion of identical T-34s which clanked forward to meet the Wehrmacht symbolized, as much as anything, this commitment.

Hitler, on the other hand, was Nazism. What he built in Germany was a sort of mock totalitarianism, almost a satire on the concept. Therefore, even though the Germans were among the most technologically advanced of peoples, war production was, even considering the titanic labors of Albert Speer, essentially a hoax.

Being ground down by one weapons colossus and about to be assailed by another (America), Hitler characteristically took refuge in the realm of fantasy. Secret weapons were to be his salvation. As with most tyrants, Hitler's thanatotic imagination and scant combat ethics predisposed him toward arms innovations. Yet personal experience and his lack of real scientific and technical awareness led him to undermine a number of initiatives.

As far back as 1936, Dr. Gerhard Schrader, searching for new insecticides, discovered tabun and later sarin, fantastically deadly chemical agents which block acetylcholinesterase, the substance which allows muscles to relax. A factory was duly built at Dyhernfurth, near the Polish border, and over twelve thousand tons of nerve agent were stockpiled there. Yet Hitler, the World War I gas victim, took little notice, and never pressed for it to be used. (Meanwhile, the Allies had no equivalent and only discovered the existence of German nerve agents at war's end.) Apparently, insecticide for humans had little appeal even for a Hitler.[62]

Yet there were other cases much more in the mainstream. For example, he would insist that the brilliantly conceived Me-262—a jet-powered interceptor with over a hundred-mile-per-hour top-speed advantage over the fastest Allied fighters—be inappropriately converted to a bomber, wasting nearly a year of developmental time.[63] Similarly, he and Speer overlooked the potential of the C-2 Waterfall antiaircraft rocket in favor of the FZG-76 and A-4 (V-1 and V-2) rockets. As Speer points out, while Allied bombers during several months of 1944 were dropping an average of three thousand tons of bombs a day on Germany, the maximum explosives delivery that could be expected from an optimal thirty V-2 launchings per day was twenty-four tons. Nonetheless, the V-2 was given equal priority with tank production, and vast quantities of the potato crop were diverted out of the mouths of hungry Germans into alcohol to fuel the rockets.[64] In the end, V-1 and V-2 rockets would be responsible for around thirty thousand British casualties and would have no appreciable effect on the outcome of the war.[65]

Yet Hitlerian advanced weaponry amounted to more than escapism. In its last feverish burst of creativity, Nazi war technology forged virtually a complete prototype arsenal for a new era of weaponry. Besides developing and mass-producing the first tactical ballistic missile, German rocket scientists at war's end were groping toward models with true intercontinental ranges and had schemes on the drawing board for launching modified V-2s from submarine-towed canisters.[66] While the C-2 Waterfall pioneered the important category of surface-to-air missiles, the Ju-287 prototype was the first heavy jet bomber to be flown successfully. In addition to the Me-262, the world's first operational jet fighter, the Luftwaffe also fielded the even-faster rocket-powered Me-163 Komet and was working with prototypes incorporating such advanced features as variable-sweep and delta wings. There was even an antitank guided missile, the Red Riding Hood. Seen in this light, postnuclear arms acquisition takes on a somewhat different cast, for virtually all subsequent avenues of development were defined, even prior to the moment of nuclear inception, in the blueprints and experimental design bureaus of the desperate Nazi war machine.

The major exception, of course, had to do with that very moment of inception. In the late thirties, Germany had led the world in nuclear physics. Yet many of the best scientists had been Jews, and they would flee. So the German bomb program went nowhere and was scrapped in the fall of 1942. Later Hitler would occasionally refer to the principles on which it was based as "Jewish physics."[67] In a way he was right. Because of the Jews' departure, the bomb would be developed elsewhere, and the world would be spared the specter of nuclear-armed Nazis.

So the war in Europe ended with the destruction of Adolph Hitler and all that he stood for. Those who complain that the conflict was unnecessarily prolonged by the Allied commitment to "unconditional surrender" do not fully consider the totality of the struggle, the utterly predatory manner in which it was waged, particularly in what was its central theater, Russia. There was no room for compromise here. The end could only come in the total obliteration of one of the two opponents. Then there was the matter of Germany, the fate of that "army possessing a state," the twisted creation of the Hohenzollerns and the Krupps. There could be no repetition of Versailles, no business left unfinished for the Germans. While it would not be deemed necessary to sow their fields with salt, the political message of the great European double war would be made absolutely clear. Once and for all it was decided that the future did not include *Deutchland uber alles.*

III

Both in the minds of the participants and in subsequent judgments, Europe was the central theater of World War II. Certainly, by conventional standards this is the case. But if pure hatred and enthusiasm for violence are taken into account, the Pacific war deserves serious consideration. For it was here, in a blinding flash of light, that mankind entered the era of nuclear weapons.

Pyrrhus the Epirot would have understood Pearl Harbor. For he learned while fighting against the Romans that to win against such an opponent is to lose. So it was on 7 December 1941.

First there was the matter of the battleships. The raid on Hawaii was one of the most brilliantly conceived and executed operations in naval history. The first true combat test of the carrier task force concept, it was a textbook example of how this new weapon should be employed—wielded like a samurai sword in a sudden slashing blow which left no time for response.

Yet strategically it was a victory of profound futility, aimed at a target of negative utility. Jutland and the Washington Naval Treaty had stripped the dreadnought of the crown of seapower, and the aerial destruction of battleship row and the *Prince of Wales* and the *Repulse* three days later in the Gulf of Siam did little more than confirm this judgment. The Allies would hardly miss their sunken dreadnoughts.[68] In fact, the elimination of the Pacific battle fleet insured that American carriers would henceforth operate in task forces and no longer be obliged to guard dreadnoughts, the remainder of which were relegated to escort and patrol duty between Hawaii and California.[69] Meanwhile, a parallel shift in the command structure circumvented the die-hard battleship supporters, and left the navy largely in the hands of men like Ernest J. King and William Halsey, whose broad experience with destroyers, submarines, and naval aviation put them much more in touch with technological reality.[70] So the attack can be seen to have actually had a salutary effect on U.S. naval power.

Yet its impact was still broader. John Toland makes the point that the Japanese attack was rooted in the same impulse which brought forth their favorite literary form, the haiku, a seventeen-syllable equivalent of a coup de grace.[71] That was the problem. A sumo or kendo match might be finished by a sudden burst, but not the Americans. To them Pearl Harbor marked the beginning, not the end.

The surprise attack provoked a rage like no other in American history. It was to this country, as Franklin Roosevelt described it, "a day of infamy." And most would have agreed with William Halsey when he vowed to fight a war, at the end of which Japanese would be spoken only in hell. While the results fell somewhat short of these aspirations, four years later Japan would lay in ruins and two million of her sons and daughters would be dead.

The two sides had begun eyeing each other balefully shortly after the Treaty of Portsmouth ended the Russo-Japanese War in 1905, and the enmity had grown ever since, fueled on both sides by racism, fear, greed, and ambition. Historians as diverse as Charles A. Beard and John Toland have argued that the clash was needless, and even Herbert Feis, after charting the accelerating currents of the prewar vortex, wondered aloud if the parties might not have escaped its pull.[72] Yet the astonishing hatred and viciousness which boiled up on both sides once the shooting began argues the contrary.

It must be conceded that the actual focus of the war—a series of island-hopping campaigns and supporting sea actions, the targets chosen as much for political as strategic reasons—contributed to the harshness. Amphibious operations are characteristically fraught with risk and prone to high casualties, while the vast distances over which carrier battles and submarine sweeps were conducted naturally thwarted rescue operations.

Nonetheless, these factors, like statistics, miss the qualitative aspect of how merciless the fighting really was. For example, it was a truism among Western war correspondents that the fighting in the Pacific exceeded in savagery the combat in Europe.[73] From the beginning it was kill or be killed. This was compounded by the Japanese view that it was a disgrace for a soldier to surrender. Thus in April 1942, the *Japan Times and Advertiser* advised its readers: "To show them [Allied prisoners] mercy is to prolong the war." Conversely, U.S. Marines were briefed: "Every Japanese has been told it is his duty to die for the Emperor. It is your duty to see that he does."[74]

Not surprisingly, slaughter became a hallmark of the conflict. The Japanese were clearly the worst offenders, and virtually everywhere they fought they indulged their most brutal instincts. As John Dower observes, "Their atrocities frequently were so grotesque . . . that it is not surprising that they were interpreted as being an expression of deliberate policy."[75] Yet a few examples of American conduct should suffice to show that this was not a one-sided activity. Thus, the day after the Battle of the Bismarck Sea, U.S. and Australian planes systematically searched for Japanese survivors and shot up every lifeboat they found. "You can't be too sporting in a war," wrote an American major in his official report of the operation.[76] Similarly, the commander of the American submarine *Wahoo*, after sinking a Japanese troop transport, spent an hour killing hundreds of survivors with his deck guns, an act for which he was decorated.[77]

The exaggeratedly predatory nature of the combat brought forth among the Americans continued evocations of the hunt. Thus, one ad for telescopic sights pictured a Japanese soldier framed in the cross hairs beneath the heading: "Rack up another one." "Tanks are used to flush Japanese out of the grass," wrote a Pulitzer Prize–winning journalist of Guadalcanal, "and when they are flushed, they are shot down like running quail."[78] Similarly, but on a much larger scale, the notable slaughter of Admiral Ozowa's attacking planes off Saipan in June 1944 by the pilots of Mark Mitchner's Task Force 58 has been known ever since as "the great Marianas turkey shoot." While there were also frequent analogies to the extermination of vermin, the hunting metaphor is more significant since it relies on a very traditional justification for indiscriminate killing, seeking to place it in a context that is at least in some respects heroic.

Complementing this and resorted to by both sides was an unrelenting dehumanization of the adversary, meticulously chronicled by Dower in his excellent book *War without Mercy*. This species distancing in the Western context most frequently fell back on Darwinian analogies, relegating the Japanese to subhuman status, particularly apes, gorillas, baboons, or monkeys (dogs, mice, rats, vipers, rattlesnakes, and cockroaches were also used, but apparently with less frequency).[79] The Japanese, lacking a cultural equivalent to the apish stigmata, tended to portray their adversaries as generally bestial or satanic. Thus, Anglo-Americans were described as demons, devils, evil spirits, and monsters.[80] It is important to note that these were not isolated references but very widely and frequently used, particularly among Americans. Moreover, the purpose can logically be assumed to be the same on both sides. As we have seen in earlier exceedingly predatory conflicts, species distancing served to ease the killing and to some extent justify it. The fact that two separate races were engaged only made this more convenient and superficially plausible. Thus, the killer is not murderer, but hunter, or alternately, demon dispatcher. But if this device can be shown to be functional, its ubiquity also serves to underline the nature of the war in the Pacific.

Not unexpectedly, weapons played a central role in the slaughter and were used in a manner calculated to intensify it. At the infantry level, Americans, as an alternative to the rifles and carbines which were standard issue in Europe, frequently employed submachine guns (advertised in the United States as "blasting big red holes in little yellow men").[81] After July 1943, when they were introduced, flamethrowers were used to broil Japanese defenders in pillboxes. On the other hand, as Dower notes, "For the Japanese enlisted man, the bayonet was the poor man's counterpart to the samurai sword . . . and for the Freudian analyst, the wanton frenzy with which these conscripts plunged this weapon into Allied prisoners as well as defenseless people everywhere in Asia must be of more than passing interest."[82]

On 7 December, just a few hours after Pearl Harbor, an order went out to U.S. naval commanders in the Pacific to "Execute Unrestricted Air and Submarine Warfare against Japan."[83] That quickly, Americans embraced the very policy which led to their entry into the Great War in 1917 and more recently spurred a confrontation with Hitler. For nearly two years, however, the subsequent campaign was severely handicapped by the Mark-14 torpedo, which because of its expense had never been tested with live warheads in peacetime and now refused to explode when it hit something. At first the Bureau of Ordnance declined to reevaluate the defective torpedo, and it was not until September of 1943 that this and other kinks were worked out of the Mark-14.

Suitably armed, American submariners immediately began operating in wolf packs, and went on a rampage of destruction. By war's end, U.S. submarines had sunk over 8 million tons of Japanese shipping, leaving less than 1.8 million tons, mostly small, wooden craft, afloat. Underlining the campaign's lethality, a force constituting under 2 percent of U.S. naval manpower racked up fully 55 percent of Japan's losses at sea, virtually cut her supply of oil, and lowered overall imports by 40 percent.[84]

Remarkably, the Japanese did little to respond. Antisubmarine warfare remained woefully inadequate, and calls by a few officers to establish a submarine counteroffensive were basically ignored. Instead, submarines were increasingly used to supply isolated garrisons, a task which could have been done better by destroyers but was not because they were considered too valuable. Yet Japan's passive approach to submarine warfare seems to have been founded more on a basic dislike of these vessels than on any particular compunctions.

Whatever their outlook at sea, the Japanese were certainly pragmatic in the air. For their major innovation during the war, the kamikaze, bore witness to their willingness to use available weaponry in any way possible to inflict harm on the enemy. A sort of reductio ad absurdum guided missile (or the ultimate "smart bomb"), the kamikaze was first used on an organized basis in the Battle of Leyte Gulf in 1944, immediately inflicting severe damage on two carriers and sinking another. By April 1945, American forces invading Okinawa found nearly a thousand kamikaze awaiting them, and in the attacks which followed scores of American ships were sunk or damaged. Because a crash-diving plane had to be completely destroyed, not just damaged, they were inherently hard to stop and remained so. Also, although a rocket-powered glide bomb, the cherry blossom, was specially developed for these missions, basically any plane—even the most obsolescent, flown by fledgling pilots—would do. For the hard-pressed Japanese the concept of "one plane, one warship" was exceedingly attractive. For the Americans it was a nightmare, and one that served to convince them that literally any means of attacking the Japanese was appropriate.

Americans had entered the war violently opposed to the bombing of civilians, and during the campaign in Europe had generally opposed British terror bombing in favor of the costly but less indiscriminate technique of daylight "precision" air raids. As we have seen, with the order of 7 December, this changed in principle almost immediately in the Pacific. Even a month prior to Pearl Harbor, George Marshall had instructed aides to develop contingency plans for "general incendiary attacks to burn up the wood and paper structures of the densely populated Japanese cities."[85] Three years later, with the arrival of the very long-range B-29 heavy bomber, the M-47 and M-69 naplam bombs, and General Curtis LeMay to command the Twentieth Air Force, these plans came to fruition. On the night of 9 March 1945, 334 B-29s armed only with incendiaries would attack Tokyo at low levels, and in the ensuing fires 267,000 buildings would burn and over eighty-three thousand people would die.[86] Japanese air defense against such night attacks was almost nonexistent, nor would it improve. By June, over 40 percent of Japan's six most important industrial cities had been gutted and millions dehoused. Yet the Americans had a better way.

In December 1938, two German physicists, Otto Hahn and Fritz Strassman managed to split a uranium atom by bombarding it with neutrons. Unaware of exactly what they had done, they wrote fellow physicist Lise Meitner, a Jew who had fled to Sweden. She soon realized that not only had they broken apart the uranium atom but that a small amount of its matter had been transformed directly into energy. Using Einstein's formula $E = mc^2$, she calculated that one pound of fully fissioned uranium would yield the equivalent of burning seven million pounds of coal. Meitner immediately informed Nobel laureate Niels Bohr. At a Washington meeting of theoretical physicists in January 1939, he relayed this information to a refugee from Mussolini's Italy, Enrico Fermi, who quickly realized that a sufficient amount of uranium (called a critical mass) could generate enough neutrons to sustain fission through a chain reaction. By early March, Leo Szilard, a Hungarian expatriot, demonstrated that Fermi's contention was correct by bombarding uranium with neutrons to produce more neutrons. An atomic bomb was possible, and these refugees from Fascist Europe realized that Hitler might be building one. They persuaded Albert Einstein, also a refugee from Germany, to sign a letter warning President Roosevelt. Further work demonstrated feasibility, and on 6 December 1941 the president ordered that everything possible be done to build an atomic bomb. By the summer of 1942 the Manhattan Project was born.[87]

It is clear that the primary motive for the program was fear that Nazi Germany would develop nuclear weapons first. However, Ronald Powaski points out that, as early as November 1944, American officials were aware that Germany had no viable nuclear program, and the surrender in May 1945 made this a certainty.[88] Despite this, work on the Manhattan Project not only continued but accelerated. No one considered the Japanese a threat to develop a bomb. Rather, the bomb was being built to be used. On 1 June President Truman accepted recommendations that it be dropped on Japan as soon as possible—"without specific warning," he recalled in his memoirs, "and against a target that would clearly show its devastating strength."[89] Kamikaze attacks and fanatical Japanese resistance on Iwo Jima and Okinawa had convinced the president and his advisors, over the protests of key scientists, that the bomb was the only alternative to an extraordinarily bloody invasion of the home islands. On 6 August 1945 a uranium bomb, "Little Boy," was dropped by the B-29 *Enola Gay* on the industrial city of Hiroshima. On 9 August, Nagasaki was similarly bombed with a plutonium device, "Fat Man." "When you deal with a beast," wrote Truman several days after, "you have to treat him as a beast."[90]

Less than a month earlier, the bomb's chief designer, J. Robert Oppenheimer, as he watched its first test, remembered some lines from the Bhagavad Gita: "Now

I am become death, destroyer of worlds; waiting the hour that ripens to their doom.''[91] These are considered remarkably prescient now, but probably were not then. For only a very few had any idea that a major era in history had passed. Instead, most would wander into the nuclear age much as Charles VIII had sauntered into Italy, under the impression that the rules of the previous era still applied. They didn't, and perhaps this was a good thing. The era of the gun had been a time of death and instability from its inception. It closed with mankind in the midst of an orgy of killing. Of all the arms conceived of by Leonardo, only chemical weapons were still being handled with some forbearance. Yet, in the future, forbearance would be the key to survival. So we would have to change.

✳ ——— Chapter 16 ————————————————

CONCLUSION:
THE ERA OF NUCLEAR WEAPONS

I

A nuclear explosion is impossible to ignore. Unlike the portentous *gonne* of Bertholdus Schwartz, the blast at Hiroshima instantly put the world on notice that an extraordinarily powerful weapon had been added to the arsenal of man. Yet just how powerful, and the true implications of a nuclear future, remained open to question even for those appropriately awed by a mushroom cloud bursting into the stratosphere.

Only a few months after Hiroshima, a Yale University professor, Bernard Brodie, and several colleagues published a book entitled *The Absolute Weapon*, which set forth the startling proposition that not only were nuclear weapons here to stay, but that their unprecedented destructiveness and the unlikelihood of effective counters might act as a "powerful inhibitor to aggression." Henceforth, the chief purpose of military establishments would no longer be "to win wars" but "to avert them." [1] So was born the doctrine of nuclear deterrence.

At almost the same time Brodie was writing, Paul Nitze, subsequently adviser to five presidents, was touring the ruins of Hiroshima and wondering if the bomb was indeed the absolute weapon everyone thought it was. This outlook was reflected in the Strategic Bombing Survey's 1946 volume on Hiroshima and Nagasaki, which Nitze supervised. While taking the enormous damage inflicted on the two cities fully into account, the survey still appeared to view it as finite and potentially reducible through measures such as evacuation, shelters, and industrial decentralization. [2] Thus, as Gregg Herken has pointed out, "the lines were drawn" very early; emphasis would shift, as would individual positions, but the two basic

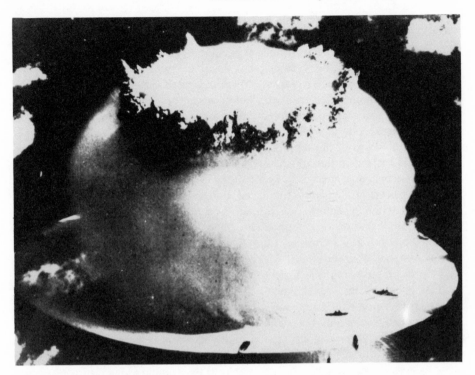

Figure 14. Atomic bomb test amidst several old battleships, Bikini Island, 1946. Courtesy of the U.S. Department of Energy.

poles of the nuclear age, deterrence and war fighting, were in place from the beginning.[3]

To be sure, the semblance of a total dichotomy in the two positions is more apparent than real. In the abstract, at least, they must run together since deterrence, to be credible, requires the means and at least the appearance of willingness to wage nuclear warfare. Also, beneath the generally bifurcated conceptual framework, it is possible to accommodate a range of strategies, institutional variables, and interpretations of adversarial capabilities and intentions. Nevertheless, even taking into account these and other complicating factors, the course of arms during the first four decades of the nuclear era can still be explained in terms of the two basic strategies, their respective destinies in the face of technology, and the inevitable tendency toward weapons symmetry.

In the main, technology has not been kind to the war fighters and their conception that cities and populations might be spared in favor of discrete exchanges against military objectives. For within seven years of Hiroshima, nuclear weapons had shown themselves to be colossally more lethal than it had appeared initially. While considerable progress was made in making atomic bombs more powerful and less consumptive of fissionable material, it was understood even prior to the first nuclear test that a potentially awesome alternative might exist. Such a device would take advantage of the one-hundred million degree heat generated by a fission event to fuse hydrogen nuclei into helium—the same process that fuels the sun—thereby releasing very large amounts of energy. Yet the real key to the weapon's potential was its composition. Being based on nature's most abundant element, the contemplated hydrogen bomb would not only alleviate the scarcity of fissionable material, making many more weapons possible, but it promised to allow the construction of nuclear devices virtually as small as desired—or as large. MIKE, the first test of the resultant device, took place on 1 November 1952 on a small Pacific island in the Marshall chain. When the huge fireball cleared ground zero, spectators were amazed to find that the whole island, one mile in diameter, had disappeared. Calculations indicated the blast had amounted to the energy equivalent of ten megatons (ten million tons of TNT), or a yield roughly one thousand times that of the device at Hiroshima. "Everything worked," explained one of the H-bomb's architects, Luis Alvarez, attempting to account for the device's unexpected power almost with an intellectual shrug of the shoulders.[4] Suddenly, the atomic bomb was a mere firecracker.

Compounding this development, a growing understanding of the long-term effects of radiation exposure, combined with actual fallout problems generated by American and Soviet atmospheric testing programs, produced a steady shift in the perception of nuclear weapons from primarily explosive implements to something much more insidious, almost akin to chemical or biological weapons. While military men were presumably less susceptible to the common vision of a few postnuclear survivors wandering amid the wreckage, slowly being poisoned by unseen radioactive effluvia, the reality of fallout persistently frustrated the operational goal of the so-called surgical strike against purely military targets.[5] To be effective, such attacks had to be directed at a full military target set, which in turn would require sufficient numbers of weapons to create massive clouds of civilian-killing radioactivity, thereby defeating the intent of the strike. Though it did become possible to build cleaner—though far from radioactivity-free—bombs, they were inherently bulky, and in fact technology has moved in the opposite direction to relatively dirty fission-enhanced devices.[6] So fallout remains a problem.

Then there was the matter of delivery. So long as nuclear attack forces were confined to high-flying manned bombers, the proposition of defending against them continued to appear reasonable and viable. Yet the German V-2 opened new vistas of offensive possibility, quickly capitalized upon by both sides. By the mid-1950s, a combination of improved rocketry and guidance, along with technology devoted to reducing the size and weight of warheads, made it apparent that nuclear weapons could and would be delivered at seventeen thousand miles per hour over intercontinental ranges. Strategic warning shrank to a matter of minutes, and quite suddenly the logic of the offensive became overwhelming.

Making it even more compelling, the United States in the early 1960s began deploying a somewhat shorter-range sea-launched ballistic missile (SLBM), the Polaris, aboard submarines whose nuclear power plants enabled them to remain submerged and virtually undetectable for months at a time. Armed with missiles with very short flight times and accuracy only sufficient to hit cities, and presenting basically nothing to shoot at, these submarines were floating embodiments of deterrence's central message. So much so that their existence, combined with that of intercontinental ballistic missiles (ICBMs), housed in blast-resistant silos, helped to give rise in American to a very pure form of deterrence theory known as mutually assured destruction (MAD). MAD posited that since both sides could endure an attack and still mount a devastating counterblow (presumably against enemy cities), neither side would be foolish enough to initiate what would amount to a suicidal assault.[7] In essence, each side's population was held hostage by the other, a paradoxical but apparently robust inhibitor to war. Thus, for a brief moment, the nuclear arms competition reached a logical plateau which, because of the theoretical unprofitability of preemptive attack, was fairly insensitive to numerical accretions. In theory, at least, the pressure was mainly in the opposite direction, toward reducing the numbers of offensive systems to some level of minimum deterrence.[8]

But, in fact, technology did not move in one direction, and a number of innovations during the sixties and seventies seemed to add weight to war fighting. Some of the most important had to do with missile accuracy. Because the blast area necessary to kill a hard target (a military objective such as a buried command post or a missile silo) increases at a rate determined by πr^2 (with r equal to the distance from the central aim point), progressive gains in accuracy allowed for inordinate decreases in warhead size and yield. Thus, the magnitude of the individual explosions in a projected nuclear exchange decreased dramatically, and after 1965 total megatonnage—though not warheads—declined on both sides.[9] Complementing missile accuracy was the development of satellite technology which allowed for the assembly of very complete lists of military targets, along with precise data on their locations.

Nevertheless, so long as it basically required one missile to kill another missile, the potential of a counterforce attack remained decidedly limited. This, however, would soon change with the evolution of multiple warhead technology—initially to be delivered in a close pattern around a central aim point and later capable of true independent targeting (MIRVs). Now one missile armed with a dozen or even more very accurate, and therefore small, warheads could threaten multiple targets, providing a prospective war fighter a significant strategic multiplier—particularly if he was interested in preemption.

The logical answer to MIRVs was some form of defense against incoming warheads. Because ICBM fields were inherently robust and had to be destroyed one missile at a time, such a system need not be perfect. Also, although a missile defense, if fielded unilaterally, could allow an aggressor to attack and then defeat a weakened adversary's retaliatory strike, so long as such a system was deployed on both sides it could in fact discourage preemption by frustrating precise calculations as to how many enemy missiles might be taken out in an initial assault. Therefore, research and development has been pursued continuously, and since the Soviet Griffon project of the mid-1950s, a succession of antiballistic missile systems have been slated for deployment. Yet with one exception—the Galosh, a limited network around Moscow—the magnitude and difficulty of the task eventually aborted every one.

The problems were indeed formidable. The inherent small size and high speed of the warheads, along with multiple possibilities for decoys and other counter-measures, made them difficult targets to begin with. Then there was the intrinsic vulnerability of the radars and other sensors necessary to detect incoming projectiles. Further complicating the problem was the almost exponential growth in the number of warheads which had to be defended against. Yet ultimately the key difficulty was probably more psychological than technical. The expense and arduousness of antimissile systems demanded that they protect something less abstract than ICBM fields and command facilities. The effective defense of population centers was required for these systems to be sold as truly cost-effective. Yet cities are inherently soft targets, requiring a "leakage" of only one or a very few warheads to do enormous damage. Thus, defensive systems have continued to fall prey to the same basic problem which defeated the Maginot Line. To justify the effort, they must be quite literally perfect and must provide assurances of remaining so over a reasonable length of time in a highly volatile technical environment. So like the roots of the blighted North American chestnut, they remain alive but in perpetual abeyance.

On the whole, war fighting has been and remains a very dubious proposition. There are numerous technical and operational problems. For example, to avoid a piecemeal response, the timing of a preemptive attack would have to insure that all targets were destroyed simultaneously, a task requiring incredible precision and compounded by the fact that no ICBM has ever been used in earnest. A related problem has to do with testing patterns, which on both sides all have been west-to-east or east-to-west. Nonetheless, an actual strike would require warheads and their sensitive guidance systems to fly over the North Pole, an area of extreme magnetism. With weapons whose required accuracy is measured in tens of yards over five thousand miles, magnetic perturbations might be sufficient to render them useless against hard targets.[10]

Viewed from a more general perspective, war-fighting scenarios appear even more sterile and farfetched. For example, since counterforce strategies are based on the preemption of an adversary committed to riding out a strike, they potentially fall prey to the simple doctrinal expedient of ordering the threatened missiles to be launched on warning of attack, leaving only empty silos as targets. Because radars, sensors, and other indications and warning technologies are subject to malfunction, this would be a dangerous and unsavory option.[11] But it serves to illustrate the fragility of war-fighting scenarios, not to mention their narrowness.

For war fighting is essentially about land-based systems. And, in fact, ICBMs in silos, like dreadnoughts, have come to exist primarily to fight themselves. Simply remove them, even unilaterally, and you remove what amounts to a strategic magnet for attack. Mobile systems are presently being considered as an alternative. Yet if they are to be confined to geographically limited military reservations, they will invite barrage assaults, bound to create vast clouds of radioactivity.[12] Still more unrealistic is the tendency of war-fighting strategies to address the submarine-borne retaliatory component as an afterthought, with what amounts to wishful thinking. Hence, it is argued that a preempted strategic player would not use these missiles, useful primarily as "city busters," because they would inevitably call down a devastating counterblow. As a means of dealing more directly with the problem, it has been recently proposed that, at the first signs of aggression, a number of ballistic missile submarines might be destroyed at or near their bases using "nonprovocative" conventional weapons.[13]

To work, all of this would require incredible forbearance and rationality by the party under attack. Whatever the protestations of both sides' strategists, war fighting as it is presently contemplated would be unlikely to involve a few nuclear explosions in isolated quarters.[14] Even the slightest loss of control could plausibly lead to the launching of literally thousands of warheads, aimed at targets virtually everywhere in enemy territory. Even presuming that it will be possible to differentiate between this and an all-out attack, what really would be the difference? Here, ultimately, is the crux of the problem. With each strategic permutation, the number of candidate weapons has risen and the chances of segregating population centers has diminished. Thus even if we totally discount the unproven, but potentially catastrophic possibilities of "nuclear winter," war fighting has choked on its own logic. And in the process it has served the purpose of pure deterrence by forcing the penalties of warfare to such outlandishly high levels that only the truly insane could contemplate it as a viable national option. It has been suggested that this could have the effect of "making the world safe for conventional warfare" by precluding escalation. Yet this line of reasoning fails to consider the possibility of large-scale, long-term radioactive contamination resulting from the incidental or planned destruction of nuclear power plants by conventional weapons.

A retrospective examination of strategic thinking during the first four decades of the nuclear era reveals a sterility and abstract quality which belies its seriousness. Gradually, one comes to the conclusion that these are truly the war plans of the absurd, and that the explanation lies with the means. Arms have literally waged war against war. This is not a new phenomenon. Weapons have always been the unruly ally of organized human conflict, and during the twentieth century, particularly in the Great War, armaments were clearly the major impediment to tactical and strategic success. The difference in the nuclear era is that now they have won. War has been vanquished, but weapons live on.

This can be seen through the deployment patterns themselves. Whatever the strategists thought they were doing, in point of fact, strategy followed weapons and not the reverse. In its essence, operational planning has been an accommodation to technical reality.[15] On the other hand, weapons acquisition has almost uniformly been driven by the rule of symmetry.

This is not to say it followed the lockstep pattern posited by the early proponents of action-reaction. Any societal activity as massive and complex as this one is bound to be affected by a number of factors. Thus, the bureaucratic and political peculiarities of each strategic player can be demonstrated to have placed a distinctive stamp on their respective arsenals. For example, interservice rivalry within the U.S. defense establishment was responsible for several duplicative weapons systems (e.g., the Thor and Jupiter programs),[16] while the proverbial Soviet suspicion of individual initiative and fear of mutiny led to relatively less emphasis on ballistic missile submarines and a greater reliance on land-based ICBMs. It is also true that at the conventional end of the weapons spectrum the urge for symmetry has proved weaker. Therefore, it can be shown that until very recently the paramount force behind Soviet land arms acquisitions has been doctrinal, and not the perceived need to respond to U.S. initiatives.

Nevertheless, at the level of truly strategic weaponry, where parochial service interests and traditions count less, the pattern of interactive symmetry is clear. Consequently, although today's respective arsenals differ considerably in numerical emphasis, virtually every weapons type represented in one can be found in the other.[17] Moreover, this has been generally true of the entire nuclear era, beginning with the Soviet Tu-4, a carbon copy of the American B-29s which crash-landed near Vladivostok during the latter stages of World War II. It is in this context that the series of real and imagined "gaps" (the "bomber gap," the "pre-1960 Soviet missile gap," the "post–Cuban missile crisis U.S. missile gap," and the "window of vulnerability") is best understood—a panic induced by one side perceiving itself outnumbered by the other in a key category of strategic armament. Doubtless, the weapons symbolized certain operational capabilities. Yet it was the arms themselves which were at the heart of the matter; they constituted the essential imbalance. Thus, gaps were not addressed with counters aimed at impinging on the operational capabilities of the subject weapon, but redressed and frequently overcorrected by building more of the same type.

A good example of how this has worked is the latest generation of Soviet land-based ICBMs, particularly the system we call SS-18. It would appear that these very powerful rockets were originally designed for fairly inaccurate and therefore large warheads. When, however, the Soviets later achieved unexpected levels of missile accuracy, they became the recipients of a "throw-weight bonus" allowing them to fill their commodious missile nose cones with large numbers of smaller MIRVs, thereby granting themselves an implied first-strike, counterforce capability. The impetus was not primarily strategic but technological. Nonetheless, the United States perceived a "window of vulnerability" and felt compelled to field a ten-MIRV land-based counterforce system of its own, MX.

So the arms competition lurched forward, confounding the schemes of both the war fighters and those wed to the concept of minimal deterrence and strategic stability. What has emerged is satisfactory to neither camp—two arsenals configured to preempt but thrust into the role of pure deterrent. Because the ability to ride out an attack and the strategic warning time of both have eroded dramatically, peace and safety are poised on a hair trigger. Plainly, this was not an intended outcome but, rather, a logical conclusion of the weapons themselves. There can be no question that it is an exceedingly dangerous situation.

The early eighties was a particularly frightening time. Apparently goaded by Reagan rhetoric and the immanent deployment of the fast-flying Pershing IIs, the Soviets appeared to be edging toward panic. Thus, in a 1982 *Time* interview, Georgi Arbatou warned that "some of our military people and even some members of the Central Committee believe America is preparing for nuclear war."[18] This was clearly not the case. Yet the fact that the Russians could give it credence testifies to the volatility of the environment.

Having apparently come to realize the magnitude of the peril, both sides finally have been driven to eliminate the most dangerous class of missiles, the INFs, in a first modest step toward reestablishing a more stable base of deterrence. Just how far this newfound spirit of cooperation can carry us toward that goal remains to be seen, however. Meanwhile, a great many extremely lethal systems remain, including weapons such as the highly accurate and nearly operational Trident D-5, which in a depressed trajectory mode could mimic the fast-flying INFs.

II

The definitive testimony to the historical importance of nuclear weapons has been their transcendent impact upon geopolitics. While some changes were foreshadowed by earlier events and others may not yet be apparent, it is now clear that the international system operates in a fundamentally different way. The search for hegemony and the extreme personalization of high politics, the most salient political features of the era of the gun, have largely passed from the scene—the former because the goal no longer justifies the danger and the latter because deterrence is vulnerable to individual madness. In their place we now find a mutual, though at times rhetorically grudging, commitment to survival and a leadership cadre hedged in by watchful colleagues. Reaching this point was not automatic, but required considerable evolution of thought and several truly dangerous crises. Nevertheless, the accommodation was rapid in both relative and absolute terms. It required Europe nearly 150 years (from roughly 1500 to 1648) to reach an equivalent level of awareness of the gun's political implications.

Initially, Americans dealt with the bomb from the perspective of their own enormous postwar national power and the presumption of a nuclear monopoly of some considerable duration. Thus, U.S. offers to share the secrets of nuclear energy, culminating in the Baruch Plan, were founded on the implicit hegemonic assumption that the resultant international control of the bomb would faithfully reflect U.S. interests.[19]

Yet it quickly became apparent that a world wrought in our image was not emerging out of the rubble of World War II. For the Soviet Union, though prostrate and bled white, was nonetheless a victor and a repository for a political philosophy which likewise claimed sole possession of the future. To make matters worse, on 3 September 1949 a B-29 flying over the South Pacific detected higher-than-normal radiation levels explicable only in terms of a Russian atomic bomb test. After only four years, the nuclear monopoly had ended. A new kind of world order was taking shape, and Americans would have to accommodate themselves to it.

Probably the most enduring feature of the resulting nuclear standoff is the continuing state of enmity short of massive violence, originally labeled the cold war. Subject to repeated mood swings and variable levels of intensity, this peculiar condition persists to this day. Earlier, when the prospect of war was still considered a real one, geopolitics in the First and Second Worlds tended toward the rigidly bipolar. Now that this perceived danger has receded, political behavior is more fluid. Nonetheless, the functional nature of the coercive structure has not changed fundamentally. History can provide examples of extended political antipathy and bipolarity (Rome and Antiochus III, eighteenth-century France and England), but none in which two such basically antithetical systems avoided war for so long.

Few now question that nuclear weapons are at the root of this unprecedented condition. In essence, they have frozen politics in the developed world. Yet because they have done so by making war impossible, power in its ultimate sense has become unusable. This is the primary frustration of the strong in the nuclear age. For as they grow stronger, they grow, if not exactly weaker, then at least stiffer and more tightly bound to the status quo. Rhetoric aside, each side has a major stake in the stability, even well-being, of its adversary. Further, there are now indications that if Britain and France go through with their latest contemplated nuclear modernization, they may find themselves with sufficient deliverable warheads to be considered serious strategic players. Yet there is no change that, as such, they will fundamentally alter the structure of deterrence—nor will China, for that matter. On the other hand, an essentially demilitarized state such as Japan is now free to pursue its interests, among them very aggressive commercial and technological policies, while being criticized for making weakness into an unfair commercial advantage by escaping the cost of an appropriate military establishment!

Like the military-technical foundation of deterrence, the peace we now know is not the peace either side expected or would have chosen. Unlike hegemony, it is based not on strength but on strength negated. Therefore, it can only effectively enforce itself at the highest level of potential violence. Beneath this superstructure we continue to live in dangerous times. As noted at the outset, full-scale combat remains possible in the Third World, among "the weak and the poor." Similarly, contemporary revolutionaries, like the Spanish guerrillas who confounded Napoleon's conventional forces, have found the natural habitat for a seemingly endless string of wars of national liberation in the power vacuum which exists below the girders of deterrence. While such conflicts are frequently costly to the point of being self-defeating, they remain possible to wage even against superpowers, as Vietnam and Afghanistan testify.

Further compounding matters, domestic tranquility has been increasingly beset by a range of subnational violence running the gamut from revolutionary terrorism to the purely criminal. Here, again, the inability of well-organized societies to cooperate effectively to check such acts further drives home the powerlessness of the powerful. Even the massive increases in criminality and a related societal fascination with individual violence can be attributed to a general perception that accepted mores, the value of human life, and even society itself are transitory in a nuclear environment.

This is not necessarily an idle point. It is not only possible but logical that a political structure founded on the threat of random and ultimate violence should have a corrosive effect upon everything it touches. Despite the sunny assurances of politicians steeped in the lore of mass psychology, there is a darkly cynical side to our lives of which only the very young are unaware. And this is not simply a preoccupation of intellectuals. As William McNeill notes: "Perhaps the most fundamental shift of the postwar decades was a widespread withdrawal of loyalty from constituted public authorities." Nor, he adds, is Soviet society immune.[20] There are clearly other reasons, particularly in the latter instance. Yet the possibility of nuclear disaster and the knowledge that these weapons are part and parcel of the political order raise grave contradictions to common sense which are not easily dismissed by official protestations that weapons are there to defend us. Yet there is also a fundamental awareness that the politicians are only partly to blame, that the arms themselves have played a major role in defining our curious reality. So they loom like a dark, brooding presence, mocking our existence, threatening it—but also, in a paradoxical way, underwriting it. And in the main we have been able to adjust. But we have done so at a price.

III

Finally, it remains to look more closely at our perceptions of contemporary weaponry, what might be done about them, and the future course of arms.

Not surprisingly, nuclear weapons have not proved easy to fit into a frame of reference relevant to human nature, and, in fact, contradictions abound. Never have there been such predatory armaments, such nonpareil tools of genocide. And, appropriately enough, they have evolved in a fashion which keeps them hidden. Like fangs behind jowls and retractable claws, they are buried in silos, banished beneath the sea in submarines, or consigned to "stealth" bombers carefully shielded from the public eye and designed to be invisible to radar. As with predatory arms in general, these weapons are indiscriminate by nature, configured for sudden, not ceremonial, aggression and frankly aimed at killing. Yet this is largely a matter of potential.

In reality, because their own enormous lethality has rendered them virtually useless for actual fighting, nuclear weapons have become preeminently instruments of threat; as such, a strong intraspecific residuum also hangs about them. Accordingly, comparisons of numbers and, in particular, size have assumed an importance that is beyond purely rational explanation. There is something almost touching about Pentagon graphics which illustrate, side by side, the large and numerous models of Soviet ICBMs and the relatively puny Minuteman III and the MX. If such comparisons say virtually nothing about relative capabilities, they do say a good deal about the tenacity with which certain ideas about weapons are held. Also, it is perhaps accidental but still notable that these consummate symbols of potency should so resemble a phallus. Although exaggerated in modern missiles, the phallic nature of numerous weapons seems more than just a coincidental function of aerodynamic and operational necessity, and therefore may be representative of some of the themes which cluster around intraspecific aggression.

No such metaphor is totally consistent, but there is a real sense of profound ambivalence in the surmisable attitudes toward contemporary strategic armaments. On one level there is a perceptible admiration for the technical virtuosity of what

are unquestionably awesome mechanisms, and ones which retain the hitherto favorable profile of relatively large size, high speed, and the capacity for making
loud noises. Yet more manifest is an exaggerated fear and dislike of devices which
strike many as truly evil and obscene. The fact that, with the exception of the
bomber, modern strategic delivery systems are inertially guided and require no
human pilot seems to make them appear still more sinister. This particular automation of random death and destruction can be seen to epitomize the inhuman
ends of the arms competition and the ultimate removal of all vestige of the heroic
from warfare. Moreover, this last impression seems to have had something of a
spillover effect in the area of chemical and biological weapons. For these very
marginal and disliked armaments were the subject of large-scale U.S. and Soviet
deployments during the 1950s and 1960s, apparently in the moral vacuum formed
by the judgment that nuclear weapons had already rendered restraints on arms
acquisitions, even realistic ones, irrelevant.

At the other end of the spectrum of armaments, conventional weapons of
choice—fighter aircraft, armored vehicles, and large surface naval combatants—
are viewed with some of the same mixed feelings but, on the whole, in a much
more positive light. Here, at least, the forces of technology have proved relatively
manageable, and consequently traditional combat ethics and attitudes retain at least
some congruence with reality. Thus, in the United States stylish combat planes
incorporating the latest in materials and techniques retain considerable allure not
only among their users but, if the popularity of films such as *Top Gun* and *Iron
Eagle* are any measure, among large segments of the civilian population. In the
USSR tanks, as noted in the previous chapter, exude much of the same panache,
and their regular appearance along with other armored vehicles in political parades
seems to indicate a real affection and genuine sense of security derived from them.
Meanwhile, in the tradition of Assyria, Rome, Spain, France, and Germany, the
Soviets have taken to the sea with the misplaced enthusiasm of an imperial land
power, creating a fleet for little more than its own sake and as a symbol of their
ambition. It is also apparent that modern conventional arms, particularly aerospace
items, are firmly established in the Third World as symbols of modernity. Consequently, arms imports in developing nations more than doubled between 1975
and 1982, reaching the astonishing figure of thirty-five billion dollars per year.
And although the numbers have dropped slightly since, they continue at levels out
of all proportion to general economic well-being.[21]

This last point is both telling and symptomatic. In whatever economic context,
conventional arms are expensive—more expensive than even their nuclear cousins. Thus, like strategic weaponry, they are almost universally considered a burden. The term *arms race* has come to symbolize a pointless, draining, and highly
dangerous process. Even among those who dispute the accuracy of the label and
the intensity of the phenomenon it represents, there is a general consensus that it
should be brought under closer and more rational supervision. So it is that arms
control has become a major preoccupation.

Recent experience and historical precedent indicate that arms control, particularly the negotiated variety, is an inherently limited process—good at circumscribing weapons deemed suspect and, less overtly, promoting more promising repre-

sentatives of the species, but not as a means to millennial solutions. Thus, the Church Edict of 1139 outlawed the crossbow's use against Christians but not Muslims, much as the Washington Naval Treaty thinned the ranks of dreadnoughts while encouraging aircraft carriers. It is probably no accident that in the nuclear era so much effort has been devoted to limiting antiballistic missile systems, ICBMs, and intermediate-range ballistic missiles, since all are unsatisfactory to either or both sides' strategic conceptions. Defensive systems are not cost-effective; ICBMs are vulnerable; and intermediate-range ballistic missiles are such fast flyers that they encourage strategic players to "use rather than lose" their assets.

In spite of these incentives, contemporary arms control has not lived up to expectations. In part this is because these expectations run so high. It is apparent that arms control negotiations have become as much a symbol as a process. For many, progress here is equated with safety, or at least its promise. This is a delusion. No seriously contemplated arms control agreement would render either side incapable of delivering a devastating nuclear strike. Yet the fantasy of nuclear disarmament and an escape from deterrence, fanned by politicians' daydreams, has enervated the process and stirred disillusionment with tangible but limited accomplishments, such as the termination of atmospheric testing.

Yet it is also true that the process is a faulted one. For one thing, it takes too long. Since the beginning of SALT the length of negotiations and proposed agreements has increased dramatically. Meanwhile, technology has continued to march on, at times undermining or rendering irrelevant settlements over which much diplomatic blood has been shed. Thus, as the negotiators fiddled (with details), MIRVs were deployed. Another suspect feature has been the staffing of both sides' delegations and support bureaucracies with high percentages of professional military men. While they do bring with them necessary expertise and a hardheaded appreciation of arms control's finite potential, this is very much like asking the foxes to guard the henhouse. Moreover, there has been a tendency, particularly in the United States, to allow arms control proposals to be formulated in a competitive interagency environment where parochial bureaucratic interests often outweigh much more important national and international concerns. What has frequently emerged are "line of least resistance" positions advocating new weapons as potential "bargaining chips," supposedly aimed at inducing the other side to compromise so as to preclude deployment but actually addressing internal motives. Experience has shown that if the process is to work well, it requires support not only at the highest levels of government, but major initiatives must originate where there is an ability to keep real objectives in perspective. Finally, the negotiations themselves consistently have been pursued in an excessively adversarial fashion. This is largely the fault of the Soviet Union. Until very recently its obsession with military secrecy, propagandistic proposals, and cynical pursuit of strategic advantage has gravely hindered both the progress and the permanence of arms control. Meanwhile, the United States, having initially shown considerable generosity and been victimized, then approached the bargaining table with extreme caution and skepticism. Lately, there have been indications that both sides are now bargaining in better faith. Yet it is not yet clear if anything fundamental has changed.

To succeed, arms control must be a cooperative endeavor. On the face of it, this may sound naive and far easier to advocate in the abstract than to achieve in reality. Yet the only alternative, unilateral national strategy, has produced dangerous and unsatisfactory results largely because it is inherently adversative. Arms control does offer a potential remedy, but only if both sides truly believe it is in their mutual interest to partake, and do so in this spirit. In certain cases this should be apparent. A class of arms so sui generis and of such marginal military utility as chemical weapons is an obvious candidate for a negotiated ban. Yet because both sides view each other with such suspicion and continue to base their positions on hypothetical scenarios in which chemical weapons might be useful, this has proved impossible. To some degree the problem can be approached through better verification and careful stipulation of the terms of an agreement. Yet in the long run the solution to this and other issues will depend on an acceptance by all major players that in the nuclear era a meaningful weapons-derived advantage is virtually a contradiction in terms. For the risks and potential penalties associated with the exercise of this advantage will always outweigh contemplated gains—so long as the actors remain rational.

Fortunately, there is a clear historical precedent for such an acceptance. With the advent of the gun, Europeans faced the basic problem of controlling arms a great deal more lethal than those which had come before, and, for two centuries after 1648, largely succeeded. They did so through a rigidly enforced limitation of ends which required that all significant players concede that hegemony was simply not worth the price firearms demanded. Qualitative improvements in weaponry virtually ceased, and the gun's use in battle was subject to numerous restraints.

Though the system worked well, it has been largely forgotten. For the most part this is because it was implicit rather than explicit, being based on a number of shared but unspoken assumptions. Yet it could be argued that the example is irrelevant since it was based on a fragmented but conceptually uniform political system, whereas our own situation is dominated by two almost diametrically opposed politico-economic models. Nonetheless, the essential life-and-death issues have not changed. Furthermore, it should be remembered that eighteenth-century armies fought and fought frequently, thereby necessitating that the system of controls endure the heat of battle and the passions of warfare. In this regard our own mechanism of mutually enforced peacefulness should be much less demanding. Arms control is no panacea. But if pursued in a spirit of cooperation, with its limitations clearly in mind, it can be a powerful stabilizing force.

We live on the edge of destruction. The situation is not hopeless, but it does require a realistic appraisal of the possibilities. Presidents Carter and Reagan, along with Mikhail Gorbachev, have all spoken recently of eliminating nuclear weapons. It is difficult to know if this is a product of naïveté or dissimulation. But it is not a realistic possibility. Their inception marked a major watershed in our history, and they now form the bedrock of the international security system. Such changes are not reversed. The real challenge is not nuclear disarmament but learning to live with these weapons. Many are pessimistic. It is argued that while the chances of Armageddon resulting from any particular crisis situation are low, eventually the odds will catch up with us. This is why the example of the Great War has such poignancy. Yet this interpretation seems too negative. In 1914 there were a number of positive incentives for going to war, while the leadership remained largely unaware of the dangers they faced. These conditions do not exist today, although complacency or recklessness could still prove fatal. Nonetheless, each year which passes without nuclear war further reinforces deterrence and increases our safety. Thus, it is reasonable to assume that a century past Hiroshima restraint will be sufficiently integrated into international behavior patterns that the prospect of nuclear holocaust on this planet will be literally unthinkable.

Meanwhile, what of the course of arms? While it does not seem likely that economics or arms controls will bring it to a halt, it may well be that its pace will slow. The emergence of the gun provides some historical perspective. Its early evolution was extremely rapid and involved geniuses of the first order, such as Leonardo and Michelangelo. Yet after a relatively short period of time, development stagnated, and these matters were left to craftsmen. The parallels with the nuclear era are suggestive. The development of the bomb drew a constellation of brilliant physicists including Bohr, Bethe, Kapitsa, and perhaps the greatest theoretician of all time, Albert Einstein. Meanwhile, virtually the entire arsenal of ancillary armaments for the new era was taking shape in Nazi Germany during its last frenzied days. Since 1952 and the first H-bomb test, the course of arms has largely been a matter of refinement, conducted by a legion of anonymous engineers. Nor is there any immediate prospect of major change, except perhaps strategic defense, which also can be traced to the 1950s. So it may well be that we are already upon a plateau.

Yet what is the meaning of this plateau? Why do we have nuclear weapons? These are questions seldom asked and virtually incapable of being answered in any ultimate sense. Yet it is important that they be addressed.

Here, again, the development of the gun is suggestive. It is interesting that its widespread use in Europe coincided with the first major era of colonization and exploration. Sailing forth in their new, roomy, wind-powered warships, themselves made possible by the gun, Europeans discovered a New World and overawed its inhabitants with firearms. Now it is quite possible, even probable, that we are poised on the brink of another great leap outward, this time into space. It is an adventure that is both longed for and particularly unnerving. For the general theory of relativity and the speed of light will insure that those who venture into deep space can never return, at least not in time to see those they leave behind. Traveling through the vast reaches of nothingness and across the face of time, these explorers will be alone in a way no humans have ever been before.

Seen in this context, it is extraordinary that the protestations of the Soviets and many concerned Americans over the necessity of keeping nuclear weapons out of space have been taken so literally. It is true that near earth–orbiting devices do pose some danger to the planet below. Yet, if these weapons have to exist, it seems appropriate that their venue be deep space rather than our small, blue planet. The problem of nuclear arms is one of radioactivity and blasts out of all proportion to the environment. In space, scale and contamination make no difference; there is nothing to poison, nothing to destroy. A central aim of arms control has always been to segregate organized violence from noncombatants. If men come to blows in space, it is hoped, at least, this end will be served.

Then there is the other possibility. As yet there is no indication, beyond that of our own imaginations, that we will meet alien life forms or other hostile forces. Yet man has always conducted his explorations well armed. It seems unlikely that this latest and most frightening venture will be any exception. Whatever our protestations about coming in peace, we should ask ourselves: "When have we ever come in peace?" Man is an imperial beast, born with a weapon in his hand. It may always be so. Perhaps weapons will be needed to preserve our kind. If not, then we can only hope we do not destroy ourselves.

NOTES

Chapter 1 Mechanisms

1. Karl von Clausewitz, *On War,* ed. Michael Howard and Peter Paret (Princeton, N.J. 1976), bk. 1, Ch. 1, 24.

2. Cited in Russell Warren Howe, *Weapons: The International Game of Arms, Money, and Diplomacy* (Garden City, N.Y.: 1980), 731. Quote confirmed by Brzezinski over telephone, November 5, 1987.

3. Robert L. O'Connell, "Putting Weapons in Perspective," *Armed Forces and Society* vol. 9, no. 3 (Spring 1983): 442, 454 n.1.

4. Trevor Depuy has divided his book, *The Evolution of Weapons and Warfare* (Fairfax, Va.: 1984), into "The Age of Muscle," "The Age of Gunpowder," and "The Age of Technological Change." However, he appears to have missed much of the wider significance of the typology and has limited its use to a scheme of organization.

Chapter 2 Dialogue With the Sphinx

1. Jess Stein, ed., *The Random House Dictionary of the English Language: The Unabridged Edition* (New York: 1967), 1616.

2. It appears that chimpanzee flailing, clubbing, and rock throwing also fall into this category. Jane Goodall, *The Chimpanzees of Gombe: Patterns of Behavior* (Cambridge, Mass.: 1986), 550–59.

3. The destruction of plant life has normally been excluded from the study of aggression. This precedent will be followed here for farm and forestry implements except, as noted earlier, where dual utilization is clearly significant.

4. The degree to which intraspecific aggression has been emphasized is illustrated by the fact that several authorities (Roger N. Johnson, *Aggression in Man and Animals* [Philadelphia: 1972], 5–6; Ashley Montagu, ed., *Man and Aggression* [New York: 1973], 6–7; and D. E. Davis, "The Physiological Analysis of Aggressive Behavior," in *Social Behavior and Organization Among Vertebrates,* ed. W. Etkins [New York: 1964] deny the fact that predation is actually a form of aggression at all. Yet the undeniably violent nature of

most predatory acts has led others, notably Edward O. Wilson (*Sociobiology: The New Synthesis* [Cambridge, Mass.: 1975], 243), to the more logical conclusion that predation is indeed a form of aggression. With regard to victims, Wilson (ibid., 94) noted that the youngest and oldest have the lowest reproduction value and are therefore the least subtraction from the exploited population. See also William S. Laughlin, "Hunting: An Integrating Biobehavior System and Its Evolutionary Importance," in *Man the Hunter*, Richard B. Lee and Irven De Vore (Chicago: 1966), 313.

5. Edward O. Wilson, *Sociobiology: The Abridged Edition* (Cambridge, Mass.: 1980), 12.

6. Edward S. Deevey, Jr. "Life Tables for Natural Populations of Animals," *Quarterly Review of Biology* 22 (1947), 283–314.

7. David McFarland, ed., *The Oxford Companion to Animal Behavior* (Oxford: 1981), 461; Johnson, *Aggression in Man and Animals*, 17.

8. McFarland, *Animal Behavior*, 129.

9. E. O. Wilson, *Sociobiology: The New Synthesis*, 242–43; Dolf Zillman, *Hostility and Aggression* (Hillsdale, N.J.: 1979), Ch. 2 and 3.

10. N. Tinbergen, "Fighting and Threat in Animals," *New Biology* 14 (1953): 9–24.

11. Cited in Irenaus Eibl-Eibesfeldt, *The Biology of Peace and War: Man, Animals and Aggression* (New York: 1979), 38.

12. E. O. Wilson, *Sociobiology: Abridged Edition*, 118–19.

13. Ibid., 120–22; Johnson, *Aggression in Man and Animals*, 14–15.

14. McFarland, *Animal Behavior*, 7.

15. I. Eibl-Eibesfeldt, "The Fighting Behavior of Animals," *Scientific American* 205 (1961): 112–22; C. E. Shaw, "The Male Combat Dance of Crotalid Snakes," *Herpetologia* 4 (1948): 137–45.

16. L. Harrison Matthews, "Overt Fighting in Mammals," in *The Natural History of Aggression*, ed. J. D. Carthy and F. J. Ebling (London: 1964), 27; Eibl-Eibesfeldt, *Biology of Peace and War*, 37; McFarland, *Animal Behavior*, 7.

17. Eibl-Eibesfeldt, *Biology of Peace and War*, 38–39.

18. J. P. Scott, "Biological Basis of Human Warfare: An Interdisciplinary Problem," in *Interdisciplinary Relationships in the Social Sciences*, ed. M. Sherif and C. Sherif (Chicago: 1969); Zillman, *Hostility and Aggression*, 90.

19. E. O. Wilson, *Sociobiology: Abridged Edition*, 158–62; Goodall, *Chimpanzees of Gombe*, 341–50; Zillman, *Hostility and Aggression*, 69.

20. Matthews, "Overt Fighting in Mammals," 25–26. See Zillman, *Hostility and Aggression*, 64. S. A. Barnett, "Attack and Defense in Animal Societies," in *Aggression and Defense: Neural Mechanisms and Social Patterns, vol. 5*, ed. C. D. Clemente and D. B. Lindsley (Berkeley, Calif.: 1967), 45.

21. E. O. Wilson, *Sociobiology: Abridged Edition*, Fig. 15-2. (160–161).

22. Konrad Lorenz, *On Aggression*, trans. Marajorie K. Wilson (New York: 1967), 105–12; E. O. Wilson, *Sociobiology: Abridged Edition*, 121–22.

23. R. A. Rappaport, "The Sacred in Human Evolution," *Annual Review of Ecology and Systematics* 2 (1971): 23–44.

24. E. O. Wilson, *Sociobiology: Abridged Edition*, 290–92: Zillman, *Hostility and Aggression*, 96.

25. E. O. Wilson, *Sociobiology: Abridged Edition*, 293.

26. I am grateful to George N. Appel for clarifying the several anthropological perspectives and their shortcomings.

27. The Sphinx, a creature from Greek mythology, asked the question, on pain of

death, of all travelers: "What walks on four legs at dawn, two at noon, and three at dusk?" The answer, which Oedipus guessed, was a man.

28. Clifford Jolly, "The Seed Eaters: A New Model of Hominid Differentiation Based on a Baboon Analogy," *Man* 5, no. 1 (1970): 5–26; E. O. Wilson, *Sociobiology: The New Synthesis*, 565.

29. E. O. Wilson, *Sociobiology: Abridged Edition*, 291–92; Zillman, *Hostility and Aggression*, 96.

30. See Zillman, *Hostility and Aggression*, 96.

31. L. S. B. Leakey, "Development of Aggression as a Factor in Early Human and Pre-Human Evolution," in *Aggression and Defense*, ed. Clemente and Lindsley; R. A. Dart, "The Predatory Transition from Ape to Man," *International Anthropological and Linguistic Review* I (1953): 201–19; Zillman, *Hostility and Aggression*, 96–97.

32. E. O. Wilson, *Sociobiology: The New Synthesis*, 567–68.

33. Glynn L. Isaac, "Traces of Pleistocene Hunters: An East African Example," in *Man the Hunter*, ed. Lee and De Vore, 259; Leakey, "Development of Aggression,"; R. A. Dart, "The Predatory Implemental Technique of Australopithecus," *American Journal of Physical Anthropology* 7 (1949): 1–38, or "The Predatory Transition from Ape to Man," *International Anthropological and Linguistic Review* 1, no. 4 (1953): 201–13; E. O. Wilson, *Sociobiology: The New Synthesis*, 567.

34. Francis Bourliere (1963) (cited in Sherwood L. Washburn and C. S. Lancaster, "The Evolution of Hunting," in *Man the Hunter*, ed. Lee and De Vore, 295) demonstrated that 75 percent of the meat available to hunters in the eastern Congo was elephant, buffalo, and hippopotamus. See also Jared Diamond, "The American Blitzkrieg: A Mammoth Undertaking," *Discover* 8, no. 6 (1987): 86.

35. Diamond, "American Blitzkrieg," 88.

36. L. S. B. Leakey, "A New Fossil Skull from Olduvai," *Nature* 183 (1959): 491–93.

37. Zillman, *Hostility and Aggression*, 99–100; E. O. Wilson, *Sociobiology: The New Synthesis*, 573; Washburn and Lancaster, "Evolution of Hunting," 296.

38. Among others, Richard Leakey and Roger Lewin, (*Origins: What New Discoveries Reveal about the Emergence of Our Species* [New York: 1977]), along with Roger Lowe and Bernard Tower (*Naked Ape or Homo Sapiens?* [New York: 1969]), have suggested that early man might have been without aggressive tendencies before learning to use weapons. On the other hand, Zillman (*Hostility and Aggression*) and Leakey ("Development of Aggression"), while appearing to acknowledge the preexistence of intraspecific aggression, basically ignore its possible influence on weapons development and use.

39. K. R. C. Hall, "Aggression in Monkey and Ape Societies," in *Natural History of Aggression*, ed. Carthy and Ebling, 50–64.

40. Lorenz, *On Aggression*, 233–34.

41. Goodall, *Chimpanzees of Gombe*, 503–34.

42. Zillman, *Hostility and Aggression*, 99.

43. Dart, "Predatory Transition from Ape to Man," 209.

44. M. K. Roper, "A Survey of the Evidence for Intrahuman Killing in the Pleistocene," *Current Anthropology* 10 (1969): 427–59.

45. See, for example, David Pilbeam, "An Idea We Could Live Without: The Naked Ape" in *Man and Aggression*, ed. Montagu, 118–20; E. O. Wilson, *Sociobiology: The New Synthesis*, 137; and Richard B. Lee, "What Hunters Do for a Living, or, How to Make Out on Scarce Resources," in *Man the Hunter*, ed. Lee and De Vore, 30–43.

46. See Eibl-Eibesfeldt, *Biology of Peace and War*, 129–87, for a good summary of

primitive warfare. Also, on the basis of this information it is interesting that, with the exception of weapon use, these raids do not differ significantly in terms of observed behavior from the chimpanzee "war" observed by Jane Goodall.

47. A number of authorities, including Raymond Dart and Dolf Zillman, have carried the predatory origins of violence among men to this logical conclusion by placing heavy emphasis on cannibalism as a strong motivation behind intraspecific violence. If this could be shown to be true, the world of early man might well be perceived as a much more violent place than the preceding paragraphs indicate. Yet there are strong reasons for doubting the validity of this hypothesis. For one thing, cannibalism is something of an aberration among higher organisms. Apart from humans, lions are the only large mammals which on occasion deliberately eat one another. Although cannibalism is thought to have been practiced in all parts of the world where primitive societies existed, in modern times no tribe includes human flesh as a regular part of its diet. When it is reported to have been eaten, the act was described as having taken place under highly controlled conditions. While there is no necessary link to the behavior of early man, in the absence of more compelling evidence, the nature of the contemporary evidence seems to cast doubt on the prevalence of cannibalism among our progenitors.

48. Charles Singer, E. J. Holmyard, and A. R. Hall, eds., *A History of Technology*, vol. 1 (Oxford: 1954), 31, 33, 69.

49. P. Lieberman, "Primate Vocalization and Human Linguistic Ability," *Journal of the Acoustic Society of America,* 44 (1968): 1574–84; P. Lieberman, E. S. Crelin, and D. H. Klatt, "Phonetic Ability and Related Anatomy of the Newborn and Adult Human, Neanderthal Man, and the Chimpanzee," *American Anthropologist* 74, no. 3 (1972): 287–307.

50. Singer, Holmyard, and Hall, eds., *History of Technology,* vol. I, 31.

51. The Plains Indians used the bow against the American bison with considerable success. However, they were greatly aided by the fact that they were mounted on horses, and could thereby inflict multiple wounds.

52. Photographs of cave painting at Morela la Vella in Eibl-Eibesfeldt, *Biology of Peace and War,* 128. Original H. Kühn, *Kunst und Kultur der Vorzeit. Das Paläolithikum* (Berlin: 1929).

53. Ibid., 170–71.

54. Zillman, *Hostility and Aggression,* 100–104; Sally Carrighan, "War Is Not in Our Genes," in *Man and Aggression,* ed. Montagu, 134–35; Geoffrey Gorer, "Ardrey on Human Nature: Animals, Nations, Imperatives," in *Man and Aggression,* ed. Montagu, 163.

Chapter 3 Genesis

1. Quincy Wright, *A Study of War,* vol. 1 (Chicago: 1942), 32–35, 39.

2. As Stanislav Andreski notes ("Origins of War," in *The Natural History of Aggression,* ed. Carthy and Ebling, 130), there must always be considerable imprecision surrounding this topic. However, the defensive fortifications at Jericho have been accurately dated as having been built somewhat before 7000 B.C. Yigael Yadin, *The Art of Warfare in Biblical Lands: In Light of Archaeological Study,* vol. 1 (New York: 1963), 34; Arthur Ferrill, *The Origins of War: From the Stone Age to Alexander the Great* (London: 1985), 28. It can be further assumed that Jericho was one of the first such sites and that war's spread was largely subsequent to this time.

3. Jacob Bronowski, *The Ascent of Man* (Boston: 1973), 86–88. Ferrill (*Origins of War,* 28–29) raises the possibility that urban fortification may have preceded agriculture, with populations gravitating to defensible spots first for safety and then resorting to eco-

nomic means suitable for settled habitation. While Ferrill does make the point that the evidence does not allow anyone to say with certainty that agriculture was introduced before the walls, Bronowski's sequence of events seems more logical and is therefore more convincing.

4. Arnold J. Toynbee, *A Study of History,* vol. 1 (London: 1955), 305–306; Karl Wittfogel, *Oriental Despotism: A Comparative Study of Total Power* (New Haven, Conn.: 1957), 34.

5. Yadin, *Art of Warfare,* vol. 1, 33–34.

6. Singer, Holmyard, and Hall, eds., *History of Technology,* vol. 1, 600, 614–15: Yadin, *Art of Warfare,* vol. 1, 45, 60.

7. Singer, Holmyard, and Hall, eds., *History of Technology,* vol. 1, 592; Yadin, *Art of Warfare,* vol. 1, 40.

8. Singer, Holmyard, and Hall, eds., *History of Technology,* vol. 1, 594.

9. Stanislav Andreski, *Military Organization and Society* (Berkeley, Calif.: 1968), 40–41, 88.

10. Ibid., 95.

11. Wittfogel, 27, 34, 61. Karl Wittfogel, in his book *Oriental Despotism,* maintains the reverse—that the regimentation necessary to construct the irrigation works of so-called hydraulic societies spilled over into the creation of armed forces. This, however, seems to ignore the need for a considerable coercive capacity in order to recruit the labor for irrigation projects in the first place. More likely, it was an interactive process, with military and civilian regimentation reinforcing each other. See also Lewis Mumford, *The Pentagon of Power* (New York: 1964), 29–30, 99.

12. On the predominance of military affairs in ancient societies and the frequency of war, see Yvon Garlan, *War in the Ancient World: A Social History* (London: 1975), 15–16. For an example of an approach based on demographics, see William McNeill, *The Pursuit of Power: Technology, Armed Force, and Society since A.D. 1000* (Chicago: 1982), 213–15, 308–15.

13. Richard Humble, *Warfare in the Ancient World* (London: 1980), 13–15.

14. Ibid., 15.

15. William Ellery Leonard, *Gilgamesh: Epic of Old Babylonia* (New York: 1934), ix.

16. "Gilgamesh and the Land of the Living," lines 54–55, 88 cited in James Pritchard, *Ancient Near Eastern Texts: Relating to the Old Testament* (Princeton, N.J.: 1955), 48–49.

17. "Gilgamesh and the Land of the Living," lines 56–58, op. cit. Pritchard, *Ancient Near Eastern Texts,* 48.

18. "Gilgamesh and Agga," lines 1–40, op. cit. Pritchard, *Ancient Near Eastern Texts,* 45–46.

19. The "Stele of Vultures" from Yadin, *Art of Warfare,* vol. 1, 134–35. For those overlooking the Sumerian phalanx see, for example, Toynbee, *Study of History,* vol. 1, annex I, 428; R. Ernest Depuy and Trevor N. Depuy, *The Encyclopedia of Military History* (New York: 1970).

20. Andreski, *Military Organization and Society,* 87–88, 98–99.

21. "The Legend of Sargon," *Cuneiform Texts from Babylonian Tablets in the British Museum* (London: 1896), 42–43; "Texts from the Beginnings to the First Dynasty of Babylon," cited in Pritchard, *Ancient Near Eastern Texts,* 266–267.

22. Pritchard, *Ancient Near Eastern Texts,* 268.

23. Samuel Noah Kramer, *The Sumerians: Their History, Culture, and Character* (Chicago: 1963), 60–61; Humble, *Warfare in the Ancient World,* 19.

24. Humble, *Warfare in the Ancient World,* 19–20.

25. Andreski, *Military Organization and Society,* 100.

26. Yadin, *Art of Warfare*, vol. 1. 47, 150.

27. See, for example, Garlan, *War in the Ancient World*, 118; Humble, *Warfare in the Ancient World*, 28–29.

28. Garlan, *Warfare in the Ancient World*, 118. See Yadin, *Art of Warfare*, vol. 1, 193, 240–41 for graphic representation of fighting chariots.

29. See, for example, Yadin's description of the Battle of Kadesh, *Art of Warfare*, vol. 1, 103–10.

30. Cited in Kramer, *Sumerians*, 63–64.

31. A. T. Olmstead, *The History of Assyria* (New York: 1923), 648–49.

32. Humble, *Warfare in the Ancient World*, 24.

33. Olmstead, *History of Assyria*, 604; Yadin, *Art of Warfare*, vol. 2, 293.

34. Yadin, *Art of Warfare*, vol. 2, 295.

35. Ibid., vol. 2, 295–96; Olmstead, *History of Assyria*, 605; Humble, *Warfare in the Ancient World*, 27.

36. Yadin, *Art of Warfare*, vol. 2, 299; Olmstead, *History of Assyria*, 604.

37. Cavalry is first depicted in the reliefs of the northwestern palace of Ashurnasir-pal (883–859 B.C.) (see Yadin, *Art of Warfare*, vol. 2, 381–83), though experiments may have preceded this date considerably. McNeill (*Pursuit of Power*, 15) hypothesizes that nomads may not have come first, but that the Assyrians may well have introduced military horse riding. He bases this argument solely on physical evidence (i.e., the Assyrians provided the first depiction of horsemen). While this is impossible to refute, the literalist approach is somewhat illogical here since nomads would have far greater use for swift horses and probably had little access to materials to make chariots, assuming they would want them.

38. See plates depicting Assyrian cavalry (Yadin, *Art of Warfare*, vol. 2, 382–85, 402, 456–59).

39. John Childs, *Armies and Warfare in Europe 1648–1789* (Manchester, Eng.: 1982), 144–45.

40. Yadin, *Art of Warfare*, vol. 1, 20, 147. Yadin is able to show evidence for a very primitive battering ram ca. 1900 B.C. in Egypt, yet its later disappearance argues that it was not well enough developed to be truly effective (70, 159).

41. Yadin, *Art of Warfare*, vol. 2, 314, 388–91.

42. Cited in Olmstead, *History of Assyria*, 97. See also similar acts in annals of Ashur-nasir-pal's "Expedition to Carchemesh and Lebanon," Pritchard, *Ancient Near Eastern Texts*, 276.

43. Olmstead, *History of Assyria*, 207.

44. Humble, *Warfare in the Ancient World*, 33.

45. 1 Sam. 8:11.

46. This translation cited in Olmstead, *History of Assyria*, 642. The translation in the King James Bible, Nah. 3:7, reads: "Nineveh is laid waste, who will bemoan her?"

Chapter 4 The Greeks

1. Xenophon, *The Anabasis* (London: 1918), 3.4.10–12.

2. Ibid., 1.7.18–21, 1.10.4, 11; N. L. G. Hammond, *A History of Greece to 322 BC* (Oxford: 1959), 451.

3. M. I. Finley, *The World of Odysseus* (New York: 1965), 19, 126–27; F. E. Adcock, *The Greek and Macedonian Art of War* (Berkeley, Calif.: 1957), 2.

4. Jasper Griffin, *Homer* (Oxford: 1980), 1; Finley, *World of Odysseus*, 3.

5. Homer, *Iliad*, trans. Richmond Lattimore (Chicago: 1951), 3.70.

6. See Yadin, *Art of Warfare*, vol. 1, 172–73.

7. 1 Sam. 17.

8. Homer *Iliad* 3.380–82, 4.445–49.

9. Ibid., 4.121–236.

10. See, for example, *Iliad* 8.174, 11.286, 5, 13.5, 15.509–10.

11. Ibid., 21.108.

12. Ibid., 13.130–35.

13. Ibid., 18.478–615.

14. Ibid., 2.385–87.

15. Ibid., 13.262–63.

16. Hammond, *History of Greece,* 62.

17. Sun Tzu, *The Art of War,* ed. Lionel Giles (Taipei: 1946), xlii–xlix.

18. See, for example, Thucydides, *The History of the Peloponnesian War,* trans. Richard Crawley (Chicago: 1952), 3.104.

19. Garlan, *War in the Ancient World,* 18–24.

20. Finley, *World of Odysseus* 49, 54–55; G. S. Kirk, *The Iliad: A Commentary,* vol. 1, Cambridge, Eng.: 1985), 336.

21. Hammond, *History of Greece,* 81, 98.

22. The persistent reference to *hippeis* (horsemen of the wealthiest class) in later census rolls is one such example. See Andreski, *Military Organization and Society,* 44–45; Fustel de Coulanges, *La Cite Antique* (Paris: 1923), 326. P. A. C. Greenhalgh's conclusion (*Early Greek Warfare: Horsemen and Chariots in the Homeric and Archaic Ages* [Cambridge, Eng.: 1973], 146–51) that these horsemen were actually mounted heavy infantry does not really contradict this political point, although it does blur somewhat the lines between hoplite and aristocrat.

23. Hammond, *History of Greece,* 110, plate IV; A. Andrews, *The Greek Tyrants* (New York: 1963), 31.

24. Humble, *Warfare in the Ancient World,* 170; Charles Oman, *A History of the Art of War in the Middle Ages: A.D. 378–1278,* vol. 2 (London: 1924), 257.

25. Adcock, *Greek and Macedonian Art of War,* 4.

26. Garlan, *War in the Ancient World,* 120.

27. Adcock, *Greek and Macedonian Art of War,* 16.

28. Hammond, *History of Greece,* 160, 299; Andrews, *Greek Tyrants,* 34.

29. Archilochus, frag. 6, E. Diehl, *Anthologia Lyrica Graeca* (Leipzig: 1925).

30. Garlan, *War in the Ancient World,* 61–63; W. K. Pritchett, *The Greek State at War: Part II* (Berkeley, Calif.: 1974), 272–73; Adcock, *Greek and Macedonian Art of War,* 7, 57.

31. Herodotus, *The Histories,* trans. Aubrey de Selincourt (Baltimore: 1950), 7.9.417–18.

32. Polybius 29.17.

33. Adcock, *Greek and Macedonian Art of War,* 10–11. On Spartan composure, see J. F. Lazenby, *The Spartan Army* (Warminister, Eng.: 1985), 4.

34. Adcock, *Greek and Macedonian Art of War,* 8.

35. Herodotus *Histories* 1.82.45–46. See also Garlan, *War in the Ancient World,* 26–31.

36. Strabo 10.1.12, 448. There is also a passage in Polybius, 13.3.2–7, to the same effect.

37. Yadin, vol. 2, 340–41.

38. See Thucydides, 1.5.350; Finley, *World of Odysseus,* 67.

39. Homer, *Odyssey* trans. Richmond Lattimore (New York: 1967), 8.30–55, 11.5, 12.165–180; Homer, *Iliad* 14.1–90.

40. Hammond, *History of Greece,* 109. See also plate III A.

41. Lionel Casson, *The Ancient Mariners: Seafarers and Sea Fighters of the Mediterranean in Ancient Times* (New York: 1959), 83–84.

42. J. S. Morrison and J. F. Coates, *The Athenian Trireme: The History and Reconstruction of an Ancient Greek Warship* (Cambridge, Eng.: 1986), 8 n. 3, 25, 35.

43. J. S. Morrison and R. T. Williams, *Greek Oared Ships: 900–322 B.C.* (Cambridge, Eng.: 1968) 29, 38–40. Lionel Casson, *Ships and Seamanship in the Ancient World* (Princeton: 1971), 53–56.

44. Although the debate over the nature of the trireme goes back to the fifth century A.D., its modern incarnation can be attributed largely to the vigorous pen of W. W. Tarn. In 1905 ("The Greek Warship," in *Ancient Ships,* ed. Cecil Torr (Chicago: 1964), 154–95) he argued that previous models of triremes employing rowers on three levels—and the so-called Lenormant relief upon which they were based—were all false interpretations since they required oars of differing lengths for each level. Not only were such sweeps impossible to row together, but it was known absolutely that the oars of the three types of trireme rowers were of the same length. As an alternative, Tarn suggested a one-level ship with the crew arranged in echelin on the order of a Venetian galley but with shorter oars. This, however, when reconstructed by Cook and Richardson (in *Ancient Ships,* ed. Torr, 196–206), proved too long to fit into excavated Athenian ship sheds and still retained oars of differing lengths. Nonetheless, Tarn's work stimulated thought and a gradual refinement of hypothetical designs. In 1940, Sinclair Morrison (Morrison and Coates, *Athenian Trireme,* xiv) was able to demonstrate a three-level design which, by employing an outrigger, accommodated oars all of the same length. Subsequently, J. F. Coates and J. S. Morrison conducted an increasingly complex series of experiments with larger and larger sections of such a trireme design. This process culminated in the construction of a full-sized three-level trireme by the "Trireme Trust" and its successful test in the summer of 1987. This would seem to end the debate.

45. Torr, ed., *Ancient Ships,* 5.

46. Adcock, *Greek and Macedonian Art of War,* 33–35; Morrison and Coates, *Athenian Trireme,* 109, 115–16.

47. Casson, *Ancient Mariners,* 99–100; Morrison and Coates, *Athenian Trireme,* 161.

48. A tradition cited by Clement of Alexandria states that Phoenicians from Sidon invented the trireme. Cited in Donald Harden, *The Phoenicians* (New York: 1962), 125.

49. Morrison and Coates, *Athenian Trireme,* 157.

50. Garlan, *War in the Ancient World,* 17.

51. C. Hignett (*Xerxes Invasion of Greece* [Oxford: 1963], 267ff.) states that there is no agreement among modern sources as to the size of the Persian army other than that it was at least sixty thousand. Herodotus *Histories.* 7.89.444, 7.184–86.480–81.

52. Hammond, *History of Greece,* 466–67; Carleton L. Brownson, "Introduction to the Anabasis," in *Anabasis* (London: 1918), xii.

53. Hammond, *History of Greece,* 345–47.

54. Thucydides, 2.83–84.409–10.

55. Ibid., 2.58, 76.

56. Ibid., 4.100.

57. Diodorus Siculus 14.51–53.

58. Thucydides 7.36; Morrison and Coates, *Athenian Trireme,* 167–68.

59. W. W. Tarn, *Hellenistic Military and Naval Developments* (Cambridge, Eng.: 1930), 130. Morrison and Coates (*Athenian Trireme,* 46) note that Aristotle attributed the invention of the "four" to the Carthaginians, while Diodorus (14.41–42) credits Dionysius with the creation of the "five."

60. Thucydides 4.40.457.

61. J. K. Anderson, *Military Theory and Practice in the Age of Xenophon* (Berkeley, Calif.: 1970), 26, 41–42, 125–26, 138. It strikes me that Anderson takes a somewhat extreme position as to the extent and rapidity with which hoplites shed their armor and even helmets. The general thrust of his argument, however, seems well supported by the evidence. See also Humble, *Warfare in the Ancient World*, 149.

62. Hammond, *History of Greece*, 534–35.

63. Ibid.

64. Justin 7.5.2; Humble, *Warfare in the Ancient World*, 169; Hammond, *History of Greece*, 537.

65. Adcock, *Greek and Macedonian Art of War*, 26; Hammond, *History of Greece*, 536.

66. Humble, *Warfare in the Ancient World*, 170.

67. Ibid., 171.

68. Hammond, *History of Greece*, 538, 561–62, 564–65.

69. Ibid., 570.

70. W. W. Tarn, *Alexander the Great: Narrative* vol. 1 (Cambridge, Eng.: 1948), 7.

71. Xenophon *The Anabasis* 1.8.17–20; Hammond, *History of Greece*, 451.

72. Tarn, *Alexander the Great*, 10–12, Hammond, *History of Greece*, 603.

73. Tarn, *Alexander the Great*, 16, 27, 50; John W. Snyder, *Alexander the Great* (New York: 1966), 45, 73, 119.

74. Tarn, *Alexander the Great*, 16; Snyder, *Alexander the Great*, 44–45.

75. This view of Alexander is most evident in the otherwise excellent work of W. W. Tarn. See, in particular, W. W. Tarn, "Alexander the Great and the Unity of Mankind," in *Alexander the Great: The Main Problems*, ed. G. T. Griffith (Cambridge, Eng.: 1966), 243–306.

76. Hammond, *History of Greece*, 570.

77. Tarn, *Alexander the Great*, 7.

78. Ibid., 40.

79. Tarn, *Alexander the Great*, 115; W. W. Tarn, *Hellenistic Civilization* (Cleveland: 1952), 14–15.

80. Andreski (*Military Organization and Society*, 159) notes that the replacement of the upper stratum is typical of oriental, particularly Chinese, political upheavals.

81. Snyder, *Alexander the Great*, 87; Tarn, *Hellenistic Military and Naval Developments*, 112, 105.

82. Tarn, *Hellenistic Military and Naval Developments*, 119.

83. Adcock, *Greek and Macedonian Art of War*, 54.

84. Tarn, *Hellenistic Civilization*, 6; Tarn, *Alexander the Great* 134–35, 137, 147.

85. Tarn, *Hellenistic Civilization*, 14, 47, 58.

86. Tarn, *Hellenistic Military and Naval Developments*, 24.

87. Ibid., 61.

88. Ibid., 73, 78.

89. Stobaeus *Flor* 4.13.46.

90. McNeill, *Pursuit of Power*, 69–70 n.4.

91. E. W. Marsden, *Green and Roman Artillery: Technical Treatises* (Oxford: 1971), 47–49; Tarn, *Hellenistic Military and Naval Developments*, 104, 113–14.

92. Tarn, *Hellenistic Military and Naval Developments*, 117.

93. Ibid., 118; Marsden, *Greek and Roman Artillery*, 153; A. R. Hall, "Military Technology," in *A History of Technology*, vol. 2 (Oxford: 1959), 713.

94. McNeill, *Pursuit of Power*, 36 n. 27.

95. Lionel Casson, *Ships and Seamanship in the Ancient World* (Princeton, N.J.: 1971), 103–4.

96. Diodorus Siculus 19.62, 20.49.

97. Memnon 13; F. Jacoby, *Die Fragmente der griechischen Historiker no. 434, 8.5.* vol. 3B (Leiden: 1958), 344.

98. Athenaeos 5.36.

99. Casson, *Ships and Seamanship,* 108–112.

100. Tarn, *Hellenistic Military and Naval Developments,* 110–11; Plutarch *Demetrius* bk. 21.

101. Tarn, *Hellenistic Military and Naval Developments,* 28.

102. Tarn, *Hellenistic Civilization,* 22.

103. Livy 31.34.4–6.

Chapter 5 Rome

1. Ancient casualty figures are notoriously inaccurate. Nonetheless, the nature of the weapon, the wounds it inflicted, and the state of medical technology all argue that the toll of the *gladius* was enormous.

2. Flavius Vegetius Renatus, "The Military Institutions of the Romans" in *The Roots of Strategy,* ed. Major Thomas R. Phillips (Harrisburg, Pa.: 1940), 75, 91.

3. Garlan, *Warfare in the Ancient World,* 119; Andreski *Military Organization and Society,* 54.

4. Lawrence Keppie, *The Making of the Roman Army: From Republic to Empire* (Totowa, N.J.: 1984), 17.

5. Livy 1.43.

6. H. H. Scullard, *A History of the Roman World from 753 to 146* (London: 1953), 47.

7. Ibid., 74; G. R. Watson, *The Roman Soldier* (Ithaca, N.Y.: 1969), 89.

8. Livy 5.38; Diodorus Siculus 14.113, 114; Plutarch *Camillus* 18.

9. Livy 5.42.

10. Scullard, *History of the Roman World,* 96–100.

11. Keppie, *Making of the Roman Army,* 21–22; Scullard, *History of the Roman World,* 128–29.

12. Keppie, *Making of the Roman Army,* 19; F. E. Adcock, *The Roman Art of War under the Republic* (Cambridge, Mass.: 1940), 8–11.

13. Harry Pratt Judson, *Caesar's Army* (New York: n.d.), 32–35; Garlan, *Warfare in the Ancient World,* 126; H. M. D. Parker, *The Roman Legions* (Oxford: 1928).

14. Cornelius Cossus won the *spolia opima* by killing Tolumnius, Prince of Veii (Livy 4.20).

15. Scullard, *History of the Roman World,* 338; Dupuy, *The Evolution of Weapons and Warfare,* 17.

16. Humble, *Warfare in the Ancient World,* 189; Adcock, *Roman Art of War,* 8–12; Depuy, *Evolution of Weapons,* 19.

17. Vegetius, in *Roots of Strategy,* pp. 83–84.

18. Livy, summary of lost bk. 16. We also know from Valerius Maximus (2.3.2) that in 105 B.C. Rutilius introduced instructors from the gladiatorial school of C. Aurelius Scaurus to train his troops in advanced swordplay. Marius was said to be so impressed by troops trained by Rutilius that he preferred them to his own.

19. Vegetius, *Roots of Strategy,* pp. 85–86.

20. Dupuy, *Evolution of Weapons,* 19.

21. In large part the terrible Roman defeats at Cannae and Carrhae were caused by this very failing.

22. Humble, *Warfare in the Ancient World,* 189.

23. Edward Luttwak, *The Grand Strategy of the Roman Empire* (Baltimore: 1976), 16. Watson, *(Roman Soldier,* 13) set the total legionary strength at 160,000, excluding the Praetorian Guards and urban cohorts.

24. Plutarch *Pyrrhus* 16.5, cited in Scullard, *History of the Roman World,* 12, 446.

25. Livy 22.19–20.

26. See Adcock's comments on the psychological overtones of castrametation (*Roman Art of War,* 13–16); see also Luttwak, *Grand Strategy of the Roman Empire,* 56–57.

27. Scullard, *History of the Roman World,* 80.

28. Livy 2.17 (on Rome's siege prowess); Andreski, *Military Organization and Society,* 77.

29. Livy 5.5.8, 19–20.

30. B. H. Warmington, *Carthage* (Baltimore: 1960), 144–49.

31. Scullard, *History of the Roman World,* 136–37.

32. Harden, *The Phoenicians,* 130.

33. Polybius 1.20. Hundreds of years before, the Assyrians fought a naval battle almost immediately upon reaching the Asia Minor coast and the sea for the first time.

34. Polybius 1.20–21; Scullard, *History of the Roman World,* 148; Warmington, *Carthage,* 185.

35. T. Frank, *Cambridge Ancient History,* vol. 8 (Cambridge, Eng.: 1926–32), 685. Warmington (191) places Roman and allied losses at ninety-five thousand.

36. Scullard, *History of the Roman World,* 155–56. Warmington (*Carthage,* 195) notes that in the year 247 a census of those living in the city of Rome showed that over the previous twenty years the number of adult males had decreased by fifty thousand.

37. While Carthaginian casualties are even less certain, Warmington (*Carthage,* 177) states that the combined total was greater than that of any war to date. Polybius (1.63) also called it "the longest most continuous and most severely contested war known to us in history." He puts Roman losses at seven hundred quinqueremes and those of the Carthaginians at five hundred.

38. Polybius 3.62.

39. Ibid., 3.114.

40. Arnold J. Toynbee, *Hannibal's Legacy: The Hannibalic War's Effects on Roman Life,* vol. 1 (Oxford: 1965), vi–vii.

41. Keppie, *Making of the Roman Army,* 63–64.

42. Watson, *Roman Soldier,* 58–59; Keppie, *Making of the Roman Army,* 66–67; Humble, *Warfare in the Ancient World,* 207.

43. Ronald Syme, *The Roman Revolution* (Oxford: 1939), 2, 53–54, 60.

44. Ibid., 296–97.

45. Luttwak, *Grand Strategy of the Roman Empire,* 2.

46. For Augustus's warning against further conquest, see Tacitus *Annals* 2.46; Ronald Syme, *Cambridge Ancient History,* vol. 10, 353.

47. Watson, *Roman Soldier,* 37, 39.

48. Josephus 3.5.

49. Cited in H. H. Scullard, *From the Gracchi to Nero: A History of Rome from 133 B.C. to A.D. 68* (London: 1970), 267.

50. Edward Gibbon, *The Decline and Fall of the Roman Empire,* vol. 1 (New York: 1932), ch. 2, particularly pp. 38, 50.

51. Luttwak, *Grand Strategy of the Roman Empire,* 128.

52. T. Pekary, "Studien zur romischen Wahrungs und Finanzgeschichte von 161 bis 235 n. Chr.," *Historia* 8 (1959): 472–73; Luttwak, *Grand Strategy of the Roman Empire,* 16.

53. Mikhail Rostovtzeff, *The Social and Economic History of the Roman Empire* (Oxford: 1926), xi–xiii, 353–55, 413.

54. Luttwak, *Grand Strategy of the Roman Empire,* 121; Watson, *Roman Soldier,* 141.

55. A. R. Hall, "Military Technology," 703, 719.

56. Baron de Jomini, *The Art of War,* trans. G. H. Mendell (Westport, Conn.: 1971), 63.

57. E. A. Thompson, ed. and trans., *A Roman Reformer and Inventor: Being the New Text of the Treatise De Rebus Bellicus* (Oxford: 1952), 22.

58. Vegetius, *Roots of Strategy,* 75.

Chapter 6 Eques

1. F. E. Adcock, *Marcus Crassus, Millionaire* (Cambridge, Eng.: 1966), 48–49, 52–54; E. G. Heath, *Archery: A Military History* (London: 1980), 42.

2. Plutarch *Crassus* 31.

3. H. M. D. Parker, *A History of the Roman World: From* A.D. *138 to 337* (London: 1958), 18–20, 69–70.

4. Toynbee, *Study of History* (London: 1934–54), vol. 5, 240, vol. 7, 95–96, 111, 199, vol. 8, 443.

5. Vic Hurley, *Arrows Against Steel: The History of the Bow* (New York: 1975), 151, 201.

6. Tarn, *Hellenistic Military and Naval Developments,* 73–74; Plutarch *Crassus* 24.

7. Tarn, *Hellenistic Military and Naval Developments,* 79.

8. Tacitus *Histories* 1.79; Plutarch *Crassus* bk. 25.

9. Lynn White, Jr., *Medieval Technology and Social Change* (Oxford: 1962), 7–9.

10. Tarn, *Hellenistic Military and Naval Developments,* 76, 91–92.

11. John Keegan, *The Face of Battle* (New York: 1976), 95, maintains that a large hunter-type horse with an armored rider and saddle (250 pounds), could make twelve to fifteen miles per hour. It is reasonable to assume that an infantryman with half armor could make around five to seven miles per hour.

12. D. J. A. Ross, "L'originalité de 'Turoldus': Le maniement de la lance," *Cahiers de civilization médiévals* 6 (1963): 127–38; White, *Medieval Technology,* 1–38 and nn. 135–53; H. Brunner, "Der Reiterdienst und die an Fange des Lehnwesens," *Zeltschrift der Savigny-Stiftung fur Rechtsgeschichte,* German Abt., 8 (1887): 1–38. Andreski (*Military Organization and Society,* 58) also sees the stirrup as critical.

13. For critiques see J. R. Strayer, "Feudalism in Western Europe," in *Feudalism in History,* ed. R. Coulborn (Princeton, N.J.: 1956), 15–25; Philippe Contamine, *War in the Middle Ages,* trans. Michael Jones (Oxford: 1984), 181–84; John Beeler, *Warfare in Feudal Europe: 730–1200* (Ithaca, N.Y.: 1971), 10–11.

14. White, *Medieval Technology,* 27–28; Contamine, *War in the Middle Ages,* 183.

15. White, *Medieval Technology,* 27; Oman, *Art of War in the Middle Ages:* A.D. *378–1278,* vol. 1, 126–29; Contamine, *War in the Middle Ages,* 184–88.

16. Beeler, *Warfare in Feudal Europe,* 25–26.

17. White, *Medieval Technology,* 29.

18. Georges Duby, *The Chivalrous Society* (London: 1977), 6.

19. Oman, *Art of War in the Middle Ages:* A.D. *378–1278,* vol. 1, 104.

20. Michel Bur, "The Social Influence of the Motte-and-Bailey Castles," *Scientific*

American, vol. 248, no. 5 (May 1983), 132 ff. Contamine, *War in the Middle Ages,* 31. William Anderson (*Castles of Europe from Charlemagne to the Renaissance* [New York: 1970], 51) provides a somewhat different interpretation and dates the motte-and-bailey technique considerably later, at least among the Normans.

21. Charles T. Wood, *The Age of Chivalry* (New York: 1970), 45, 47; Marc Block, *Feudal Society* (London: 1961), 39.

22. R. Allen Brown, Michael Prestwich, and Charles Coulson *Castles: A History and Guide* (Poole, Eng.: 1980), 14.

23. A. W. Brogger and Haakon Shetelig, *The Viking Ships* (Oslo, Norway: 1951), 224, 226, 230.

24. Oman, *Art of War in the Middle Ages:* A.D. *378–1278,* vol. 1, 92, 96–97, 105, 108.

25. White, *Medieval Technology,* 30; Duby, *Chivalrous Society,* 75–76, 86.

26. F. M. Stenton, *First Century of English Feudalism* (Oxford: 1932), 131.

27. White, *Medieval Technology,* 32.

28. Duby, *Chivalrous Society,* 115–18.

29. Ibid., 119.

30. Sidney Painter, *William Marshal: Knight Errant, Baron and Regent of England* (Baltimore: 1933), 58–59; Georges Duby, *William Marshal: The Flower of Chivalry* (Boston: 1986), 100–101.

31. Duby, *William Marshal,* 73–74; Painter, *William Marshal,* vii.

32. Duby, *William Marshal,* 70. To back up this point, Contamine (*War in the Middle Ages,* 256) cites a war waged for more than a year after the murder of Count Charles the Good in which about one thousand knights were involved but only seven were killed, almost all accidentally.

33. White, *Medieval Technology,* 32.

34. Gerard J. Brault, ed., *The Song of Roland: An Analytic Edition,* vol. 2 (University Park, Pa.: 1978), 2304–5, 2316–17.

35. *The Poem of the El Cid,* trans. Rita Hamilton and Janet Perry (Manchester, Eng.: 1975), First Cantar, 43 (p. 65).

36. *The Romance of Tristan and Iseult* (New York: 1945), 65, 148.

37. Painter, *William Marshal,* 162, 165–166.

38. Duby, *Chivalrous Society,* 126–27.

39. Ibid., 130–31.

40. Charles Oman, *The Art of War in the Middle Ages:* A.D. *378–1515* (Ithaca, N.Y.: 1953), 31, 47–53; Vic Hurley, *Arrows against Steel* 127–130; Dupuy, *Evolution of Weapons,* 52–57.

41. E. J. King, *The Knights Hospitallers in the Holy Land* (London: 1931); Contamine, *War in the Middle Ages,* 74–77.

42. Dupuy, *Evolution of Weapons,* 64.

43. Ibid.

44. Ibid.

45. Contamine, *War in the Middle Ages,* 71; Dupuy, *Evolution of Weapons,* 65; Robert Hardy, *Longbow: A Social and Military History* (Cambridge, Eng.: 1976), 35.

46. Kate Norgate, *Richard the Lion Heart* (New York: 1924), 326–27.

47. Oman, *Art of War in the Middle Ages:* A.D. *378–1515,* 67; Beeler, *War in Feudal Europe,* 44.

48. Oman, *Art of War in the Middle Ages:* A.D. *378–1515,* 70; Beeler, *Warfare in Feudal Europe,* 44–45. For the recourses of those under siege, see Norgate, *Richard the Lion Heart,* 325–26.

49. Dupuy, *Evolution of Weapons*, 69–70.

50. Oman, *Art of War in the Middle Ages:* A.D. *378–1515*, 55; Dupuy, *Evolution of Weapons*, 66–67.

51. Richard W. Unger, *The Ship in the Medieval Economy: 600–1600* (Montreal: 1980), 83; Brogger and Shetelig, *The Viking Ships*, 89, 133–34, 179, 181, 187.

52. Romola Anderson and R. C. Anderson, *The Sailing Ship: Six Thousand Years of History* (London: 1926), 78, 82; Brogger and Shetelig, *Viking Ships*, 178.

53. Unger, *Ship in the Medieval Economy*, 43, 46, 47–49; Oman, *History of the Art of War in the Middle Ages:* A.D. *378–1278*, vol. 2, 46–48.

54. Unger, *Ship in the Medieval Economy*, 120.

55. Ibid., 140, 150.

56. Ibid., 149.

57. White, *Medieval Technology*, 16.

58. J. J. Saunders, *The History of the Mongol Conquests* (New York: 1971), 44–45; Hurley, *Arrows against Steel*, 148–49; H. Desmond Martin, *The Rise of Chingis Khan and His Conquest of Northern China* (New York: 1977), 37.

59. Martin, *Rise of Chingis Khan*, 17–21; Dupuy, *Evolution of Weapons*, 72–73.

60. *The Secret History of the Mongols*, trans. Francis Woodman Cleaves (Cambridge, Mass.: 1982), 14.

61. Saunders, *Mongol Conquests*, 49; op. cit. Martin, *Rise of Chingis Khan*, 90.

62. Saunders, *Mongol Conquests*, ch. 4, n. 11; BYa. Vladimirtov, *The Life of Chingis-Khan* (New York: 1930), 63–64.

63. Saunders, *Mongol Conquests*, 46, 53–54.

64. Dupuy, *Evolution of Weapons*, 71; Saunders, *Mongol Conquests*, 54, 64.

65. Saunders, *Mongol Conquests*, 57.

66. Ibn al-Athīr, *sub anno* 628/1231, trans. in E. G. Browne, *A Literary History of Persia*, vol. 2 (Cambridge, Eng.: 1902–24), 430.

67. Hurley, *Arrows against Steel*, 160–61.

68. See, for example, Saunders, *Mongol Conquests*, 59; Oman, *Art of War in the Middle Ages:* A.D. *378–1278*, vol. 2, 326; Dupuy, *Evolution of Weapons*, 71–72; Hurley, *Arrows against Steel*, 161–62.

69. Oman, *Art of War in the Middle Ages:* A.D. *378–1278*, vol. 2, 329; Saunders, *Mongol Conquests*, 85.

70. Oman, *Art of War in the Middle Ages:* A.D. *378–1278*, vol. 2, 330–31; Hurley, *Arrows against Steel*, 161–62; Saunders, *Mongol Conquests*, 86.

71. Saunders, *Mongol Conquests*, 139, 155.

72. Saunders, *Mongol Conquests*, 13.

73. Oman, *Art of War in the Middle Ages:* A.D. *375–1515*, 77.

74. Ibid.; Oman, *Art of War in the Middle Ages:* A.D. *378–1278*, vol. 2, 254.

75. Ibid., vol. 2, 255; Oman, *Art of War in the Middle Ages:* A.D. *375–1515*, 76.

76. Oman, *Art of War in the Middle Ages:* A.D. *375–1515*, 82.

77. Op. cit. Oman, *Art of War in the Middle Ages:* A.D. *378–1278*, vol. 2, 280.

78. Ibid.

79. Oman, *Art of War in the Middle Ages:* A.D. *375–1515*, 75–76.

80. Oman, *Art of War in the Middle Ages:* A.D. *378–1278*, vol. 2, 274–75.

81. Niccolo Machiavelli, *The Art of War*, in *Machiavelli: The Chief Works and Others*, vol. 2 (Durham, N.C.: 1965), bk. 2, 600.

82. Hardy, *Longbow*, 38–41; Hurley, *Arrows against Steel*, 170; Heath, *Archery*, 112–15; Contamine, *War in the Middle Ages*, 152–53.

83. Magna Carta, 51; Contamine, *War in the Middle Ages*, 247.

84. Hardy, *Longbow*, 18–20.

85. Ibid., 30.

86. Hurley (*Arrows against Steel*, 22) notes that a bodkin-point arrow shot from a seventy-five-pound longbow will penetrate a quarter inch of steel plate. The power of the longbow is also testified to by a wound received by William de Briouse in which the arrow passed through the skirts of his mail shirt, his mail breeches, his thigh, and the wood of his saddle frame, and finally dealt his horse a mortal blow. Oman, *Art of War in the Middle Ages: A.D. 378–1278*, vol. 2, 59. On rate of fire, see Dupuy, *Evolution of Weapons*, 82. See also Keegan, *Face of Battle*, 98; Hardy, *Longbow*, 43–44.

87. Hardy, *Longbow*, 42–43; Heath, *Archery*, 115; Oman, *Art of War in the Middle Ages: A.D. 378–1278*, vol. 2, 61–65.

88. Keegan, *Face of Battle*, 92, 98, 104.

89. Oman, *Art of War in the Middle Ages: A.D. 378–1278*, vol. 2, 168–74; Hardy, *Longbow*, 93–95.

90. Hardy, *Longbow*, 99, 125–30; Oman, *Art of War in the Middle Ages: A.D. 378–1278*, vol. 2, 375.

91. Hardy, *Longbow*, 127; Oman, *Art of War in the Middle Ages: A.D. 375–1515*, 149.

92. Oman, *Art of War in the Middle Ages: A.D. 378–1278*, vol. 2, 377–78. See illustration, Hardy, *Longbow*, 129.
tration, Hardy, *Longbow*, 129.

93. Contamine, *War in the Middle Ages*, 140.

94. Unger, *Ship in the Medieval Economy*, 191.

95. Ibid., 176, 179.

96. F. C. Lane, *Navires et constructeurs à Venise pendant la Renaissance* (Paris: 1965), 93–97, 125–29.

97. Unger, *Ship in the Medieval Economy*, 191–92.

98. Ibid., 176–78.

99. Ibid., 192.

100. T. C. Lethbridge, "Shipbuilding," in *History of Technology*, vol. 2, ed. Singer, Holmyard, and Hall (Oxford: 1954), 587.

Chapter 7 Guns

1. Michael Howard, *War in European History* (London: 1976), 13, 19.

2. Robert Boyle, *Works*, vol. 2 (London: 1772), 65. Boyle states that the "invention of gunpowder hath quite altered the condition of martial affairs over the world, both by sea and land."

3. Henry W. Hime, (*The Origin of Artillery* [London: 1915], 124–27) dates the first firm European reference to cannon as not until 1313. A. R. Hall ("Military Technology," 726) states that the gun was certainly in use by 1325. For Chinese invention, see McNeill, *Pursuit of Power*, 81.

4. McNeill, *Pursuit of Power*, 24–116.

5. Bernard Brodie and Fawn Brodie, *From Crossbow to H-Bomb* (Bloomington, Ind.: 1972), 43; McNeill, *Pursuit of Power*, 83–86.

6. John U. Nef, *War and Human Progress: An Essay on the Rise of Industrial Civilization* (New York: 1950), 27–28; Maurice Daumas, ed., *Histoire général des techniques*, vol. 2 (Paris: 1965), 487.

7. McNeill, *Pursuit of Power*, 86–87; Dupuy, *Evolution of Weapons*, 98. The French army, for example, was equipped with bronze cannon in the War of 1870.

8. Brodie and Brodie, *From Crossbow to H-Bomb*, 43; McNeill, *Pursuit of Power*, 71.

See also C. N. Bromehead, "Mining and Quarrying to the Seventeenth Century," in *History of Technology,* vol. 2, ed. Singer, Holmyard, and Hall 13, 24.

9. Nef, *War and Human Progress,* 43.

10. Ibid.

11. McNeill, *Pursuit of Power,* 87–88.

12. Howard, *War in European History,* 17.

13. McNeill, *Pursuit of Power,* 113–14; Howard, *War in European History,* 31; Nef, *War and Human Progress,* 66–67.

14. A. R. Hall, "Military Technology," 360; Brodie and Brodie, *From Crossbow to H-Bomb,* 49; Howard, *War in European History,* 61.

15. Michael Roberts, *Gustavus Adolphus: A History of Sweden: 1611–1632,* vol. 2 (London: 1958), 228; Frederick L. Taylor, *The Art of War in Italy: 1494–1529* (Cambridge, Eng.: 1921), 82.

16. McNeill, *Pursuit of Power,* 87. For a description of the casting of the Constantinople gun, see A. R. Hall, "Military Technology," 363.

17. McNeill, *Pursuit of Power,* 87–88; Brodie and Brodie, *From Crossbow to H-Bomb,* 51.

18. Niccolo Machiavelli, *The Prince,* trans. Luigi Ricci (New York: 1940), ch. 4 "Why the Kingdom of Darius, Occupied by Alexander Did Not Rebel against the Successors of the Latter after His Death."

19. Ibid., 53.

20. Machiavelli, *Art of War,* 625, 634–40.

21. Machiavelli, *Prince,* 52–53.

22. Charles Oman, *Art of War in the Sixteenth Century* (New York: 1937), 12.

23. Ibid., 140, 158–59; Oman, *Art of War in the Middle Ages: A.D. 378–1278,* vol. 2, 309.

24. Taylor, *Art of War in Italy,* 56.

25. Blaise de Montluc, *Commentaries* (Paris: 1911), bk. 1, 50.

26. C. W. Wedgewood, *The Thirty Years War* (New Haven, Conn.: 1939), 516.

27. Howard, *War in European History,* 33; Dupuy, *Evolution of Weapons,* 113.

28. Dupuy, *Evolution of Weapons,* 116; A. R. Hall, "Military Technology," 355; Howard, *War in European History,* 34.

29. Roberts, *Gustavus Adolphus,* vol. 2, 174–75, n. 5; Dupuy, *Evolution of Weapons,* 114.

30. Howard, *War in European History,* 60–61; McNeill, *Pursuit of Power,* 141.

31. Contamine, *War in the Middle Ages* 210–16 (pre-1500); Machiavelli, *Art of War,* bk. 2. Also see McNeill's comments on *Pursuit of Power,* 128) on Maurice of Orange's debt to Vegetius and Aelian.

32. Oman, *Art of War in the Sixteenth Century,* 133; Roberts, *Gustavus Adolphus,* vol. 2, 172.

33. Oman, *Art of War in the Sixteenth Century,* 54.

34. Howard, *War in European History,* 21.

35. Oman, *Art of War in the Sixteenth Century,* 146; George Gush, *Renaissance Armies: 1480–1650* (Cambridge: 1982), 7.

36. Oman, *Art of War in the Sixteenth Century,* 147–48.

37. Taylor, *Art of War in Italy,* 50–52 (Marignano, La Bicocca); Oman, *Art of War in the Sixteenth Century,* 202–3.

38. Hans Delbruck, *History of the Art of War: Within the Framework of Political History,* vol. 4 (Westport, Conn.: 1975), 38; Roberts, *Gustavus Adolphus,* vol. 2, 176–78; Nef, *War and Human Progress,* 34.

39. Miguel de Cervantes Saavedra, *Don Quixote*, ed. H. Bohn (London: 1925) I, 402.

40. J. L. Motley, *The Rise of the Dutch Republic*, vol. 3 (New York: 1856), 555–56.

41. McNeill, *Pursuit of Power*, 89.

42. Christopher Duffy, *Siege Warfare: The Fortress in the Early Modern World, 1494–1660* (London: 1979), 8–9.

43. Brodie and Brodie, *From Crossbow to H-Bomb*, 71; McNeill, *Pursuit of Power*, 90; Duffy, *Siege Warfare*, 20.

44. Taylor, *Art of War in Italy*, 89–93, 139–41.

45. McNeill, *Pursuit of Power*, 90.

46. See diagrams in McNeill, *Pursuit of Power*, 92–93. J. R. Hale, *Renaissance War Studies* (London: 1983), 1–29.

47. J. R. Hale, "The Development of the Bastion, 1440–1534," in *Europe in the Late Middle Ages*, ed. John R. Hale (Evanston, Ill.: 1965), 466–94.

48. McNeill, *Pursuit of Power*, 91.

49. Taylor, *Art of War in Italy*, 132–33, 143–45; Howard, *War in European History*, 36–37.

50. Nef, *War and Human Progress*, 47–48; Dupuy, *Evolution of Weapons*, 100.

51. *A History of Technology*, vol. 3, ed. Charles Singer, E. J. Holmyard, and A. R. Hall, (Oxford: 1959) 361, 368.

52. Ibid., 355, 358, 362; Brodie and Brodie, *From Crossbow to H-Bomb*, 59.

53. Edward MacCurdy, *The Notebooks of Leonardo da Vinci* (New York: 1939), 808, 810–11, 813–14, 816, 822–23, 826, 831, 841, 844, 846.

54. Nef, *War and Human Progress*, 48, 120–21, 132–33.

55. Letter, Leonardo da Vinci to Ludovic Sforza ca. 1492, in MacCurdy, *Notebooks of Leonardo da Vinci*, 1152–53.

56. MacCurdy, *Notebooks of Leonardo da Vinci*, 850.

Chapter 8 Harvest of Blood

1. J. V. Polisensky, *War and Society in Europe 1618–1848* (Cambridge, Eng.: 1978), 77, 154, 217.

2. Nef, *War and Human Progress*, 114–15.

3. David Ayalon, *Gunpowder and Firearms in the Mamluk Kingdom* (London: 1978), 4, 46, 49–50, 108.

4. Ibid., 63–69, 58; Oman, *Art of War in the Sixteenth Century*, 619.

5. Ayalon, *Gunpowder and Firearms*, 98–99; Stanford Shaw, *History of the Ottoman Empire and Modern Turkey*, (Cambridge, Eng.: 1976), vol. 1, *Empire of the Gazis: The Rise and Decline of the Ottoman Empire*, 1280–1808, 21.

6. S. Shaw, *Empire of the Gazis*, 123.

7. Arnold Toynbee, *A Study of History*, vol. 3 (London: 1934), 33–34, 37–41.

8. Sir Edward Casey, (*History of the Ottoman Turks* [London: 1877], 138), states that by 1515 the Turkish army had elaborate artillery and that a portion of the Janissaries bore firearms. Flemish scholar and diplomat Ogier Ghiselin de Busbecq observed in 1559 that few Janissaries "carried any weapon except muskets, which was their regular arm" (*Exclamatio, sive de Re Militari contra Turcam instituenda comsilium* (Leyden, 1633), letter 3, 246; S. Shaw, *Empire of the Gazis*, 46.

9. Oman, *Art of War in the Sixteenth Century*, 611–13, 615 (Persia), 618–26 (Mamluks), 657, 662 (Mohács); Ayalon, *Gunpowder and Firearms*, 109.

10. Charles Wilson, *The Transformation of Europe 1558–1648* (Berkeley, Calif.: 1976), 131–35, 244.

11. Toynbee, *Study of History*, vol. 3, 47.

12. Fray Bernadino de Sahagun, *Codex Florentine*, in *The War of Conquest: How It Was Waged in Mexico*, ed. Arthur J. O. Anderson and Charles E. Dribble (Salt Lake City: 1928).

13. William H. Prescott, *A History of the Conquest of Peru*, in *History of the Conquest of Mexico and Peru* (New York: 1936), 941.

14. See, for example, Bartolomé de Las Casas, *History of the Indies*, trans. Andree Collard (N.Y.: 1971), bk. 3, Ch. 4 and 5, 182–89.

15. William H. Prescott, *The Conquest of Mexico*, in *History of the Conquest of Mexico and Peru*, 609–10.

16. Winthrop Jordan, *White over Black: American Attitudes Toward the Negro, 1550–1812* (Chapel Hill, N.C.: 1968), 55–56.

17. C. Wilson, *Transformation of Europe*, 116–26, 157–58, 231–33; Oman, *Art of War in the Sixteenth Century*, 393–94, 459–60.

18. Garrett Mattingly, *The Armada* (Boston: 1959), 157.

19. La Noue, *Discourses*, 502–19, cited in Oman, *Art of War in the Sixteenth Century*, 396.

20. Cited in Edward Grierson, *The Fatal Inheritance: Phillip II and the Spanish Netherlands* (Garden City, N.Y.: 1969), 50.

21. C. Wilson, *Transformation of Europe*, 63, 144–45.

22. John L. Motley, *The Rise of the Dutch Republic*, vol. 2 (New York: 1906), 129.

23. Dupuy, *Evolution of Weapons*, 112–14; Roberts, *Gustavus Adolphus*, vol. 2, 173–74.

24. Motley, *Rise of the Dutch Republic*, vol. 2, 151–52.

25. Oman, *Art of War in the Sixteenth Century*, 555–57.

26. Ibid.

27. Ibid., 542–43, 548, 546–47.

28. Motley, *Rise of the Dutch Republic*, vol. 3, 28.

29. McNeill, *Pursuit of Power*, 109.

30. Ibid.; C. Wilson, *Transformation of Europe*, 136.

31. See, for example, Motley, *Rise of the Dutch Republic*, vol. 2, 344, 382–83.

32. Geoffrey Parker, "The Military Revolution 1550–1660—a Myth?" *Journal of Modern History* 48 (1976): 206.

33. McNeill, *Pursuit of Power*, 113.

34. Claude Gaier, *Four Centuries of Liège Gunmaking* (London: 1977), 29–31; McNeill, *Pursuit of Power*, 113.

35. McNeill, *Pursuit of Power*, 159–60. McNeill also cites official Prussian statistics compiled after the Seven Years' War showing that weapons, powder, and ammunition accounted for only 1 percent of that country's total expenditures.

36. C. Wilson, *Transformation of Europe*, 175–76.

37. Roberts, *Gustavus Adolphus*, vol. 2, 181; Brodie and Brodie, *From Crossbow to H-Bomb*, 92.

38. Dupuy, *Evolution of Weapons*, 104; Brodie and Brodie, *From Crossbow to H-Bomb*, 83.

39. McNeill, *Pursuit of Power*, 128; Roberts, *Gustavus Adolphus*, vol. 2, 185; Oman, *Art of War in the Sixteenth Century*, 570.

40. Roberts, *Gustavus Adolphus*, vol. 2, 183.

41. Dupuy, *Evolution of Weapons*, 132.

42. McNeill, *Pursuit of Power*, 131–33.

43. Ibid., 131.

44. Roberts, *Gustavus Adolphus*, vol. 2, 187–88.

45. Mattingly, *Armada*, 141, 323; Brodie and Brodie, *From Crossbow to H-Bomb*, 68.

46. Motley, *Rise of the Dutch Republic*, vol. 2, 384–85.

47. Ibid., 503.

48. C. Wilson, *Transformation of Europe*, 134.

49. Motley, *Rise of the Dutch Republic*, vol. 2, 285.

50. Ibid., 264–265, 306–07.

51. Mattingly, *Armada*, 84, G. P. B. Naish, "Ships and Shipbuilding," in *History of Technology*, vol. 3, ed. Charles Singer, E. J. Holmyard, and A. R. Hall (Oxford: 1959) 474.

52. Michael Lewis, *The Spanish Armada* (New York: 1968), 62–63.

53. Ibid., 51, 68.

54. David Howarth, *The Voyage of the Armada: The Spanish Story* (New York: 1981), 93–94.

55. Mattingly, *Armada*, 196; Howarth, *Voyage of the Armada*, 97–98. Geoffrey Parker, "Why the Armada Failed," *MHQ: Quarterly Journal of Military History* 1, no. 1 (1988): 18–27.

58. Mattingly, *Armada*, 367–70; Howarth, *Voyage of the Armada*, 206–10.

59. Howarth, *Voyage of the Armada*, 215; Mattingly, *Armada*, 368–69.

60. Polisensky, *War and Society in Europe*, 139; Nef, *War and Human Progress*, 92.

61. Wedgewood, *Thirty Years War*, 86–88, 123, 275, 301, 449.

62. Ibid., 257.

63. S. H. Steinberg, *The Thirty Years War and the Conflict for European Hegemony 1600–1660* (London: 1967), quoted in C. Wilson, *Transformation of Europe*, 263. See also T. K. Robb, ed., *The Thirty Years War* (Boston: 1969) for the main point of Steinberg's argument.

64. Geoffrey Parker, *The Thirty Years War* (London: 1984), 211.

65. See G. Parker, *Thirty Years War*, 208–15; C. Wilson, *Transformation of Europe*, 264.

66. Father Roger Mols, *Introduction à la démographie historique des las villes d'Europe: du XIV au XVIII siècle* (Louvain: 1954), vol. 2, *Les résultats*, cited in C. Wilson, *Transformation of Europe*, 264.

67. Wedgewood, *Thirty Years War*, 256–57.

68. Ibid., 316.

69. McNeill, *Pursuit of Power*, 121; Wedgewood, *Thirty Years War*, 346–47.

70. Roberts, *Gustavus Adolphus*, vol. 2, 191–201.

71. Howard, *War in European History*, 57.

72. Ibid., 59.

73. Roberts, *Gustavus Adolphus*, vol. 2, 237–38.

74. Ibid., 227; Dupuy, *Evolution of Weapons*, 135.

75. Howard, 59; Gush, *Renaissance Armies*, 113.

76. Dupuy, *Evolution of Weapons*, 135; Roberts, *Gustavus Adolphus*, vol. 2, 223–24.

77. Roberts, *Gustavus Adolphus*, vol. 2, 234–35.

78. Ibid., 231–33.

79. Ibid., 232.

80. Ibid., 234.

81. Wedgewood, *Thirty Years War*, 307–19; Roberts, *Gustavus Adolphus*, vol. 2, 674.

82. Frederick Schiller, *History of the Thirty Years War* (New York: 1885), 365.

83. Hugo Grotius, *De Jure Belli ac Pacis (The Law of War and Peace,)* vol. 1, ed. William Whewell (Cambridge: 1853), lix.

Chapter 9 When Time Stood Still

1. Childs, *Armies and Warfare in Europe,* 174–77.
2. Huigh de Groot (Grotius), *The Law of War and Peace* (Washington: 1901), 318.
3. Ibid., 321.
4. Ibid., 294–95.
5. Ibid., 326, 328–30.
6. Ibid., 361.
7. Ibid., 366–67.
8. McNeill, *Pursuit of Power,* 139. See also Childs, *Armies and Warfare in Europe,* 42, Table I: Comparative Sizes of European Armies, 1690–1789.
9. Childs, *Armies and Warfare in Europe,* 77–78; H. W. Koch, *The Rise of Modern Warfare: 1618–1815* (Englewood Cliffs, N.J.: 1981), 69; Theodore Ropp, *War in the Modern World* (Durham, N.C.: 1959), 41.
10. Childs, *Armies and Warfare in Europe,* 98–106; Koch, 80.
11. Schaumburg cited in Childs, *Armies and Warfare in Europe,* 101.
12. Childs, *Armies and Warfare in Europe,* 102.
13. David Chandler, *The Art of Warfare in the Age of Marlborough* (London: 1976), 38.
14. Ropp, *War in the Modern World,* 30–35; Howard, *War in European History,* 70; McNeill, *Pursuit of Power,* 141; Dupuy, *Evolution of Weapons,* 145.
15. Childs, *Armies and Warfare in Europe,* 107.
16. Childs, *Armies and Warfare in Europe,* 41.
17. Lorenzo Sabine, *Notes on Duels and Duelling* (Boston: 1855), 6–7, 9–10, 14. J. G. Mullingen (*History of Duelling* [London: 1941], 153) notes that during the reign of Louis XIV no less than ten edicts against dueling were issued. However, Nef (*War and Human Progress,* 308) cites these admonitions as evidence that duels were actually growing less frequent. This is doubtful.
18. B. C. Truman, *The Field of Honor* (New York: 1844), 23. The code of Galway specifically prohibits fisticuffs on the grounds that "gentlemen" should not indulge in such behavior.
19. Sabine, *Duels and Duelling,* 29–30.
20. Compte de Saint-Germain, *Mémoires* (Paris: n.d.), 178.
21. Robert Ergang, *The Potsdam Fuhrer: Frederick William, Father of Prussian Militarism* (New York: 1941), 84–96, 101–2, 218.
22. Childs, *Armies and Warfare in Europe,* 65–67.
23. Childs, *Armies and Warfare in Europe,* 43–45; Ropp, *War in the Modern World,* 37.
24. Frederick II, "Testimony Politique," 1768, cited in Christopher Duffy, *Frederick the Great: A Military Life* (London: 1985), 335.
25. Robert B. Asprey, *Frederick the Great: The Magnificent Enigma* (New York: 1986), 485; Ergang, *Potsdam Fuhrer,* 90–93. See also Voltaire's classic description of the eighteenth-century recruitment in which Candide is dragooned into the Bulgarian Army (*Candide,* ch. 2).
26. Nef, *War and Human Progress,* 204–5; Ropp, *War in the Modern World,* 25–26; Howard, *War in European History,* 71–72.
27. Childs, *Armies and Warfare in Europe,* 80.
28. Childs, *Armies and Warfare in Europe,* 43; Maurice de Saxe, "'My Reveries,'" in *Roots of Strategy,* ed. T. R. Phillips (Harrisburg, Pa.: 1950), 194. See Ropp, *War in the*

Modern World, 38. See also McNeill (*Pursuit of Power,* 130–33) for the transformation of men subjected to this training.

29. de Guignard, *Ecole de Mars,* cited in Chandler, *Warfare in the Age of Marlborough,* 103–4.

30. Howard, *War in European History,* 64.

31. Cited in Pierre Gaxotte, *Frederick the Great,* trans. R. A. Bell (New Haven, Conn.: 1942), 104.

32. Chandler, *Warfare in the Age of Marlborough,* 29, 145, 165; Childs, *Armies and Warfare in Europe,* 49, 63.

33. Childs, *Armies and Warfare in Europe,* 49; Chandler, *Warfare in the Age of Marlborough,* 165–66.

34. Chandler, *Warfare in the Age of Marlborough,* 30, table on percentage of cavalry in armies by nationalities; Child's Table I: Size of French Army over Time 1690–1789 compared with Chandler's table (159) showing Size of French Artillery Establishment, 1689–1748.

35. Brodie and Brodie, *From Crossbow to H-Bomb,* 80–83.

36. Chandler, *Warfare in the Age of Marlborough,* 82–84.

37. Ibid., 76–77.

38. Ibid., 80.

39. Howard, *War in European History,* 60–61.

40. McNeill, *Pursuit of Power,* 142; Chandler, *Warfare in the Age of Marlborough,* 80–81.

41. Chandler, *Warfare in the Age of Marlborough,* 80.

42. Ibid., 150.

43. Ibid.; figures taken from Table of Artillery Present at Selected Engagements.

44. Ibid., 178.

45. E. Picard and L. Jouan, *L'Artillerie Française au 18ieme siècle* (Paris: 1906), 44–46.

46. Picard and Jouan, *L'Artillierie Francaise,* 54–59; Chandler, *Warfare in the Age of Marlborough,* 189.

47. Brodie and Brodie, *From Crossbow to H-Bomb,* 101.

48. McNeill, *Pursuit of Power,* 167–68. It required around twenty years for cannon-boring machines to proliferate.

49. Chandler, *Warfare in the Age of Marlborough,* 206–8.

50. Dupuy, *Evolution of Weapons,* 104–5.

51. Brodie and Brodie, *From Crossbow to H-Bomb,* 115.

52. Chandler, *Warfare in the Age of Marlborough,* 185.

53. Brodie and Brodie, *From Crossbow to H-Bomb,* 93; Nef, *War and Human Progress,* 189.

54. Chandler, *Warfare in the Age of Marlborough,* 223–24; Nef, *War and Human Progress,* 190; Brodie and Brodie, *From Crossbow to H-Bomb,* 93–94.

55. Childs, *Armies and Warfare in Europe,* 134.

56. Childs, *Armies and Warfare in Europe,* 136.

57. Circular to all governors from Louis XIV, 6 April 1705, reprinted in Sebastian le Prestre de Vauban, *Traite de la défense des places* (Paris: 1779), 301–3.

58. Ropp, *War in the Modern World,* 27.

59. Brodie and Brodie, *From Crossbow to H-Bomb,* 94.

60. Chandler, *Warfare in the Age of Marlborough,* 183.

61. Julian S. Corbett, *Some Principles of Maritime Strategy* (London: 1960), 100.

62. P. K. Kemp, *History of the Royal Navy* (New York: 1969), 120.

63. Sir Richard Hawkins, *Observation* (London: 1622), 190.

64. Ropp, *War in the Modern World*, 55.

65. de Guiche cited in Kemp, *History of the Royal Navy*, 39.

66. Michael Lewis, *The Navy of Britain* (London: 1948), 432; Ropp, *War in the Modern World*, 53.

67. Robert L. O'Connell, "Dreadnought? The Battleship, the United States Navy and the World Naval Community," unpublished doctoral dissertation, University of Virginia, 1974, 61–64, 141–51.

68. E. J. Archibald, *The Wooden Fighting Ship in the Royal Navy: 892–1860* (New York: 1968), 24.

69. John Ruskin cited in Lewis Mumford, *Technics and Civilization* (New York: 1934), 208–9.

70. Archibald, *Wooden Fighting Ship*, 59.

71. Ropp, *War in the Modern World*, 54.

72. Archibald, *Wooden Fighting Ship*, 33, 65.

73. I. F. Clarke, *Voices Prophesying War: 1763–1984* (London: 1966), 4–5.

74. Saxe, "My Reveries," 212–13.

Chapter 10 A World Destroyed

1. Childs, *Armies and Warfare in Europe*, 104; Ropp, *War in the Modern World*, 25.

2. Nef, *War and Human Progress*, 189–90. The normally sarcastic Saint Simon referred to Vauban as "without question the finest man of his century where sieges and fortifications were concerned," cited in Chandler, *Warfare in the Age of Marlborough*, 272.

3. Koch, *Rise of Modern Warfare*, 117; Chandler, *Warfare in the Age of Marlborough*, 128.

4. Chandler, (*Warfare in the Age of Marlborough*, 304) states that Swedish casualties amounted to 9,600 of 21,500 engaged, or almost 45 percent. Childs (*Armies and Warfare in Europe*, 44) is more conservative, rating casualties at four thousand out of thirteen thousand, or 31 percent.

5. See Childs, *Armies and Warfare in Europe*, 155–56.

6. Cited in Nef, *War and Human Progress*, 305.

7. Asprey, *Frederick the Great*, xvi–xvii; Duffy, *Frederick the Great*, 2; Ergang, *Potsdam Fuhrer*, 163.

8. Howard, *War in European History*, 68.

9. Ropp, *War in the Modern World*, 29.

10. Ergang, *Potsdam Fuhrer*, 94.

11. Ibid., 88–89.

12. Gaxotte, *Frederick the Great*, 80.

13. Childs, *Armies and Warfare in Europe*, 160–69; Gaxotte, *Frederick the Great*, 343–51, 382.

14. Ropp, *War in the Modern World*, 30.

15. Childs, *Armies and Warfare in Europe*, 42, Ch. 5.

16. Howard, *War in European History*, 73.

17. Daniel J. Boorstin, *The Americans: The Colonial Experience* (New York: 1958), 347.

18. Ibid., 347–48.

19. Erhard Geissler, *Biological and Toxin Weapons Today* (Oxford: 1986), 8; Francis

Parkman, *The Conspiracy of Pontiac and the Indian War after the Conquest of Canada:* vol. 2 (Boston: 1901), 44; C. H. Sipe, *The Indian War after the Conquest of Canada* (Harrisburg, Pa.: 1929), 424.

20. Brodie and Brodie, *From Crossbow to H-Bomb,* 104; op. cit. Boorstin, *Americans,* 351.

21. Boorstin, *Americans,* 351.

22. Ibid., 370.

23. Ropp, *War in the Modern World,* 75–76 n. 18; ed. E. B. Potter, *The United States and World Sea Power* (Englewood Cliffs, N.J.: 1955), 104–105.

24. Brodie and Brodie, *From Crossbow to H-Bomb,* 116.

25. Howard, *War in European History,* 99.

26. Ropp, *War in the Modern World,* 86 and n. 5.

27. Koch, *Rise of Modern Warfare,* 198–99; Nef, *War in Human Progress,* 312.

28. Ropp, *War in the Modern World,* 90.

29. Ibid., 91; Gunther E. Rothenberg, *The Art of War in the Age of Napoleon* (London: 1977), 35.

30. Rothenberg, *War in the Age of Napoleon,* 115; H. Nickerson, *The Armed Horde* (New York: 1940), 91.

31. Ropp, *War in the Modern World,* 84. Rothenberg, *War in the Age of Napoleon,* 23.

32. Howard, *War in European History,* 81; Brodie and Brodie, *From Crossbow to H-Bomb,* 106–7.

33. Dupuy, *Evolution of Weapons,* 158; McNeill, *Pursuit of Power,* 170–71, 194.

34. Cited in Ropp, *War in the Modern World,* 92.

35. Ibid.

36. David G. Chandler, *The Campaigns of Napoleon* (New York: 1966), 10, 12–14.

37. Ibid., 25–27.

38. Cited in Lord Russell of Liverpool, *Knight of the Sword* (London: 1964), 40.

39. Napoleon Bonaparte, *Correspondence de Napoleon I:* vol. 1 (Paris: 1858), nos. 91, 107.

40. Dupuy, *Evolution of Weapons,* 155–157; *War in the Modern World,* 82–83; Rothenberg, *War in the Age of Napoleon,* 115.

41. McNeill, *Pursuit of Power,* 198; Brodie and Brodie, *From Crossbow to H-Bomb,* 110.

42. M. de Bourienne, *Memoirs of Napoleon Bonaparte* vol. 1 (London: 1836), 349.

43. Rothenberg, *War in the Age of Napoleon,* 71–72.

44. Chandler, *Campaigns of Napoleon,* 236.

45. Napoleon, *Correspondance,* vol. 31, 328–29.

46. Dupuy, *Evolution of Weapons,* 152; Chandler, *Campaigns of Napoleon,* 1149.

47. Dupuy, *Evolution of Weapons,* 157–58.

48. Rothenberg, *War in the Age of Napoleon,* 69.

49. Chandler, *Campaigns of Napoleon,* 352.

50. Napoleon, *Correspondance,* vol. 32, 27.

51. Ropp, 55; Archibald, *Wooden Fighting Ship,* 24.

52. Chandler, *Campaigns of Napoleon,* 226.

53. Ropp, *War in the Modern World,* 97; Oliver Warner, *Nelson's Battles* (Newton Abbot, Eng.: 1971), 50–64.

54. Henry A. Kissinger, *A World Restored* (New York: 1964), 63.

55. Chandler, *Campaigns of Napoleon,* 366, 599.

56. Ibid., 512, 594.

57. McNeill, *Pursuit of Power*, 210–211, 214.

58. David Howarth, *Trafalgar: The Nelson Touch* (New York: 1969), 19.

59. Cited in Howarth, *Trafalgar*, 130.

60. Warner, *Nelson's Battles*, 204, 232–34.

61. Cited in Chandler, *Campaigns of Napoleon*, 597.

62. Ibid., 603.

63. Cited in Chandler, *Campaigns of Napoleon*, 611.

64. Kissinger, *World Restored*, 18; Chandler, *Campaigns of Napoleon*, 664–66.

65. Chandler, *Campaigns of Napoleon*, 756, 763.

66. General de Caulaincourt, *Mémoires*, vol. 1 (London: 1950), 108.

67. General M. de Marbot, *Mémoires du General Baron de Marbot* (Paris: 1891).

68. Kissinger, *World Restored*, 7–8, 18–19.

69. Ibid., 120–33, 203.

70. Ibid., 201.

71. Ibid., 203.

72. Howard, *War in European History*, 57; Ropp, *War in the Modern World*, 38–39.

73. McNeill, *Pursuit of Power*, 200. Rothenberg, *(War in the Age of Napoleon)* puts the number conscripted and enrolled between 1800 and 1815 at 1.5 million men.

74. Rothenberg, *War in the Age of Napoleon*, 81–82; McNeill, *Pursuit of Power*, 213.

75. J. Houdaille, "Pertes de l'armée de terre sous le premier empire," *Population* 27 (1972): 50.

76. McNeill, *Pursuit of Power*, 213–14, 310–17.

77. Nef, *War and Human Progress*, 330–37.

78. McNeill, *Pursuit of Power*, 211.

79. Ibid., 202–3, n. 37.

80. Brodie and Brodie, *From Crossbow to H-Bomb*, 115.

81. Ibid.; Dupuy, *Evolution of Weapons*, 218–19; Rothenberg, *War in the Age of Napoleon*, 77–78.

82. Cited in Brodie and Brodie, *From Crossbow to H-Bomb*, 127; Willy Ley, *Rockets, Missiles, and Men in Space* (New York: 1968), 61–75.

83. Cited in Brodie and Brodie, *From Crossbow to H-Bomb*, 118.

84. Karl von Clausewitz, "Plan of Operations," *Strategie aus dem Jahr 1804*, 51.

85. Clausewitz, *On War*, bk. 5, Ch. 4 "Relation of the Three Arms."

Chapter 11 Death Machine

1. Brodie and Brodie, *From Crossbow to H-Bomb*, 9.

2. Ibid., 131–32, J. F. C. Fuller, *Armament and History; A Study of the Influence of Armament on History from the Dawn of Classical Warfare to the Second World War*, (New York: 1945), 110; Dispatch of Lieutenant-General Lord Viscount Gough, *London Gazette*, 8 October 1841.

3. Brodie and Brodie, *From Crossbow to H-Bomb*, 132; Fuller, *Armament and History*, 110; J. W. Fortescue, *A History of the British Army*, vol. 12 (London: 1927), 180.

4. McNeill, *Pursuit of Power*, 235–36; Larry Addington, *The Pattern of War Since the Eighteenth Century* (London: 1984), 85; J. F. C. Fuller, *The Conduct of War: 1789–1961* (New Brunswick, N.J.: 1961), 89.

5. Dennis Showalter, *Railroads and Rifles: Soldiers, Technology, and the Unification of Germany* (Hamden, Conn.: 1975), 81–82, 95–98.

6. McNeill, *Pursuit of Power*, 233–34.

7. O. F. G. Hogg, *The Royal Arsenal: Its Background, Origins, and Subsequent History,* vol. 22 (London: 1963), 792–93.

8. On Fitch see McNeill, *Pursuit of Power,* 235 and n. 17; J. D. Scott, *Vickers: A History* (London: 1962), 25.

9. McNeill, *Pursuit of Power,* 238 n. 27.

10. Brodie and Brodie, *From Crossbow to H-Bomb,* 115–16, 125; Lewis, *Navy of Britain,* 575.

11. Commander A. Angas, *Rivalry on the Atlantic* (New York: 1939), x–xi, 75, 88, 90, 100.

12. James P. Baxter, *The Introduction of the Ironclad Warship* (New York: 1920), 13–14; Harold Sprout and Margaret Sprout, *The Rise of American Naval Power: 1776–1918* (Princeton, N.J.: 1959), 126.

13. Grady McWhiney and Perry D. Jamieson, *Attack and Die: The Civil War, Military Tactics, and Southern Heritage* (Montgomery, Ala.: 1982), 6, 49, 56, 60.

14. *U.S. War Department, Report of the Secretary of War and Accompanying Documents for the Year 1854* (Washington, D.C.: 1854), 20.

15. McWhiney and Jamieson, *Attack and Die,* 27–40. James M. McPherson, *Battle Cry of Freedom: The Civil War Era* (New York: 1988), 4–5.

16. McWhiney and Jamieson, *Attack and Die,* 5, 7.

17. General Daniel H. Hill cited in McWhiney and Jamieson, *Attack and Die,* 4.

18. McWhiney and Jamieson, *Attack and Die,* 7.

19. Lincoln cited in Bruce Catton, *This Hallowed Ground: The Story of the Union Side of the Civil War* (New York: 1956), 228.

20. Cited in Bruce Catton, *Grant Takes Command* (Boston: 1968), 253.

21. Ibid., 262.

22. Stephen Crane, *The Red Badge of Courage* (New York: 1963), 28.

23. Catton, *This Hallowed Ground,* 339–40.

24. Lyman cited in McWhiney and Jamieson, *Attack and Die,* 75.

25. Ulysses S. Grant, *Personal Memoirs of U.S. Grant,* vol. 2 (New York: 1886), 307–15.

26. Gilbert W. Beebe and Michael DeBakey, *Battle Casualties* (Springfield, Mass.: 1952), cited in Dupuy, *The Evolution of Weapons,* Table 4, 171.

27. John L. Collins, "When Stonewall Jackson Turned Our Right," in *Battles and Leaders of the Civil War,* vol. 3, ed. Robert U. Johnson and Clarence C. Buel (New York: 1956), 183.

28. John S. Mosby, *The Memoirs of Colonel John S. Mosby* (Bloomington, Ind.: 1959), 30.

29. Cited in Jay Luvaas, *The Military Legacy of the Civil War* (Chicago: 1959), 56.

30. Letter, Stephen Mallory to C. M. Confrad, chairman of Committee on Naval Affairs, Confederate States House of Representatives, 8 May 1861, cited in Sprout and Sprout, *American Naval Power,* 156.

31. Frank M. Bennett, *The Monitor and the Navy under Steam* (Boston: 1900), 132–33.

32. Luvaas, *Military Legacy of the Civil War,* 12, 226–29.

33. Fuller, *Conduct of War,* 113; Ropp, *War in the Modern World,* 114, 137–39.

34. Dupuy, *Evolution of Weapons,* 179–80; McNeill, *Pursuit of Power,* 248.

35. Howard, *War in European History,* 99.

36. Ropp, *War in the Modern World,* 143; McNeill, *Pursuit of Power,* 253–54, Michael Howard, *The Franco-Prussian War* (London: 1961), 3.

37. Howard, *The Franco-Prussian War*, 249; Ropp, 143; Howard, *Franco-Prussian War*, 43–44.

38. Howard, *Franco-Prussian War*, 2.

39. Kissinger, *World Restored*, 157.

40. William Manchester, *The Arms of Krupp* (Boston: 1968), 38–41.

41. Manchester, *Arms of Krupp*, 83–84; Peter Batty, *The House of Krupp* (London: 1966), 70.

42. Manchester, *Arms of Krupp*, 65–66.

43. Ibid., 84–88.

44. McNeill, *Pursuit of Power*, 252.

45. Cited in Edward Crankshaw, *Bismarck* (London: 1981), 122.

46. Ibid., 133. In fact, it appears that the original phrase was "iron and blood," which was later turned around for euphony.

47. Letter to Johanna (wife), 9 July 1866, in *Bismarck: Die gesammelten Werke*, vol. 14, ed. H. von Petersdorff et al. (Berlin: 1923), 717.

48. McNeill, *Pursuit of Power*, 253–54; Eric J. Leed, *No Man's Land: Combat and Identity in World War I* (Cambridge, Eng.: 1979), 16–17, 51–55.

49. Howard, *Franco-Prussian War*, 27–28; McNeill, *Pursuit of Power*, 247; Crankshaw, *Bismarck*, 172–73.

50. Crankshaw, 213–14; Ropp, *War in the Modern World*, 151; McNeill, *Pursuit of Power*, 249–50.

51. Howard, *Franco-Prussian War*, 229–32, 249–56, 434–39.

52. Ibid., 35.

53. Ibid., 212–13.

54. Ardant du Picq, *Battle Studies: Ancient and Modern Battles* (New York: 1921), 101–2, 113, 181, 229.

55. Fuller, *Armament and History*, 118; Manchester, *Arms of Krupp*, 119–22.

56. Ropp, *War in the Modern World*, 145; Fuller, *Conduct of War*, 119–20.

57. Howard, *Franco-Prussian War*, 36 n. 6.

58. George H. Quester, *Offense and Defense in the International System* (New York: 1977), 79–80.

59. Stephen Van Evera, "Why Cooperation Failed in 1914," *World Politics* 38 (October 1985): 85–88, 90–95, 101–3.

Chapter 12 On the High Seas and Out of Sight

1. Reinhard Scheer, *Germany's High Seas Fleet in the World War* (London: 1920), 3.

2. John Toland, *The Rising Sun in the Pacific: The Decline and Fall of the Japanese Empire: 1936–1945* (New York: 1970), 477.

3. Annual Report of the Secretary of the Navy, 38th Cong. 2d sess. 1864, Executive Documentation no. 1, vol. 6, xxii; ed. Potter, *United States and World Sea Power*, 393; O'Connell, "Dreadnought?" 99.

4. William Hovgaard, *Modern History of Warships: Comprising a Discussion of the Present Standpoint and Recent War Experiences* (New York: 1920), 96.

5. Cited in Elting Morison, *Admiral Sims and the Modern American Navy* (Cambridge, Mass.: 1942), 19.

6. Alfred Thayer Mahan, *From Sail to Steam* (New York: 1907), 197.

7. Alfred Thayer Mahan, *The Influence of Sea Power upon History: 1660–1783* (New York: 1890), 2.

8. Letter, Theodore Roosevelt to Mahan, 12 May 1890, Mahan Papers, Library of Congress; Ernest R. May, *American Imperialism* (New York: 1968), 198, 201–2; Sprout

and Sprout, *Rise of American Naval Power* 207; Letter, Hilary A. Herbert to Mahan, 4 October 1893, Mahan Papers.

9. W. D. Puleston, *The Life of Admiral Mahan* (New Haven, Conn.: 1939), 149; Louis Hacker, "The Incendiary Mahan," *Scribner's Magazine,* April 1934, 318.

10. Arthur J. Marder, *Anatomy of British Sea Power* (New York: 1940), 47.

11. History of the United States War College: 1884–1958 (Newport, R.I.: 1959), 3 (document on file at Operational Archives, Washington Naval Yard).

12. Francis J. McHugh, "Gaming at the Naval War College," *U.S. Naval Institute Proceedings* (March 1964): 49–50; Bradley A. Fiske, *The Navy as a Fighting Machine* (New York: 1917), 152–53; A. P. Niblack, "The Jane Naval Game," *U.S. Naval Institute Proceedings* 29, no. 3 (September 1903): 581.

13. Fiske, *Navy as a Fighting Machine,* 126–27.

14. Rear Admiral Stephen B. Luce, "Our Future Navy," *U.S. Naval Institute Proceedings* 15, no. 4 542–43.

15. Lieutenant Commander Richard Wainwright, "Tactical Problems in Naval Warfare," *U.S. Naval Institute Proceedings* 21, no. 2, (1895): 257.

16. Hovgaard, *Modern History of Warships,* 15, 71.

17. H. M. Le Fleming, *The ABC Warships of World War I* (London: 1962), 11.

18. Letter, Home Poundstone to William S. Sims, 15 August, 1905, William S. Sims Papers, Library of Congress.

19. Richard Hough, *The Death of the Battleship* (New York: 1963), 6.

20. Hovgaard, *Modern History of Warships,* 452.

21. Ibid.

22. Theodore Ropp, "Continental Doctrines of Sea Power," in *The Makers of Modern Strategy,* ed. Edward M. Earle (Princeton, N.J.: 1943), 447.

23. Hovgaard, *Modern History of Warships,* 264; ed. Potter, *United States and World Sea Power,* 392.

24. Hovgaard, *Modern History of Warships,* 263.

25. O'Connell, "Dreadnought?" 188.

26. Richard Knowles Morris, *John P. Holland* (Annapolis, Md.: 1966), 89.

27. Testimony of Admiral George Dewey taken by the House Committee on Naval Affairs, 23 April 1900, Dewey Papers, Library of Congress.

28. Hovgaard, *Modern History of Warships,* 310; Philip K. Lundeberg, "Undersea Warfare and Allied Strategy in World War I, to 1916," *The Smithsonian Journal of History* 6, no. 3, (1966): 6.

29. Bernard Brodie, *A Layman's Guide to Naval Strategy* (Princeton: 1942), 252; Report of the Reconciling Committee on Question 21, U.S. Naval War College, 21 August 1909, Sims Papers.

30. Cited in Arthur J. Marder, *From Dreadnought to Scapa Flow: The Royal Navy in the Fisher Era,* vol. 1 (London: 1961), 332.

31. John A. Fisher, *Memories and Records:* vol. 2 (New York: 1920), 175.

32. E. Morison, *Admiral Sims,* 84.

33. Ibid., 81–86, 132. See also W. S. Sims, "The Remarkable Record Target Practice, H.M.S. Terrible," 15 March 1901, Sims Papers.

34. E. Morison, *Admiral Sims,* 142, 241–42; Letter, Scott to Sims 19 August 1906, Sims Papers.

35. O'Connell, "Dreadnought?" 216; Letter, Theodore Roosevelt to Poundstone, 27 December 1902, Poundstone Papers, Naval Museum, U.S. Naval Academy.

36. Vitorio Cuinberti, "An Ideal Battleship for the British Fleet," *Jane's Fighting Ships* (London: 1903), 407.

37. Fisher, *Memories and Records,* vol. 2, 197.

38. Hough, *Death of the Battleship,* 19–20.

39. O'Connell, "Dreadnought?" 223; Arthur J. Marder, *The Anatomy of British Sea Power* (New York: 1940), Ch. XXVII; Arthur J. Marder, "Fisher and Genesis of the Dreadnought," *U.S. Naval Institute Proceedings* (October 1956).

40. Hovgaard, *Modern History of Warships,* 443; Charles Domville-Fife, *The Submarine and Seapower* (New York: 1923), 198.

41. E. Morison, *Admiral Sims,* 172–73; Letter, Poundstone to Sims, 15 August 1905, Sims Papers; Hovgaard, *Modern History of Warships,* 139–40.

42. Hovgaard, *Modern History of Warships,* 228; Marder, *From Dreadnought to Scapa Flow,* vol. 1, 44; Richard Hough, *The History of the Modern Battleship: Dreadnought* (New York: 1964), 84.

43. Hough, *History of the Modern Battleship,* 24.

44. Cited in Barbara Tuchman, *The Guns of August* (New York: 1962), 6.

45. Letter, Baron Friedrich von Holstein to Paul Hatzfeld, 9 April 1987, cited in Jonathan Steinberg, *Yesterday's Deterrent: Tirpitz and the Birth of the German Battle Fleet* (London: 1965), 117.

46. Steinberg, *Yesterday's Deterrent,* 330.

47. Walter Millis, *Arms and Men* (New York: 1960), 189.

48. Alfred T. Mahan, "Reflections Historic and Other, Suggested by the Battle of the Sea of Japan," *U.S. Naval Institute Proceedings* (June 1906): 452.

49. Winston S. Churchill, *The World Crisis,* vol. 1 (New York: 1923), 33.

Chapter 13 Prelude

1. St. Petersburg Convention, Renouncing the Use, in Time of War, of Explosive Projectiles under 400 grams Weight, in Adam Roberts and Richard Guelff, eds., *Documents on the Laws of War* (Oxford: 1982), 29.

2. Ibid.

3. Speech by Sir John Ardagh, 22 June 1899, *The Proceedings of The Hague Peace Conference* (London: 1920), 286–87.

4. Edward M. Spiers, "The Use of the Dumdum Bullet in Colonial Warfare," *The Journal of Imperial and Commonwealth History* (1975): 9.

5. John Ellis, *The Social History of the Machine Gun* (New York: 1975), 46.

6. Ibid., 70.

7. G. W. Steevens, *With Kitchener to Khartoum* (London: 1898), 300.

8. Ellis, *Social History of the Machine Gun,* 89.

9. Ibid., 98–99.

10. Hilaire Belloc, "The Modern Traveler," cited in Ellis, *Social History of the Machine Gun,* 94.

11. Cited in T. Ranger, *Revolt in Southern Rhodesia: 1897–98* (London: 1967), 121.

12. Cited in Ellis, *Social History of the Machine Gun,* 96.

13. Christopher Hibbert, *The Great Mutiny: India 1857* (New York: 1977), 47, 55.

14. Ibid., 61, 64, 73–74.

15. Ibid., 392. See also Percival Spear, *India* (Ann Arbor, Mich.: 1961), 270.

16. Pat Barr, *The Coming of the Barbarians: The Opening of Japan to the West* (New York: 1967), 15–16, 26–27.

17. E. H. Norman, *Japan's Emergence as a Modern State: Political and Economic Problems of the Meiji Period* (New York: 1940), 65–66.

18. Ibid., 132.

19. Clive Trebilcock, "British Armaments and European Industrialism," *Economic History Review* 26 (1973): 254–72; McNeill, *Pursuit of Power*, 292.

20. Norman, *Japan's Emergence*, 128, 132–33.

21. Ibid., 194–96.

22. Ropp, *War in the Modern World*, 202.

23. Clarke, *Voices Prophesying War*, 64, 68.

24. Roberts and Guelff, *Documents on the Laws of War*, 35; William I. Hull, *The Two Hague Conferences and their Contributions to International Law* (Boston: 1908), 2–3.

25. Hull, 45–46; Joseph H. Choate, *The Two Hague Conferences* (Princeton, N.J.: 1913), 13.

26. Hull, *Two Hague Conferences*, 48.

27. Choate, *Two Hague Conferences*, 13–15; Declaration (IV, 2) Concerning Asphyxiating Gases, in Roberts and Guelff, *Documents on the Laws of War*, 35.

28. Cited in Hull, *Two Hague Conferences*, 87.

29. Declaration (IV, 3) Concerning Expanding Bullets (1899), and Convention VIII Relative to the Laying of Automatic Submarine Contact Mines (1907), in Roberts and Guelff, *Documents on the Laws of War*, 40–42, 86–92.

30. I. S. Bloch, *The Future of War in its Technical, Economic, and Political Relations*, abridged (Boston: 1902), xvi, lxi–lxii.

31. Ibid., 251, 266, 293, 315.

32. Ibid., 103, 109–10, 121.

33. A. Conan Doyle, *Danger* (London: 1913), 16.

34. Ibid., 40.

35. Fitzgerald cited in Clarke, *Voices Prophesying War*, 105.

36. Ibid., 101–2.

37. Ibid., 102.

38. H. G. Wells, *The World Set Free* (London: 1926), 116.

Chapter 14 The Great War

1. Bernadotte E. Schmitt and Harold Vedeler, *The World in the Crucible* (New York: 1984), xv.

2. Ibid., 24, 296; D. J. Goodspeed, *The German Wars: 1914–1915* (Boston: 1977), 254.

3. Jack L. Snyder, *The Ideology of the Offensive: Military Decision Making and the Disasters of 1914* (Ithaca, N.Y.: 1984), 39.

4. Steven Van Evera, "Why Cooperation Failed in 1914," 83; Scott D. Sagan, "1914 Revisited: Allies, Offense, and Instability," *International Security* vol. 2, no. 2 (Fall 1986): 166–67.

5. Snyder, *Ideology of the Offensive*, 199.

6. Quester, *Offense and Defense*, 112.

7. Snyder, *Ideology of the Offensive*, 21, 150–55.

8. Henri Isselin, *The Battle of the Marne* (New York: 1966), 11, 239.

9. Ibid., 236.

10. Cited in Isselin, *Battle of the Marne*, 252–53.

11. Keegan, *Face of Battle*, 229–30.

12. Fuller, *Conduct of War*, 160.

13. Dupuy, *Evolution of Weapons*, 217.

14. Richard Hough, *The Great Dreadnought: The Strange Story of the H.M.S. Agin-*

court (New York: 1967), 13; Winston S. Churhill, *The World Crisis,* vol. 2 (New York: 1923), 545.

15. Milne cited in Thomas G. Frothingham, *The Naval History of the Great War,* vol. 1 (Cambridge, Mass.: 1924), 84.

16. Telegram, Tirpitz to Souchon, 4 August 1914, cited in Geoffrey Bennett, *Naval Battles of the First World War* (New York: 1969), 30.

17. Wray's testimony, Troubridge court-martial, cited in Marder, *From Dreadnought to Scapa Flow,* vol. 2, 35.

18. Alfred P. von Tirpitz, *My Memoirs,* vol. 2 (New York: 1919), 82.

19. Marder, *From Dreadnought to Scapa Flow,* vol. 3, 189.

20. Ibid., vol. 2, 42; Scheer, *Germany's High Seas Fleet,* 25.

21. Geoffrey Bennett, *The Battle of Jutland* (Philadelphia: 1965), 36.

22. Churchill cited in Hough, *History of the Modern Battleship,* 147; John Rushworth Jellicoe, *The Grand Fleet, 1914–1916: Its Creation, Development, and Work* (New York: 1919), 397–98.

23. Sir David Beatty, cited in Marder, *From Dreadnought to Scapa Flow,* vol. 2, 398.

24. Jellicoe, *Grand Fleet,* 207; A. A. Hoeling, *The Great War at Sea* (New York: 1965), 59.

25. Kenneth Edwards, *We Dive at Dawn* (London: 1924), 369.

26. Marder, *From Dreadnought to Scapa Flow,* vol. 2, 349.

27. Bernard Brodie, *Sea Power in the Machine Age* (New York: 1941), 71.

28. Frothingham, *Naval History of the Great War,* Vol. I, 102.

29. Letter, John Jellicoe to the Admiralty, 30 October 1914, cited in G. Bennett, *Naval Battles of the First World War,* 152.

30. Tirpitz, *My Memoirs,* vol. 2, 415; memorandum by Hugo von Pohl, 7 November 1914, cited in Scheer, *High Seas Fleet,* 222.

31. Marder, *From Dreadnought to Scapa Flow,* vol. 2, 345.

32. Colin Simpson, "Lusitania," *Life Magazine,* 13 October 1972, 58–80.

33. Samuel Dumas and K. O. Vedel-Petersen, *Losses of Life Caused by War* (London: 1923), vol. 2, *The World War* 139.

34. Diary, George von Muller, 9 February 1916, cited in Walter Gorlitz, *The Kaiser and His Court: Diaries, Notebooks, and Letters of George von Muller* (London: 1961), 133–34; Tirpitz, *My Memoirs,* vol. 2, 202, 424.

35. Kitchener cited in Fuller, *Conduct of War,* 160.

36. Ropp, *War in the Modern World,* 227; Addington, *Pattern of War,* 135–36.

37. Schmitt and Vedeler, *World in the Crucible,* 76–77.

38. Robert Harris and Jeremy Paxman, *A Higher Form of Killing* (New York: 1982), 1–2; L. F. Haber, *The Poison Cloud: Chemical Warfare in the First World War* (Oxford: 1986), 34.

39. Ulrich Trumpener, "The Road to Ypres: The Beginnings of Gas Warfare in World War I," *Journal of Modern History* 47 (September 1975): 464, 466, 471.

40. Ibid., 470, 472–73.

41. Ian V. Hogg, *Gas* (New York: 1975), 25–28.

42. Stockholm International Peace Research Institute, *The Problem of Chemical and Biological Warfare* (Stockholm: 1971), vol. 1, *The Rise of CB Weapons,* 36; Hogg, *Gas,* 136.

43. Tappen to Reichsarchiv, 16 July 1930, cited in Trumpener, "Road to Ypres," 468.

44. McNeill, *Pursuit of Power,* 317.

45. Ibid., 319–22 (France); 322–24 (Germany); 329 (Russia).

46. Leed, *No Man's Land,* 104.

47. Keegan, *Face of Battle*, 231–36.

48. Ibid., 245.

49. Leed, *No Man's Land*, 116.

50. On the paradox see Paul Fussell, *The Great War in Modern Memory* (London: 1975), 115; Leed, *No Man's Land*, 115.

51. Leed, *No Man's Land*, 108.

52. Donald MacIntyre, *Jutland* (New York: 1958), 100; Bennett, *Battle of Jutland*, 50.

53. Bennett, *The Battle of Jutland*, 84.

54. MacIntyre, *Jutland*, 143–44; G. Bennett, *Battle of Jutland*, 50.

55. Jellicoe cited in Marder, *From Dreadnought to Scapa Flow*, vol. 3, 85.

56. G. Bennett, *Naval Battles of the First World War*, 78.

57. Jellicoe cited in Marder, *From Dreadnought to Scapa Flow*, vol. 3, 104.

58. Holloway Frost, *The Battle of Jutland* (Annapolis, Md.,: 1936), 328; MacIntyre, *Jutland*, 173; G. Bennett, *Battle of Jutland*, 113.

59. Scheer, *Germany's High Seas Fleet*, 155.

60. George von Hase, *Kiel and Jutland* (London: 1921), 286.

61. Ibid., 289.

62. G. Bennett, *Battle of Jutland*, 121; Frost, *Battle of Jutland*, 384.

63. Marder, *From Dreadnought to Scapa Flow*, vol. 3, 203; G. Bennett, *Battle of Jutland*, 203.

64. Frost, *Battle of Jutland*, 205.

65. Scheer cited in A. A. Hoeling, *The Great War at Sea*, 150–51. G. Bennett, *Battle of Jutland*, 163.

66. Memorandum, John Jellicoe to the First Lord of the Admiralty, 20 October 1916, cited in Marder, *From Dreadnought to Scapa Flow*, vol. 3, 256.

67. E. Morison, *Admiral Sims*, 341–42.

68. W. S. Sims, First Detailed Report on the Allied Naval Situation, 19 April 1917, Sims Papers; cable, Woodrow Wilson to Sims, 4 July 1917, Sims Papers.

69. Ray Stannard Baker, *Woodrow Wilson: Life and Letters*, vol. 7 (New York: 1939), 140, 147.

70. John Jellicoe, *The Crisis of the Naval War* (New York: 1921), 59–60; Marder, *From Dreadnought to Scapa Flow*, vol. 4, 71.

71. Arthur Hezlet, *The Submarine and Sea Power* (New York: 1967), 93; Philip K. Lundeberg, "Undersea Warfare and Allied Strategy in World War I: 1916–1918," *The Smithsonian Journal of History* vol. 6, no. 4 (Winter 1966–67), 62–63.

72. E. Morison, *Admiral Sims*, 413–17.

73. Schmitt and Vedeler, *World in the Crucible*, 305.

74. Ezra Bowen, *Knights of the Air* (Alexandria, Va.: 1980), 37.

75. Ibid., 39.

76. Lloyd George cited in Bowen, *Knights of the Air*, 18.

77. Edward V. Rickenbacker, *Rickenbacker* (Englewood Cliffs, N.J.: 1979), 106.

78. Ibid., 116.

79. Leed, *No Man's Land*, 134.

80. Herbert Sulzbach, *With the German Guns* (Hamden, Conn.: 1981), 113; A. Stuart Dolden, *Cannon Fodder: An Infantryman's Life on the Western Front* (London: 1980), 87.

81. Cited in Bowen, *Knights of the Air*, 19; Rickenbacker, *Rickenbacker*, 110.

82. Leed, *No Man's Land* 116, 123, 135.

83. Raymond Fredette, *The Sky on Fire: The First Battle of Britain: 1917–1918* (London: 1976), 39–40, 133–36.

84. Ibid., 212, 239–40.

85. Tirpitz cited in Fredette, *Sky on Fire,* 160.

86. B. H. Liddell Hart, *The Revolution in Warfare* (London: 1946), 95.

87. Isaac Don Levine, *Mitchell: Pioneer of Air Power* (New York: 1943), 143.

88. Ibid., 147.

89. Winston Churchill, *The World Crisis,* vol. 2, 61.

90. Ibid., 63–68.

91. Memorandum, E. D. Swinton, 6 February 1916, cited in Dupuy, *Evolution of Weapons,* 221–22.

92. Dupuy, *Evolution of Weapons,* 222–23.

93. Schmitt and Vedeler, *World in the Crucible,* 299–300.

94. Ibid., 299.

95. I. B. Holley, *Ideas and Weapons: Exploitation of the Aerial Weapon by the United States during World War I* (New Haven, Conn.: 1953), 171.

96. Schmitt and Vedeler, *World in the Crucible,* 195–96.

97. Cited in N. N. Golovin, *The Russian Army in the World War* (New Haven, Conn.: 1931), 281.

98. Ropp, *War in the Modern World,* 247; Dupuy, *Evolution of Weapons,* 225–27.

99. Cited in Schmitt and Vedeler, *World in the Crucible,* 260.

100. Arno J. Mayer, *Politics and Diplomacy of Peacemaking: Containment and Counterrevolution at Versailles, 1918–1919* (New York: 1967), 3.

Chapter 15 Sequel

1. Toynbee, *Hannibal's Legacy,* vol. 1, 1–2.

2. Robert Goralski, *World War II Almanac: 1931–1945* (New York: 1981) 425–29.

3. E. Morison, *Admiral Sims,* 504–05.

4. Letter, W. S. Sims to Brigadier General William Mitchell, 8 April 1921; Letter, Mitchell to Sims, 14 April 1921, Sims Papers.

5. Letter, C. E. Hughes to W. F. Fullam, 2 January 1923; Letter, Fullam to Hughes, 22 December 1923, Charles Evans Hughes Papers, Library of Congress.

6. For negotiations leading up to aircraft carrier allotments, see diary of Theodore Roosevelt Jr., 4–11 January 1922, Theodore Roosevelt, Jr., Papers, Library of Congress.

7. Raymond G. O'Connor, *Perilous Equilibrium: The United States and the London Naval Conference of 1930* (Lawrence, Kans.: 1962), 61, 105; Edward Arpee, *From Frigates to Flat-Tops: The Story of the Life and Achievements of Rear Admiral William Adger Moffett* (Lake Forest, Ill.: 1953), 173–78.

8. George V. Fagan, "FDR and Naval Limitation," *U.S. Naval Institute Proceedings* 81, no. 4 (April 1955): 416.

9. Remarks of Admiral W. V. Pratt, Fleet Problem IX, cited in Arpee, *From Frigates to Flat-Tops,* 155.

10. Ronald H. Spector, *Eagle against the Sun: The American War with Japan* (New York: 1985), 43; Toland, *Rising Sun,* 476–77; Stephen Roskill, *Naval Policy between the Wars,* vol. 1 (New York: 1968), 530.

11. Jiro Horikoshi, *Eagles of Mitsubishi: The Story of the Zero Fighter* (Seattle: 1980, trans. from the 1970 Japanese edition), 93–109.

12. Hovgaard, *Modern History of Warships,* 298; Toland, *Rising Sun,* 477.

13. Letter, C. C. Bloch to W. D. Leahy, 12 April 1938; Letter, Leahy to Bloch, May 13, 1938, Claude C. Bloch Papers, Library of Congress.

14. Toland, *Rising Sun,* 477.

15. Samuel Elliot Morison, *History of the United States Naval Operations in World War II* (Boston: 1948), vol. 3, *The Rising Sun in the Pacific,* 23.

16. Linus Pauling, ed., *Encyclopedia of Peace,* vol. 1 (Oxford: 1986), 359.

17. Marion W. Boggs, *Attempts to Define and Limit "Aggressive" Armaments in Diplomacy and Strategy* (Columbia, Mo.: 1941), 46–60.

18. Barton Whaley, *Covert German Rearmament, 1919–1939: Deception and Misperception* (Frederick, Md.: 1984), 1.

19. Manchester, *Arms of Krupp,* 320.

20. Whaley, *Covert German Rearmament,* 29; Manchester, *Arms of Krupp,* 353–54; Anthony Fokker and Bruce Gould, *Flying Dutchman: The Life of Anthony Fokker* (New York: 1931), 222–26.

21. John Erickson, *The Soviet High Command: A Military Political History* (Boulder, Colo.: 1984), 157.

22. Ibid., 260.

23. Ibid., 274.

24. Heinz Guderian, *Panzer Leader* (London: 1952), 30.

25. Albert Speer, *Inside the Third Reich* (New York: 1970), 163.

26. Goodspeed, *German Wars,* 355.

27. Alistair Horne, *To Lose a Battle: France 1940* (Boston: 1969), 78–79; Whaley, *Covert German Rearmament,* 65.

28. John Strawson, *Hitler as a Military Commander* (London: 1971), 61.

29. Ronald H. Bailey, *The Air War in Europe* (Alexandria, Va.: 1979), 26–27.

30. Bernard Brodie and Fawn Brodie, *From Crossbow to H-Bomb,* rev. ed. (Bloomington, Ind.: 1973), 207.

31. Bailey, *Air War in Europe,* 22; Bernard Fitzsimons, ed., *Warplanes and Air Battles of World War II* (London: 1973), see British bomber chart.

32. Brooke quoted in Horne, *To Lose a Battle,* 107–8.

33. Strawson, *Hitler as a Military Commander,* 244.

34. Ibid., 240. A. J. P. Taylor argued implacably against this point of view. However, Albert Speer's *Erinnerungen* makes it clear he planned to wage war from the beginning.

35. Speer, *Inside the Third Reich,* 209, 213.

36. Martin van Creveld, *Fighting Power: German and U.S. Army Performance, 1939–1945* (Westport, Conn.: 1982), 5–6.

37. Eberhard Jackel, *Hitler's Weltanschauung: A Blueprint for Power* (Middletown, Conn.: 1972), 61.

38. Hitler quoted in Strawson, *Hitler as a Military Commander,* 213.

39. Horne, *To Lose a Battle,* 102.

40. William L. Shirer, *The Rise and Fall of the Third Reich* (New York: 1960), 734–35.

41. Erich von Manstein, *Lost Victories* (London: 1955), 166.

42. Brodie and Brodie, *From Crossbow to H-Bomb,* 217; Edward Jablonski, *Airwar* (Garden City, N.Y.: 1971), vol. 1, *Terror from the Sky,* 40.

43. Brodie and Brodie, *From Crossbow to H-Bomb,* 218.

44. Ibid., 217–21; Charles B. MacDonald, *The Mighty Endeavor: The American War in Europe* (New York: 1986), 61.

45. Strawson, *Hitler as a Military Commander,* 148.

46. Bader quoted in Jablonski, *Airwar,* vol. 1, 161.

47. Cherwell quoted in Bailey, *Air War in Europe,* 54.

48. Montgomery quoted in Strawson, *Hitler as a Military Commander,* 132.

49. Hitler quoted in Manchester, *Arms of Krupp,* 431. See also Goodspeed, *German Wars,* 388–89.

50. Guderian, *Panzer Leader,* 151.

51. Erickson, *Soviet High Command,* 587–600; Alan Clark, *Barbarossa: The Russian-German Conflict, 1941–1945* (New York: 1965), 31, 50.

52. Cited in Clark, *Barbarossa,* 43. See also Manstein, *Lost Victories,* 180–81.

53. Erickson, *Soviet High Command,* 655.

54. Clark, *Barbarossa,* 182; Strawson, *Hitler as a Military Commander,* 144–47.

55. Von Hardesty, *Red Phoenix: The Rise of Soviet Air Power, 1941–1945* (Washington, D.C.: 1982), 61.

56. Clark, *Barbarossa,* 207.

57. S. L. Mayer, ed., *The Russian War Machine, 1917–1945* (London: 1977), 44, 195; Hardesty, *Red Phoenix,* 146.

58. Mayer, *The Russian War Machine,* 116.

59. Ibid., 117.

60. Guderian, *Panzer Leader,* 143.

61. Ibid., 233.

62. Seymour M. Hersh, *Chemical and Biological Warfare: America's Hidden Arsenal* (Indianapolis: 1968), 8–9; Stockholm International Peace Research Institute, *Problem of Chemical and Biological Warfare: Rise of CB Weapons* 71–3, 317.

63. Bailey, *Air War in Europe,* 185.

64. Speer, *Inside the Third Reich,* 365, 368; Walter Dornberger, *V-2* (London: 1952), 241.

65. MacDonald, *Mighty Endeavor,* 317.

66. Basil Collier, *The Battle of the V-Weapons, 1944–1945* (New York: 1965), 150–51; Dornberger, *V-2,* 245–47.

67. Speer, *Inside the Third Reich,* 225–29.

68. S. E. Morison, *United States Naval Operations,* vol. 3, 131–32; Arthur R. Hezlet, *Aircraft and Sea Power* (New York: 1970) 200–2; Spector, *Eagle against the Sun,* 83.

69. Spector, *Eagle against the Sun,* 147–48.

70. Ernest J. King, *Fleet Admiral King: A Naval Record* (New York: 1952), 291; William F. Halsey and J. Bryan, *Admiral Halsey's Story* (New York: 1947), 15, 52.

71. Toland, *Rising Sun,* 150.

72. Charles A. Beard, *President Roosevelt and the Coming of the War, 1941* (New Haven, Conn.: 1948), Ch. 1 and 7, 240; Toland, *Rising Sun,* 147; Herbert Feis, *The Road to Pearl Harbor* (Princeton, N.J.: 1950), 319.

73. John W. Dower, *War without Mercy: Race and Power in the Pacific War* (New York: 1986), 10.

74. Cited in Toland, *Rising Sun,* 301; cited in Dower, *War without Mercy,* 53.

75. Dower, *War without Mercy,* 42.

76. Martin Caidin, *The Ragged, Rugged Warriors* (New York: 1966), 36–37; Spector, *Eagle against the Sun,* 228.

77. Clay Blair, *Silent Victory: The U.S. Submarine War against Japan* (New York: 1975), 384–86.

78. Cited in Dower, *War without Mercy,* 89–90.

79. Ibid., 81.

80. Ibid., 244.

81. Ibid., 162.

82. Ibid., 43–44.

83. Cited in Spector, *Eagle against the Sun,* 478.

84. Samuel Eliot Morison, *The Two-Ocean War: A Short History of the United States Navy in the Second World War* (Boston: 1963); 511. Spector, *Eagle against the Sun*, 486–87.

85. Dower, *War without Mercy*, 40; 19 November 1941, order quoted in John Costello, *The Pacific War, 1941–1945* (New York: 1982), 105.

86. Statistics cited in Spector, *Eagle against the Sun*, 505.

87. This account is taken from Ronald E. Powaski, *March to Armageddon: The United States and the Nuclear Arms Race, 1939 to the Present* (New York: 1987), 3–5.

88. Ibid., 12.

89. Harry S. Truman, *Memoirs* (Garden City, N.Y.: 1955), vol. 1, *Year of Decisions*, 419.

90. Truman cited in Spector, *Eagle against the Sun*, 555.

91. Cited in Len Giovannitti and Fred Freed, *The Decision to Drop the Bomb* (New York: 1965), 194–95.

Chapter 16 Conclusion: The Era of Nuclear Weapons

1. Bernard Brodie, ed., *The Absolute Weapon: Atomic Power and World Order* (New York: 1946), 73, 76.

2. U.S. Strategic Bombing Survey, *The Effects of Atomic Bombs on Hiroshima and Nagasaki* (Washington, D.C.: 1946), 18–22.

3. Gregg Herken, *Counsels of War* (New York: 1985), 6.

4. Ibid., 59.

5. Ibid., 138–39; Fred Kaplan, *The Wizards of Armageddon* (New York: 1983), 270–72.

6. Brodie and Brodie, *From Crossbow to H-Bomb*, rev. ed., 294.

7. Robert S. McNamara, "The Dynamics of Nuclear Strategy," 18 September 1967, *U.S. Department of State Bulletin* 57 (9 October 1967), 445.

8. Herken, *Counsels of War*, 149–50; Kaplan, *Wizards of Armageddon*, 259–60.

9. Albert J. Wohlstetter, "Legends of the Strategic Arms Race: Part II," *Strategic Review* vol. 3, no. 1 (Winter: 1975), 76–77.

10. Mathew Bunn and Kosta Tsipis, "The Uncertainties of Preemptive Nuclear Attack," *Scientific American* 249 (November 1983): 38–47; Powaski, *March to Armageddon*, 189.

11. Thomas Powers, "Choosing a Strategy for World War III," *Atlantic Monthly*, November 1982, 98–99.

12. U.S. Congress, House and Senate Joint Committee on Foreign Affairs and Foreign Relations, *Fiscal Year 1986 Arms Control Impact Statements: ICBMs* (Washington, D.C.: April 1985), 151–52.

13. Jack Beatty, "In Harm's Way," *The Atlantic Monthly*, May 1987, 38–39.

14. Powers, "Strategy for World War III," 108, 110.

15. Ibid., 98.

16. Powaski, *March to Armageddon*, 64; Herbert York, *Race to Oblivion: A Participant's View of the Arms Race* (New York: 1970), 98–102.

17. Powaski, *March to Armageddon*, 224–45.

18. *Time*, 6 December, 1982, 30.

19. Ibid., 30–34, 40–45.

20. McNeill, *Pursuit of Power*, 377.

21. U.S. Arms Control and Disarmament Agency, *World Military Expenditures and Arms Transfers: 1986* (Washington, D.C.: 1986), 6; Gavin Kennedy, *The Military in the Third World* (London: 1974), 174–89.

INDEX